Language, Discourse, Society
General Editors: Stephen Heath, Colin

Recent titles include:

Stanley Aronowitz
THE CRISIS IN HISTORICAL MATERIALISM
SCIENCE AS POWER: Discourse and Ideology in Modern Society

John Barrell
THE BIRTH OF PANDORA AND THE DIVISION OF KNOWLEDGE

Norman Bryson
VISION AND PAINTING: The Logic of the Gaze

Lesley Caldwell
ITALIAN FAMILY MATTERS: Women, Politics and Legal Reform

Teresa de Lauretis
ALICE DOESN'T: Feminism, Semiotics and Cinema
FEMINIST STUDIES/CRITICAL STUDIES (editor)
TECHNOLOGIES OF GENDER: Essays on Theory, Film, and Fiction

Mary Ann Doane
THE DESIRE TO DESIRE: The Woman's Film of the 1940s

Jane Gallop
FEMINISM AND PSYCHOANALYSIS: The Daughter's Seduction

Peter Gidal
UNDERSTANDING BECKETT: A Study of Monologue and Gesture in the Works of Samuel Beckett

Peter Goodrich
LEGAL DISCOURSE: Studies in Linguistics, Rhetoric and Legal Analysis

Piers Gray
MARGINAL MEN: Edward Thomas; Ivor Gurney; J R Ackerley

Ian Hunter
CULTURE AND GOVERNMENT: The Emergence of Literary Education

Ian Hunter, David Saunders and Dugald Williamson
ON PORNOGRAPHY: LITERATURE, SEXUALITY AND OBSCENITY LAW

Andreas Huyssen
AFTER THE GREAT DIVIDE: Modernism, Mass Culture and Postmodernism

Colin MacCabe (editor)
JAMES JOYCE AND THE REVOLUTION OF THE WORD
THE TALKING CURE: Essays on Psychoanalysis and Language

Christian Metz
PSYCHOANALYSIS AND CINEMA: The Imaginary Signifier

Jean-Claude Milner
FOR THE LOVE OF LANGUAGE

Jeffrey Minson
GENEALOGIES OF MORALS: Nietzsche, Foucault, Donzelot and the Eccentricity of Ethics

Angela Moorjani
THE AESTHETICS OF LOSS AND LESSNESS

Laura Mulvey
VISUAL AND OTHER PLEASURES

Douglas Oliver
POETRY AND NARRATIVE IN PERFORMANCE

Michel Pêcheux
LANGUAGE, SEMANTICS AND IDEOLOGY

Denise Riley
AM I THAT NAME?: Feminism and the Category of 'Women' in History
POETS ON WRITING: BRITAIN 1970–91

Jacqueline Rose
THE CASE OF PETER PAN or THE IMPOSSIBILITY OF CHILDREN'S FICTION

Brian Rotman
SIGNIFYING NOTHING: The Semiotics of Zero

Michael Ryan
POLITICS AND CULTURE: Working Hypotheses for a Post-Revolutionary Society

David Trotter
CIRCULATION: Defoe, Dickens and the Economics of the Novel
THE MAKING OF THE READER: Language and Subjectivity in Modern American, English and Irish Poetry

Jean-Marie Vincent/translated by James Cohen
ABSTRACT LABOUR: A Critique

Peter Womack
IMPROVEMENT AND ROMANCE: Constructing the Myth of the Highlands

ON PORNOGRAPHY
Literature, Sexuality and Obscenity Law

Ian Hunter
Senior Lecturer, Division of Humanities,
Griffith University, Australia

David Saunders
Senior Lecturer, Division of Humanities,
Griffith University, Australia

Dugald Williamson
Senior Lecturer, Division of Humanities,
Griffith University, Australia

M
MACMILLAN

© Ian Hunter, David Saunders, Dugald Williamson 1993

All rights reserved. No reproduction, copy or transmission of this publication may be made without written permission.

No paragraph of this publication may be reproduced, copied or transmitted save with written permission or in accordance with the provisions of the Copyright, Designs and Patents Act 1988, or under the terms of any licence permitting limited copying issued by the Copyright Licensing Agency, 90 Tottenham Court Road, London W1P 9HE.

Any person who does any unauthorised act in relation to this publication may be liable to criminal prosecution and civil claims for damages.

First published 1993 by
THE MACMILLAN PRESS LTD
Houndmills, Basingstoke, Hampshire RG21 2XS
and London
Companies and representatives
throughout the world

ISBN 0-333-39895-5 hardcover
ISBN 0-333-39896-3 paperback

A catalogue record for this book is available from the British Library.

Printed in Hong Kong

Contents

Preface	viii
Acknowledgements	xiii
1 An Introduction	1
2 The Pornographic Field	12
3 Nineteenth-Century English Obscenity Law	57
4 Literary Erotics	92
5 Twentieth-Century English Obscenity Law	135
6 The Limits of Law Reform	162
7 United States Obscenity Law	198
8 Feminism and Law Reform	229
Notes	247
Bibliography	265
Table of Cases	275
Table of Statutes	278
Reports and Parliamentary Debates	280
Index	282

Preface

The reader who picks up a book on the history of the policing of pornography has every right to demand of its authors a clear statement of their approach to the subject. After all, few subjects of historical and cultural enquiry are more contentious and leave less scope for detached observation and disinterested analysis. The development of research into pornography and its legal regulation obeys none of the comforting models for the evolution of scholarly fields. It is characterised neither by the patient accumulation of historical facts and progressive refinement of disciplinary frameworks, nor by the sudden and momentous theoretical breakthrough that grounds the object of enquiry in a revelation of its fundamental conditions. Knowledge of pornography is too deeply embedded in its auto-erotic use, in the medical and pedagogical categories of its legal regulation, and in campaigns for its aesthetic emancipation or moral eradication for the researcher to be able to approach it in a Kantian manner as the universal subject of reason. From D. H. Lawrence's attempt to distinguish erotic art and pornography to the feminist denunciation of Lawrence as a pornographer, from the specification and regulation of pornography as a social harm by jurists in the 1860s to the debunking of this claim by their liberal colleagues in the 1960s, from this debunking to the reinstatement of the social harmfulness of pornography as the instrument of sexism, knowledge of pornography has been inseparable from the competing agencies of its use and regulation, its discrediting and valorisation. For this reason all attempts to provide a general statement of the truth of pornography – whether to discover its origin in the puritanical repression of healthy sexuality, its essence in the patriarchal objectification of women, or its rightful place in the sphere of private morality or in that of literary emancipation – must be greeted with a degree of scepticism. Invariably and perhaps inevitably, such statements are driven by particular interests formed in the heterogeneous spheres of private erotics and public policy, cultural projects and governmental programmes. For the same reason, however, strict limits are imposed on the scope of sceptical enquiry. In acknowledging the interested character of various reasonings about pornography, we can neither claim to see through them in a purely disinterested manner to a new truth, nor indeed suspend all judgement and wait for the marching orders of history.

We have responded to this problem in a number of ways. In the first place we have not attempted to overcome the interested character of knowledge in the field but have treated it as establishing limits and parameters for our

Preface

own investigations. In this regard, the speed with which the liberal debunking of the Victorian conception of the harms of pornography has itself been debunked by the feminist reinscription of the older conception in a new form has proved salutary. These shifts are exemplary of the circumstantial character of pornography as an object of knowledge and a target of policy. For this reason we have not attempted to describe pornography in terms of a single origin, underlying essence or general function. Instead, we have concentrated our attentions on the shifting historical circumstances in which it has emerged as an eroticising instrument, a saleable commodity, a crime, an object of governmental concern and medical regulation, an ethical occasion or an aesthetic phenomenon.

This methodological strategy has in its turn alerted us to the dominant rhetorical forms through which books on pornography address their readers and their object. Whether in the name of 'man's' long-repressed erotic being, or in the name of a marginalised feminine desire, these books find their voices in a speaking for that which has been silenced, a discovery of that which has been hidden. This rhetoric disables analysis in several ways. First, it activates the 'fable' of repression, as it is termed in Michel Foucault's work on the history of sexuality. In the wake of this work, we must suspect that the so-called 'silence' surrounding sexuality exists only in order to be endlessly broken, our 'hidden' sexuality being in practice a stalking-horse for a remorseless engine of discovery and industry of publication. Repression undoubtedly occurs, but it is also a tactic within a confessional mechanism, a tactic for getting us to treat sexuality as the great secret of ourselves. Most books on pornography treat sexuality in just this way, relaying the mechanism of confession rather than describing it.

Second, in purporting to break the silence surrounding sexuality the authors of such books lay claim to what Foucault has called 'the speaker's benefit'. This is the claim to a certain moral authority flowing from the courage displayed in breaking taboos, transgressing prohibitions, and speaking up for the silenced. No doubt this helps explain the portentous and momentous aura surrounding much of the writing on pornography, as well as the immense reservoir of indignation that feeds into it. Unfortunately, it also suggests why so much of this writing is basically uninformative. When the 'silence' of sexuality is in fact a device in a ritual for getting people to break it, little is achieved by speaking up, except to draw attention to one's own claim to moral courage. The level of moral heroism in writing about pornography has thus tended to be inversely related to its informational content.

Third, the rhetoric of speaking out is typically accompanied by the textual strategy of copious quotation from erotic and pornographic works.

Indeed, there is a sense in which such books as the Kronhausens' *Pornography and the Law*, Stephen Marcus' *The Other Victorians* and Andrea Dworkin's *Pornography* are as much anthologies of pornographic writing as they are analyses of it. The rhetoric of taboo-breaking that dictates copious quotation simultaneously deprives these books of the intellectual capacity to subordinate the excitatory power of pornography to the explanatory power of its analysis. This is what makes their reading such an ambiguous experience.

Cognisance of these rhetorical problems goes some way towards explaining why our book takes the form that it does. We eschew the confessional mode and mechanism in order to constitute sexual confession itself as an object of historical description and cultural analysis. We have done our best not to be courageous or indignant in speaking of pornography so that we can speak of it in a more historical and descriptive manner. The reader will find very little direct quotation of pornographic writing here but a good deal of quotation from writings about it. While this no doubt makes for a less exciting book it also, we believe, makes for a more informative one.

Our central reorientation of existing scholarship, however, lies in the *positive* character of our descriptions of pornography and its regulation. 'Positive' does not mean 'approving'. It refers to our attempt to describe the object in its own terms, as the autonomous product of irreducible historical conditions. By contrast, pornography has to date been analysed in a largely negative manner, that is, as a by-product of history, a phenomenon possessed only of a half-existence and that due solely to the malfunctioning of more fundamental forces and mechanisms. Psychologists have treated it as a perversion of the primary drives, a failed sublimation brought about by a too-rigorous application of norms and laws. For cultural historians pornography originates in epochs of repression which, in refusing the social expression of desire, drive it underground where it assumes mutant forms. And for their part literary critics treat pornography as the product of the aesthetic failure to mediate fantasy and real experience, the sensuous and the moral – a failure manifest in the obsessive detail of pornographic description accompanied by skeletal plots and characters.

In departing from these well-worn accounts we shall investigate pornography as a historically specific practice, not as a distortion of 'man's' timeless erotic being. This practice did not originate from a predictable collision of the drives with society's norms and laws. Rather, it emerged unforeseen from the unplanned interactions of a series of historical forces. In the studies that follow, four factors in particular play preeminent roles. First, the technology of confession and ethical self-scrutiny which, it is argued, permitted an ever-increasing number of individuals to treat their self in a new manner as the harbinger of a secret and hence endlessly discoverable sexual desire. Second, the communications technology of literacy and the printed book. It was this which allowed an otherwise esoteric and religiously-based interrogation of the 'flesh' a broader dissemination as a profane auto-erotics in book form. Third, the legal regulation of obscenity. This displaced the religious codification of confessional erotics when, at the beginning of the eighteenth century, the printed book permitted this erotics to find a new home – and a new use – in a literate and reading public. Finally, a series of later and less visible 'governmental' policings – medical, pedagogic, welfarist and aesthetic – that have constituted pornography as a social problem, their norms coming to inform the legal regulation of obscenity as a social harm.

Pornography thus does not have a single point of origin in the exemplary dialectic of body and mind inside the human subject. It appeared on a variety of surfaces – as an instrument of desire, an ethical failing, a crime, a medical problem, a pedagogic threat, an aesthetic challenge and occasion – when the contingent interaction of the factors just listed gave birth to a novel historical phenomenon: biblio-erotics or book sex. Book sex is not the negative symptom of an incomplete human subjectivity; it is the positive artefact of a complex cultural technology and as such marks the addition of a particular practice of life to the human repertoire.

This last point enables us to acknowledge that we have written this book not as amanuenses for the universal subject but as men. Today it might seem impossible for men to write about the regulation of pornography except in defiance of or in obeisance to feminist analysis. We adopt neither posture. We acknowledge the significance of our gender as writers not in a spirit of confession but in order to situate our studies in the context of an important historical fact: once we see that biblio-erotics is not an attribute of human subjectivity *per se* but the result of the historical formation and distribution of a specific erotic technology, then it is impossible not to see that this distribution has been overwhelmingly skewed towards men and, moreover, towards literate men. This is not to mark a deficiency in the masculine psyche; it is to observe that the repertoire of modern western masculinity has been decisively informed by the historical transmission of the auto-erotic techniques of book sex. It is the transmission of these techniques that forms the proper object of legal, ethical and social regulation; the male psyche is only a dependent reality.

Since the late nineteenth century feminism has been properly concerned with the consequences of this masculine auto-erotics for women. This concern – together with the legal, medical and pedagogical categorisations on which it has drawn – has been the single most important factor in the modern problematisation of pornography. It is no detraction from this concern to conclude by noting that ours is not identical.

I. H., D. S., D. W.

Acknowledgements

The debts we have incurred during the course of this work have been largely institutional. Its origins lie in our teaching in the erstwhile Forms of Communication programme in the Division of Humanities at Griffith University. To the students of this programme whose presence obliged and whose interest inspired our initial work on the relations between literature, sexuality and the law, our thanks are due. To Waddick Doyle, Jenny Freeman and Bronwyn Hammond, who at different times worked with us as research assistants, we offer our particular gratitude. We should also like to record our appreciation of the work done by the Division's general staff who with good nature and great efficiency have worked on the typescript at various times between 1986 and 1991. The staff of Griffith University's Inter-Library Loan service have been similarly helpful over this same period. Finally, we should like to acknowledge the material support of the Division and the University which has made the writing of this book possible.

1 An Introduction

We can set the scene with two citations. The first is well known, being taken from Samuel Pepys, a government official of some standing and a posthumously famous diarist. Writing early in 1668, Pepys describes his encounter with what we now call pornographic literature:

> Thence homeward by coach and stopped at Martins my bookseller, where I saw the French book which I did think to have had for my wife to translate, called *L'escholle de Filles;* but when I came to look into it, it is the most bawdy, lewd book that ever I saw, rather worse than *putana errante* – so that I was ashamed of reading in it . . .
>
> Thence away to the Strand to my bookseller's, and there stayed an hour and bought that idle, roguish book, *L'escholle des Filles;* which I have bought in plain binding (avoiding the buying of it better bound) because I resolve, as soon as I have read it, to burn it, that it may not stand in the list of books, nor among them to disgrace them if it should be found . . .
>
> Lords day. Up, and at my chamber all the morning and the office, doing business and also reading a little of *L'escholle des Filles,* which is a mighty lewd book, but yet not amiss for a sober man once to read over to inform himself in the villainy of the world . . . We sang till almost night, and drank my good store of wine; and then they parted and I to my chamber, where I did read through *L'escholle des Filles;* a lewd book, but what doth me no wrong to read for information sake (but it did hazer my prick para stand all the while, and una vez to decharger); and after I had done it, I burned it, that it might not be among my books to my shame; and so at night to supper and then to bed.
>
> (Pepys, 1976, IX, pp. 21–2, 57–9)

Our second text is assembled from the confessions of William Chidley, an obscure Australian commercial artist turned sex reformer. Completed in the first decade of the twentieth century, Chidley's confessions also record pornographic encounters. However, these are described by a figure who did not exist prior to the nineteenth century – the aspiring sexual healer who is himself sick with sex:

> Martin liked reading Reynolds's *Mysteries of Paris* in which girls, naked

as the moon, danced in perfumed apartments before young, handsome and rich men of that and other cities. These scenes affected me with an odd mixture of feelings – a sense of Divine beauty and youth (the naked girls with long hair waving in the moonlight) – and a sense of something evil, akin to the sensations I knew now, alas, if only feebly and pervertedly. This same boy lent me Smollett's *Roderick Random*. I soon learnt where to find lewd passages to excite me while I was abusing myself. They were not very lewd – that was not necessary. I gloated over trifles, even looked up words in a lexicon hoping to find some reference to a woman's vulva. The latter became a mysterious and unattainable prize . . .

Mother took the house in Dover Street Richmond: it was there that she warned me against self-abuse. I shall have to speak again of indecent cards – 'French cards' we called them – and their influence.

One day when I was abusing myself in a urinal the semen came for the first time. I knew so little that I thought I had injured myself. It gave me what might have been a salutary turn, had not the habit now hold of me past hope.

I grew stiff in the neck, my spine clogged, and I had unholy sweats. The pupils of my eyes were like pin-heads – so small and weak I could not look at the sun, or a healthy lad or lassie in the eyes . . .

In six months Williams taught me all that was useful to him, then he left me to my own devices. But it just suited me also, as it gave me time to read novels during his absence, which was nearly all day. So for five years, when Mother and Father thought I was learning a good profession, I was reading novels, drawing caricatures – and abusing myself.

(Chidley, 1977, pp. 38–9, 45, 46)

Each of these passages represents a particular configuration of two of the factors – literature and sexuality – which, together with law and policing, constitute the object of our enquiry. It would be unwise to assume, however, that the relation between these factors in the cited passages is immediately clear, or that the path to such a difficult and problematic object as pornography lies open before us.

Thirty years ago, in the 1960s – that period of cultural liberalisation which we are told produced a new attitude to obscenity and less restrictive laws governing its circulation – these things were clear, or so it seemed. Pornography, it was discovered by a host of literary critics and psychologists, formed part of 'man's' attempt to give literary expression to the truth of his sexuality. Pornography, like sex itself, had been repressed and stig-

An Introduction 3

matised for centuries but society was now mature enough to accept the truth about itself told by the literature of sexuality. Driven perhaps by the heritage of Puritanism, or by capitalism's will to harness sexual energy to its own economic ends, or perhaps simply by the fear of sex itself, the law from this point of view had imposed itself in an area that was the proper preserve of the artist or the therapist.

Even reforming jurists accepted this view. True, the centuries of repression had distorted sexual instincts and pornography could be seen as the revenge of sex on the society that had injured it: a perverse, fantasmatic, even pathological reflux expression of true sex. The law might, therefore, have to continue to draw the line of prohibition around pornography, or at least restrict access to it. But now it would do so with the help of literary critics and psychologists whose project of fostering the true literary expression of sex would surely lead to the withering away of both pornography and its legal regulation.

As for our historians of culture, they provided this account of repression and liberation with a periodisation and a telos. They assured us that from the relative freedom of sexual expression in Elizabethan England flowed a literature of sexuality both frank and healthy, a state of affairs which continued well into the seventeenth century. With the rise of Puritanism, however, and successive waves of stigmatisation and legal repression during the eighteenth and nineteenth centuries, sexual expression was driven underground where, divorced from reality, it went bad, finally to re-appear in the form of the pornography of perversions.

It is with regard to just this historical framework that the relation between our two cited passages would be typically understood. Donald Thomas (1969, pp. 26–7; 1972, p. 55), for example, regards *L'Ecole des filles* as an open and realistic portrayal of the joys of sex, and Pepys' reading of it as characteristic of the uninhibited period prior to the Puritan revival – the revival which produced the fantasmatic and perverse pornography of the Victorians. Chidley's pathological auto-erotic use of lewd literature, on the other hand, would be fitted neatly into the analysis of the cultural repression and perversion of sexuality that we find in Peter Gay's (1984, pp. 328–402) account of Victorian pornography. Of course, on our side of Chidley – seen as a late victim of a repression he struggled to overcome – lay the dawn of a free, realistic, and joyous erotica into whose light we were about to step.

That bright day did not arrive. Indeed, the kindest words one could use to describe the state of the erstwhile liberal intellectual consensus on obscenity – until so recently the vehicle of sexual enlightenment and historical progress – would be confusion and disarray. Far from being a sign of cultural backwardness, the concept of obscenity has today resumed its place as a central category in the analysis of pornography. Today, in some circles, pornography is less likely to be regarded as an expression of the truth of sex than as a harm or discrimination perpetrated by a systematic campaign to cast women as sexual, according to the *diktat* of male interest, imagination and desire. The idea that pornography constitutes a 'social harm' and is hence eligible for legal suppression – the very idea that the 1960s liberals and libertarians sought to laugh out of court as a Victorian prejudice – is once again gaining ground.

What is more, the project through which literary critics, psychologists, and jurists sought to protect true erotic expression by legally distinguishing it from pornography is itself under attack. The remark of an English magistrate that the 'most splendidly painted picture in the Universe might be obscene' – once a benchmark for ignorance and illiberalism – now finds a ready if somewhat discomforting echo in those who seek to bring erotic art (and advertising) within the sphere of obscenity law in order to combat sexism.

This reversal in the axis of progressive politics is a salutary lesson for anyone tempted to follow the stars of cultural enlightenment and historical progress. It was brought about, of course, by the rise of feminism and is the result of an attempt to include pornography in the general analysis of sexism and thereby target it for eradication, or at least radical transformation. This reversal – as disorienting as it was rapid – provides an avenue to the central concerns of these studies. This is not because we have adopted a feminist strategy for dealing with pornography. Rather, it is because the fact of the reversal itself – in its very speed and apparent completeness – suggests the instability in the erstwhile consensus, without necessarily signifying the truth of the position that seeks to displace it. Under these circumstances the question to formulate is not: What was wrong with the liberal approach to pornography? or: To what extent is the feminist analysis correct? It is rather: What is it about the field in which pornography appears as an object of knowledge and regulation that permits such sudden reversals of ethical and political polarity?

Our central concern is therefore not to provide yet another description of what pornography *is* – whether expression of sexuality or armature of sexism. Rather it is to describe the material circumstances in which pornography has assumed a variety of forms – for example, as a device of sexual intensification, as a problem of conscience, as a pathological agent in the sphere of sexual medicine, as an aesthetic category, as a species of illegal conduct – without deciding in advance, or on general theoretical grounds, which if any of these forms represents the 'truth' about pornography.

This epistemological reserve is more a sign of the circumstances in which

An Introduction

we find ourselves than of a praiseworthy modesty on our part. In a field so multi-faceted, so unstable, so prone to polar reversals, a concern with the field itself comes as a tactical imperative rather than as philosophical nicety. In such a field the will to speak the truth and be on the right side becomes a disabling liability. We can, however, specify our concern with this field in terms of three interests which the reader will discern as themes running through the studies which compose this book.

First, a *theoretical* interest. If erotic art and pornography are representations of an abiding human sexuality, how is it that for us they have so quickly and readily been denounced as lies and transgressions? Can we really afford to think that the alliance of psychologists, jurists and literary critics which invaded the press and the courts in order to defend the freedom of erotic expression was simply mistaken, duped by a naive politics, a cunning libido or an exploitative book trade? No doubt this would be a comforting thought, if we were among those now sure they are on the right side. But is it not the case that what is complained of in current denunciations of erotica and its liberal defenders is less the accuracy of pornography (as a representation) and more its harmful normalising effects (as a conduct)? And is it not true that the feminist campaign against pornography – whether it dreams of displacing pornography altogether, or of having it conform to the contours of 'women's pleasure' – is a campaign to disseminate new norms of sexual conduct and pleasure? In other words, can we not begin to explore the possibility that what pornography confronts us with is not a representation of sexuality at all – true or false – but a definite apparatus for transmitting norms of sexual conduct and feeling relayed in certain techniques and practices?

When Pepys' secret little book, *L'Ecole des filles*, was translated into English at the end of the seventeenth century it appeared under the title *The School of Venus: or, the Ladies Delight reduced into rules of practice*. This title was more than usually accurate. As we shall see in more detail below, drawing on a powerful sexualising machinery which had formed around the religious direction of conscience in relation to sins of the flesh – a machinery easily transposed into the erotic register – this book transmitted a rhetoric of sexual postures, a lexicon of erotic names, and a thematics of initiation and sexual discovery. What Pepys found in *L'Ecole des filles* was not a true or false representation of some general human sexuality but an incitatory manual of norms, techniques, and fantasy scenarios for acquiring and putting into practice a very specific form of sexual conduct.

If this is the case, it is not difficult to detect a certain naivety in Thomas' attempt to rescue this book from the category of pornography on the basis of its 'realism'. But this does not mean that it is sufficient to denounce the work as pornography by alleging its *failure* to provide a true representation of sex or by pointing to its fantasmatic objectification of women. We shall argue that the words and fantasies of such a work do not exist in a relation of (mis)representation to a true sexuality. Rather they form part of an ensemble of techniques, practices, and institutions which, during the seventeenth century, was bringing a definite form of sexuality into being, in part through the distribution and consumption of certain books. Once we cease to treat pornography as having a purely negative relation to sexuality – as its transparent representation or its tendentious or pathological distortion – we can begin to explore the alternative possibility that it has formed part of an apparatus that in a positive sense directly installs interests and capacities for actual forms of sexuality.

Second, a *historical* interest. If we look at historical treatments of pornography, it is not hard to detect the presence of a model which our cultural historians had earlier applied to the history of sexuality. According to this model there is first a golden age in which – despite differences as to its date – erotic texts and pictures reconciled the unrestrained joys of fantasy and the sobering limits of experience, thereby achieving the difficult mediation of what desire demands and social norms allow. In this harmonious state, where desire accommodates itself to norms while norms are softened to receive the shape of desire, erotic expression is in touch with 'man's' true sexual being or with the forces shaping this being over time. Then comes the split. Owing to a too-violent expression of desire or a too-repressive imposition of social norms, fantasy is divorced from experience and driven underground, finding a distorted expression as pornography. Alternatively, it is possible to provide the golden age with a more synchronic location, as Peter Gay (1984, pp. 71–168, 328–402) does when he contrasts the inclusive and balanced erotic expressions and gestures of his high-bourgeois Victorian couples with their repressed and distorted counterparts in Victorian pornography. Either way, it is this model which allows Thomas (1972, pp. 54–60) to treat *The School of Venus* as a late flowering of erotic expression; and for Gay to describe the desolating winter of Victorian pornography as the result of a failed mediation that left erotica both too repressed and too uninhibited.

No doubt this history with its promise of better erotic times to come – or perhaps already within reach – has its comforts. This should not stop us asking some questions of it. In the first place, is it possible to conceive of pornography in terms of a single historical reality, into which it is born as the result of the tension between fantasy and experience, private desires and public norms? Consider again the case of *The School of Venus*. That this book should have emerged in the sphere that we now call pornographic was, we shall argue, the contingent outcome of events taking place in quite disparate departments of existence. Without anticipating too fully the investigations which follow, we can point to: the transposition of a sexualising rhetoric, lexicon, and fantasia – developed in the context of religious confession – into an auto-erotic register; the emergence of printing, the book trade, and print literacy which permitted the dissemination of the self-eroticising concerns and techniques beyond their initial religious and court milieus into the world of the urban middle classes; and, alongside these, the development of legal (and later medical and pedagogical) forms of regulation which sent this dissemination down particular social channels, thus permitting sexualities differentiated by gender, class, and age to emerge.

In the second place, given that these separate historical developments do not appear to obey the one dialectical logic of desire and norm, fantasy and experience, is it possible to punctuate the history of pornography by dividing periods of successful from periods of failed reconciliation? Is the fact that William Chidley's auto-erotic use of pornography was deeply pathological, while Pepys' was not, indicative of the difference between an epoch of erotic expression incapable of integrating desire and norm and one that could? Again the answer has to be in the negative. We shall see that by Chidley's time not only had the literary, technical, and legal elements composing the field of pornography undergone significant changes, they had also been joined by two forces unknown to Pepys: the governmental policing of obscenity as one of the social problems affecting the decency, order, and health of the urban popular classes; and the medicalisation of pornography as a pathological agent afflicting the now delicately balanced sexuality of the bourgeois household, particularly that of its sons. It was this latter development in particular that permitted Chidley to give the auto-erotic use of pornography such a central and pathological place in the organisation of his life – to trace its effects in the degeneration of his body and demeanour and in the sexual misery accompanying his relations with women.

In other words, we can suggest that what separates the mid-nineteenth century problem of pornography from its appearance at the end of the seventeenth century is less the epochal failure of true sexual expression than a series of mutations in what might be called the deployment or apparatus of pornography. If we are to describe such mutations it will be necessary to shift our gaze from the great movements of the sexual dialectic, which have thus far transfixed the historians of obscenity, and focus instead on the shifting and contingent relations between the elements of this deployment or apparatus. Rather than the great cycles of sexual expression – with their movements towards a true reconciliation of desire and norm, or away, in the direction of repression and unleashed pornographic fantasy – the object of historical description becomes the relations between the array of factors (literary, legal, technical, social) which happened to compose the field in which pornography emerges.

Finally, an *ethical* and *legal* interest. In the 1960s the issues in this regard seemed fairly clear. Armed with a set of distinctions between morality and law, the private and the public – between the individual's right to freedom of expression and society's right to suppress harmful conduct – a team of liberal jurists, supported by psychologists and literary critics, set out to reform a tangle of criminal statutes, common law procedures and administrative regulations which they took to be choking the sources of authentic erotic expression. By attempting to give legal force to a distinction between erotic art and pornography, they sought to rescue the literature of sexuality from legal suppression by placing it in the sphere of private morality or (in the American case) in the domain of constitutionally protected speech. To say that today the results of this reforming project are uncertain would be a decided understatement. For one thing, it is not clear that the *cordon sanitaire* between protected and suppressible erotica has been drawn with any uniformity or completeness. For another – and this is largely due to the impact of feminist campaigns – the very idea that it is possible to separate private fantasies from public norms, or art from pornography, or protected from suppressible erotica, no longer seems self-evident. Far from seeking to contract the domain of legally suppressible erotica, feminism today seeks to expand it to include forms of erotic art and advertising.

Once again, this reversal opens a space in which we can put some questions to the liberal consensus. Above all it permits us to ask whether in the area of obscenity it is possible to draw the kind of distinction between morality and law, private and public, art and pornography, on which the reform of the law was to be based? We can recall the situation of Samuel Pepys locked away in his chamber, in one hand a copy of *L'Ecole des filles*. Given our description of the dependence of Pepys' feelings and conduct on the printed dissemination of a particular sexualising device, it would be a mistake to conflate Pepys' architectural privacy and the philosophical privacy of his moral judgement. In other words, it would be a mistake to treat the space of the chamber in which Pepys cannot be seen by others as a physical sign of a space of conscience in which Pepys' actions can be seen by his self.

It is really only in the architectural sense that Pepys was in private. We shall see that with regard to his sexual ethics, Pepys' desires and gestures – as well as the ambivalent judgement he brings to bear on them – are products of a quite public apparatus of sexual self-formation. Indeed, we shall argue that Pepys' capacity to make himself into an object of knowledge and pleasure for himself – and to do so by himself in a closed chamber – is inseparable from a specific component of this apparatus: the technology of the printed book. We have already isolated as a topic for further discussion the ease with which the manuals of sexual confession could be converted into repositories of self-eroticisation and thus used for ends quite other than but just as definite as a seeking of grace. As far as Pepys in Protestant England is concerned, the literate techniques of Puritan self-examination – spiritual journalism and autobiography (of which Pepys was a virtuoso exponent) and casuistical reasoning – could just as easily support the eroticising confessions of *Fanny Hill* as the pious life of *Robinson Crusoe*, both texts serving exemplary roles for their readers.

The constitutional ambivalence of this sexual conscience – the ease with which the scrutiny of the soul could assume the form of an erotic search for sexual grace – as well as its dependence on the printed dissemination of a specific set of ethical techniques, both bode ill for the project to draw an essential line between erotica that should be left to judgments of the private conscience and those other publications which should fall under the public regulation of the law. If that project is in fact ill-conceived, the distinction between morality and law begins to look less like a basic philosophical boundary than a tactic of demarcation. Moreover, this tactic might itself have depended on the practical forms of ethical education and on the variable thresholds which have marked the 'juridification' of conducts, that is, their administration by specifically legal means and instruments. In short, the distinction between morality and law may not be open to a general philosophical account or adjudication.

Similar remarks apply to the attempt to reform obscenity law on the basis of a fundamental distinction between art and pornography. Censorious judges and campaigning feminists join forces in pointing out that such a distinction has no necessary pertinence for the sphere of erotica. Chidley's auto-erotic use of Reynolds and Smollett suggests that this distinction, far from being an aesthetic or ethical foundation on which the law can build, itself depends on the positive formation of particular cultural and ethical capacities that may be unevenly disseminated in a given historical population.

If this is so, we might suspect that the global advance of the philosophical-legal categories informing the movement of liberal reform will bog down in the practical and variable distribution of the ethical capacities actually responsible for the appropriation of erotica. Small wonder, then, that the categorical distinctions which were to have provided a clear basis for the new law – between private and public, morality and law, art and pornography – should have become so entangled in the array of institutions and professions (pedagogical, medical, aesthetic) responsible for the uneven ethical qualification and skilling of different social groups and categories of person.

Damaging as this suspicion may be for the liberal attempt to free erotica once and for all from legal interference, it is by no means automatically supportive of the feminist project to expand the domain of legal regulation. To the extent that this latter project also bases itself on a single general form of subjectivity – the 'objectifying' male psyche – it too risks faltering amidst the sheer variability and practicality of ethical competences. For we shall see that obscenity law has no interest in the quality of the consciousness lying behind pornography; it is wholly concerned with the uneven ethical abilities of the populations 'into whose hands pornography might fall'. In the modern West, such abilities are the objectives of pedagogic, medical and other socially therapeutic agencies; hence, it is in relation to these objectives that legal regulation takes place, with scant regard for the sovereignty of the subject of representation. The legal recognition of 'variable obscenity' – the idea that works are obscene only relative to particular channels of distribution and audience type – is one indication of this important fact.

It now become possible to formulate a different kind of ethical and legal interest in pornography. This is not an interest which seeks to found legal or social interventions in a set of philosophical-legal universals, whether those invested in the distinctions between morality and law, art and pornography, or those which claim a basis in the rights and prerogatives of a complete and self-determining human subject. Our starting point is the proposition that ethical and legal interventions make sense only within the limits imposed by specific configurations of what we shall call the 'pornographic field'; that is, the field of disparate institutions historically responsible for the channels through which erotica have been disseminated and the cultural interests and abilities through which erotica have been consumed.

The studies of the pornographic field that follow are defined, then, by the intersection of three interests:

- a *theoretical* interest in the role of pornography as a relay for the norms, techniques, and practices of instituted sexualities;
- a *historical* interest in the field of (literary, legal, communicational, medical) forces which has seen the emergence of pornography as an object of pleasure, knowledge, and regulation;

- finally, an *ethical and legal* interest that seeks to remain within the range of the actual ethical and legal capacities supported by this field; that is, within range of ethical intelligibility and legal possibility.

In what follows, these interests are brought to bear simultaneously, rather than serially, on a number of historical and theoretical problems drawn from this field in which, along with law and the policing of the streets, the institutions of medicine, education and literature have played their parts.

2 The Pornographic Field

HARM AND CHARM

In 1879 Elizabeth Blackwell, a medical practitioner who had also written works advocating Christian socialism, women's rights and moral and sanitary 'rescue work', published a small manual entitled *Counsel to Parents: On the Moral Education of their Children in Relation to Sex*. This book is not exceptional in relation to similar advice books, if anything, it tends to be more enlightened in acknowledging the sexuality of women and in stressing the mutuality of the conjugal relation. Nonetheless, in finding in sex the hidden key to personal and social improvement *and* degeneration, in treating it as both the source of moral and physical health and of numberless pathologies, Doctor Blackwell's little book is resolutely representative.

If sex is woven into the moral and physical economy of the individual body, it also has – through the transmission of hereditary or acquired morbidities and weaknesses – profound consequences for the social body. As the mediator of these two bodies – responsible for the sexual health of its individual members and custodian of the vitality of the nation and the race – the family required concerted ethical and legislative protection if the dangers and evils of sex were to be avoided. For the doctor certain matters were beyond question:

> The evils resulting from a violation of Nature's method of growth by a life of early dissipation, are both physical and mental or moral . . . Amongst the physical evils, the following may be particularly noted. The loss of self-control reacting upon the body, produces a morbid irritability (always a sign of weakness) which is a real disease, subjecting the individual to constant excitement and exhaustion from slight causes. The resulting physical evils may be slow in revealing themselves, because they only gradually undermine the constitution. They do not herald themselves in the alarming manner of a fever, or a convulsion, but they are not to be less dreaded, from their masked approach. The chief forms of physical deterioration are nervous exhaustion, impaired power of resistance to epidemics or other injurious influences; and the development of those germs of disease, or tendencies to some particular form of disease, which exist in the majority of constitutions. The brain and spinal marrow and the lungs, are the vital organs most frequently injured by loose life. But whatever be the weak point of the constitution, from

inherited or acquired morbid tendencies, that will probably be the point through which disease or death will enter.

(Blackwell, 1879, pp. 38–9)

It was in the context of this fragile and highly charged moral physiology – in which sexual medicine had joined the health of the body to the purity of the mind and the pathology of the individual to that of society – that the harms of pornographic literature could be known and calculated:

> The dangers arising from vicious literature of any kind, cannot be overestimated by parents. Whether sensuality be taught by police reports, or by Greek and Latin literature, by novels, plays, songs, penny papers, or any species of the corrupt literature now sent forth broadcast, and which finds its way into the hands of the young of all classes and both sexes, the danger is equally real. It is storing the susceptible mind of youth with words, images, and suggestions of vice, which remain permanently in the mind, springing up day and night in unguarded moments, weakening the power of resistance, and accustoming the thoughts to an atmosphere of vice. No amount of simple caution, given by parents or instructors, suffices to guard the young mind from the influence of evil literature. It must be remembered that hatred of evil will never be learned by intellectual warning. The permanent and incalculable injury which is done to the young mind by vicious reading, is proved by all that we now know about the structure and methods of growth of the human mind . . . Physiological inquiry is constantly throwing more light upon our mental as well as physical organization . . . All that we observe of these processes, shows us that different physical changes are produced in the brain, by different classes of ideas, and that the moral sense itself, may be affected by the constant exercise of the brain in one direction or another, so that the actual individual standard of what is right or what is wrong, will be quite changed, according to whether low or high ideas have been constantly recorded in the retentive substance of the brain.
> These important facts have a wide and constant bearing on education, showing the really poisonous character of all licentious literature, whether ancient or modern, and its destructive effect on the quality of the brain. (pp. 89–90)

Writing some eighty years after our doctor of sexual medicine, two American professors of law take as their task the reformation of the tangle of laws that had grown up around the literature of sexuality in the eighteenth and nineteenth centuries. The profound centrality of sex to humanity remains in their account, but its fragile and pathological qualities seem to have vanished. Now the problem for these reforming jurists is to permit 'man' to explore his sexual potential in erotic literature by extending to it the protection of the First Amendment:

> Here is an area of life that immediately concerns all of mankind. It creates problems that vitally affect most individuals. It is an area in which man has often groped in the dark, because of periodic taboos on intelligent discussion. The ready response in recent years to the wider distribution of literature dealing with this area demonstrates great interest in the serious concern with problems that so closely affect the lives of all, and the widespread desire for more information, light, and understanding. There are many differing and conflicting viewpoints and opinions concerning the place that sex should play in the life of individuals, and what is acceptable human conduct. This is exactly the type of subject matter on which freedom of expression is essential – because of this great human interest and the great variety of viewpoints. Unrestricted censorship over the expression of ideas in this area would defeat the very purpose of the guarantees of free expression – 'that men shall be free to express themselves on, and to consider and choose between, conflicting viewpoints in matters of vital concern to themselves.
>
> (Lockhart and McClure, 1954, pp. 361–2)

At the same time the professors are well aware that the right of free expression cannot be extended to pornography. They therefore concentrate their energies on formulating a legal mechanism for distinguishing between pornography and legitimate sexual expression. This cannot be achieved, they argue, by using the armory of common law tests and definitions of obscenity, reliant as these had been on conceptions of harm that do not stand the test of modern knowledge, and scattered as they were across a patchwork of administrative and legal jurisdictions that robbed them of consistency and left sexual literature to the mercies of sectional extremism and local ignorance.

The solution, they argue, is to acknowledge the aesthetic specificity of this literature: to acknowledge that it too is a vehicle for important ideas, albeit ideas expressed in a manner that is unique to literature – embodied in story, character, and setting. Once this is done it will be possible to draw the protective circle of the Constitution around sexual literature by building aesthetic criteria into legal statutes (courts must concern themselves with the aesthetic place and role of erotic passages in the work as a whole), and by affording literary critics the standing of expert witnesses to the work's aesthetic (and hence social) value. 'Consideration of literary criticism and other expert appraisal is probably not a constitutional requirement, but is essential for adequate fulfilment of the judicial function in constitutional adjudication of obscenity charges against literature' (p. 393). Our professors are not too concerned about whether – on the other side of this rational boundary – pornography might be subject to a certain vestigial policing, or whether it can be left to die a natural death once sexual expression was in full aesthetic bloom.

Until yesterday we were in no doubt as to the meaning of this little historical drama, in which reforming jurists escorted sexual medicine to the courtroom door, bade it farewell and welcomed in its place literary criticism and psychology. There was no shortage of participants in this ritual of enlightenment in which pornography lost its power to harm and became at worst the sign of a certain personal or cultural immaturity. After all, had it not been shown that the old law had predicted its prosecution of the harm of obscenity on groundless conceptions of personal and social pathology laughable to modern knowledge? Furthermore, in assuming connections between erotic ideas and pathological effects and between sexual expression and social harms, had not the law been guilty of a fundamental confusion between values and facts and between the spheres of private aesthetic or ethical judgement and public legal regulation? Yesterday it was clear that a work like Elizabeth Blackwell's was at best a quaint relic and at worst a sinister reminder of an age in which the fear of sex had obscured our knowledge of it and curtailed its full and true literary expression by legal suppression.

Today, however, we are not so sure; and this, as we have indicated, is in part due to the emergence of feminist campaigns against pornography. Through an analysis of sexism and the patriarchal oppression of woman, feminists have sought to re-establish links between erotic ideas and pathological conduct ('pornography the theory, rape the practice') and between sexual literature and social harms. Without reverting to Elizabeth Blackwell's moral physiology, contemporary feminism is just as sceptical that erotic art can be separated from pornography or that modes of sexual expression are purely a matter of private ethical judgement and therefore of no concern to the legal regulation of public life. Today it is possible to see the reforming jurists of the 1960s and 1970s as dupes who, in the name of freeing sexual expression from the law, collaborated in the dissemination of materials that infringe women's civil rights or violate the integrity of their persons.

Yet this view of the liberal reformers may turn out to be as uncomprehending and condescending as their view of the likes of Elizabeth Blackwell. In the liberal consensus feminism finds a naive de-regulatory strategy ultimately complicit with sexism. Without disputing the charge of naivety, there are a number of reasons for rejecting this analysis.

In the first place, the goal of those who sought to reform obscenity law was, we shall argue, not to free pornography from regulation but to change the form of its regulation. In this regard it is important not to be taken in by the reform movement's own view of itself. We have heard our American professors wondering about whether it would be necessary to have any regulation of pornography at all, once true sexuality was allowed unfettered expression. Yet at the same time were they not in fact proposing a new and more sophisticated mechanism for regulating the dissemination of pornography? To be sure, Lockhart and McClure proposed that the old 'deprave and corrupt' test be replaced by statutes recognising the legitimate aesthetic role of erotic passages – statutes to be applied on the advice of literary experts. But they also recommended that in deciding the obscenity of a work, courts should simultaneously take into account the character of the audience to whom it was addressed, and the channels of advertising and distribution through which it reached this audience. Even the work of an acclaimed artist might be obscene in some circumstances of distribution and reception; that is, obscene for some audiences. From the very beginning, then, the tactic to establish an aesthetic threshold for obscenity formed part of a strategy that would allow this threshold to vary with the cultural or psychological 'maturity' of particular audiences.

Second, it is quite unrevealing to attribute such complex and specific strategies to general social or political forces like patriarchy or sexism, or capitalism for that matter. Such attributions do not tell us *how* – through what precise configuration of discourses and institutions – the new regulatory strategy was formed. We can catch a glimpse of this configuration in Norman St John-Stevas' 'Obscenity, Literature and the Law', published in the same period as Lockhart and McClure's article, and making a similar argument for the removal of the law from the sphere of sexual expression and ethics. Liberalisation not only bestows rights, argues St John-Stevas (1956, p. 45), it also imposes responsibilities: 'If a great literature cannot be created without freedom, neither can it be sustained without a sense of responsibility on the author's part. The greater the power and the less the external restraint, the more urgent the need of interior sanctions voluntarily imposed'.

In this balanced partnership of freedom and restraint, which is inseparable from the pairing of desire and norm, fantasy and utility, we can detect the presence of a familiar dialectical practice – equally powerful in the domains of psychology and aesthetics – that contributed to forming the new regulatory threshold for obscenity. Moreover, St John-Stevas argues that even if erotic artists achieve this difficult reconciliation by an interior asceticism, it may still be necessary to impose external restraint (in the form of legally differentiated circulation networks) on those sectors of the public whose sensibilities are not 'fully formed': 'When this practice is extended to deprive the general public of literary works it is indefensible, but the protection of the mass of the people from the corrupting effects of pornography is not so much class prejudice as a realistic recognition that the present educational level leaves them open to victimisation' (p. 47). It is thus implied that the interior sanctions provided by aesthetic discrimination – the sanctions that allow the law to withdraw from the sphere of morality – themselves have public and material conditions of distribution through the apparatus of popular education. We need not, however, suspect St John-Stevas of being aware of this implication. In short, it begins to look as if the move to establish an aesthetic threshold for obscenity depends not on patriarchy but on a certain calculation made in terms of a 'governmental' distribution of aesthetic and ethical competences to different audience types.

Finally, it is by no means clear to what degree the feminist critique itself exists outside the liberal strategy. To be sure, feminism is sceptical of the art-pornography distinction and with it the move to extend to sexual expression the protection of conscience or Constitution, and some feminists seek instead to have pornography policed as a social harm. Yet the arguments supporting this position are anything but uniform. On the one hand there are arguments which aim to show the harm of pornography by using sociology and psychology to demonstrate causal relations between pornography and criminal or undesirable conduct like rape or sexual discrimination. These causal arguments, underscoring the gendered nature of pornography, are indeed outside the intellectual and institutional parameters of the liberal strategy. They remain, however, irredeemably contentious. Of great importance, on the other hand, are those arguments which locate the harm of pornography in its false objectification of women. Pornography, we are told, objectifies women because it fails to achieve the full reconciliation of fantasy and utility, desire and norm. Instead it represents women frozen in the image of masculine fantasy and subservient to the imperatives of patriarchal interest and social utility. Yet these arguments, as we shall see, are products of the same aesthetic and ethical dialectic deployed by the liberal reformers, but which is here directed to speaking of the destruction of women's experience by the excess of unconstrained male fantasies and norms. By contrast, liberals have used this dialectic in a positive sense, taking pornography as the sign of a need to pursue the search for a true representation of sex.

Feminism has thus used the same aesthetic and ethical threshold for obscenity as the liberal strategy, while seeking a different deployment of it. Feminists are understandably sceptical that the interior sanctions or cultural competences necessary to remove pornography from external legal restraint (and transform it into a matter of conscience) are distributed purely according to levels of cultural and psychological maturity. Pressing home the fact that pornography belongs overwhelmingly to the masculine cultural repertory, they have attempted to make gender the central determinant of this distribution. Scepticism regarding the art-pornography and morality-law distinctions is therefore not a sign that the feminist campaign against pornography exists outside the tactics and forms of calculation of the liberal strategy. Rather, it indicates the attempt to deploy the aesthetic-ethical threshold – above which pornography is harmful to development and in need of legal restraint or pedagogical intervention – such that the entire male audience falls beyond it. Not surprisingly, on this side of the threshold the old call for a true, that is, feminist erotic art continues to be heard.

It seems clear, then, that we cannot regard the liberal strategy as marking a definitive moment of cultural maturation in which the forces of reason – armed with the distinction between art and pornography, morality and law – ejected the pathological conception of pornography from the courtroom and freed sexual expression from the long night of obscurantism and repression. But neither can we see it as heralding a new wave of sexual oppression in which a transfer of pornography from the legal to the ethical domain would unleash the full degrading force of male fantasy.

Our object is thus to question the pertinence of any general philosophical division between a private sphere of sexual ethics (interior sanctions) and a public sphere of social and legal regulation (external restraint). Seen less in conceptual than in historical terms, the domain of sexual ethics is inseparable from a variegated field of institutions and discourses – including those of sexual medicine and pedagogy but also of pornography itself – responsible for a specific distribution of ethical-sexual competences across the population. This is the field of the 'social' (Donzelot, 1979), in which a mix of governmental, legal and ethical provisions and their associated disciplines have elaborated a specific domain of 'social' problems. These traverse the public-private boundary at every step. If the liberals' philosophical differentiation of morality from law and art from pornography is in fact dependent on some such practical and variable distribution of ethical-sexual competences, then it cannot form the basis for a general withdrawal of the law from an area said to be intrinsically not its business.

On the other hand, if the ways individuals use pornography are dependent on the actual distributions of ethical and cultural competences, then these uses need not be conceptualised as driven by unleashed male fantasy and hence intrinsically in need of legal restraint. There may be no single general threshold defining the limits of obscenity law (the line bounding art and morality) nor, contrawise, establishing the circumstances in which that law must come into play (causing social harm, infringing rights). Instead, the threshold across which the law makes its entrances and exits – the threshold of juridification of sexual writing – will vary with the distribution of specific ethical abilities, the law itself being part of the complex of institutions overseeing this distribution.

In the light of these preliminary remarks we can formulate two broad hypotheses which the following studies will develop and explore:

- First, that the deployment and use of erotica has no general form (deriving from 'man's' true or fantasmatic desire) but varies with the distribution of erotic interests and competences within the variable mix of institutions and discourses (religious discipline, sexual medicine, the erotic book trade, pedagogy, policing, social reform campaigns, legislative and judicial decisions) which has constituted the pornographic field.
- Second, that this field is not characterised by intrinsic differences between art and pornography or morality and law, but by the contingent and shifting historical configurations of its elements: these forming mobile thresholds for the juridification, pathologisation and aestheticisation of erotica.

It is the task of this chapter to provide a broad survey of the pornographic field in its variable configurations, some of which are selected for more detailed treatment in subsequent chapters.

The argument thus far can be summarised as follows: the liberal strategy is best understood not as a moment of cultural maturation or regression but as the sign of a specific historical mutation in the pornographic field: one which has seen a shift in the composition of regulatory forces away from a medical-legal configuration (as represented by Elizabeth Blackwell) and towards an aesthetic and pedagogical one (as represented by Lockhart and McClure).

THE LIBERAL STRATEGY

Almost all current discussion of obscenity law and pornography takes place within the horizons of the liberal strategy. If, however, we are to understand this strategy as itself a specific historical mutation occurring in a much wider field, we must first learn how to detach ourselves from it. How are we to understand that proliferation of articles, books, and legal testimony through which, in the 1950s and 1960s, a variety of experts sought to lift the legal restraints on erotic art, or at least restrict their scope? The phenomenon is all the more striking, given the silence of these experts today.[1] What was it that permitted them to change the status of erotica from a legally controlled 'toxic' substance to that of the most important agency in 'man's' quest for sexual and personal truth, in need of policing only when more essential and inward forms of restraint broke down?

The liberal strategy emerges at the intersection of three distinct forces. First, *psychology* with its theme of an optimum form of sexual development; second, *aesthetics*, in particular a romantically-derived literary criticism with its theme of an ideal mode of organic personality and sexual expression; lastly, *jurisprudence* with its project for a rational rectification of the boundary between morality and law. Taking shape within this set of coordinates, the liberal strategy harnessed a therapeutics of sexual maturation to an aesthetics of the erotic text, thereby transforming the problem of pornography and relocating the threshold of its legal regulation.

As far as *psychology* is concerned, pornography is symptomatic of a breakdown in the mechanism of sexual development, not harmful in itself but indicative of a harm occurring elsewhere, in a fundamental maturational process. In what was perhaps the single most influential psychological account of pornography in the 1960s – *Pornography and the Law: The Psychology of Erotic Realism and Pornography* – Eberhard and Phyllis Kronhausen tell a familiar fable of human sexual development. Emerging between inborn sexual drives and the countervailing force of social mores and customs, the process of maturation is said to be governed by a fundamental dialectic of desire and norm. As the ageless product of this eternal dialectic, the literature of sexuality is presented with the difficult dual task of satisfying 'the natural and desirable interest in sex, without turning it into morbid channels, confusing and linking it with violence, or keeping it antiseptically detached from the physical sensations which should accompany it, and by connecting the sexual impulse with those love feelings which are its highest perfection' (Kronhausen and Kronhausen, 1959, p. 260). It is with reference to the options presented by this dialectic that the psychologists draw a line through the field of sexual literature separating what they call 'erotic realism' from 'hard core pornography'.

Erotic realism, they say, has only goal: 'To depict life as it is, including man's basic biological needs' (p. 28). We should note, however, that the criterion for success in this regard is that erotic writing function as a vehicle for the dialectic of psycho-sexual maturation; that is, that it permit a full

The Pornographic Field 21

expression of the sex drive without allowing it to become tyrannical, while admitting the shaping force of social norms without allowing them to become repressive. The value of this realism lies in the therapeutic possibilities that it offers: '[I]t reflects a basically healthy and therapeutic attitude toward life' (p. 23). This must be kept in mind when the Kronhausens offer as a touchstone for recognising erotic realism the presence of anti-erotic detail (dirt in Henry Miller, philosophy in D. H. Lawrence, humour in Mark Twain) that keeps erotic fantasy in touch with the balancing norms of experience and aesthetic judgment.

Pornography, for its part, and especially the pornography of perversions, is what results when this dialectic fails. In our age, the authors claim, social norms in the form of literary censorship have imposed a one-sided repression of the drives, forcing them underground where – paradoxically – they achieve enormous power and return in uninhibited and perverse forms. For this reason pornography is simultaneously fantasmatic and aphrodisiacal, a succession of inadequately sublimated sex scenes, each one a little theatre of forbidden and perverse acts. Once again, it is important to note that in offering as the touchstone of pornography the absence of anti-erotic details and digressions – of characterisation, setting, philosophy – the Kronhausens are lamenting the lack of material for a certain psycho-therapeutic action: the playing off of fantasy and desire against experience and norm.

It should be clear why the law can be accorded no positive role in this new division of the field. At best it appears as a somewhat clumsy institutional expression of social norms which, if they are not to deny 'man' his sexual truth, must be kept flexible enough to receive the shape of desire:

> In its attempts to suppress the sexual needs of the individual, society has always exercised a certain amount of literary and artistic censorship. In defiance of this limitation, erotic realism insists on giving the sexual interests . . . their proportionate share in the particular medium of the artist. (p. 26)

At worst – but typically – the law is treated as complicit with the fearful and repressive imposition of such norms which, in blocking the appropriately sublimated expression of desire, actually produces the pornography of perversions that it attempts to eradicate. Psychology therefore shows the law how to withdraw from what is claimed to be the psycho-therapeutic domain of erotic literature, leaving it only a residual function at the margins, to handle cases of bad development, which will become fewer and fewer as the yoke of repression is lifted.

In the case of *aesthetics* (and literary criticism), pornography is the sign of an aesthetic rather than a psychological failure. However, we are immediately aware that this failure is specified according to a dialectic that bears a striking resemblance to the one we have just examined. It was Friedrich Schiller who in the late eighteenth century first differentiated between 'naive' and 'sentimental' poetry, declaring that the former was indicative of the tyranny of the senses over the imagination while the latter was the product of ideas and fantasies given free reign at the expense of the senses and experience. The truly aesthetic work or disposition, however, achieves a dialectical reconciliation of what Schiller called the 'form drive' and the 'sense drive':

> Melting beauty, so it was maintained, is for natures which are tense; energizing beauty for those which are relaxed. I call a man tense when he is under the compulsion of thought, no less than when he is under the compulsion of feeling. Exclusive domination by either of his two basic drives is for him a state of constraint and violence, and freedom lies only in the co-operation of both his natures. The man one-sidedly dominated by feeling, or the sensuously tensed man, will be released and set free by means of form; the man one-sidedly dominated by law, or the spiritually tensed man, will be released and set free by means of matter. In order to be adequate to this twofold task, melting beauty will therefore reveal herself under two different guises. First, as tranquil form, she will assuage the violence of life, and pave the way which leads from sensation to thought. Secondly, as living image, she will arm abstract form with sensuous power, lead concept back to intuition, and law back to feeling. The first of these services she renders to natural man, the second to civilized man.
>
> (Schiller, 1795, pp. 119–21)

In this process 'melting beauty' effects an ideal reciprocity between feeling and idea, subject and object, desire and norm.

Through an historical overlapping (examined in more detail in Chapter 4) it became possible to transpose this aesthetic and ethical dialectic into the sexual register, thereby producing the aesthetic specification of pornography publicised by D. H. Lawrence. For Lawrence – preoccupied as he was with the image of the over-civilised or 'spiritually tensed' man – the defining characteristic of pornography is predictably its sentimentality, a tyranny of mentality and fantasy which, at the expense of the senses and the 'body' of language, traps the subject in a purely auto-erotic relation to the self:

The Pornographic Field

The sentimentalism and the niggling analysis, often self analysis, of most of our modern literature, is a sign of self abuse. It is the manifestation of masturbation, the sort of conscious activity stimulated by masturbation, whether male or female. The outstanding feature of such consciousness is that there is no real object, there is only subject. This is just the same whether it be a novel or a work of science. The author never escapes from himself, he pads along within the vicious circle of himself.

(Lawrence, 1936, p. 180)

Lacking the resistance of experience or norms, the 'pornographic imagination' is manifest in endless erotic fantasy. Recognisable in the absence of developed characters and setting, it transmits the single-minded intention of sexual arousal.

Erotic art or literature, on the other hand, is characterised – the pattern should by now be clear – precisely by its success in reconciling the aestheticosexual opposites. Bringing fantasy up against the complexity of experience and forcing the imagination to embody itself in the senses (which are in their turn refined by it), erotic art – the sexual novel in particular – permits the single-mindedness of sex to encounter the human totality and allows self and other, subject and object, to enter into a truly reciprocal relation. It is through such a reconciliation, we are told, that the literature of sexuality is justified by its realism and wins the right to represent the truth of sex:

We have to be sufficiently conscious, and self-conscious, to know our own limits and to be aware of the greater urge within us and beyond us. Then we can cease to be primarily interested in ourselves. Then we learn to leave ourselves alone, in all the affective centres: not to force our feelings in any way, and never to force our sex. Then we can make the great onslaught on the outside lie, the inside lie being settled. And that is freedom and the fight for freedom. (p. 185)

Once again, however, the criterion for this realism – the co-presence of erotic detail with developed characters, setting, 'philosophy' – signifies neither more or less than the textual availability and deployment of the materials of the aesthetic-ethical dialectic.

We can observe in passing, and mark for future comment, the fact that the aesthetic specification of pornography also provides the basis for much feminist analysis. Despite Lawrence's claim that both men and women are susceptible to the 'sentimentalism' that leaves them locked in an auto-erotic relation to the self – and despite the bestiary of Lawrence's female characters, many of whom are indeed masturbatory and wilful – it was possible from the outset to identify the pornographic tyranny of fantasy with the male imagination, and to replace the one-sidedness of masturbation with that of rape. For example, in a general article on 'Literature and Pornography', Colin Wilson (1982, p. 212) is quite happy to write that 'Pornography is a more civilised version of rape. That is to say, it is an appeal to this masculine desire to conquer and penetrate, without personal involvement . . . Rape has been transposed into the world of the imagination'. With this, we are already in that quirky domain where – like masturbation before it – rape will be used as a general metaphor for any failure of aesthetic reciprocity and thus of sexual mutuality, bringing the stigma of crime to an ethical failing but thereby threatening to turn the crime into a matter of aesthetics and ethics.

In either case, it is clear that, like psychology, literary criticism provides a powerful means for rolling back the area of sexual literature open to legal regulation: this time by making the aesthetic-ethical dialectic central to the realisation of true sexuality and by reconstructing the problem of pornography as a failure in 'man's' aesthetic education. The claims of aesthetics to adjudicate in this matter are given their full romantic charge in the following remarks:

> One point seems evident, that literary standards should not be regulated by law. Literature is creative, imaginative and aesthetic, with no extrinsic purpose, its one criterion being fidelity to its own nature. It is the study of the universal, but in the light of the individual and the particular, an expression of man's creative faculty, intent on beauty not on utility. Law is not creative but regulative, seeking not a special ideal harmony but a generalized justice and the application of universally valid principles. Thus it is impossible to attempt to confine literature within the Procrustean bed of the law.
>
> (St John-Stevas, 1956, p. 51)

Pictured as the vehicle of an inflexible social normativity, the law continually threatens to foster that which it would suppress, by driving the erotic imagination from the realms of open and publishable experience into a private fantasy world where it goes bad. Again, it is argued that the law itself cannot draw the line between art and pornography. Moreover, it can enter the scene only to deal with residual pornographic failures in aesthetic education.

It is not yet our business to enquire into the depth of this reciprocity

The Pornographic Field

between the psychological and aesthetic specifications of pornography; or into whether it results from a common lineage or the contingent overlapping of adjacent fields. For the moment it is enough to say that in the area of our concern the psychological dialectic of drive and norm and the aesthetic dialectic of experience and form duplicate each other perfectly, and in doing so have produced a powerful psycho-aesthetic schema for the intelligibility of erotica.

The psycho-aesthetic analysis of pornography dominates the general academic and cultural arena. For example, Steven Marcus' (1964) much-cited study describes Victorian pornography in terms of the breakdown of the aesthetic mediation of fantasy and experience. Its leading characteristic, therefore, 'is its quality of dissociation; it is dissociated from itself, from experience, from literature' (p. 228). Hence in Marcus' view pornography is both too 'abstract' (because nothing diversifies the over-narrow purpose of sexual arousal) and too 'concrete' (because nothing gives shape to the proliferation of organs, positions, and events with which the fantasy feeds itself). But, at the same time, this aesthetic failure to reconcile fantasy and experience, ideas and feelings, goes proxy for a psycho-therapeutic failure to achieve an appropriate reconciliation of sexual drive and social norm. Pornography, says Marcus, is the result of a repressive culture which, in denying sexual desire, displaces it into perverse and fantasmatic forms instead of the appropriate sublimation achieved by erotic realism.[2]

Peter Gay's (1984) general study of Victorian sexuality simply transposes this same dual dialectic more fully into the historical register. Here a whole range of historical institutions – from law and education to sexual medicine – are explained in terms of a repressive failure to reconcile drive and norm that leads desire into the perverse forms of pornography and away from its highest expression in the sexual mutuality of the high-bourgeois couple.

This alliance of psychology and aesthetic has contributed decisively to the liberal campaign to reform obscenity law. It was, as subsequent chapters will show, responsible for recasting the problem of pornography from one of suppressing a pathological substance to one of projecting and protecting an optimum sexual development – even if the form in which the law could offer such protection was in the event quite unlike that graceful withdrawal from the aesthetic scene envisaged by St John-Stevas.

The role of the third force in the liberal strategy – *jurisprudence* – is both more complex and more ambivalent than those of psychology and aesthetics. Attached on one side to a philosophical analysis of the law and a project to subject its errors and excesses to a rational rectification and, on the other, to the historical array of statutes and case law, procedures and agencies actually responsible for the judicial regulation of obscenity, jurisprudence has been forced to negotiate a more exacting 'dialectic'.

There is no doubt that during the 1950s jurisprudential reasoning about obscenity was opening itself to the discourses of psychology and aesthetics, finding in them a new way of knowing about pornography as a problem in need of resolution. The role of the psycho-therapeutic dialectic is quite evident in the American Law Institute's attempt to develop a new obscenity statute – based on a particular conception of 'appeal to prurient interest' – for its Model Penal Code. In Lockhart and McClure's paraphrase:

> To the American Law Institute, 'prurient interest' is a 'shameful or morbid interest in nudity, sex, or excretion'; it is 'an exacerbated, morbid, or perverted interest growing out of the conflict between the universal sexual drive of the individual and equally universal social control of sexual activity.' Material 'appeals' to this interest when, 'of itself, the material has 'the capacity to attract individuals eager for a forbidden look behind the curtain of privacy which our customs draw about sexual matters'. The Institute's primary purpose in adopting this definition was to prevent exploitation of the psychosexual tension created by the conflict between the individual's normal sexual curiosity and drive, and the powerful social and legal inhibitions that restrain overt sexual behavior.
>
> (Lockhart and McClure, 1960, p. 56)

But the impact of aesthetics is no less clear. Lockhart and McClure (pp. 58–68) draw in equal measure on Lawrence and the Kronhausens, seeking to construct the boundary between 'erotic realism' and 'hardcore pornography' in terms of the latter's fantasmatic and retardational properties. 'Pornography is daydream material, divorced from reality, whose main or sole purpose is to nourish erotic fantasies or, as the psychiatrists say, psychic autoeroticism' (p. 65).

Existing American obscenity law was organised around the 1868 English definition of obscenity (in *Regina* v. *Hicklin*) in terms of its 'tendency to deprave and corrupt those whose minds were open to such immoral influences and into whose hands it might fall'. In the new cultural-legal environment, however, this law appeared to be beset by a fundamental weakness. The existing law, it was argued, defined obscenity in terms of certain alleged *causal effects* (and in particular its harmful effects on the most vulnerable) instead of in terms of the *aesthetic and psychological responses* of which it is susceptible. In so doing it confused the unethical with the harmful and failed to distinguish erotic literature (necessary for 'man's' ethical-sexual development) from 'worthless pornography'. As a result, it was suggested that the *Hicklin* test be abolished, that courts be forced to contextualise erotic passages in the 'work as a whole', so that their aesthetic integrity could be judged in terms of the author's intentions; and that literary critics be empowered to help clarify whether a work was a true aesthetic expression of human sexuality or whether it simply nourished erotic fantasies. In this way a reforming jurisprudence drew on psychology and aesthetics to propose what it imagined was a rational correction of the law. The effect of these reforms would be the law's withdrawal from an ethical and aesthetic sphere into which it had trespassed at the behest of the forces of sexual ignorance and cultural repression.

There is equally no doubt, however, that the closer the reform movement came in government reports and legal statutes to operationalising the new threshold for obscenity, the more difficulties it encountered. It was all very well to talk about the 'work as a whole' and about respecting the author's intentions, but given that these intentions could only be ascertained in the work itself, and given that the work was dependent on the kind of response it received, the location of the new threshold was far less easy. But this was only a curtain-raiser to a more general and profound problem.

In attempting to free erotica from laws aimed at protecting the most vulnerable, the liberal strategy had begun using as its benchmark 'contemporary community standards' and 'the average person'. However, as Lockhart and McClure (1960, pp. 68–87) were quick to see, in simultaneously moving to replace causal *effects* with psychological and aesthetic *responses* the reformist strategy could not in fact avail itself of these universal agents of judgement, for the inescapable reason that such responses vary. In short, it became clear that the *kind of response* to erotic literature, which was to determine its obscenity, would vary with the *kind of person* who was responding.[3] Hence, so too would the obscenity of the work.

The proposed and actual reforms of the 1960s and 1970s have not in the event attempted to directly enact the psycho-aesthetic threshold in a general form. Rather, emerging in the gap between the clear idea of this threshold and the actual uncertainty imposed by the variability of audience response, a number of compromise solutions have been produced, ranging from exemption clauses (for materials of literary merit) to proposals for a variable test of obscenity itself. We investigate the character of these compromises in more detail below. For the moment it is enough to draw out their consequence for our exposition thus far: namely, that in determining obscenity the law can take as its point of reference not a general-purpose or universal human subject but an array of kinds of person. These are differentiated according to the possession of cultural capacities that must be legally recognised. Individuals are equipped with these capacities – that can affect their legal personhood – by a complex infrastructure of other institutions adjacent to the law and overlapping it.

The jurisprudential project to withdraw obscenity law from the ethical sphere is simply utopian, to the degree that this project assumes that ethical capacities inhere in a private realm of subjectivity independent of social provision and regulation. As far as psychology and aesthetics are concerned, it follows that sexual attributes and ethical abilities do not derive from the dialectical division of a general human subject but are variably acquired in the disparate passages of individuals and groups through cultural institutions. Acknowledgement of the fact that the 'appropriate' psychological and aesthetic response to erotica will vary with the cultural level of the audience means that these responses are themselves contingent capacities differentially distributed in actual populations.

This helps to make sense of our earlier remarks that in speaking of the 'realism' of legitimate erotica the liberal strategy is in fact referring to the contingent presence of a particular aesthetic-ethical practice and skill. It also allows us to propose that mastery of this particular practice and skill, in which desire is played off against norm and fantasy against experience, by no means exhausts the historical field in which erotic capacities have been acquired and pornography has circulated. Once we see the liberal strategy as a recent configuration of the pornographic field, we can begin to pursue our investigation outside the specific form of psycho-aesthetic intelligibility which that strategy has imposed upon the field.

THE POSITIVITY OF PORNOGRAPHY

A principal limitation of the psycho-aesthetic analysis is that it treats pornography as a purely negative phenomenon. Pornography, we are told, is the result of some artificial blockage in the mediation of drive and norm, fantasy and experience. It is the retort of a repressed sexuality that assumes auto-erotic, perverse, and fantasmatic forms only because this sexuality has been silenced, denied access to its legitimate objects, and removed from the shaping pressures of reality and norm. Pornography's consumers are alleged to be emotionally immature, under-educated, retarded by 'psychic auto-eroticism' or, in blunter language, 'pathetic dirty-minded old men'.

Of course this view has its attraction, dependent as it is on the promise of a true sexuality to be made good at the end of our personal or cultural history, when we have learned to integrate sexual desire and social norms. However, the assumption on which it is based – that our sexuality has been

The Pornographic Field

disfigured by a long history of silencing and repression – has been more or less destroyed by Michel Foucault's history of sexuality. The history of sexuality since the seventeenth century, argues Foucault (1979, pp. 17–35), has not been marked by silencing and repression but by the converse: a multiplication of inducements to speak about sex, discourses on sex, and institutions requiring their utterance.

Foucault's account turns on a remarkable inversion of the cornerstone of the standard histories: we in the West are not beings characterised by a repressed sexuality; we are beings characterised by the fact that we *say* that our sexuality is repressed. This discourse on repression, for Foucault, is a 'fable' which emerged as part of the apparatus of confession and spiritual direction between the fifteenth and seventeenth centuries. In this context the discourse did not behave as a (true or false) description of sex but as a device with particular application to conduct. To teach individuals that the truth of their sex was hidden was a means of getting them to look for it and, in looking for it, expose more of their self to correction. We learn to say that our sex has been silenced as part of an instituted process of speaking about it. In other words, the discourse on repression and the confessional technology to which it belongs are responsible for getting individuals to behave as if their conduct was determined by secret and silent desires, which must of course be revealed and spoken. In this manner, our sexuality is not *expressed* but *achieved*. Foucault summarises his functional displacement of the theme of repression in the following remarks:

> But this often-stated theme, that sex is outside of discourse and that only the removing of an obstacle, the breaking of a secret, can clear the way leading to it, is precisely what needs to be examined. Does it not partake of the injunction by which discourse is provoked? Is it not with the aim of inciting people to speak of sex that it is made to mirror, at the outer limit of every actual discourse, something akin to a secret whose discovery is imperative, a thing abusively reduced to silence, and at the same time difficult and necessary, dangerous and precious to divulge? We must not forget that by making sex into that which above all else had to be confessed, the Christian pastoral always presented it as the disquieting enigma: not a thing which shows itself, but one which always hides . . . . Doubtless the secret does not reside in that basic reality in relation to which all the incitements to speak of sex are situated . . . . It is a question rather of a theme that forms part of the very mechanics of these incitements: a way of giving shape to the requirement to speak about the matter, a fable that is indispensable to the endlessly proliferating economy of the discourse on sex. What is peculiar to modern societies, in fact, is

not that they consigned sex to a shadow existence, but that they dedicated themselves to speaking about it *ad infinitum*, while exploiting it as *the* secret. (pp. 34–5)

And to emphasise the peculiarity of our western sexual technology, Foucault reminds us that in the East sexuality is less a dark secret to be endlessly brought into the light of knowledge than a set of pleasure techniques in which one might be successfully instructed, like yoga.

From Foucault's account of the discourse on repression we can draw a number of coordinates for re-orienting the approach to pornography. In the first place, we can suggest that in attributing pornography to the repression of sexuality, modern histories and psychologies show themselves to be active *extensions* of the apparatus of western sexuality rather than independent reflections on it. By ignoring the fact that western societies have developed elaborate mechanisms for speaking about sex, and by re-telling the fable of the long centuries during which we have supposedly repressed sex and condemned it to silence, these modern histories reactivate in their own registers the very same means deployed by the technology of confession. If they ascribe pornography to repression, this is less a description of historical fact than a device ensuring that we will continue to approach pornography as if it were the dark secret of our sexuality and the hidden truth of our self. Not only does the fable of repression thus activate a powerful incentive to talk about pornography, it also ensures that this discourse will present itself as an emancipation, the breaking of a silence and the penetration of an enigma. Our own discourse on pornography in these studies, therefore, will not forget that it takes place in one of the most garrulous fields imaginable. Far from requiring sagacity and courage in order to be spoken of, the secret of pornography is something that anyone can speak of in order to be attributed sagacity and courage.

Second, setting limits to the concept of repression helps to draw out the *positive* character of pornography. Foucault's hypothesis is that western sexuality – far from being a timeless expression of the dialectic of drive and norm, fantasy and experience – is a historical product of the emergence and proliferation of confessional techniques, discourses and institutions. Let us say that pornographic writing is one device in this confessional technology. The technology of confession is not an apparatus revealing the existence of sexuality to knowledge; it is a means of bringing western sexuality into existence by attaching it to an apparatus of knowledges in which it must be revealed. As a result, argues Foucault, our knowledges of sex – even the most scientific – are also a means of obtaining sexual pleasure, just as pleasure in sex is for us to tied to the gesture of knowing its mystery. As part of the confessional apparatus, pornographic writing is not a negative reflex of real sexuality but a repository of positive techniques for making a specific kind of sexuality real.

Finally, as a result, we can begin to discuss the emergence of modern pornography in the seventeenth century in terms of the action of confession seen as a particular cultural technology. Confession was a means of getting individuals to organise their feelings and conduct around the principle of a hidden desire: a desire which they were obliged to reveal in an exchange establishing the interdependence – among us – of knowledge of sex and pleasure in it. The religious 'confession of the flesh' was thus itself a powerful eroticising mechanism which, under ideal operational circumstances, used the erotic sensibility that it created as an anchor for spiritual intensity and religious discipline. Operational circumstances are rarely predictable, however, and the border between the mastery of sexual self-interrogation for spiritual purposes and as an avenue to erotic intensities proved to be easily crossed. Most important, it is at the crossing of this border that we can locate the emergence of pornography. Foucault comments:

> One could plot a line going straight from the seventeenth-century pastoral to what became its projection in literature, 'scandalous' literature at that. 'Tell everything', the director would say time and again: 'not only consummated acts, but sensual touchings, all impure gazes, all obscene remarks . . . all consenting thoughts'. Sade takes up the injunction in words that seem to have been retranscribed from the treatises of spiritual direction: 'Your narrations must be decorated with the most numerous and searching details; the precise way and extent to which we may judge how the passion you describe relates to human manners and man's character is determined by your willingness to disguise no circumstances; and what is more, the least circumstance is apt to have an immense influence upon the procuring of that kind of sensory irritation we expect from your stories'.
>
> (Foucault, 1979, p. 21)

To do historical justice to pornographic writing, we must not see it as emerging from the thwarting of a universal and ideal process of sexual maturation – a phantom that would turn to dust when the first rays of sexual liberation broke through the long dark of repression. Rather, it acquired a positive and autonomous existence as an ethos or means of conducting the self in a certain way, that is, as the 'profane' form of what had been a 'spiritual' ethic.

We can now see what it means to say that sexuality is not the possession of a generalised psychological subject – the expression of a timeless dialectic between drive and norm – but the artefact of a limited set of institutional and discursive arrangements, initially focused in the practice of confession. Far from silencing and repressing sexuality, the Christian churches were the initial locus of a powerful machinery for sexualising larger sectors of the population; for disseminating the techniques of sexual conscience; for 'putting sex into discourse'.

Since the confession of the flesh was not simply a matter of doctrine and belief but the product of a whole technology of instituted relationships, regulated practices, and types of discourse, there was no guarantee that this technology would remain within the limits and purposes of its initial religious deployment. Even here the eroticising effects of confession and the direction of conscience could not be strictly controlled. The unstable exchange between excitation and restraint often broke down, sometimes with spectacular and alarming effects, as in the phenomenon of demonic possession. We should not too surprised then, if outside its religious deployment, the intensification of desire produced by the confessional technology could easily assume 'lewd and lascivious' forms. This was not the subversive retort of a repressed sexuality rooted in the body and its drives, however. It was a sign that, transposed beyond its religious deployment through the agency of print and print literacy, this migrating technology continued to produce its effects of desire in other milieus governed by other norms. It is to this transposition that we must look for the emergence of early modern pornography, which was both its instrument and its effect.

Consider, for example, this extract from a confessional manual published in the early seventeenth century. Giving directions for confessing the sin of lust, the manual states that:

> With respect to the confession of bad gestures the penitent must describe:
> a. exactly what he was thinking at the time of the pollution
> b. whether he made use of any instrument
> c. whether he made use of the hand of another
> d. which part of the body was used to make the gesture
> e. was the reason for using this part of the body uniquely for reasons of utility, or was it for reasons of particularity?
>
> (quoted in Foucault, 1975, p. 32)

Under this kind of pressure, comments Foucault:

The complex and floating notion of carnality, of the flesh, begins to detach itself from the materiality of the body. The flesh is both the domain and the exercise of power and of objectivation; it is the site of the multiple intensities of desire and delectation, the sensitive and complex body of concupiscence. (p. 29)

It is not so remarkable, then, that early modern pornography should have emerged from the Christian technology of the flesh. More specifically, we can understand why, towards the end of the seventeenth century, the table of contents from *The School of Venus* should have both duplicated and parodied the spiritual interrogation of the flesh, containing these entries amongst others:

> Special names of those organs which are primarily the ones to minister to love's desires, beginning with another description of the yard . . . . A discussion of mounting and the various ways of riding, as well as others which can be imagined . . . Care which must be taken in approaching the climax of love-making. Brief description and classification of all the pleasures which should precede and accompany it, in words and thoughts, as well as actions . . . . The aim of love is physical pleasure. Reason for this with a charming explanation of the subject . . . Reasons why the buttocks are clenched during intercourse. An explanation of this. A further enquiry as to why men experience more pleasure when women touch the yard with their hands than with any other part of their bodies. The special virtue of this pleasure attributed to the female hand . . . . Necessary means to ensure the enjoyment of perfect bliss by two lovers during copulation. An exhortation to follow this method. Those girls who wish to learn this lesson will please take the trouble to read what is written here.
>
> (Millot and L'Ange, [1655] 1972, pp. 67–75)

In these answers addressed to a reader who accedes to pleasure through the ritual of instruction in its secrets, we can recognise the central features of the spiritual interrogation of the flesh: its minute mapping and naming of the sexual body, its precise specification of pleasures, and its exacting codification of desire. The concupiscent body – saturated with desire and charted by a complex cartography of pleasures and gestures – was not something that pornography found ready-made in the psycho-sexual drives; neither was it something that pornography manufactured from them as a revenge on a too-puritanical society. It was, instead, something which pornography inherited when it emerged unforeseen as a profane relay for the Christian technology of the flesh which had brought this body into being.

Giving it this genealogy clarifies a number of features of what we might call – although not without a degree of retrospective formulation – England's first commercial pornography. First, it makes sense of the fact that this literature was almost wholly imported (from France and Italy) and was relatively rare, both in terms of titles and dissemination. David Foxon's (1964) bibliographical survey confines itself to Aretino's 'Postures', *Ragionamenti* and (the attributed) *La Puttana Errante*, as well as Millot and L'Ange's *L'Ecole des Filles (The School of Venus)*, Chorier's *Satyra Sotadique (L'Académie des Dames, a Dialogue Between a Married Woman and a Maid, or The School of Women)*, and Barrin's *Vénus dans le Cloître (Venus in the Cloister, or the Nun in her Smock)*. Although Wagner (1985, p. 33) expands this list to twenty-four titles (largely by including a number of borderline erotic romances), the fact remains that here we are not dealing with the late flowering of a prolific pre-repression sexuality, nor the first dark blooms of pornography that would spread with the onset of Puritanism. Instead, we are observing a limited but definite process of cultural transmission. Having migrated from its initial religious deployment, along the profane channels of translation, authorship and dissemination opened by print and the book trade, the confessional interrogation of the flesh crossed the English Channel as a highly specialised literary species addressing a small sector of the literate public: aristocratic and middle-class men, predisposed to self-cultivation and possessing sophisticated literate abilities.

Second, we can understand why this literature is so dependent on the religious milieu, in particular on the practices of confession and the direction of conscience. Not only does it draw on these for setting and characters (overheated nuns, seducing confessors) but, more importantly, for the ethical-literary techniques with which it addresses its audience. These works are overwhelmingly in dialogue form. They are in fact erotic transpositions of the dialogical direction of conscience in which a sexual 'director' conducts a novice through a series of erotic interrogations, following a logic of intensification and refinement of desire and pleasure.

This also explains the educative rhetoric of much of this literature. The question and answer form of the dialogue has of course a long history and the quasi-parodic invocation of pedagogical address is clear enough in the 'answers' cited from the preface to *The School of Venus*. What Pepys found in this 'mighty lewd book' was a typology of sexual postures and erotic zones; a repertoire of techniques; a sophisticated erotic lexicon ('A refined and subtle explanation of such words as *thread, impale, belabour, mount* and *ride'*); and a whole encyclopedia of pleasures and imaginings. But of equal if not greater importance is the fact that what *The School of Venus* found in the great diarist was a master of spiritual 'book-keeping'; that is, a reader adept in the ethical-literary techniques through which Protestants had learned to scrutinise their own lives for the signs of inner grace and thereby expanded and intensified the private sphere.

Should we be surprised, then, if at the meeting point of a literature transmitting a new erotics of the flesh, and a practice of reading through which individuals opened up the relation to the inner self, there should have emerged a specifically auto-erotic deployment of literature? A conscientious sexuality? Pepys' masturbatory use of pornography is not the surrogate form of a sexuality denied its true object, a symptom of psychic auto-eroticism. Instead, it can be regarded as one of an ensemble of positive techniques through which a special class of individuals redefined their relation to the self through an interrogation-incitation of the sexual body. The old joke that pornography is literature read with one hand yields up its grain of truth. In Pepys' secretive use of it, we find a small emblem for the emergence of pornography as the instrument and effect of the profane redeployment of the spiritual technology of the flesh. That psychologists now interpret the auto-erotic application or use of literature as symptom of retarded or incomplete maturation does not signal the discovery of the truth about pornography. It is simply a sign that in the two centuries following Pepys, this particular application would come to be increasingly managed by a medical apparatus and its norms, as we shall see.

BIBLIO-EROTICS

Given their reciprocity and interdependence, we can predict that what we have called the positivity of pornography will be as problematic for aesthetics as it is for psychology. It will be recalled that in the aesthetic analysis pornography is understood in terms of the breakdown of a fundamental aesthetic-ethical dialectic, that is, a result of the failure to reconcile the tyrannical fantasies of the will and the equally peremptory imperatives of the senses and experience. Pornography is said to be the outcome of twin failures: of the inability to realise and embody the abstract intention to arouse in an imagery that would put it in touch with the potential totality of human experience; and of the symmetrical inability to subject the chaotic and excitatory imagery of the senses to the shaping force of the moral will. As such, pornography is paradoxically held to fail in two different directions at the same time. It is too abstract, being nothing more than a didactic vehicle for the intention to arouse, and hence recognisable by a mechanical aggregation of sex scenes allowing for no organic development of character and plot. But it is also too concrete: freed from the inhibitions of the moral will, the imagery of the senses gushes forth unconstrained, allowing pornography to be recognised by the torrent of sexual detail flooding over its mechanical plot.

There is no doubt that this model – in which psychology's maturational and therapeutic analysis of pornography is recapitulated and tranformed by an aesthetics of the text – is the most powerful one currently available. But if, as we have just seen, the psychological analysis runs foul of the historical specificity and positivity of pornography, things are no easier on the aesthetic side of the psycho-aesthetic model, and for similar reasons. Three questions must be raised.

1. Is pornography failed art?

What are we to make of the attempt to specify a pornographic genre – one in which aesthetic failure would go proxy for psychological immaturity – in terms of the plethora of erotic detail and the mechanical nature of the sexual narrative and its characters? While not wishing to reject their descriptive value out of hand, have we not seen that these features of pornography emerge from cultural circumstances more local, technical and contingent than the failure of some great dialectic between fantasy and experience, senses and will? Dwelling on erotic details might be a characteristic of the 'pornographic imagination', but there can be little doubt that this is a capacity formed initially in the institutions and for the purposes of confession and spiritual guidance. The confession of the flesh took hold not as a theological doctrine, nor as a moral code, but as a network of regulated practices, controlled techniques, and constrained discourses; one that permitted the adept to locate desire in the smallest impulses, in the most ramified complicity of the body's gestures and the mind's imaginings. For example, in requiring the penitent to describe 'exactly what he was thinking at the time of the pollution', the confessional manual cited above also required the priest to inquire as to whether thoughts of incest or of fornication accompanied the act, as this affected the sort of sin committed. Transposed into the pornographic register the same technique affected the intensity of desire stimulated and pleasure realised. In both cases the degree of sexual detail registers the extent to which the practice of a confessional erotics has transformed the body into that complex cultural object of spiritual anxiety and carnal pleasure known as 'the flesh'.[4] Adopting Foucault's terminology, we might say that what the confession of the flesh provided was a 'micro-technics of delectation' whose redeployment in pornography relied upon a sensitivity to erotic detail that – far from signifying the uncontrolled tyranny of fantasy or the senses – had been painstakingly forged through mastery of the techniques of spiritual self-interrogation. That this is so can be seen from two very different events.

First, by the end of the seventeenth century the Catholic church was itself attempting to moderate the incitatory effects of confession and spiritual direction, precisely by urging on priests a new discretion with regards to the details sought in the confession of sins of the flesh. Second, the work that we find at the centre of the *Hicklin* case in 1868 – the nineteenth-century case responsible for producing the 'deprave and corrupt' test – is a pamphlet entitled *The Confessional Unmasked*. This is a compilation from the great confessional manuals of Dens, Liguori, Bailly, and Cabassutius. The intimate relation between the profane delectation of erotic detail and the minute spiritual interrogation of desire may have remained a mystery to psychologically inclined literary critics; not so, however, to Chief Justice Cockburn, who found in this relation the crux of the obscenity of this anti-papist pamphlet:

> The very reason why this work is put forward to expose the practices of the Roman Catholic confessional is a tendency of questions, involving practices and propensities of a certain description, to do mischief to the minds of those to whom such questions are addressed, by suggesting thoughts and desires which otherwise would not have occurred to their minds. If that be the case between the priest and the person confessing, it manifestly must equally be so when the whole is put into the shape of a series of paragraphs, one following upon another, each involving some impure practices, some of them of the most filthy and disgusting and unnatural description it is possible to imagine.

> (*Regina* v. *Hicklin*, p. 371)[5]

So much for the question of delectable details. What of the so-called repetitive and mechanical quality of pornographic narrative and characterisation? Once again it is not difficult to show relations of filiation and transposition between the structure of sexual confession and that of the erotic text. An erotic dialogue like *The School of Venus*, for example, is organised by the confessional imperative to tell another all one's secret temptations and sins, now given a positive value as the key to sexual knowledge and pleasure. Equally, the dialogical form of this erotic direction of conscience imposes a serial and repetitive organisation. The director questions the novice regarding her feelings, command of sexual technique and idiom, which produces further disclosures, prompting further questions and so on.

Recent scholarship has discerned a similar relation between Puritan techniques of conscience and the structure of the early novel.[6] Here the focus has been on a specific ensemble of ethical-literary techniques – spiritual autobiography in particular – but also diary-keeping, conduct books, providence literature, and popular casuistry. Robbed of the certitude of salvation provided by sacramental rituals like confession, Puritans found in these techniques a means for giving their own conduct the structure of a 'life' and for scrutinising it for signs of grace. In this way specific ethical and literate competences were developed which formed a cultural sub-stratum common to both devotional literature and those books which were eventually called novels. Two features of this cultural overlap are of particular importance for our argument.

First, because the function of spiritual autobiography was essentially exemplary – to show readers how to organise their lives around the search for signs of grace – pseudo-memoirs like *Robinson Crusoe* and *Tom Jones* could be put to the same ethical use. Second, this secular transposition of spiritual autobiography also provided the memoir-novel with a particular structure. This was one in which events were organised into the stages of a life: a succession of critical moments in which the memorialist either discovered the workings of grace in their own life and hence moved closer to that blessed state, or else failed to do so and remained in anxiety.

Once again, the important thing about this structure is that, as a functional component in a specific ethical-literary practice – a device for recording and scrutinising conduct which permitted norms to be internalised as conscience – it was relatively autonomous of any particular doctrinal investment. Under these circumstances it was quite possible for the pleasures of the flesh to occupy the structural position of 'grace', and for memoirs to appear in which the events of the 'life' were organised around the search for sexual grace and the cultivation of erotic conscientiousness.

Underwriting the 'editor's' prefatory claim that Robinson Crusoe's story

> is told with modesty, with seriousness, and with a religious application of events to which wise men always apply them, viz. to the instruction of others by this example, and to justify the wisdom of Providence in all the variety of our circumstances . . .

(Defoe, 1719, p. 25)

and Fanny Hill's promise to

recall to view those scandalous stages of my life, out of which I emerged at length, to the enjoyment of every blessing in the power of love, health and fortune to bestow . . .

(Cleland, 1748, p. 39)

we find a single structure linking one of the most pious novels in English to one of the most erotic. That Fanny Hill's life should lead her only from one erotic encounter to the next is not a sign of the author's inability to achieve an exemplary reconciliation of the imperatives of fantasy and the pressures of experience. Instead, it indicates that – once redeployed as an erotics of the flesh – the autobiographical schema (awakening, search for grace, conversion) could promise a different kind of election; one in which each event in the exemplary life revealed a new level of pleasure and took one a step closer to erotic grace:

For my part I was so enchanted with my fortune, so transported with the comparison of the delights I now swarmed in, with all the insipidity of my past scenes of life, that I thought them sufficiently cheap even at the price of my ruin, or the risque of their not lasting. (pp. 80–1)

2. Is there a subject of pornography?

Pornography, it is said, is read and written by those who have not yet learned to mediate between the power of fantasy and the resistance of experience; it is essentially a symptom of an aesthetic immaturity. Its appeal signifies the retardation of a formative process – Peter Gay's 'education of the senses' – rooted deep in the divisions of the human ethical substance and whose culminating point is represented by the true artist and true erotic art. Or so we are told.

What, then, are we to make of Samuel Pepys who, in order to read pornography, not only had to possess a relatively scarce cultural competence – print literacy – but had to possess it in a foreign language if he was to consume this rare literary import? What are we to make of the fact that his reading of pornography overlapped with a quite different cultural accomplishment: the discipline of the diary which permitted him to open the space of inner reflection on his daily conduct? Finally, what are we to make of the fact that the literary channel through which Pepys shaped his auto-erotic desire not only required specific cultural abilities, but was also gender specific? (Pepys had picked up *L'Ecole des Filles* as a possible translation exercise for his wife, but found in it a device for a practice of erotic intensification from which she was excluded.) All these questions suggest that the auto-erotic interest in pornography, far from originating in the (retarded) aesthetic organisation of the human subject, was (at least initially) a relatively rare cultural competence dependent on a definite and limited social distribution.

This competence depended on particular kinds of institution transmitting specific ethical techniques. The direction of conscience, for example, was a practice largely of seminaries and convents, so that in the first instance it was only the spiritual aristocracy who could acquire a 'concupiscent body'. And even when, through Protestantism, certain ethical techniques were spread more widely, they remained unevenly distributed, depending on the degree of proselytizing and pastoral surveillance, general cultural levels, and mastery of discursive literacy. The schema of the spiritual autobiography in which both Robinson Crusoe and Fanny Hill recorded their respective stages of grace was a cultural device whose mastery not every one acquired.

Moreover, pornography did not emerge until these instituted ethical techniques were joined by a particular cultural technology, the printed book. As Elizabeth Eisenstein (1979) has argued, it was print technology that permitted ethical techniques to migrate from their closed religious environments – to spread along the channels opened up by the book trade where they were transformed by new uses and purposes. Indeed, we have seen that it was precisely in this process of migration that early modern pornography was able to emerge as a profane improvisation on the spiritual interrogation of the flesh.

This permits us to see that the ability to achieve sexual pleasure through books and a certain practice of reading is neither incidental to – nor a regressive surrogate for – the real thing. Pornography is not so much a representation of sexuality as a specific practice of it. We can, therefore, quite properly speak of pornography as emerging at that point where the ethical and literary techniques of conscience-formation were re-deployed as a *biblio-erotics* or book sex. The outcome of this transposition, in which techniques for the intensification of desire are relayed through specific practices of reading and writing, is clear enough in the address to the reader prefaced to the English translation of *L'Ecole des filles*:

> In the second dialogue Susanne, having come back several days later to inquire of Fanchon how she enjoyed the sport of love and being made a woman of, got the girl to give her a complete account of what had gone on. The two girls being thus absorbed in a conversation which they found so delightful, stop to investigate and examine all the aspects of the game of love. They do this with enquiries which are so choice, and stimulating,

The Pornographic Field 41

and appealing, so unusual, so ingenious, and so persuasive that a mere reading of them is enough to rouse love's passions, and I guarantee that even the most fastidious ladies will find something here to give them pleasure.

(Millot and L'Ange, [1655] 1972, p. 66)

At the intersection of the instituted techniques of the flesh and the communicational technology of the book we find the phenomenon of the audience. It should now be clear that to speak of the audience for pornography is not to speak of a general human subject characterised by aesthetic immaturity. Instead, it is to refer to a specific historical distribution of the cultural competences responsible for the practice of biblio-erotics. For this reason the audience cannot go proxy for 'the subject', defined by generalised processes of subject formation; for 'class', as the bearer of certain economically-determined interests and attributes; or for 'men', as a class for whom pornography is both symptom and weapon of a rapacious sexual imagination. Rather, the audience is the terminal point for an array of criss-crossing and overlapping cultural techniques and practices. It is always the plural locus of a patchwork of cultural competences whose bearer is not the human subject but differentiated categories of person.

This reconstruction of the interest in and audience for the first pornography enables us to avoid a number of problems endemic to aesthetic discussions of pornography. It enables us to sidestep the problems posed by attempts to specify pornography in terms of a general category of aesthetic value, for example 'erotic realism'. The point is not just that the application of such categories provokes endless and sterile debate about which erotic works should be included in the privileged domain of literature, but also that the use such categories is premised on the existence of a generalised aesthetic-sexual subjectivity; one whose truth can only be represented by a literature that dialectically reconciles the fantasies of the will and the norms of experience. However, the audience is not the locus of such a subjectivity. It is the target for an array of cultural techniques, *one* of which is indeed the specific technique of dialectical reconciliation. The audience is the bearer not of representations but of techniques and practices. And the effect of these techniques and practices is, broadly speaking, to intensify and sensitise. For this reason it is necessary to replace the single division between 'erotic realism' and pornography with a more flexible and differentiated descriptive schema; one oriented to the variety of ways in which a biblio-erotics engages the disparate cultural competences of its audience network.

Specifying the audience in this way also enables us to relegate the attempt to treat pornography as symptomatic or expressive of a (negatively) exemplary subjectivity. This relegation not only applies to liberal endeavours to treat pornography as a sign of aesthetic immaturity but also to feminist attempts to identify this immaturity with masculinity. We have observed that the audience for pornography is not the locus of a deficient subjectivity but the bearer of particular erotic-ethical interests and competences which are not evenly distributed. The fact that this distribution has been gender specific suggests that the masculine erotic repertory is at least in part a historical *product* of the deployment of pornography, not its source. The masculinity of the audience for pornography is a sign not of the latter's gender-specific essence but of its gender-specific distribution. Nothing in principle stands in the way of the blurring of this distributional boundary and the emergence of mixed-gender audiences for pornography.

Lastly, we can see why political and legal interventions in the pornographic field cannot draw a single exemplary line between art and pornography or between morality and law, guaranteed by the potential of the human subject for self-mastery. From the very beginning, the point of reception for pornography – the sphere of its eroticising functions – was not a general subject or consciousness but a definite and limited audience in which erotic competences were differentially distributed according to age, gender, familial position, and cultural ability. Small wonder, then, that the attempt to reform obscenity law by distinguishing between erotica in need of legal regulation and erotica which could be left to the private conscience immediately encountered the problem that the scope of conscience (and hence of obscenity) fluctuated, depending on the audience addressed.

3. How should pornography be historicised?

Our final question to the aesthetic model concerns its history of pornography. In tandem with its historical twin, cultural history, aesthetics has managed to bring this rather inglorious cultural product within the great schema of Romantic historicism. While the aesthetic model depicts pornography as emerging from the crucial mediation of fantasy and experience, of sexual drives and social conventions, cultural history projects this dialectical schema on to the 'whole culture'. Pornography is thus held to emerge from an imbalance in the historical dialectic: typically from epochs of social repression in which social norms, too forcefully imposed, deny desire its true object and force it into a surrogate outlet. This produces the standard periodisation: pornography is alleged to arise at the end of the seventeenth century with the onset of Puritanism and to take on new and fantasmatic forms in the Victorian era, itself understood in terms of the resurgence of

The Pornographic Field 43

Puritan repressiveness. Subtending this periodisation is, of course, the historical version of the aesthetic education of the senses in which – whether it is actualised or not – the history of sexuality acquires an ethical direction from the telos of an ideal reconciliation of private desires and social norms.

The commitment of this historiography to the view that pornography is an essentially negative phenomenon – its indebtedness to what Foucault (1979) calls 'the repressive hypothesis' – is clear enough. There is some irony in the importance attached to Puritanism as a repressive agency, given the eroticising role of Puritan ethical techniques, but this is only a particular instance of the difficulties confronting any attempt to read off a history of pornography from the dialectical development of the 'whole culture'. Yet pornography did not appear on the historical stage as a truant from the great school of culture whose mission is the complete sexual education of 'man'. It emerged from a group of local and contingent historical developments: roughly speaking, from that unexpected overlap in which the eroticising machinery of the confession of the flesh was redeployed through the technology of the book as a biblio-erotics.

This pragmatic and pluralist perspective shows why biblio-erotics cannot be taken as the (true or distorted) expression of a sexuality originating in the human subject, or promised by the latter's historical development. From the outset pornography functioned as a profane relay for the confessional technology through which some learned to refer all their conduct and feelings to the hidden spring of desire. For this reason the deployment of pornography has undergone the same series of historical mutations as the technology of confession.

Foucault's (1979, pp. 17–49) analysis of the field in which these transformations have occurred is thus focussed on a specific series of historical developments. During the second half of the eighteenth century the Christian confessional, through which individuals had learned to make their self and their 'flesh' into objects of spiritual knowledge and desire, was itself penetrated by and taken up within a range of other instrumentalities and discourses. These included demography, medicine, pedagogy, and psychiatry. This redeployment produced a network of institutions that multiplied the situations in which one had to talk about sex; it also multiplied the social forces and powers whose anchorage became the constantly reiterated mystery and danger of sex. In this way the formerly esoteric minority practice of sexual self-interrogation became aligned with the more general governmental administration of a new entity, the population. This changed organisation of the field, Foucault argues, was responsible for a decisive transformation in western sexuality.

Inside the new institutional network, an old pastoral regulation of conjugal desire – organised around the division between licit and illicit sex – underwent a sea-change. The new demographic, medical and pedagogic deployments of sexuality were less concerned with policing conjugal desire as a law governing the couple than with establishing it as a population-wide norm in relation to which various non-conjugal sexualities could be specified as deviations in need of expert intervention and correction. Against deviancy theory, Foucault argues that these perverse sexualities – of children, the homoerotic, the insane – were not negative refluxes of their social stigmatisation and repression. They were in fact directly positive outcomes of the newly normalised field that specified them, classified them, 'implanted' them in bodies and personalities as so many definite forms of life.

Power, in Foucault's terms, did not attempt to take charge of sexuality through the negative means of prohibiting its marginal forms. On the contrary, generated within the expanding institutional network of the apparatus of sexuality, power was exercised in a series of strategies which were in fact responsible for a proliferation and intensification of perverse sexualities. Because of their importance in organising the pornographic field we should take a brief note of these strategies, again drawing on Foucault's (1979, pp. 41–6) account.

1. The marginal sexualities were not objects of eradication but props or supports for strategies of inquiry and management which, in using these sexualities to expand ever further into social space, in fact required their multiplication. For example, in constituting masturbation as an aberration to which all children were prone, sexual medicine and pedagogy could enter the home and the school, reorganising these spaces of conduct around the constant surveillance of a 'vice' which was thereby rendered indispensable to new medical, pedagogical and familial arrangements.
2. Non-conjugal acts and desires were not banished but targetted by programmes of (medical, psychiatric, criminological) codification and incorporated into personality types. Practices like sodomy and mutual masturbation, once illicit acts anyone might be tempted to commit, became instead signs of unique personages. They were attached to exemplary biographies and identified with exotic sensibilities, as medicine and psychiatry expanded their field by making available a new sexual characterology: not just homosexuals but zoophiles, fetishists, necrophiles, exhibitionists, masochists, and so on.
3. Without forfeiting their own methods and objectives, medicine, psychiatry and pedagogy – in absorbing the technology of confession – took over the ritual in which one individual is relieved of the burden of their

The Pornographic Field

secret sexuality by telling it to another. So, the technique of knowledge that permitted these disciplines to claim rights to the continent of sexuality was simultaneously a technique of pleasure, as confession brings desire to the light of knowledge only by inciting it. The power of the new disciplines of sexuality was thus inescapably wedded to the strategic exchange linking knowledge and pleasure in the mechanism of confession. In the case of medicine, for example, therapeutic confession gave the doctor access to the concupiscent body of the patient and was responsible for a profound medicalisation of sexuality. At the same time, by ensuring that this body could only be reached through the eliciting of sexual secrets, therapeutic confession eroticised the doctor-patient relation and was responsible for a significant sexualisation of medicine. The power of the new discipline was thus not the expression of a will or principle acting through them. It was formed only through particular techniques and relationships, through participation in what Foucault (1979, p. 45) calls a particular 'game'. 'Capture and seduction, confrontation and mutual reinforcement: parents and children, adults and adolescents, educators and students, doctors and patients, the psychiatrist with his hysteric and his perverts, all have played this game continually, since the nineteenth century'.

In the complex field to be organised by these three operations or programmes, early-modern pornography was itself subject to a number of decisive mutations. In the first place, caught up in the strategies through which the apparatus of sexuality colonised new regions of social space, pornography too, like the marginal sexualities with which it was increasingly identified, underwent ever greater specification and expansion. Identified with the problem of precocious sexuality and made a target of the great anti-masturbation campaigns undertaken by nineteenth-century sexual medicine and pedagogy in home and school, pornography became pathologised as a secret cause of the vice that robbed youth of its physical and mental health and threatened the future of the family and the race. Pornography thus entered the realm of 'social problems' as a pathological agent. When we come to investigate the terms in which Victorian judges spoke of the harms caused by pornography, we should be strict enough historians to recall its contemporary medical and pedagogical specification and to avoid the habit of mind which simply falls back on notions of prejudice and hypocrisy. At the same time, because pornography was so closely identified with the evil of masturbation, it too came to function as an indispensable support for the expansionist strategies of the apparatus of sexuality. In this way, during the nineteenth century, pornography became a far more important phenomenon that it had ever been before. The more it became the hidden cause of the dormitory ailment – the guilty secret that any boy might confess – the more thoroughly consciousness of it took hold in the new spaces of sexual surveillance.

Second, with the codification of aberrant sexual acts into personality types a pornography of perversions became possible. This was not, as Stephen Marcus assumes, a fantasmatic reflux of increased repression. It resulted from a particular cultural exchange. On the one hand, pornography absorbed the medical and psychiatric specification of perverse personalities. It transposed and re-valorised these new types, acquiring in the process a vastly expanded erotic characterology, as the compact libertines of early-modern pornography – typified by Fanny Hill – fragmented into specialised pederasts, masochists, fetishists and so on. On the other hand, the machinery of the novel was itself a powerful force in this codification and proliferation of perverse personalities. Not only was it to permit the migration of medical characterologies to new milieus where they could be put to erotic and self-affirmatory uses, the novel was also the popular vehicle for those techniques of conscience through which readers learned to organise their feelings and conduct around the incitation-interrogation of the flesh. It was through this unforeseen exchange that certain acts which in libertine literature had obeyed a logic of the progressive intensification of pleasure – for example, mutual masturbation which Fanny Hill learns as simply one skill or element of the erotic repertory – reappeared in the pornography of perversions as the identifying traits of proudly inverted sexual personalities.

Third, the scientific coding of the confessional pleasure-power-knowledge nexus – accompanying the emergence of sexual medicine and psychology – is also a key feature of the modern deployment of pornography. Continuing to function as a profane variation on the now scientifically re-coded technology of sexual confession, pornographic writing itself acquired a scientific character. Hence the appearance during the nineteenth century of a whole catalogue of erotic books, memoirs and letters in which the intensification of pleasure is attached to perverse yet methodical forms of recording, measurement and classification. Such are the writings whose heroes and authors are pictured as enthusiastic sexual sociologists and anthropologists, adept in the methods of participant observation, or – like poor William Chidley – doctors of sexual medicine obsessed by the pathology of their own desire.

At the same time, because the new sciences of sexuality could approach their object only through the writings of their subjects – whether fantasies, therapeutic dialogues, diaries, published and unpublished memoirs – they themselves acquired a certain pornographic character. We have noted that the object of knowledge of the new sexologies – deviant sexuality in particular – existed only through the constant application of incitatory technique. The fact that pornography was a major repository of such technique meant that auto-erotic reading and writing were not simply dispassionate objects of study for sexology, they were also its indispensable instruments. For this reason, sexological studies have not been able to reveal the secret of pornography except through excitatory quotation and rhetoric. The discourse on pornography is always in part a pornographic discourse.

Today, in the exchanges of knowledge and pleasure that link a scientific pornography and a pornographic science, it is difficult to separate the diagnosis of pornography from its symptoms. In this twilight world, erotic literature provides a symptomatology for sexological classification (as in the case of Masoch's *Venus in Furs* and the works of Sade), while sexological studies are themselves disseminated as erotic bestsellers – consider the whole series of sex reports and surveys from Havelocks Ellis (1922) and Krafft-Ebing (1965) through Kinsey (1948) and the Kronhausens (1959) to Shere Hite (1976, 1981) and Andrea Dworkin (1981).

It would be naive to treat these transformations as indicative either of the scientific abuse of literature or of the popular misuse of scientific knowledge. They are simply signs that pornography and sexology have both gained access to sexuality through a discursive mechanism in which the interdependence of examination and excitation, knowledge and pleasure, is inescapable. The fact that the first volume of Havelock Ellis' *Studies in Sexual Psychology* was threatened with prosecution under the obscenity statutes is not necessarily symptomatic of legal obscurantism and puritanism.

Instead of the model of cultural history – where the place of pornography as the retort of a repressed sexuality is always redeemed by the goal of an epoch promising the true reconciliation of desire and norm – we can therefore propose a more multivalent history of the pornographic field. In the modern apparatus of sexuality – formed when the technology of confession was dispersed through a new governmental network, and the law of conjugal desire was redeployed as a norm specifying a new spectrum of perverse sexualities – the pornographic field took shape around three main co-ordinates. Pornography spread along the same axis along which the medical and pedagogical administration of sexuality was expanding. Like the aberrant sexualities with which it was identified, pornography was an indispensable support for this process, and for this reason the interest in it expanded at the same rate as its pathologisation. Pornography also functioned as a relay and support for the new specification of perverse sexual personalities produced by the apparatus. It transposed the pathological characterology into an affirmative erotic register and disseminated the techniques of sexual-ethical identification to an expanding array of specialised audiences. Finally, there is the fact that the interrogation of sexuality was the product of a limited number of techniques of examination in which knowledge was linked to pleasure. Forced to share these techniques, pornography and the emergent sciences of sexuality entered into a reciprocal relation. In this exchange the pursuit of knowledge was inseparable from the charge of pleasure and the pursuit of pornographic pleasure borrowed the interrogative forms of the science of sexuality.

LAW AND ETHICS

To say that the role of the law in the pornographic field has outstripped the public understanding of it would be a decided understatement. Lawrence's early *cri de coeur* 'The law is a dreary thing, and its judgements have nothing to do with life' (Lawrence, 1936, p. 170) might seem a little exaggerated, but it still echoes in St John-Stevas' already cited contrast of a law which is 'regulative' and a literature which, being 'creative, imaginative and aesthetic, with no extrinsic purpose', cannot be confined 'within the Procrustean bed of the law'. Moreover, as we have seen, these ideas are at work in jurisprudence itself where they have informed the attempt to disengage the law from morality precisely along the line alleged to separate pornography from erotic art.

Jurisprudential reasoning about obscenity law has been disabled by its openness to the psycho-aesthetic analysis of pornography, an analysis which is in fact barely legally literate. Placing it at the intersection of erotic desires and social utility, private fantasies and public norms, this analysis has allowed the law a very narrow field of action indeed. What is more, this action has been typically and overwhelmingly seen in negative terms, as a matter of censorship.

The law, we are told, silences and prohibits. Fuelled by a norm-fed fear of the drives whose psychological repression it duplicates at the social level – or else by a utilitarian straitjacketing of the fantasy whose aesthetic reconciliation with experience it blocks – obscenity law is made to appear as a monolithic refusal of sexual expression. It is for this reason that even our best history of it – Donald Thomas' *A Long Time Burning* – is subtitled *The History of Literary Censorship in England*, and places the legal regulation of obscenity in the same series as the law controlling blasphemy and sedition.[7]

The Pornographic Field

Until the 1970s, the only option allowed to the law was that it convert this repressive and censorious function into one of true mediation and reconciliation. In effect this meant leaving the field of erotic expression to the intrinsic dialectics of human subjectivity, except for some residual policing along the line which marked the occasional failure of this dialectic; that is, the line separating erotic art and pornography. We have already noted the problems which the liberal reformers faced when they attempted to draw such a line through an organisation as shifting and ambivalent as the pornographic field. We will return to these problems below. Our prior task, however, is to address the limitations of the psycho-aesthetic understanding of obscenity law itself. Here we must pose the following question: Does obscenity law emerge from a fundamental conflict between desire and norm, fantasy and utility, in which it has played the role of censor? A number of considerations suggest an answer in the negative.

First, there is the organisation of the field in which obscenity law initially appeared. We have argued that in its technical complexity and historical contingency this field does not share the exemplary dialectical structure of the human subject, or its collective surrogate, culture. As a result we must be sceptical concerning the existence of a general repressive function – the tyranny of norm over drive and fantasy – to which the law supposedly gives social expression and force. This scepticism is borne out if we look at the creation of the offence of obscene libel in early eighteenth-century English common law. We can be brief here as the following chapter deals with this topic in more detail.

Typically this event is discussed in terms of the early eighteenth-century resurgence of Puritanism, manifest in the formation of the Societies for the Reformation of Manners. There is no denying the importance of this event with regard to the policing of obscenity. We have, however, already cast doubt on the existence of a uniformly repressive relation between the Puritan conscience and the deployment of sexuality; what is more, the sparse obscenity case law of the period reveals no clear evidence for such a relation. There was, for example, none of the legal mobilisation of the reforming societies which was to be characteristic of the nineteenth-century Societies for the Suppression of Vice. The circumstances permitting the first emergence of obscenity law lie elsewhere.

As a preliminary we need to note that the first book to cause its publisher to be convicted of obscene libel in a major court – Jean Barrin's translated *Venus in the Cloister, or The Nun in Her Smock*, printed and sold by Edmund Curll in 1724 – had in fact been freely available in London since 1683, just as Millot and L'Ange's *L'École des filles* and Chorier's *Satyra Sotadique* had been sold openly, apparently without legal interference, since the 1670s.[8] What was it that brought such books to the attention of the common-law courts in the first decades of the eighteenth century? What made the criminal law assume a form, in 1727, that permitted it to attend to them? There seem to be two key factors, tied to the concepts of 'public' and 'public morality'.

1. The question of jurisdictions. Curll's defence argued that to count as a libel in a temporal court a work must either undermine public order or defame 'some private person': 'Whatever tends to corrupt the morals of the people ought to be censured in the Spiritual Court, to which properly all such cases belong' (*R.* v. *Curll*, p. 849). And indeed it was precisely on these grounds that the Court of King's Bench had quashed a conviction for obscene libel in *Queen* v. *Read* in 1707. The majority of the judges in *Curll*, however, accepted a new disposition of public morality, one which cut across the existing division of jurisdiction between the civil and ecclesiastical courts. This new disposition was based on bringing morality within the sphere of government:

> As to morality. Destroying that is destroying the peace of the Government, for government is no more than publick order, which is morality .... I do not insist that every immoral act is indictable, such as telling a lie, or the like; but if it is destructive of morality in general, if it does, or may, affect all the King's subjects, it then is an offence of a publick nature. (p. 850)

Accepting this reasoning by the Attorney General prosecuting, the court broke with the old boundary between spiritual and temporal jurisdictions and instituted a new division between private ethics and public morality. It was with this expansion of the governmental sphere that the crime of obscene libel came into being.

2. The question of the audience. What pushed Curll's book across this threshold in 1727 was the formation of a public for pornography. No such public existed in the middle of the seventeenth century, when works such as *Vénus dans le cloître* first appeared in England. Published in French for a linguistically sophisticated specialist audience – Pepys is again representative – they did not constitute a *public* problem. Their translation into English, however, together with the rapid expansion of print literacy and the popular book trade in the late seventeenth and early eighteenth centuries, changed this situation. That this change was crucial to the formation of the crime of obscene libel is evident in one judge's claim that '[t]he Spiritual Courts punish only personal spiritual defama-

tion by words; if it is reduced to writing, it is a temporal offence' (p. 850); and in Justice Reynolds' remark that 'This is surely worse than *Sir Charles Sedley's* case, who only exposed himself to the people then present, who might choose whether they would look upon him or not; whereas this book goes all over the kingdom' (p. 851).

We will return to this prescient linking of the public domain to the apparently coercive immediacy of a new technology of communication. For the moment we can say that obscenity law first emerged in a complex technical environment formed by the overlap of a new governmental distinction between public and private spheres and the spread of a specific cultural technology and competence. It was this unforeseen overlap, not an access of Puritan repressiveness, which first saw the law concern itself with a corruption of public morality by written publications judicially deemed obscene. Even if the expansion of government had specified a public whose morality might be corrupted, a public which might be corrupted by pornography could not in fact exist without the prior dissemination of a specific cultural technology and the competence to use it: the book and print literacy.

Second, we should note the specific forms of action open to obscenity law in the pornographic field. The law did not supervene in an exemplarily repressive swoop on a field occupied only by the drives and erotic fantasies. Rather, through a single and uncertain common-law court decision, the law entered a field already *dense* with specific forms of social and ethical regulation derived from the religious technology of the flesh and the direction of conscience. This occurred only when a new governmental distinction was drawn between private ethics and public morality. Finding its object here – with a judicial reassessment of the possibility of a corruption of public morality by printed dissemination of the techniques of the flesh and the erotic conscience – obscenity law has been substantially dependent on those other forms of regulation (first religious and then, in the nineteenth century, medical and pedagogical) which have supported the deployment of sexuality. The objective of the law was not – and can never be – the complete suppression of biblio-erotics. Rather, obscenity law has provided legal codification and sanction for a specific 'infra-legal' distribution of ethical-sexual competences ('infra-legal' refers to fields of knowledge and institutions which have overlapped with the legal domain, and carried regulatory functions of various sorts). In using this term, our intention is to establish a historical sense of the on-going negotiations between law and other forms of regulation – religious, ethical, medical, pedagogical, aesthetic – of which law might codify certain elements. In the early eighteenth century, then, a governmental concern with the policing of the population was made over into a specific legal creation – the new crime of obscene libel – which marked the juridification of obscene publication.[9] This is not to say that law served as a simple vehicle for state power. In advance of the finding in *Curll*, the jurisdictional transfer to which we have referred was in no way predictable.

It should be clear why the action of obscenity law cannot be understood as fundamentally repressive or censorious. Particular acts of restriction form part of a juridification of those channels – differentiated by age, gender, class and culture – through which the literature of erotic formation circulates. These acts signal a larger strategy that is *distributive* rather than repressive. This – not the hypocrisy of the judiciary – explains not only why Curll was still advertising *Venus in the Cloister* in 1735, eight years after his exemplary prosecution, but also why Victorian authorities turned a blind eye to the trade in privately-published pornography. It also enables us to provide an appropriate analysis of the fact that when, in the nineteenth century, the legal policing of pornography escalated in scale and intensity, it did so along specifically differentiated social channels.

Consider in this regard two crucial moments in the development of the nineteenth-century law of obscenity, Lord Campbell's Bill of 1857 and the landmark *Hicklin* judgement of 1868. In a moment that was anything but fortuitous, Campbell raised the matter of the trade in obscene literature during a House of Lords' debate on the unregulated sale of poisons in the metropolis:

> He [Lord Campbell] was happy to say that he believed the administration of poison by design had received a check. But, from a trial which had taken place before him on Saturday, he had learned with horror and alarm that a sale of a poison more deadly than prussic acid, strychnine, or arsenic – the sale of obscene publications and indecent books – was openly going on.
>
> (*Parliamentary Debates*, 1857, p. 103)

Even in these preliminary remarks it is clear that the cause for concern is the unregulated and indiscriminate character of a dissemination. Through the metaphor of pornography as social toxin, Victorian jurists and legislators articulated two different elements of the pornographic field: the medical and pedagogical specification of pornography as a pathological agent invading bourgeois homes and schools and whose emblem was the masturbatory child; and the Malthusian campaigns and moral reform movements which identified cheap pornography – along with advertisements for abortificients, lotteries, drink and incest – as a threat to the procreative behaviour, well-being and public decency of the popular classes.

Negotiating and systematising these infra-legal specifications of pornography, Victorian obscenity law emerged not as a monolithic repression of sexual expression but as a sophisticated and discriminating mechanism of regulation. Tactics of suppression were involved, certainly, but always as part of larger strategies of distribution. Chief Justice Cockburn's famous dictum in *Hicklin*:

> I think the test of obscenity is this, whether the tendency of the matter charged as obscenity is to deprave and corrupt those whose minds are open to such immoral influences, and into whose hands a publication of this sort may fall.
>
> (*Regina* v. *Hicklin*, p. 371)

should, therefore, no longer be read as a self-condemnatory expression of Victorian sexual hypocrisy. Instead, we must learn to see it as indicative of the law's regulatory role in a broader machinery of dissemination in which erotica were differentially treated according to an infra-legal specification of types of susceptible persons and dangerous places.

At one end of the scale we find the uncontrolled urban haunts and resorts of the popular classes – above all London's Holywell Street – which were pictured as centres of pornographic contagion. At the other end we find the cultural milieus of the household and the school, specifically – yet ambivalently – targetted by sexual medicine and pedagogy as places where pornography silently attacked the minds and bodies of bourgeois youth. Lord Campbell's introduction of seize and forfeiture provisions into the law in 1857 was solely directed at policing the distribution of cheap pornography. As to the erotic literature directed at the literary middle-class, Lord Campbell said – with reference to Dumas' *The Lady of the Camellias* – that '[h]e did not wish to create a category of offences in which this book might be included, although it certainly was of a polluting character. It was only from the force of public opinion and of an improved taste that the circulation of such works could be put a stop to; but he was glad to inform their Lordships that there was a society for the Encouragement of Pure Literature, of which his noble friend, the Duke of Argyll was president' (*Parliamentary Debates*, 1857, p. 1152).

Far from prosecuting an inflexible suppression of biblio-erotics, Victorian obscenity law was in fact responsible for systematising the channels of its distribution. As the initial threshold of pornography's juridification began to diversify in accordance with the array of infra-legal instrumentalities aimed at pornography, so too did the legal specification of the boundary between private ethics and public morality. From a very early date the law did not attempt to draw this line along a single axis based on harms caused to a general human subject or reader. Rather it allowed the threshold to float according to expert medical and other norms defining particular categories of person and social milieu. Deploying its sanctions in a variable fashion along this floating threshold, obscenity law subjected cheap mass-produced pornography to a tactics of policing that constituted in effect a form of commercial regulation of an illegal economy. At the same time it created a tolerated zone for the specialised pornography of perversions as long as its distribution remained private, that is, restricted to adult bourgeois males.

Finally, we can note that the deployment of obscenity law in the pornographic field imposes definite limits on the degree to which, and the directions in which, this law can be reformed. We are now better placed to see why the weapons used by the reforming jurists of the 1960s – the aesthetic distinction between art and pornography and the philosophical-legal distinction between law and morality – were so quickly blunted by the actual machinery of obscenity law. Wielded on the assumption that it would be possible to cut sexual ethics free from the law with a single blow – a blow directed by the goal of an ideal psycho-aesthetic maturity – this reformist weaponry was harmless against a mechanism in which the thresholds between morality and law, art and pornography, private and public, floated according to a variable codification of audience capacities presided over by the law itself.

Somewhat ironically, the reform movement's campaign to rescue literature from the 'Procrustean bed of the law' was confronted by the depth of the law's own role in the deployment of literature, not least in producing and maintaining the channelled patterns of dissemination for nineteenth-century erotica. Of importance in this regard was the creation of the private circuit of distribution for the pornography of perversions, which differentiated the form and consumption of that pornography from both the popular pornography of the streets and the educative novel of the bourgeois home and school. In this way the law became a precise condition of possibility for the literary milieu. This was so particularly with the containing of a permitted biblio-erotics to the private sphere of specialised ethical and erotic capacities, an arrangement which, as we shall see, had a profound effect on the form of the 'public' educative novel.

Given the law's constitutive role in actual deployments of printed literature, there can be no question of simply withdrawing the law from the domain of biblio-erotics. In fact we must ask whether it was because of this organisation of the literary field that a figure like D. H. Lawrence could take as his project the transgression of the limits of erotic expression and the aesthetic discovery of the 'long repressed' truth of our sexuality. As we shall show in Chapter 4, Lawrence was simply the first to exploit a possibility created by the legally-buttressed systematisation of the pornographic field: that is, to merge the pornographic novel's perverse characterology and 'micro-technics of delectation' with the dialectics of self-discovery and aesthetic maturation characteristic of the educative *Bildungsroman*. Far from being the exemplary explorer of a sexual truth beyond the law, Lawrence was arguably the *product* of a distinctive and specialised nineteenth-century juridical patterning of the cultural field.

Notwithstanding that the novel of sexual education was in an important sense the product of a juridified cultural field, its appearance nonetheless triggered a change in the legal arrangements for this field. In joining the austere public dialectic of Romantic aesthetic education to the delectable private auto-erotics of the pornography of perversions, novelists like Lawrence, Miller, and Burroughs in effect created a hybrid cultural artefact moving at a tangent to the previous main lines of literary dissemination. As long as this remained merely a local mutation in advanced middle-class aesthetics and ethics – an eroticising of the old elite practice of Romantic self-culture – the problem could be contained within the existing organisation of the field. Hence Lawrence's 'banned' novels in fact circulated in the private zone of tolerated erotica throughout the 1920s and 1930s. Under these circumstances the existing infra-legal specification of the pathological character of pornography – its typology of susceptible persons and dangerous places – could remain intact. However, once it was decided to publish such works in cheap unexpurgated editions aimed at a general market something had to give.

The liberal attempt to replace the medical with an aesthetic specification of pornography was the outcome of precisely these developments. The decision to publish, however, was less an exemplary aesthetic challenge to the 'repressive' powers of the law than a sign that the forms of infra-legal regulation of biblio-erotics were in the process of changing. We can simply note here a pointer developed in detail below: the old hegemony of sexual medicine was being displaced by a new pedagogical deployment of sexually educative novels in the school system. If, then, it was proposed to replace the pathological conception of pornography with one which treated it as nothing more than the sign of a certain psychological and aesthetic immaturity, this was not an indication that culture itself had reached a level of maturity such that sex could be safely left to the privacy of the individual conscience. Rather, it indicated that the ethical dialectics of desire and norm, fantasy and utility, had themselves acquired a socially regulative deployment in the educational apparatus. Here an expanded circulation of educative erotica became possible, indeed imperative, as public policy, in keeping with the wider pedagogical distribution of specific ethical-sexual competences to the young. The new deployment, however, remained within the field in which these competences varied along specific distributive channels.

The legal threshold of obscenity continued to float. For example, in 1979 in the United Kingdom the *Report of the Committee on Obscenity and Film Censorship* (hereafter the Williams Report) recommended that no work consisting solely of printed matter should be liable to legal prosecution or restriction for obscenity. It did so on the ground that readers had to choose to read such works – an act which, it was argued, placed them in the extra-legal domain of the private conscience. This recommendation is of course a direct inversion of Justice Reynolds' decision that Curll was guilty because the speed and immediacy of print pre-empted choice and placed it and its consumption in the public domain. This should occasion no perturbation of the old judge's spirit, however. Far from signalling the abolition of the threshold between private and public, ethics and the law, the Williams recommendation simply registers one of its characteristic migrations. We shall see in Chapter 6 that the Williams Report in fact *re-invests* the notion of a coercive immediacy that defines the 'public' domain – this time in photographic images – on the basis of calculating the kind of audiences susceptible to this pornographic 'coercion of imagination'. The scope of the exercise of private conscience also thus continues to vary with changing calculations of the social distribution of particular ethical and cultural competences and with assessments of the effects of particular communicational technologies. Hence, so too must all attempts to reform obscenity law by differentiating material that can be left to individual morality from that which should be legally regulated.

3 Nineteenth-Century English Obscenity Law

BEYOND CENSORSHIP

The historical episode is perhaps ending during which published sexual writing was an important object of legal regulation. The legislative limits of the episode are set by the Obscene Publications Act of 1857 (Lord Campbell's Act) and the Obscene Publications Act of 1959, the key statutory construction being *Regina* v. *Hicklin* which in 1868 established as the test of obscenity a publication's 'tendency to deprave and corrupt'. During this episode, legal regulation of the publication of sexual writing was found both plausible and necessary. By the late 1970s, to judge from the Williams Report, this was no longer so: '[T]he printed word should be neither restricted nor prohibited since its nature makes it neither immediately offensive nor capable of involving the harms we identify, and because of its importance in conveying ideas' (1979, p. 160). If opinions such as this indicate a closing of the episode on philosophical grounds, others refer to more general shifts in cultural conditions. Thus, buoyed with aesthetic and psychoanalytic hope, Stephen Marcus argues that 'we are coming to the end of the era in which pornographers had a historical meaning and even a historical function' (Marcus, 1974, p. 285). For Charles Rembar (1968), however, the appeal of written obscenity is at an end simply because the young no longer get excited that way.

In Chapter 2 we suggested why, in writing the history of this episode, our intention is to avoid the 'censorship model' exemplified not only in classic literary historical works such as Thomas (1969) but also in recent legal scholarship, for instance Robertson (1979). Censorship histories accord a purely negative and extrinsic role to law as impeding the literary expression of human sexuality. We have begun to suspect that in practice things were somewhat less straightforward. Sexualities have a public character as specific historical and cultural artefacts. And as for making a clean break between 'literature' and the 'Procrustean bed of the law', this might not be possible once it is seen that these two fields have shared a deep reciprocity in organising the cultural environment responsible for the distribution of sexual sensibilities using print.

Our counter-history will not employ the tactic of invoking a universal sexual self as the driving but always secret force behind works written across the span from Tudor to contemporary times. Such a tactic is the sign of over-commitment to an epic narrative of censorship as the key to the nature and history of obscenity law. Under 'Origins of Censorship', Robertson (1979, p. 20) thus takes his readers back to Ezekiel, Aristophanes and Ovid before returning to modern times by way of the Puritan's 'legacy of shame and guilt about sexual pleasure which was never quite eradicated from the national conscience and which created consumer demand for the new pornography'. Doubtless a glow of historical pedigree comes with the claim to be part of the one continuous history of personal liberty (of which sexual expression is made emblematic), but this is at the price of losing the specificity not only of different regimens of sexuality but also of the historical discontinuities that mark the different regimes of English obscenity law. The problem is exemplified by the title which Thomas chooses for his concluding chapter: 'The Twentieth Century: "Plus ça change . . . "', as it is by Robertson's (1979, p. 16) claim that '[t]he only lesson we learn from the legal history of censorship is that the more the law changes, the more the social reality remains the same'. It remains to be seen, of course, where our own political calculations are concerned, whether our historical analysis will avoid the fatalism which seems to be the condition of approaching obscenity law through an undiscriminating censorship and personal liberties narrative.

Our aim – unlike Marcus (1964), Robertson (1979) and Gay (1984) – is not to indict the supposed hypocrisy and repressiveness of the Victorians and, by extension, the flawed nature of nineteenth-century obscenity legislation and law-enforcement. Instead, much of this chapter is expended on historical description of what in fact were the particular forms of institutional arrangements, infra-legal fields of knowledge, ethical practices and governmental measures that made the Obscene Publications Act 1857 and the 1868 *Hicklin* judgement intelligible to contemporaries. In our view, the chance of reconstructing in some detail the terms of intelligibility of nineteenth-century legal regulation of obscene publications more than compensates for losing the utopian option of participation in a trans-historical struggle for sexual emancipation supposedly achieved through the blossoming of sexual literature and the withering away of obscenity law. This means rejecting the approach of studies as diverse as Rolph (1969), Pearsall (1976) and Heath (1982).

Let us begin by turning the negativity of the censorship model on its head and asking: Is it possible that obscenity law played a positive role in the regulation of nineteenth-century sexualities and pornographies?

MORAL TOXINS AND SOCIAL HARMS

A major obstacle to the study of nineteenth-century obscenity law is the almost universal knowingness about it which is demonstrated by commentators and historians for whom the Obscene Publications Act of 1857 and the 'deprave and corrupt' test which gave the Act its construction simply bespeak philistinism and ignorance, notably in their failure to respect the difference between art and pornography. They also, it is said, bespeak hypocrisy and irrationality in the failure to distinguish the immoral from the socially harmful. Read in this light, the words and actions of nineteenth-century legislators, jurists, law enforcers and law reformers become the very exemplars of error, prejudice and illiberalism. Such knowingness is, however, not without some problems of its own. It assumes that the two distinctions which have come to lie at the heart of current concerns with pornography – the one between art and pornography and the other between the immoral and the harmful – should have governed nineteenth-century arrangements too. We shall therefore dispense with this anachronistic notion, incapable as it is of doing descriptive justice to the historical variability of the field in which pornography has emerged, rather than laying claim to know the truth about pornography.

Approached in this less anachronistic way, nineteenth-century English obscenity law need not be convicted of the ignorance and hypocrisy which later commentators have come to prize so highly in the Victorians. That law begins to look less flawed and self-condemnatory. In fact, to anticipate the argument, it is not the voice of ignorance and unreason which we shall recover and listen to, but that of a once powerful, rational and highly specialised domain of knowledge, law and government. This particular sphere of legal and governmental reason, in which the object of knowledge was inseparable from the objectives and norms of a particular system of social supervision, was identified with the notion of 'police'.

Following Oestreich (1982), we use the term 'police' more broadly than is usual in the Anglo-Saxon context. The continental etymology of the term stems from 'policy', and in early modern absolutist states it was used to name the general administration of all areas of life: economic, cultural, religious, social and political. In England, Colquhoun's (1797) *Treatise on the Police of the Metropolis* uses the term in this wider sense. It is notable that broadly-based police programmes such as Colquhoun's – covering everything from the medicalisation of prostitution to the regulation of food vendors – were not legislatively enacted in England or America. However, by the early nineteenth century less co-ordinated developments in a variety of regulatory milieus – public health, education, welfare, domestic economy – were linking up to form a broad network of social policing. 'Police' in the narrower sense of police forces emerged in this same context. We use the term in both the broad and narrow senses, as the context will make clear.

It was in the context of this network that conservative judges like Lord Campbell and progressive social reformers like Elizabeth Blackwell could come together in a common concern with the medical, moral and pedagogical harms caused in the street and the home by cheap auto-erotic literature. This was a commodity whose uncontrolled circulation and consumption threatened to corrupt the regenerate body and mind of the population. To have done nothing to control this circulation and consumption would have been to remain passive in the face of a disaster. We must therefore re-orient ourselves: the Obscene Publications Act of 1857 and the *Hicklin* judgement of 1868 mark the formal alliance of law to the network of social police. To describe the 1857 Act, modern aesthetic and philosophical habits of mind are unhelpful; what is needed is a sense of the objectives, knowledge and norms which informed this network and provided the historical context in which Victorian obscenity law was intelligible.

Introduced as a private member's Bill – the government, through the Lord Chancellor, Lord Cranworth, was of the view that no additional legislation was required and left the matter to Lord Campbell, the Lord Chief Justice – the Obscene Publications Act of 1857, also known as Lord Campbell's Act, was the British Parliament's first incursion into the field of obscene publication.[1] Lord Campbell's motive was to establish an effective machinery for the legal destruction of obscene publications under the provisions for the existing common law offence of obscene libel. This new machinery was to work largely through summary procedures administered by magistrates and justices of the peace as part of a routine policing of the streets.[2] The object was a statute whose provisions were directed

> exclusively to works written for the single purpose of corrupting the morals of youth and of a nature calculated to shock the common feelings of decency in a well regulated mind ... [Such were the works of] people who designedly and industriously manufactured books and prints with the intention of corrupting morals.

(146 *Hansard Parliamentary Debates*, 3rd series 1857, pp. 327 ff.)

The mid-Victorian legislature did not pass Lord Campbell's Bill with open acclamation and expressions of complete support. On the contrary, parliamentary and extra-parliamentary opposition to the proposal ranged from the

Lord Chancellor – in Lord Cranford's view the existing law was adequate to the task – to organs of the legal profession such as *The Justice of the Peace*, which voiced a characteristic criticism of the extensive powers of search and seizure which the Bill sought to grant to complainants and to the police:

> Surely it could never have been intended that the complainant and the police constable should be enabled to exercise such an irresponsible power as would thus be given to them, and that the latter should be the sole judge of whether the things which he may seize are of a kind and nature of those sworn to by the complainant .... We most strongly object to such a power being given to any constable, or, indeed, to any authority whatever, until the things seized have been judicially condemned as being obscene within the meaning of the Act; after which an officer of the court which condemns them might be entrusted to destroy them before one or more witnesses.
>
> (*The Justice of the Peace* (1857), 21, p. 467, quoted in Manchester, 1988, p. 230)

This commentator was evidently in no doubt that the strengthening of the street-policing powers proposed by Lord Campbell's Bill was a distinctly new and, from the viewpoint of the legal profession, problematic step in the regulation of pornography. Hence the concern to recall that regulation to the embrace of the judicial process in the strict sense, rather than to endorse the granting to the police of a potentially excessive power of intervention and action, given the absence of what were deemed adequate safeguards over the responsible exercise of that power. Such evidence indicates what was at most a muted enthusiasm, and in some quarters a definite lack of enthusiasm, for this private member's Bill, the legislative history of which underscores both the diversity of regulative mechanisms and agencies, and the fact that the law itself had a limited role in such regulation.

As to our specific interest in the status of serious literature and its treatment under the provisions of the Act, contemporary concern among members of the legal profession extended to the possible mis-application of the provisions of the Bill to what could be held to be reputable works of art and literature. The *Law Times* commented as follows, at the moment of debate on the Bill:

> The Obscene Publications Bill of Lord Campbell ought to have been deferred for maturer deliberation in another session .... Who would be

safe with such a weapon in the hands of fanatics? . . . . We do not fear its use by sensible men, but its abuse . . . . It is not merely possible, but probable, that two justices will be found to hold pictures, and statuary, and books, which lovers of art look upon as art, to be 'obscene' within the meaning of the Act, injurious to morals and offensive to decency. What is to restrain them from doing that which they will conscientiously believe to be a duty and 'putting down' the, to them, obnoxious objects? We fear that Lord Campbell has not sufficiently reflected upon this.

(*Law Times* (1857), quoted in Manchester, 1988, p. 235)

A variation in the capacity to judge what is obscene is here located within the legal profession itself. A certain concern was also expressed in the House on the demarcation between obscene publications and works of literary merit, Lord Brougham seeking to ensure that 'works of some of [our] most eminent poets'(*Hansard, Lords*, 11 May 1857, CXLV, p. 329) would not suffer prosecution. Lord Campbell, however, shared 'the Victorian reverence for great Books':

[N]o twentieth-century legislator could have been more positive than Lord Campbell that his proposals were in no way meant to interfere with literature and the arts. And so he produced a copy of *La Dame aux Camélias* and announced that, much as he disapproved of the book, he had no wish to see such publications banned by the new law.

(Thomas, 1969, pp. 262–3)

This gesture came at the report stage.

As to enforcement of the Act once it became law, '[i]nvoking the Act against literary or artistic works . . . proved to be the exception rather than the rule, and for the most part such works suffered no disability before the law' (Manchester, 1988, p. 237). This assessment by Manchester is of the essence; yet his account of how it was that obscenity law and serious literature came into a more intimate contact later in the century perpetuates the notion of a repressive official morality bent on censoring an expressive literary culture. Such an account and such a notion need to be radically revised if they are to fit the facts. When in the following chapter we enquire how and why towards the end of the nineteenth century and into the twentieth it became possible for works of literary merit to fall foul of nineteenth-century obscenity law, it will not be a matter of of taking an ironic distance from the supposed hypocrisy of the makers of the law (Robertson, 1979, p. 29), nor of representing the Act of 1857 as fundamentally uncertain in its definition of obscenity (Williams Report, 1979, p. 168). The fact is that at this point in its history obscenity law was too discriminating in its application to be reduced to a single mask for hypocrites; as for pornography, it was a readily recognised commodity.

The 1857 Act created no new offence, its purpose being to give magistrates authority to destroy matter which, in their judgement, was obscene. In practical terms, this authorisation established a machinery for policing pornography: a summary procedure allowing the routine seizure and destruction of offending publications. The police, armed with a magistrate's warrant, could enter premises in search of suspected matter. Where this was found, it could now be seized and brought before the magistrate, who could then issue a summons to the occupier of the premises, requiring cause to be shown why the matter should not be destroyed. Although no criminal penalty was imposed, the printer, publisher or bookseller whose stock was seized risked having that stock destroyed by order of the court. As Robertson observes, 'the burden of proving that the material was not obscene lay on the bookseller'. And he adds an important detail:

> [T]o put a pornographer in prison, the prosecutor had to give the publisher the option of trial by jury and had to prove the obscenity of his books beyond a reasonable doubt. The House of Commons inserted two further safeguards before enacting the Bill: a right of appeal to a judge at Quarter Sessions and a requirement that the prosecutor prove that the offending book was actually for sale to the public. Lord Campbell acquiesced in these amendments, and looked forward to a time 'when Holywell Street would become the abode of honest, industrious handicraftsmen and a thoroughfare through which any modest woman might pass'.
>
> (Robertson, 1979, pp. 28–9)

This reference to street life is more than an incidental image in Lord Campbell's speech. The law endows police and magistrates with powers to be exercised in the meaner streets of the metropolis and other urban centres, powers whose enforcement will enjoy a significant autonomy from the specifically judicial regulation of pornography. That the spheres of the law of obscenity and the policing of pornography overlap yet diverge illustrates the fact that we are dealing with a field in which the law plays a limited, albeit a definite role.

In Parliament, John Roebuck MP characterised Lord Campbell's Bill as 'an attempt to make people virtuous by Act of Parliament' (*Hansard*, 12 August 1857, CXLVII, p. 1475), expressing his doubt that legislation could determine moral conduct where vulnerability to or taste for obscene publications were concerned. Here a different limit to law is evoked, an appeal to an unbridgeable gap between law and morality that has not ceased to function as a powerful rhetorical ploy, as arguments for the liberalisation of obscenity law in the 1960s were to testify. However, during the nineteenth century, public legislation and private moral taste were brought into a new proximity through the emergence of social policing with its new technologies of governmental concern, investigation and supervision. Against this background of the medical, civil and assistantial network, Lord Campbell's Bill emerges as a 'police' measure, conditioned by the gradual emergence of an urban police force, and directed at a cheap pornography which by the available criteria of the time was rationally judged to constitute a threat to the moral and physical well-being of the urban popular classes.

The Act met with variable success. Late in 1857 Lord Campbell noted in his diary that its 'success has been most brilliant'. Holywell Street, he wrote, had been so decisively transformed by the policing initiative that some shops had closed while others had shifted to the alternative trade staple of 'moral and religious books' (quoted in Manchester, 1988, pp. 228–9). By most accounts, a period of vigorous enforcement accorded an initial efficacy to the move 'to give additional powers for the Suppression of the Trade in Obscene Books, Prints, Drawings, and other Obscene Articles' as set out in the Preamble to the Act. Yet by the late 1860s – in a much-cited characterisation of Holywell Street first recorded in the *Saturday Review* of 5 December 1868 – 'the dunghill is in full heat and steaming with all of its old pestilence'. At the time of the *Hicklin* judgement, the picture is therefore one of a reduced level of policing of popular pornography, or at least of a fluctuating pattern of concern with the traffic. It would be unwise to read too much into alleged failures of the Act. As a police measure, its objective was not to extirpate the publication of pornography as an illegal act but to regulate it in accordance with the objectives of a social and moral policing of the population. In this regard, the periodic failures of the measure in fact serve as testimony to the ongoing vitality of the ethical-political objective, each 'failure' signalling a new regulatory drive.

If the sensibility of certain categories of person to certain types of printed matter was being transformed into a concern of policing, this was not due to the ascendancy of a censorious and hypocritical morality on the part of the Victorians. Rather, it was a result of the fact that – having crossed into the space of governmental concern and supervision through the development of a new technology of watchfulness – the taste for pornography was becoming the target of two initially distinct but soon intersecting agencies.

First, a metaphorics of contagion and a mapping of 'dangerous places'.

These were the product of a whole series of voluntary and state investigations of the city which traced the distribution and disposition of the population in terms of a set of overlapping threats to its health, decency, good order and well-being. It was in the context of such 'moral topographies' that cheaply-printed pornography could appear as a noxious substance and a contagious threat to insufficiently socialised and self-protecting sensibilities.

Second, the specialist knowledges of moral psychology and sexual medicine. Here – as in Elizabeth Blackwell's warnings concerning the consumption of pornography by children – moral danger and physical pathology were linked at the level of the individual mind and body. This was achieved through a moral physiology which in effect transformed medical pathology into a source of admonitory images used for an ethical discipline of the self while simultaneously bringing the latter within the confessional sphere of the doctor-patient relationship. It was here, primarily in the context of the great anti-masturbation campaigns directed at the bourgeois family, that the failure to resist the incitements of erotic words and images became intelligible in terms of a general debilitation of body and soul.

Lord Campbell's references to poison and obscene publications regain their historical intelligibility when read against these dual agencies:

[F]rom a trial which had taken place before him on Saturday, he had learned with horror and alarm that a sale of poison more deadly than prussic acid, strychnine or arsenic – the sale of obscene publications and indecent books – was openly going on.

(*Parliamentary Debates*, 1857, p. 103)

The reference to poison is not symptomatic of the excesses of a Victorian mentality which erroneously conflated moral distaste with physical harm. Joining the metaphorics of moral contagion aimed at the urban popular classes to the medical specification of the middle-class individual's moral pathology, this formulation indicates the emergence of a powerful social apparatus – a new configuration of the pornographic field – in which the taste for erotic literature indeed became a then quite proper object of governmental intervention and legal regulation.

Not so long ago it was easy for us to smile knowingly at this 'repressive' and 'unscientific' stigmatisation of erotica. Today these smiles are fading. The recent return of the rhetoric of pornography as a social harm suggests that current changes represent mutations in the regulatory apparatus which first emerged in the nineteenth century, not its definitive superseding. In other words, pornography's power to join moral and physical harm was not a chimera of Victorian ignorance and irrationality. It was a sign of the pivotal place that erotic words and images came to occupy at the juncture where the policing of the streets met the government of the self.

THE *HICKLIN* DICTUM AND UNDOUBTED OBSCENITY

The Obscene Publications Act of 1857 gained its definitive construction when, in 1868, Lord Campbell's successor as Lord Chief Justice, Sir Alexander Cockburn, made some observations on the distinguishing features of that species of publication liable to the charge of criminal obscenity. These observations became ubiquitous – in England, the United States, Canada and Australia – as the standard test used in proceedings relating to the common law offence of obscene libel. They were also to acquire a statutory existence – in an only slightly altered form – as the test for obscenity under the English Obscene Publications Act of 1959. Familiar though they are, the terms of Cockburn's dictum are so central to any reconstruction of English obscenity law that quotation is imperative:

> I think the test of obscenity is this, whether the tendency of the matter charged as obscenity is to deprave and corrupt those whose minds are open to such immoral influences, and into whose hands a publication of this sort may fall.
>
> (*Regina* v. *Hicklin*, p. 371)

As the *Hicklin* test for criminal obscenity, this became authority.

The case involved a destruction order made in the Wolverhampton magistrates court, an appeal against that order to Quarter Sessions, and a review of the ruling of the Quarter Sessions by the Queen's Bench Division of the High Court. The detail is as follows: under the forfeiture and destruction provisions of the 1857 Act, the Wolverhampton Justices authorised police seizure of a pamphlet, *The Confessional Unmasked: Showing the Depravity of the Romish Priesthood, the Iniquity of the Confessional, and the Questions put to Females in Confession*. The title recalls a specific literary arrangement we have already noted: the unforeseen exchange between spiritual confession and profane detailing of sexual possibilities. The Justices were responding to a complaint by a police officer acting at the direction of the Borough Watch Committee. 252 copies of the pamphlet were seized and after inspection by the local Justices – Benjamin Hicklin among them – their destruction was ordered on the grounds that the text was in part obscene.

The publication was not new, having seen a number of editions since 1836. It contained an anthology of extracts from the Catholic theologians Dens and Liguori, together with shorter selections from Bailly and Cabassutius, focussed on the practice of confession. They were printed in Latin on one side of the page, with English translations facing. The character of the extracts was not uniform, some dealing with doctrinal and casuistical matters and others, in a manner that the magistrates had no hesitation in finding obscene, with the conditions of 'females in confession'. There was also a preface in which, as in the commentary on the extracts, the editor attacked Catholic practices and beliefs: 'In the later part of the pamphlet I have given a few extracts without abridgement, to shew into what minute and disgusting details these holy men have entered. This alone has been my object, and not the filling of the work with obscenity' (*Regina* v. *Hicklin*, p. 362n). The copies seized came from the stock of an edition of *The Confessional Unmasked* that, together with the plates from which it was printed, had been bought from a William Strange, 'very possibly the same William Strange who had been sent down for three months by Lord Campbell in 1857 for selling obscene literature' (Thomas, 1969, p. 264). The buyers were the Protestant Electoral Union, a society committed to protect the Protestant tradition and to resist Catholicism in England. A member of the Protestant Electoral Union, a Wolverhampton metal broker Henry Scott, had then purchased copies from the Union's head office in London. Scott, 'a person of respectable position and character' (*Regina* v. *Hicklin*, p. 362), was the subject of the prosecution when the pamphlets were seized in his dwelling house. Faced with the detail of the sexual confessions illustrating the immorality of Catholic practice, the Justices moved to have the material destroyed as an obscene libel.

Scott, however, appealed against the destruction order, taking his case to the Quarter Sessions where the Recorder found that publication of the pamphlet was redeemed by its moral objective, a religious conviction that was in no sense indictable. Scott's intention, it was argued, was not to corrupt public morals, but to promote the case of the Protestant Electoral Union by exposing the 'iniquity of the confessional'. Nonetheless, recognising the legal implications of the case, the Prosecution asked the Recorder to put the matter up for consideration by a Queen's Bench Divisional Court. The ruling of the Wolverhampton Justices was therefore quashed, conditional on confirmation by the Court of Queen's Bench that, on the stated facts, Scott's possession, sale and distribution of *The Confessional Unmasked* was not a misdemeanour within the meaning of the Obscene

Publications Act 1857. Such confirmation was not, however, forthcoming. Lord Cockburn and his fellow judges unanimously affirmed the original destruction order.

Despite the cardinal importance of *Hicklin* – the Williams Report (1979, p. 169) comments that 'the test thus enunciated had a tremendous effect' – errors have crept into accounts of it. Tribe (1973, p. 65) has Hicklin as the Quarter Assizes Recorder, although it was of course the Recorder who quashed Hicklin's original destruction order; also, when citing the full title of the work, Tribe gives 'Immorality' in place of 'Iniquity' (p. 64). Thomas (1969, p. 264), perhaps determined to miss no chance of depicting the repression of literature by law, makes Scott a 'Wolverhampton bookseller', not a metal broker. Even the Williams Report (1979, p. 169), having decided to mention the location from which *The Confessional Unmasked* was seized, misleadingly refers to the 'premises' of Henry Scott, when in fact the raid had been on his dwelling-house, thus losing the sense of Scott as metal broker acting as concerned private citizen rather than as someone operating commercially from 'premises'.

More than detailed rectifications of fact, however, a sense of the legal-cultural environment of *Hicklin* is required if we are to grasp the contemporary intelligibility of Cockburn's celebrated dictum. Histories of obscenity law usually accord *Hicklin* its importance in terms of dire and nefarious consequences, a characteristic account describing it for instance as 'one passing judicial comment which has survived the passage of time and which returns regularly to plague the courts and parliaments of England, America and the common-law world' (Robertson, 1979, p. 30). Putting aside its hyperbole, we can nonetheless take from this remark a pertinent fact. Cockburn's epochal definition of obscenity was indeed, in the context of the judgement as a whole, just 'one passing judicial comment'. Re-reading the legal text, we find no sense whatsoever that a definition of obscenity was what everyone was looking for.

It was the moral and religious aspect of the work in question which had led the Quarter Sessions to seek the higher court's review of the ruling. That aspect, and Scott's expressed intention in publishing the pamphlet, focusses the reasoning of the Queen's Bench judges. In other words, even though the 1857 Act had passed into law unaccompanied by any statutory definition of obscenity, the judgement in *Hicklin* does not, in the first instance, read like a calculated piece of statutory interpretation.[3] 'Obscenity' is not recognised as being problematic in its reference or in need of legal definition. The celebrated phrase – it does not even constitute a complete sentence – is lodged inside a substantial paragraph in which, both before and after the definition, Cockburn wrestles with the problem of Scott's intent. Nor does the Lord Chief Justice offer any elaboration of the terms of his definition, other than to reiterate, later in his comments, what he has already said:

> I cannot suppose but that they had that intention which constitutes the criminality of the act, at any rate that they knew perfectly well that this work must have the tendency which, in point of law, makes it an obscene publication, namely the tendency to corrupt the minds and morals of those into whose hands it might come.
>
> (*Regina* v. *Hicklin*, p. 373)

None of Cockburn's fellow judges shows any sign of recognising something epochal – or even something useful and needed – in these definitions of obscenity.

This is not surprising. The Queen's Bench had not been asked to rule on whether *The Confessional Unmasked* was or was not obscene. The point at issue was whether an honest purpose could justify a criminal act of obscene publication. The Lord Chief Justice cites precedents to support the rule whereby 'when the act is in itself unlawful . . . the proof of its justification or excuses lies in the defendant; and in failure thereof, the law implies a criminal intent' (p. 364) and 'every man, if he be a rational man, must be considered to intend that which must necessarily follow from what he does' (p. 369). Noting his disagreement with the Recorder, the Lord Chief Justice then comments:

> I think that if there be an infraction of the law the intention to break the law must be inferred, and the criminal character of the publication is not affected or qualified by there being some ulterior object in view (which is the immediate and primary object of the parties) of a different and of an honest character. (p. 370)

As an explicit construction of the 1857 Statute, *Hicklin* is in one sense rather thin. The Wolverhampton Justices had no doubt that their destruction order fell within the meaning of the Act. In his comments, Lord Cockburn refers to sections of the Act but in a quite unproblematic way, to confirm that under the Statute the mere possession or sale of a work 'in a certain sense obscene' is not in itself sufficient for an indictment, but that the *circumstantial* intention must be established: 'the question is therefore quo animo was the publication' (pp. 367–8). Justice Blackburn opened his comments by confirming that the Statute was 'for the more effectually preventing the sale of obscene books'. He read the first section of the Act and then outlined the procedures to be followed in a prosecution:

Now what the magistrate or justices are to be satisfied of is that the belief of the complainant is well founded, and also that any of such articles so published for any of the purposes aforesaid, are of such a character and description that the publication of them would be a misdemeanour, and that the publication in the manner alleged would be proper to be prosecuted; and having satisfied themselves in respect of those things, the magistrates may proceed to order the seizure of the works. And then the justices in petty sessions are also in effect to be satisfied of the three same things; first, that the articles complained of have been kept for any of the purposes aforesaid, and that they are of the character stated in the warrant, that is, that they are of such a character that it would be a misdemeanour to publish them; and that it would not only be a misdemeanour to publish them, but that it would be proper to be prosecuted as such; and then, and only then, are they to order them to be destroyed. I think that with respect to the last clause, that the object of the legislature was to guard against the vexatious prosecution of publishers of old and recognised standard works, in which there may be some obscene or mischievous matter. (pp. 373–4)

The final remark raises the possibility that the concept of obscenity might have been in need of definition, but on balance the judge's words seem to refer less to a problem than to a wise provision of the Statute. Later he recalls *Regina* v. *Moxon*, the prosecution for blasphemous libel half a century earlier involving Shelley's *Queen Mab*, but only to distance himself from that judgement ('I believe, as everybody knows, that it was prosecution instituted merely for the purpose of vexation and annoyance.'). The judge then reflects on the 1857 Act and offers the reassurance that 'I think the legislature put in that provision in order to prevent proceedings in such cases' (p. 374).

In other words, for the Bench, adequate statutory provision had been made to distinguish between obscene and non-obscene writings. No hint is given that the drawing of that boundary requires an explicit act of interpretation. Justice Blackburn makes no further mention of the Statute, but comments instead on the all-important issue of intention in terms identical to those of the Lord Chief Justice. Only in a remark of Justice Mellor on the subject matter of the pamphlet – confessional practices – might some doubt concerning the obscenity of the item seem to reside:

The nature of the subject itself, if it may be discussed at all (and I think it undoubtedly may), is such that it cannot be discussed without to a certain extent producing authorities for the assertion that the confessional would be a mischievous thing to be introduced into this kingdom; and therefore it appears to me very much a question of degree, and if the matter were left to the jury it would depend very much on the opinion which the jury might form of that degree in such a publication as the present. (p. 378)

Perhaps there is a suggestion in this hint that erotic writing cannot even be cited for the purposes of discussion without provoking a certain incitatory effect, a point made in Chapter 2, it being a peculiarity of pornography that even as an object of knowledge and judgement it cannot be entirely detached from the excitation of the knower or the judge.

The text of *Hicklin* thus provides little evidence that the judges of the Queen's Bench saw themselves confounded by the absence of a clear idea of obscenity. In assuming such a lacuna, historians of obscenity must be suspected of anachronism. It is certainty, not doubt, which characterises the court's handling of obscenity. There was no doubt because obscene publication was defined not in the abstract but concretely and circumstantially by its mode and place of dissemination, that is, by its demographic targets. However, in talking of certainty, it remains important not to imply that the judges were locked into some iron-clad ideology which blinded them to the reality of (what has since become) the slippery concept of obscenity. The question is rather: What allowed the judges of the Queen's Bench in 1868 to be so certain about obscenity that definition of the concept occupied so little of their time? From the historical viewpoint, this certainty calls for explanation, not denunciation.

The multiple answers to the question of why the court in *Hicklin* was so unconcerned with the definition of obscenity do not turn on a crude sociological characterisation of the judges as the mere vehicles of a class mentality functionally determined by the structure of mid-Victorian society. We shall look first towards explanations involving the specialist infra-legal knowledges – sexual medicine and moral psychology – which informed the network of policing agencies.

The criteria and classifications which at the time of *Hicklin* organised knowledge of moral character no longer provide us with an admissible characterology, except perhaps at the level of our common sense, that sedimentation of former knowledges. The Wolverhampton justices, the Recorder of Quarter Sessions and the Judges of Queen's Bench could identify 'obscenity' without hesitation because of their capacity to work within the knowledge that morality was positively connected to health and that, in those who lacked the appropriate prophylactic preparation, moral health was damaged by exposure to obscene words and images. The 'deprave and corrupt' formulation of *Hicklin* was anything but idiosyncratic. What was known and applied was the social-medical norm which helped organise that world of which Lord Cockburn and Elizabeth Blackwell were exemplary denizens. Sexual medicine, as suggested in Chapter 2, linked bodily health to the purity of the mind and the pathology of the individual to that of society and the population at large. Pornography had gained but not yet lost its power to harm – a power which it is perhaps regaining among us today.

It was also known that not all individuals or populations were equally vulnerable to the harms defined and treated by the moral physiologists. *Hicklin* specifies 'those whose minds are open to such immoral influences, and into whose hands a publication of this sort may fall'. More than a specification of the attributes defining what will count as a vulnerable person, the second element of this formulation is an indication of a certain social space in which that person's vulnerability will be most exposed to exploitation by the distributors of pornography. It is not just that the minds and hands in question are weak, but that in certain specified places pornography falls – more noxiously and purposively than the gentle rain from heaven – into those minds and hands. These places are the streets of the city where the vulnerable were directly exposed to the harms of pornography. Here – cognisant of the medical-moral norm we have described – the law found itself working alongside the police (the latter using measures not necessarily juridical in form) to manage the reading of the popular classes. Given her expressed concern, Dr Blackwell would have required no less.

Precisely this concern is visible in the emphasis placed in *Hicklin* on the *circumstances* of the harming done by exposure to obscene publication:

> This work [*The Confessional Unmasked*] . . . is sold at the corners of streets, and in all directions, and of course it falls into the hands of persons in all classes, young and old, and the minds of those hitherto pure are exposed to the danger of contamination and pollution from the impurity it contains. (p. 372)

Earlier, the court had made the following explicit observation on the circumstantial nature of obscene publication:

> A medical treatise, with illustrations necessary for the information of those for whose education or information the work is intended, may, in a certain sense, be obscene, and yet not the subject for indictment; but it can never be that these prints may be exhibited for anyone, boys and girls, to see as they pass. The immunity must depend upon the circumstances of the publication. (p. 367)

This is a recognition that serious works – medical treatises or literature – might indeed fall within the scope of obscenity statutes when *distributed* to those whose taste was not fully formed (schoolchildren) or in a form calculated to 'exploit' those classes outside the precincts of ethical tutelage (cheap reprints sold on the streets). No doubt some people today are inclined to mock this demographics of moral vulnerability and even the notion of vulnerability itself, despite the feminist assault on such complacency. For our part, we remain more hesitant to dismiss out of hand the nineteenth-century capacity to identify moral offence and personal harm occasioned by pornography to certain categories of person in certain cultural circumstances. The 'deprave and corrupt' criterion for obscenity does not reduce to paternalist and bourgeois moral prejudice. It is not so empty of real content. On the contrary, it is perhaps too full – of the moral, medical, psychological, demographic and administrative knowledges from where derived the specific norms to which nineteenth-century obscenity law was oriented. That law presents moral-medical aetiologies more complex than we can immediately comprehend.

Since 1868, an edifice has been built upon the words of Lord Cockburn and his colleagues. Lodged in early textbooks such as Stephen's *Digest of the Criminal Law* and Archbold's *Criminal Pleading*, the 'tendency to deprave and corrupt' became the standard criminal law test for obscene publications.[4] The important task now is to sketch its career without collapsing the historical variations of obscenity law and the policing of pornography into a single story of personal right, human sexuality and literary expression struggling against the dark forces of law and censorship. That would be a story of repression, not a history of legal regulation and policing. Given this safeguard, there is some chance of restoring to obscenity law its positive but limited place in the mid-nineteenth-century complex of state and private programmes for collective and individual welfare, a complex in which distinct strategies to regulate pornography converged, sometimes in unexpected ways.

VARIABLE OBSCENITY

One sign of the practical and para-judicial character of the nineteenth-century policing of obscenity is the miscellaneous array of instruments and institutions which supported that policing. The Obscene Publications Act of 1857 and the *Hicklin* dictum were not the only mechanisms for regulating obscene publication. Other nineteenth-century statutes relating to obscenity included the Vagrancy Acts of 1824 and 1838, the Metropolitan Police Act of 1839, the Libel Act of 1843, the Theatres Act of 1843, the Town Police

Causes Act of 1847, the Post Office Act of 1870, the Public Health Act of 1875, the Customs Consolidation Act of 1876, the Post Office (Protection) Act of 1884, and the Indecent Advertisements Act of 1889. Merely to list these titles suggests something of the heterogeneous character of the administration of pornography. This unplanned regulatory concert can be schematised as a graduated scale, at one end of which are minor offences involving indecent handbills, sandwich-boards, placards and shop-window displays. These are tried in courts of summary jurisdiction by magistrates and justices and carry relatively light sentences to a maximum of forty shillings or one month in prison. Such offences and sentences constitute the legal infrastructure for keeping public order on the streets, and are dealt with by the police, often in an informal manner by the issuing of warnings. The police develop their own tests and classificatory mechanisms. The offenders – shopkeepers, street corner sellers, itinerant pedlars – appear to have accepted this policing as part of the particular commercial system within which they operated.

At the other end of the scale are the common law provisions. Here, obscene publication is constituted as a serious misdemeanour, handled under the criteria and procedures built up by the courts since the early eighteenth century. Obscene publication is here less a street offence subject to policing by the local constable than the descendant of the common-law delict of obscene libel which, as we have already noted, emerged when an obscene libel which defamed no one was recognised to be a corruption of the morality of everyone, and when with Curll's case in 1727 the *Sedley* precedent was imported into the newly-expanding domain of print publication and dissemination. At this high end of the scale lie the ceremonial of trial by jury and the heavier penalties faced by 'grossly indecent' materials.

How does the Obscene Publications Act of 1857 relate to this spectrum? The Act retained the existing common law offence of obscene libel. It classified the conditions under which the police could enter and search premises, and seize and destroy materials found to be obscene. Proof of exhibition and sale had to be obtained by police or informants purchasing materials, following which the magistrate or justices could issue the search warrant. The police as prosecutor could then seize the materials, returning with them to the magistrate who, unless a change of mind had occurred since the issue of the search warrant, could issue a destruction order. This summary procedure was embodied in the Act for use by the police against street pornography.

However, the Act also allowed an appeal by a defendant to a judge at Quarter Sessions and provided for jury trial under the common law. It thus connected, at least in theory, the routine policing of the streets and the ceremonial trial of condemned works, where the jury could speak for the entire community on what the state of public morality was to be. Across this bridge it became possible for the objectives and norms of moral policing to meet up with laws governing public morality and health. It was here that 'classics' could become caught up in the regulation of the circulation of socially harmful and dangerous commodities. This connection is manifested in the text of *Hicklin*. In a single sweep, reference is made on the one hand to what the 'boys and girls . . . see as they pass' and to the works 'sold at the corners of streets' (*Regina* v. *Hicklin*, pp. 367, 372); and, on the other, to the dignity of Juvenal and Chaucer, Milton and Dryden, Byron and Bayle before an appropriately respectful law (p. 365).

If taken to imply that serious works could appear only at the common law end of our scale, this listing of classics is misleading. On the contrary, the evidence of prosecutions demonstrates that established literary works had no uniform condition of existence under the law. If and when they entered the 'penny edition' circuit, Boccaccio, Balzac, Maupassant and Zola could become objects of routine street corner policing. In *Regina* v. *Thomson*, for instance, a London bookseller was in 1900 charged with having published 'a certain lewd, wicked, bawdy, and obscene libel in the form of a book entitled *The Heptameron* of Margaret Queen of Navarre'. The publication had come to the attention of the Metropolitan Police, for whom Inspector Arrow testified. In opening for the prosecution, R. D. Muir 'suggested that though it was a classic in the French language it was not a classic in the English language'. However, more than with a matter of incompatible national literary canons, in the words of the Common Sergeant's summing up of the case to the Central Criminal Court jury the court had 'to deal with the time and circumstances under which the book was put forth': 'If it had been in a library to which students had access, no one would deny that the book was properly there and properly kept for a proper use' (*Regina* v. *Thomson*, p. 457). Some half-century before it dawned on literary theorists, the police were thus aware that the meaning and effects of literature varied with the circumstances of its consumption and the cultural capacities of its users. As we shall see in Chapter 6, this pragmatic dependence of obscenity on the variable strategies of its policing would later pose major difficulties for its jurisprudential definition, codification and reform. In the event, Margaret Queen of Navarre was found fit to read.

Earlier, in 1888, action had been taken against Henry Vizetelly, the London publisher of translations of Gautier, Flaubert, Daudet, Maupassant and Zola. If the Vizetelly prosecution is the first example of the successful use of the 1857 Act against works which might be deemed to be of literary merit, two comments are appropriate. If it took more than thirty years from the passage of the Act or twenty years from *Hicklin* for there to occur this first example of the law being successfully invoked against literary works, a question must be raised about the standard censorship account of the effect of Victorian obscenity law. Robertson (1979, p. 30) claims that, '[a]rmed at last with a definition of obscenity, Victorian prosecutors proceeded to destroy many examples of fine literature'. Set against the fact of a single successful literary prosecution in the twenty central years of the Victorian era, such indignation and hyperbole is simply wrong. Yet the standard account is what underpins the received historiography of obscenity law. As if indifferent to what actually happened, the 'censorship' story endlessly returns to a fundamental and unchanging dichotomy between literary subjectivity and the generalised repressive agency of obscenity law depicted as blanket censorship.

The second comment concerns the way the conduct to which obscenity law applies – publication – is habitually represented as an invariant and transparent adjunct of subjectivity. Literature and publication have their histories. What counts as literature has changed, as have the uses made of published writings. It is therefore anachronistic to set a fourteenth-century collection of satirical folk-novellas and a nineteenth-century naturalist novel alongside one another as 'literature', imagine their prosecution and conclude with the usual observation on the philistine repressiveness of Victorian obscenity law. In the following chapter, therefore, we consider the possibility that with writings such as those of Zola or – more particularly – of D. H. Lawrence, serious literature had entered into a new and unforeseen relation with sexuality and the pornographic genre. For the moment it is enough to note that the aesthetic (and ethical) certainty implied by Robertson's phrase – 'many examples of fine literature' – may turn out to be quite misplaced. As we have seen, for the police the difference between lascivious material and improving literature was not inherent. It depended on where and to whom the literature was disseminated, how and by whom it was used. In showing a pair of clean and pragmatic pair of heels to modern reader-response theories, the nineteenth-century policing of erotic writing is also more subtle and flexible than twentieth-century attempts to write the history of obscenity law in terms of the censorship of a putatively self-evident and constant phenomenon called 'literature'.

THE LAW AND THE POLICE

To the suggestion that in the nineteenth century actual prosecutions against serious literature were rare, we can imagine a response that ties this rarity to a widespread adoption of procedures of self-censorship by authors of sexually expressive works in the face of the law of obscenity. In the following chapter, we shall give some good reasons why such a response is ill-conceived. For now, however, this response is useful insofar as it directs attention to the possibility of a diversity of regulatory mechanisms. And indeed, when we look, we find a miscellany of agencies, private and public.

The Proclamation Society was founded in 1787 by William Wilberforce, following a royal 'Proclamation for the Encouragement of Piety and Virtue; and for preventing and punishing Vice, Profaneness, and Immorality'. The Society for the Suppression of Vice and the Encouragement of Religion and Virtue superseded the Proclamation Society in 1801, enjoying a long and active career as the Vice Society. In the 1860s, the Duke of Argyll's Society for Pure Literature was active, while in 1886 from the National Vigilance Committee there emerged the National Vigilance Association for the Repression of Criminal Vice and Public Immorality. This incorporated the Society for the Suppression of Vice, the Minors' Protection Committee and the Belgian Traffic Committee, and merged in 1891 with the Central Vigilance Society.

As with the array of nineteenth-century statutory provisions, there is no uniformity of concern between or indeed within these civic societies and their endeavours. Just as Elizabeth Blackwell's pathologising of exposure to erotic writing and imagery now seems to jar with her feminist and socialist aspirations, so Wilberforce's attack on such writing does not sit easily with his attack on slavery, at least for the modern assumption that unless emancipation is general we do not properly have emancipation. The same is true of the National Vigilance Association with its actions against literature on the one hand – it was instrumental in bringing the 1888 Vizetelly prosecution – and its work against child prostitution and enforced incest on the other.

The law was not, however, hostage to these civic societies. While all of the nearly forty prosecutions for obscene libel brought by the Vice Society up to 1817 were successful, the Society's request for power of arrest to be made available to private citizens to seize persons distributing or selling obscene materials was not accorded when the Metropolitan Police Act of 1839 passed into law. Indeed, despite the increased powers made available by this statute and the Obscene Publications Act of 1857, the authorities appear to have been reluctant to set the law in motion, and without such official assistance, the civic bodies were inadequate to the task they set themselves. In part because of the increasing dissemination of pornography by mail, police interest fluctuated. 'Cases were brought from time to time but not with sufficient frequency to prevent the bookshop trade from re-establishing itself around Holywell Street' (Manchester, 1988, pp. 232–3).[5] Again, too much should not be read into the supposed failure of regulatory initiatives whose object was to channel, not to eradicate, pornographic materials. Nor should we forget that such basic practical determinants of legal action in relation to obscene publication as the locus of entitlement to prosecute – are charges to be brought by private individuals or should the Crown alone have the carriage of criminal prosecution? – were not yet codified into their modern form.

The miscellany of agencies in the field is further attested by a document which affords an excellent overview of nineteenth-century arrangements. Between March and June 1908, a Joint Select Committee of the Commons and the Lords inquired into the laws on lotteries and literature, pictures and advertisements 'relating to things indecent and immoral', and in late July 1908 brought down its *Report from the Joint Select Committee on Lotteries and Indecent Advertisements* (hereafter, the 1908 Report). A single committee to review laws relating to lotteries and to obscenity is today unlikely; however, the configuration of the Committee's brief exemplifies the particular 'series' in which obscene publications could intelligibly be placed at that time. Obscene publication was located among other street dangers to be regulated for the sake of the moral and physical well-being of urban populations. Within the one sweep of concern came lotteries which took the family man's wages, advertisements for 'female ailments' – 'Dr Paterson's famous female pills which remove irregularities, suppressions, and so on by simple means in a few hours' (1908 Report, p. 42) – advertisements of the 'Malthusian kind', that is for birth control and abortificients, and exhibitions of indecent pictures through bioscopes and 'mutoscopes':

> [T]he exhibition . . . was prosecuted on a Sunday night at the Elephant and Castle, and at the very least estimate the number of persons, boys and girls, there was over 300. They are indulging in all sorts of indecent acts among themselves, and two were looking round picking out the different machines which bore the most seductive titles and which they thought contained the worst pictures – a boy and girl each spying on the payment of ^{1}/2d. in the same machine, touching one another in an indecent manner, and making use of very indecent language. (pp. 44–5)

The diverse issues before the Committee illustrate the interlocking objectives of medical, social and pedagogical policing and define the series as the system of police developed for the regulation of city populations.[6]

The scale of offences, practices and institutions which was outlined in the previous section is evident in the 1908 Report. Constables on the beat use specified criteria to recognise and deal with offences under the Vagrancy Acts of 1824 and 1838, the Metropolitan Police Act of 1839, the Town

Police Causes Act of 1847 and various local acts and by-laws. Evidence on this aspect of policing is given by Commissioners of the Metropolitan Police, by the Chief Constables of Liverpool, Manchester, Hull and Dublin, and by the Director of Public Prosecutions. Reference is also made to the Obscene Publications Act of 1857 and the common law on obscene libel. The Head Constable of Liverpool identifies the difference between routine street policing practices and the statutory and common law provisions in explaining how his officers police obscene and indecent materials. Where indecent advertisements are found, instructions are given 'to the ordinary constable on the street' on how to handle matters himself, exercising a not insignificant measure of discretion. But the Head Constable then adds: 'Of course, with regard to the Obscene Publications Act 1857, that is mostly carried out by instructions from headquarters, and there are no more instructions issued to the police on the street on the subject, except that they would report anything which seemed to them suspicious' (p. 640).

Drawing a distinction between routine street policing and the ceremony of jury trial does not imply that the police acted entirely independently of the law. The point – as the detail of the 1908 Report demonstrates – is that police regulation of pornography had its relative autonomy and developed its specific criteria and norms as appropriate to its circumstances. Hence the pragmatic and incorrigible tests that the police had locally developed for use by the constables, as instanced by Chief Inspector Drew:

> I would like at this point to inform your Lordship's Committee, what in the opinion of the police is the difference between a photograph of an obscene nude person, and one which might be considered indecent, although not obscene, and that is where the hair is clearly shown on the private parts. (p. 436)

There is not room in this practical instruction to constables for the panoply of possible exemptions and the finer evidential concerns of the jury trial. Analogously, the Chief Constable of Manchester commented on his regularly using the same stipendiary magistrate for the granting of summonses under the 1857 Act: 'We always apply to him because you get a uniform practice by applying to one man; on indecency publications, I always go to the Stipendiary, so that you get a uniform practice' (p. 964). This evidences the desirability of a predictable and 'uniform practice' at street level. By contrast, the outcome of jury trial would be quite uncertain.

Other testimony points towards this 'high' end of the scale. Thus a Mr Corfe, concerned citizen and author of letters to the papers, correspondent with the Headmaster's Conference on the matter of their *Memorial* to the

Railway Companies concerning literature available through station bookstalls, is of the opinion that 'English novels have become so indecent of late years as to be even worse than the French ones' (p. 539). Indeed, three of them – *Three Weeks, Cynthia in the Wilderness* and *The Sands of Pleasure* – were 'about as bad as they can be' (p. 540). Still other testimonies range between the concerns of street policing and high moral principle, as when William Coote of the National Vigilance Society, freshly returned from Paris – he had attended an International Conference on indecent literature, books and pictures – expresses his anxiety over indecent exhibitions, displays of rubber goods in shop windows, 'living statuary' and an Anatomical Museum in London's Oxford Street.

Most importantly, it is the police – through the Head Constable of Liverpool – who draw attention to the variable character of the distinction between serious works and popular pornography:

> I think you must consider the circumstances of the case – the circumstances of how the thing is advertised, how it is distributed, and so on; for instance, we had a case before His Majesty's Judge of Assize last year, a case of some indecent photographs, and the learned counsel who was defending the prisoner drew rather a red-herring across the scent by alluding to the fact that he kept classical books like the *Contes Drolatiques* of Balzac, but the judge said: 'Balzac's works are classic, and they would not be regarded as indecent.' I do not think he would have used that expression if he had known that the particular edition of the *Contes Drolatiques*, which was found there, were penny editions of certain of those stories, mostly sold to dirty-minded little boys. In the same way, there is the *Decameron* of Boccaccio; I think it would be very undesirable if that were split up into penny editions, although regarded as a classic, perhaps it may be all right. (p. 652)

The Head Constable's point is not that there is no distinction between the classic and the pornographic. It is, rather, that this distinction is subordinate to a more important consideration: the need to calculate the effects of literary matter relative to the circumstances of its consumption by particular social-moral categories of person. This policeman's working assumption – as we have said, it anticipates literary theory by some half a century – is that there is no inherent or fixed distinction between art and pornography. The status of a piece of literature depends upon the aesthetic and ethical abilities and disposition of its audiences or – in other words – on the actual uses to which particular categories of person put it. This is precisely the point made by many feminists today about the masculine use of erotic literature. The Head Constable gives an exemplary circumstantial definition of what would count as obscene (the classics in penny part-editions circulating in the streets) and what would not (the classics in whole editions in the hands of competent readers). It was along these variable and discretionary boundaries that obscenity law adjusted itself to uses of pornography which differed according to the uneven distribution of erotic interests and cultural capacities.

The 1908 Report is an index of the state of relations between obscenity law and serious literature at the end of the nineteenth century. The Committee's final recommendation makes explicit reference to the matter of such literature:

> A provision should also be inserted to exempt from the operations of the Act any book of literary merit or any genuine work of Art. The Committee consider that it would be almost impossible to devise any definition which would cover this exception. In their opinion the decision in such cases should be left to the discretion of the Magistrate; but they believe that, if a provision such as they recommend were inserted into the Act, a Magistrate would be enabled to take into consideration all the circumstances of the case, and would be free from a supposed obligation merely to decide upon the decency or the indecency of the particular literary or artistic work brought to his notice. (p. 46)

This eschewing of definition and the wide margins allowed for circumstance and discretion confirm our account of police objectives as sensitive to context. The provision was not in fact made law, nor was the recommendation for a single consolidated statute with explicit definitions. Nonetheless, the Committee's move towards exemption for literary and artistic merit points to the developments later in the twentieth century.

In the 1908 Report the problem of erotic literature occupies a marginal position. No men of letters testified. If the Committee sought an exemption for literature, it did the same for medical men and registered chemists acting *bona fide*. It also left the task of recognising what was pornographic and what was literary and artistic to the police, magistrates and justices. Given their predominant pattern of distribution, *Three Weeks, Cynthia in the Wilderness* and *The Sands of Pleasure* would tend to be unproblematically recognised as part of that socially harmful and thus criminal merchandise which also included gambling games, advertisements for contraceptives and abortion devices, images in mutoscopes and French postcards, a veritable canon of unseemly artefacts aimed at the moral harm and financial exploitation of the vulnerable. Circumstantially located here, erotic writings could scarcely call in their defence upon a general and unconditional right of aesthetic self-expression, any more than rubber goods can do today.

While literature is not a focus of the 1908 Report, obscenity law too fails to occupy the central ground. Or, more precisely, it does not have that central ground – the government of the national population's moral and physical welfare – entirely to itself. The Committee's recommendation that its proposed consolidated statute on obscenity be enforceable by summary jurisdiction rests on the assertion reiterated by witness after witness that the common law provisions for dealing with obscene publications are inappropriate, and that the offender should be dealt with summarily rather than only on indictment before a jury. There is an element here of the notion – dear to enforcers – that cheap, fast and easy judgement is best. These reiterations endorse a shift away from jury trial, for example in the specific recommendation that punishments should be calculated to fall below the level at which defendants could claim trial by jury.

In addition, other agencies of regulation of obscene publication make a substantial appearance in the 1908 Report. Civic rather than legal, these agencies and their presence draw attention to the ordering of commercial and personal conduct by means other than the criminalisation of pornography. These extra-legal agencies signal that at the threshold of the twentieth century a multi-institutional fabric regulated conduct across the cultural field in which lotteries, abortificients, pornography and overindulgence in mutoscopes could constitute a coherent social harm with which it was a government's proper responsibility to deal.

Agencies other than law and police were also involved, formulating routine instructions for staff having to deal with offending materials. The Committee received evidence on the routine guidelines issued to postmasters by the Postmaster-General on the handling of illegal materials.[7] Indeed, the Postmaster-General envisaged an extension of his regulatory powers and sought a new power to open suspect mail:

> [I]t is very difficult to deal with either lotteries or indecent matter, so long as the letters relating to them are put in sealed covers. There are very stringent provisions in the Post Office Acts against opening or delaying any letter, and every officer of the Post Office has to make a declaration when he is appointed that he will not open or delay, or suffer to be opened or delayed, contrary to his duty, any letter or thing sent by the post. (p. 76)

At issue is the locus of authority to take regulatory action. At the time of the 1908 Report, the Postmaster-General had no authority of his own to open suspect items. Such authority was vested in the Home Secretary. Signs of emerging boundary disputes are visible in the following exchange between the Committee Chairman and the Solicitor to the Post Office:

> Have you anything in your Post Office at all corresponding with the Bureau of Chemistry in the Washington Post Office? – No, I do not think we have. May I ask what the Bureau of Chemistry does?
>
> The Bureau of Chemistry analyses a certain number of matters or goods which are brought to their notice, and if under the report made to the Post Office they appear not to come up to the qualifications that are claimed for them by the advertisers the postmaster refuses to transmit these goods at all. (pp. 82–3)

The Solicitor then confirms that the British Post Office has no machinery comparable to the US Bureau of Chemistry. Asked whether he favoured the establishment of some such agency, he replies: 'I should hardly have thought it was necessary to have a Chemical Department to deal with these questions. Such a thing would be primarily to help the Adulteration Acts' (p. 86). An exchange of this kind testifies to the emergence of new agencies from technical fields of knowledge in which criteria and tests are developed for identifying harmful materials (here pharmaceuticals). These new agencies construct their own boundaries of judgement – the Solicitor retreats to the established legal arrangement when confronted by the prospect of a 'Chemical Department'. With the Post Office too, the fact of variable judgement arises, Mr Muskett, legal adviser to the Commissioner of Police, complaining that

> the Post Office have expressed the view that a number of photographs of nude women which came into their hands accidentally from a person who is now being prosecuted, were not obscene, whereas in my judgement they are exactly similar in every way to photographs which have always been regarded by the police authorities as obscene, and which have formed the subject of a large number of successful prosecutions. (p. 334)

This statement of the discrepancy between the pragmatic criteria and forms of judgement deployed by two interested agencies underlines the heterogeneous character of the regulatory fabric of policing that was in place by the end of the nineteenth century.

The regulation of obscene publication, it is clear, did not fall wholly within the field of criminal law. On the contrary, this regulation was diversified and marked by irregularities, boundary shifts, disputed loci of authority. The 1908 Report demonstrates the continuing role of extra-legal agencies – both professional enterprises and amateur consciences – in the regulation of obscene publication. Newspapers, for instance, were confronted with the issue since – like the national and international postal service – they enhanced the circulation of obscene publications, rendering regulation more difficult. Thus the newspaper proprietors and distributors also functioned as regulators:

> Personal representations have been made to the proprietors of more than one newspaper and to Messrs Smith and Son and Wyman and Sons, the great newsagents, in order to prevent them selling certain papers which either admittedly deal with indecent matters, or have actually been convicted of doing so. Favourable replies have been received from both those firms . . . (p. 237)

The regulation of obscene publication here passes across the boundary between public and private, into the domain of the Smiths and Wymans, the Boots and the Mudies, that is, into the domain of self-regulating book and newspaper wholesalers and retailers, and the circulating libraries.

Across this wide array of regulators and modes of regulating the problem of pornography is generally defined in terms of a social harm to be handled according to the then available medical-moral criteria. These, as we have seen, were marked by an acute awareness of the circumstantial character of this harm. The 1908 Report provides a picture of an English public whose reading is organised differentially, within a complex network of social regulation. It is not only professional administrators like Mr Byrne, Assistant Undersecretary of State in the Home Department, whose reference to the 'great newsagents' we have just quoted, who are active in this network. More than once the Committee is informed of bodies such as the Headmasters' Association and the Headmasters' Conference (pp. 191, 518–9), and their intervention with the railway companies concerning the literature available at railway bookstalls (these outlets were very largely owned by W. H. Smith and Sons). While the headmasters were policing the booksellers, the Billposters Association (p. 558), Watch Committees (p. 645), the afore-mentioned National Vigilance Society (pp. 719 ff.), the Church of England Men's Society (p. 735), the Ancient Society of Hibernians (p. 750) and the ever-alert Paris Vigilance Society were all at work on obscene publication and its channels of distribution and consumption.

So, in the late nineteenth century, the edifice of the common law was being lapped by a rising tide of other regulatory agencies – private and public, religious and administrative, ethical and commercial. The fact that censorship historians have, for their own ends, been transfixed by the grand but rare ceremonies of the courtroom should not blind us to the equally powerful but more organic and diverse regulatory currents flowing through the capillaries of the social body. An inconspicuous reference in the 1908 Report thus signals a mode of regulating individual conduct contrasting absolutely with public legal sanction. Giving evidence on behalf of the National Anti-Gambling League, a Mr Hawke advised the Committee of his idea for curbing illicit lotteries run through the post by allowing the Postmaster General

> to refuse to deliver any open or closed communications which he has reason to believe contain matters relating to lotteries contravening this Act, and, unless proof to the contrary can be shown by the persons interested, such communications shall be destroyed, and any lottery remittance therein shall be retained for the benefit of the Rowland Hill Memorial Benevolent Fund.
>
> [Postmen] are always wanting money; it is a great institution, and, my Lord Chairman, there is this to be said, that these poor postmen have to go through the valley of temptation with regard to these sorts of things, and if they were stimulated to put a stop to it, and if their fund for the decrepit and old amongst them were benefitted, I hope it might do some good. (pp. 589–90)

Mr Hawke's regulatory superannuation scheme did not see the light of day. But his image of poor postmen in 'the valley of temptation', acquiring through the promise of benevolent funds the individual self-discipline that makes a postal service possible, offers a polar opposite to the image of judicial *gravitas* presiding at the ceremonial criminal trial where, in relation to a certain publication, court and jury symbolically embody the community pronouncing on the state of public morality.

Michel Foucault's *History of Sexuality* tells of the invasion of the *law* by *norms*, and of the overlapping of the old juridical monarchy by

> new methods of power whose operation is not ensured by right but by technique, not by law but by normalization, not by punishment but by control, methods that are employed on all levels and in forms that go beyond the state and its apparatus. We have been engaged for centuries in a type of society in which the juridical is increasingly incapable of coding power, of serving as its system of representation.
>
> (Foucault, 1979, pp. 88–9)

'Not by law but by normalization, not by punishment but by control': this could be the slogan of those state and civic agencies whose active presence is recorded in the 1908 Report: the police, the Post Office, the Bureau of Chemistry, the newspapers and the newsagents, the booksellers and the headmasters, the Billposters' Association and the National Vigilance Society. Later, Foucault clarifies his proposition:

> I do not mean to say that the law fades into the background or that the institutions of justice tend to disappear, but rather that the law operates more and more as a norm, and that the juridical institution is increasingly incorporated into a continuum of apparatuses (medical, administrative, and so on) whose functions are for the most part regulatory. (p. 144)

In its characteristic dialect, Foucault's aligning of the law with the 'continuum of apparatuses' invites us to find a historical instance in the spectrum of interlocking measures for dealing with what constituted – according to governmental objectives and norms – the social problem of pornography. In nineteenth-century England, obscenity law thus found itself in regulatory partnership with a miscellany of other agencies. Given the multiple nature of this regulatory field, to seek out a single great subject of power behind it all – Victorian moralism, capital, patriarchy, the law, censorship – is to create and to pursue a shadow, a chimera. It is to risk describing nothing, when all the time the task should be to describe the actual agents which organised and managed the pornographic field.

HISTORICISING OBSCENITY LAW

The theme culled from Foucault recalls the matter of how published obscenity was brought within the common law sphere in the first place. Literary histories of obscenity law – the work of what we have termed 'censorship historians' – identify the person who creates and the person who is prosecuted. This identification is manifest in the attachment of post-Romantic criticism to the figure of the transgressive author (or text), said to embody the whole impetus of human development against the repressive powers of law and state. This identification is so profoundly established that these literary histories do not pause to digest the fact that the bulk of obscenity prosecutions have been of printers, publishers and booksellers, not of writers.

It was thus as a printer and bookseller, not as a writer, that an individual was first convicted of obscene publication. In Chapter 2 we noted that in

1727, with *Rex* v. *Curll*, the court of King's Bench created the offence of obscene libel, conceptualised as a disturbing of the King's peace by virtue of an obscene publication which does harm to public morality.[8] In 1724, the London printer, bookseller, pamphleteer, journalist, publicist, employer of hacks, pirate and pornographer Edmund Curll was charged in relation to the publication of *Venus in the Cloister; or, the Nun in her Smock*, an English translation of Jean Barrin's *Vénus dans le cloître*, together with certain other works. For the first time, obscene publication appeared within the purview of the common law, entering the criminal justice system and thereby gaining a new social generality as the object of governmental responsibility. With the sentencing of Curll in 1727, obscene publication gained legal recognition as a danger which, left unchecked by the custodial and legal powers of the sovereign, could morally harm the population at large. In effect, the judges in Curll's case adopted a new disposition of public morality, transferring a specific form of immorality from sin to crime and shifting its control from religious to legal regulation.

This shift marked a significant mutation in the existing division of jurisdiction between the temporal or common law courts and the spiritual or ecclesiastical courts which, hitherto, had dealt with matters pertaining to personal morality and sex (hence their popular appellation as the Bawdy Courts).[9] The spiritual courts had traditionally carried the responsibility for dealing with 'personal' offences *pro custodia morum* of the community and *pro salute animae* of the offender, that is, for the sake of reforming the sinner. The judges did not slip obscene publication across this jurisdictional boundary without a deal of debate about the existing demarcation of competence between the different courts and about the indications and counter-indications of such precedents as were to hand, notably *Rex* v. *Sir Charles Sedley* 1663 and *Regina* v. *Read* 1707. A solid tussle was conducted within the terms of a specific common law procedure – the construction, extension and application of precedent. This is just one sign that the judges' action was anything but automatic and driven by Puritan morality or by a reflex repression of sexual expressivity.

Curll's defence to the charge ran within established boundaries and rested, one would think, on a solid precedent in *Read*. In 1707 the King's Bench had quashed a conviction on the grounds that a written publication which did not defame some actual person was not a criminal matter. As Curll's counsel said of *Read*:

[T]here was an information for a libel in writing an obscene book called *The Fifteen Plagues of a Maidenhead*, and after conviction it was moved in arrest of judgement that this was not punishable in the Temporal

Courts; and the opinion of Chief Justice Holt was so strong with the objection, that the prosecutor never thought fit to stir it again.

(*Rex* v. *Curll*, pp. 849–50)

Yet this defence failed against an evidently successful analogy drawn by the Attorney General: just as 'particular acts of fornication are not punishable in the Temporal Courts, and bawdy houses are' (p. 850), so the action of obscene publication – if it 'tends to disturb the civil order of society' or reflect upon morality – should be considered by the court in the same terms as the running of a bawdy house.

In this unforeseen reorganisation of the institutions of moral regulation, the common law courts acquired a new responsibility: regulation of the field of obscene publication. In its early modern configuration, this field was organised around an equally unforeseen yet potent liaison between certain literate products of a confessional practice concerned with instilling an ever more detailed sense of the erotic and the sinful, and a commercial book trade beginning to exploit that same developing erotic sensitivity but for ends quite other than grace. The once specialist genre of libertine anti-clerical crotica was thereby redirected to a new audience, as English translation and publication established new circulations for works such as *Vénus dans le cloître*. In Chapter 2, in considering the question of this new audience, we thus suggested that what pushed Curll's publication across the threshold into the domain of criminal law was the formation of a new and less specialised public with a disposition for pornography in English.

This particular expansion of government and criminal law into the area of public morality did not involve an abstract specification of the existence of a public with a propensity for corruption. Without the definite means of becoming corrupt, in other words without the communications technology of the book and without the dissemination of a particular cultural competence – print literacy – a public which might be corrupted by obscene publications could not actually exist. Hence the significance of one judge's observation that '[t]he spiritual Courts punish only personal spiritual defamation by words; if it is reduced to writing, it is a temporal offence' (p. 850). More pointed still is the contrast drawn by Justice Reynolds between *Sedley*, where Sir Charles had 'only exposed himself to the people then present, who might choose whether they would look upon him or not', and the action of Curll, whose 'book goes all over the kingdom' (p. 851). The notion of the new distributional force of print, and the judges' suspicion that print exercises a certain type of direct impact upon its readers, swings the case against Curll. This had not been the decision in *Read*, and the divergence of these two decisions at common law, separated by only twenty years, says something of the instability of the pornographic field from the very start. The court in *Curll* thus set itself to weigh up whether a publication of obscene literature, the distribution and reading of *Venus in the Cloister*, could disturb the King's peace as surely as the actions of Sedley, friend of Rochester, had been found to do in 1663. In the earlier case, along with the public display of nakedness on the balcony, the defendant had, as Chief Justice Fortescue remarked in *Curll*, exercised a physical force in throwing out bottles and pissing down upon the people's heads.

Aside from the telling contrast with our own times when, in the Williams Report (1979), *books* fall by their essential nature as 'writing' into the realm of free 'choice' whereas *photographs* are excluded on the grounds of the coercive immediacy of their impact, what is the historical and theoretical interest of Curll's case for subsequent law on obscenity?[10] The judges in *Curll* realised a complex piece of lawmaking which – as the offence of obscene libel – was to endure in English criminal law for 232 years, until the Obscene Publications Act of 1959. The creation of this new offence and the judicial initiative to use the criminal law for the moral government of the kingdom were contingent on an unpredictable conjunction of legal and cultural factors: the *Sedley* precedent whereby the common law declared itself competent – as *custos morum* of all the king's subjects – to indict on the grounds of a subversion of public morals; the rise of the distribution of printed works and a rapid expansion of the cultural capacity – discursive literacy – needed to consume them; the emergence of a less specialist interest in erotic writings and the formation of a system of supply, for instance by a pornographer, printer and bookseller such as Curll, of a market providing for this new 'personal' interest.

It is in this conjunction of otherwise unrelated factors – legal, governmental, cultural, technological and commercial – that the contingency of the early modern pornographic field is displayed. Set against this background of unplanned circumstances, the attempt to account for the first emergence of the crime of obscene publication in terms of some general movement of consciousness of which the law was the pliant instrument – typically an access of 'Puritan' repressiveness – promises only a loss of historical specificity and a reduced descriptive capacity. Certainly, an expansion of the sphere of government occurred through the mechanism of the criminal law. But this unanticipated reorganisation of the institutions regulating public morality resulted from a characteristic piece of common law innovation, building up from gritty example and particularity of circumstance. The court was confronted by the possibility of a crime involving a disturbance of the peace where there was no use of physical force and a libel where no one was libelled. The question of how such an act could have become intelligible as a crime, as it evidently did with *Curll*, calls for analysis in terms of quite local circumstances, not grand philosophical schemes.

In Curll's case, a printed and published writing was recognised as constituting an obscene libel and made the object of a criminal sanction on the grounds that – left unchecked – such a publication would harm public morality and disturb the social balance by libelling the honour of the king through an exposure of his subjects to the imperious force of printed obscenity. By the time of the Obscene Publications Act of 1857 and *Hicklin* in 1868, things are very different. By then, a work counted as obscene is treated as a toxic substance having 'a tendency . . . to deprave and corrupt those whose minds are open to such immoral influences, and into whose hands a publications of this sort may fall'. If the publication is dangerous enough to be deemed a social risk and thus made subject to preventive legal regulatory measures, it is no longer as an action liable to disturb the king's peace. Rather, it has become a dangerous substance, a commodity capable of inducing the user who comes from what is deemed a category of vulnerable and non-competent persons to deviate from known norms of moral and physical health. What nineteenth-century obscenity law targetted as an essential object of governmental responsibility was no longer an act of sedition endangering the social balance, but a dangerous poison inducing moral and medical harm. To underscore such transformations is to break with the received pattern of historiography that has been imposed on English obscenity law. We have in mind accounts such as St John-Stevas (1956), Hyde (1964), Rolph (1969), Thomas (1969) and Robertson (1979). These are unitary narratives which construct a history of the legal relations of erotic writing in terms of a single trans-historical struggle between repressive external controls – censorship, obscenity law, police – and an essential subjectivity which seeks individual expression in writing the truth about sex.

What is the problem with such accounts? It is not just that they write the history backwards from the present as if a single logic, a single dark and shining path led from Ezekiel to D. H. Lawrence (Robertson, 1979) or from ancient Greece to the First Amendment and Arthur Schlesigner Jr (Widmer, 1970). More importantly, the received historiography does no justice to the substantive changes in the social organisation of subjectivity. The medicalised morality and moralised medicine which created and so minutely managed the nineteenth-century sexual personality – and thus directly informed the obscenity law of that time and cultural milieu – register a high degree of historical particularity. In our present study, historical transformations of subjectivity are taken as a necessary starting point for any attempt to put the record straight concerning the objectives and norms of obscenity law. The difference should be clear between a history which recognises the historically distinctive but impermanent arrangement of sexual, moral, medical and legal attributes in nineteenth-century England and one – the received historiography of the censorship historians – that assumes a timeless sexual subject upon which, except at rare moments of emancipation, more or less the same censorious law eternally impinges in more or less the same repressive manner. No doubt the notion of a transhistorical sexuality is convenient, providing both origin and destiny for the traditional history of erotic writing, whether for the author behind the work, the reader in front of it or the historian wanting to write his or her single story of repression.

By contrast, we have emphasised the historical and cultural differences between a crime of obscene publication defined within a series comprising sin, sedition, disturbance of the king's peace, print technology and a crime of obscene publication defined within a series comprising moral offence, medical harm, abortificients, lotteries, the Post Office, unregulated poisons and mutoscopes allowing universal access. In foregrounding the fact of historical difference, we directly confront those two traditional periodisations of English obscenity law which tie the emergence of that law either to the alleged excess of puritan moral conscientiousness or to the supposedly overweaning power of Victorian moralism. In each case, the received historiography underestimates the technical complexity and historical particularity of the legal-cultural arrangements, just as it underestimates the possibility – if, that is, it even suspects it – that western sexuality is less the locus of an essential human truth than a specialised cultural artefact into which so much work has gone. Not the least important element of this work has been a remarkable alteration in the relations between literature and sex. It is to this theme – a quite unforeseen transformation of the concerns and content of aesthetic literature and the problems which this transformation posed for obscenity law – that we now turn.

4 Literary Erotics

> Nothing is more obdurate to artistic treatment than the carnal, but it has to be got in, I'm sure: everything has to be got in . . .
>
> E. M. Forster, 1983 [1920]

TENDER IMAGINATIONS

In the late nineteenth and early twentieth centuries a significant development occurred, one which was unforeseen in earlier legislation and policing. Serious literary works began to come under the eye of police employing routine tests for obscenity, and on occasion were the cause for obscenity proceedings in the courts.[1] How is this development to be understood? When, how and to what extent did serious literature enter the field of discourses concerned with sex, in an event which signals a new orientation of literary techniques and abilities?

We can begin by separating out two relevant instances. In the nineteenth century, the educative novel and the erotic novel were defined through different channels of distribution which were maintained, partly, by law. The genre of 'curious' or perverse pornography was confined to a tolerated specialist zone, which added an erotic space, a 'habitus' of secrecy, to the definition of a true (that is, hidden) self identified with the activity of reading erotica. At that time, biblio-erotic techniques were set apart from the educative fictions of the cultivated classes. While this was the case, the law on obscenity would remain largely indifferent to questions of literary merit. The conditions for significant conflict to occur between artistic value and the criminal harms associated with obscenity did not yet exist, a fact reflected in nineteenth-century law's untroubled distinction between pornography and literature. Of course, as noted in the preceding chapter, police routinely tested the obscenity of works normally viewed as literature but republished in editions designed as pornography or collected in erotic anthologies aimed at the street market. This, however, neither collapsed the distinction between literature and pornography nor undermined the medical-legal policing of obscenity as a social pathology. Different types of publication were regulated and channelled according to a working knowledge of audiences that was maintained into the twentieth century. In general, obscene publications were easily recognisable as a particular form

Literary Erotics

and use of print literacy – and not just for the law – by the matter they contained, their mode of distribution and their sites of sale.[2] The educative novel was not a target in nineteenth-century campaigns against obscenity. It is equally important to note that serious literary writing, including criticism, was not among the array of 'infra-legal' disciplines which guided the law in administering that area. The limited political opposition to Lord Campbell's Bill which was voiced in Parliament was not matched by widescale criticisms defending literary projects and rights, of the sort which would become familiar in connection with twentieth-century obscenity law. Generally, novelists, editors and critics felt no need to mobilise opinion in order to protect their craft against supposed encroachments by obscenity law. On the contrary, the literary establishment shared the concerns of the legislature.

Consider, in this regard, the letter written by Charles Dickens to Wilkie Collins in 1867, concerning certain scenes in a novel which had become embroiled in controversy, *Griffith Gaunt, or Jealousy*, written by Charles Reade (who had initiated suits against critics attacking his novel's treatment of adultery, bigamy and seduction). With a clear sense of the difference between the serious novel and 'Holywell Street literature' or pornography, Dickens defends Reade's work against critics who have treated it as no different from the latter. However, he is also aware that there are different kinds of audience and distribution, and in this regard Dickens's views accord with those of the police. What is to be made of a book depends in part on the capacities, dispositions and habits of those who read it and the uses to which they may put it. As the editor of a widely circulating periodical, Dickens recognises that if literature can improve it can also damage its readers:

MY DEAR WILKIE, – I have read Charles Reade's book, and here follows my state of mind – *as a witness* – respecting it.

I have read it with strongest interest and admiration. I regard it as the work of a highly accomplished writer and a good man; a writer with a brilliant fancy and a graceful and tender imagination. I could name no other living writer who could, in my opinion, write such a story nearly so well. As regards a so-called critic who should decry such a book as Holywell Street literature, and the like, I should have merely to say of him that I could desire no stronger proof of his incapacity in, and his unfitness for, the post to which he has elected himself.

Cross-examined, I should feel myself in danger of being put on unsafe ground, and should try to set my wits against the cross-examiner, to keep well off it. But if I were reminded (as I probably should be, supposing the evidence to be allowed at all) that I was the Editor of a periodical of large circulation in which the Plaintiff himself had written, and if I had [*had*] read to me in court those passages about Gaunt's going up to his wife's bed drunk and that last child's being conceived, and was asked whether, as Editor, I would have passed those passages, whether written by the Plaintiff or anybody else, I should be obliged to reply No. Asked why? I should say that what was pure to an artist might be impurely suggestive to inferior minds (of which there must necessarily be many among a large mass of readers), and that I should have called the writer's attention to the likelihood of those passages being perverted in such quarters.

(David Paroissien (ed.) 1985, p. 358, footnotes omitted)

Like the Chief Constable of Liverpool, Dickens was attuned to the fact of differences in the social distribution of ethical culture and hence to the circumstantial character of literary value. In a case where erotic passages in a serious novel might prove too strong a medicine for the ethical constitution of a popular audience, Dickens accepts without hesitation the role of aesthetic policeman. The writer and publisher of educative literature, in contrast to the pornographer, must attempt to communicate edifying sentiments and conducts. The project of a writer such as Dickens could be said to help manage 'sexuality' only if we understand by this term a way of cultivating moral norms and manners which displays no interest in setting up sexual acts or erotic pleasures as containing an ultimate truth, central to the recovery and expression of personal identity.[3]

By the 1920s, the relation of some serious literature to obscenity law had become sensitised and vexed, not only for the literati but also for those administering the law. The regulation of obscenity – including the relation of its customary object, pornography, to their own enterprise – had now appeared on the agenda of advanced literary intellectuals. They responded in various ways. E. M. Forster was sufficiently interested in accommodating erotic writing in the novel to compose his study of homosexuality, *Maurice*, in 1913–4, although it was not published until after his death in 1970. In 1920 he wrote to Siegfried Sassoon the avowal, cited at the head of this chapter, to achieve an artistic treatment of the carnal. James Joyce recorded that in *Ulysses*, a work attracting legal attention in England (Robertson, 1979, pp. 35, 38) and in the USA where its publication was permitted in 1934 in *US* v. *Ulysses*, he was experimenting with 'the grossly masturbatory prose of "dirty" books' (Charney, 1981, p. 51). D. H. Lawrence, of course, wrote many erotic works and apologias for them and, in

1915, a Bow Street magistrate ordered the destruction of one thousand copies of *The Rainbow* while in 1929 several of his pictures were seized by police at an exhibition. *Lady Chatterley's Lover* opened its episode with the policing of pornography in 1928 as soon as it was written, Lawrence avoiding prosecution by having it printed in Italy and mailed to private subscribers in England. This book circulated in the same manner as pornography and was a minor catalyst to the pornographic trade since, without copyright protection, it was open to piracy. A certain set of circumstances allowed a writer such as Lawrence to occupy an ambiguous status: on the one hand he could produce works that were likely to be prosecuted for obscenity; on the other, he could figure as a progressive author entitled to comment ethically on social problems including the soundness of obscenity law itself. The mid-nineteenth century had no equivalent to this contradictory persona. In order to understand what made such as figure possible, we need to reconstruct the peculiar conditions under which literary discourse and literary careers could become marked by so intense an interest in sex.

Of course it was not that literature had never spoken of sex before. As a theme, sex is no doubt continuous from the classical period onwards. This does not mean, however, that the sex being spoken of and the manner in which the speaking was done (by whom, to whom, and for what purposes) remained constant. In Chapter 2 we outlined the emergence of a personal confessional sexuality, resulting from the deployment of religious techniques of erotic self-interrogation in early modern Europe. Paul Veyne has argued that, as the inheritors and masters of such techniques, modern writers address their sexuality and their audience in a manner quite unlike their classical forebears:

> The problem of individualism in literature gets posed more often in terms of pragmatics than content. Romanticism did not discover unknown continents of the human soul. It won the right to talk about oneself for no other reason than to express, in one's own name, truths that may have already been known, tossing into the balance the weight of personal testimony, even if it was repetitive. All of which presupposes a civilisation where every soul is held to be interesting, if it is undisguised. Greek civilization, however, was as yet unaware of the anxiety of confession, doubt, or self-exploration. Greek souls did not publicise their turmoils. If error or faults were to be published as something important, they had to stop being something negative and become, like sin, integral parts of the human condition.

(Veyne, 1988, p. 170)

During the Romantic period it became possible for authors and readers to orient themselves around the personal experience of sex. This was due to the emergence of an ethical culture that created individuals who routinely related to their 'selves' by problematising their sex. As a profane relay for this interrogation-incitement of the flesh, pornographic writing, we have argued, maintained an ambivalent and fugitive existence during the eighteenth and nineteenth centuries. Having emerged when the techniques of auto-erotic inwardness were unexpectedly caught up in a new technology of mass communication, pornographic writing was initially balanced precariously on the cusp of private ethical and public legal regulation and was bathed in the strange half-light where the sciences of pathological sexuality embraced a literature that intensifies sexuality by pathologising it. So when, at the end of the nineteenth century, serious literature began to experiment with the techniques of pornographic writing and to dice with obscenity law, it opened itself to the whole unstable play of forces that formed the pornographic field.

Serious sexual literature emerged thanks not to the independent experience and vision of individual authors, but to a complex interaction with an existing field of sexual techniques, problematisations and disciplines which already had a role in constructing sexualities. In the late nineteenth and early twentieth centuries, literature came to play a distinct part of its own in organising sexuality. This was not because it reflected the intrinsic nature of sexuality more accurately than other discourses had been able to do. It was simply that a certain kind of literature provided the techniques through which a particular group of writers and readers would be able to transform – aesthetically – a certain deployment of sexuality. In this way, early in the twentieth century, sexualised literature became the locus and the medium for a highly specialised use of sex. For a little band equipped with the cultural capacity to make them into serious ethical endeavours, erotic writing and reading became the instruments for a novel kind of work on the self.

What made this new role of literature possible? Two general factors were in play. First, as we suggested in Chapter 2, an aesthetic mode of self-fashioning – derived from the Romantic period and sustained thereafter by a highly educated minority – converged with various disciplinary knowledges and problematisations of sex. Second, in a particular development of this aesthetic interest, the serious novel took over techniques of erotic writing, especially from pornography, revalorising these as a true (because secret) means of shaping and knowing the self.

From these factors emerged a re-organisation of literary interest, identifiable in the Lawrentian project to realise and publish the truth of sex. We shall examine these general factors in more detail below, but let us note for the moment that this literary incursion into the territory of explicit sexual representations was powerful enough to blur the existing boundary between social genres. The distinction between pornography and serious literature observed by the law was no longer respected by a hybrid form of the novel which had become both literary and pornographic. This shift created a new uncertainty in the regulation of pornography. Pornographic elements began to surface in the educative novel, that much more widely disseminated social relay of norms of conduct and sentiment, which now started teaching its readers the need to experience and express erotic feeling. It was this literary intensification of the erotic and perverse which posed problems for legal regulation. Advocates of serious works about sex claimed that they should not be subject to legal interference (cf. 'The Revaluation of Obscenity', in Ellis, 1931, pp. 103–42). At the same time, many of them agreed that pornography, the very form from which they were now borrowing, was harmful and should be legally controlled (see, for example, Lawrence, 1936, p. 175 and the reviews by V. S. Pritchett and E. M. Forster reprinted in Draper, ed., 1970, pp. 287–8, 508–9).

The nascent interest of the literati in using the educative novel as a means of forming sexual identity depended on their social access to a special practice of reading. This was the practice, developed by the Romantics, in which literature is used to intensify and reconcile the antagonism between the reader's sensual and moral sides, in pursuit of a commodious, harmonised and stylised self. However, this practice and interest were anything but universal. Once on the market, serious erotica was thus available to readers not interested or schooled in applying such a method. The same text might therefore have an aesthetic use for some and a more plainly pornographic use for others. To investigate these issues further, we can consider two very different contributions on the problem of obscenity which were made in the 1920s to a Faber and Faber pamphlet series, *The Criterion Miscellany*. The inclusion of these texts on obscenity in the literary project of the *Criterion* is itself a sign of the interest which literary publishers and writers had developed in this problem by this time.

D. H. Lawrence's 'Pornography and Obscenity' (first published in 1929) was to become a definitive statement for proponents of liberal and libertarian positions on obscenity, law and literature.[4] Implicit in the essay is the new aestheticising of sex: individuals must allow themselves to be more open to the profound meanings of sex – at once sensuous and spiritual – which conventional morality suppresses. Alongside this aesthetic schema stands the accompanying historical narrative. Like the censorship historians, Lawrence imagines a period before Puritan repression when literature expressed sexual experience in a spontaneous unity of feeling and thought.

In accordance with the invariable schema of Romantic historicism, he makes the recovery of this unity a fundamental goal.

Of course, once the literati began to experiment in the serious novel with the techniques of auto-erotic writing and reading borrowed from pornography, it became necessary for them to distinguish their own interests from the common uses of erotica. To this end, they used the aesthetic dialectic as a means of problematising their own sexuality. This is evident in Lawrence's apologia for serious sexual literature. In his distinction between true creative literature and pornography, we see the aesthetic and medical conceptions of sex combine. In sexual writing worthy of the name of literature, it is said, we find a natural, fresh openness about sex, whereas pornography is the distortion of sex brought about by the tyranny of moral norms over experience (p. 177). Pornography is the dissociation of ethical being into mental consciousness on the one hand, and into sentimental fantasy on the other, in which 'there is no real object, there is only subject' (p. 180). This non-dialectical exploitation of sex is 'underworld, it doesn't come into the open' (p. 175). In that statement which was to become axiomatic for literary criticism, pornography is 'the attempt to insult sex, to do dirt on it' (p. 175) and hence 'do dirt' on life. Pornography is said to be a morbid obsession with the body and its organs and functions, in which all moral and spiritual understanding of sexuality is extinguished. At the same time, it is an obsessive moralisation of bodily sensuality in which the latter is denied all normal expression and assumes perverse forms. In Lawrence's idiosyncratic appropriation of psychoanalysis, pornography is a form of regression at once physical and psychical, in which 'the sex flow and the excrement flow' become identical and 'the profound controlling instincts collapse' (p. 176). This inner collapse is the 'dirty little secret' to which pornography panders by providing 'an invariable stimulant to the vice of self-abuse, onanism, masturbation, call it what you will . . . [which] is the one thoroughly secret act of the human being' (pp. 177–8).

Lawrence is as convinced as any nineteenth-century medical or legal authority that pornography is harmful to physical and moral health. According to him, the established powers of law, literature and the press, the 'grey ones left over from the nineteenth century' (p. 185), collude with 'the vast mob of the general public' to create 'perpetual censorship of anything that would militate against the lie of purity and the dirty little secret' (p. 186). However, any notion that might be drawn from this that there was formal censorship of literature in this period is incorrect, as we shall see from the second *Criterion* text we consider. Rather, this type of statement belongs to a strategy of *saying* that suppression and censorship exist, in order to justify a project which promises to bring liberation by truly expressing sexuality.

Literary Erotics

For Lawrence, acceptance of the literary realisation of sex is the path towards this freedom. The 'problem' of obscenity and pornography has a utopian solution: the dialectic of mind and body, consciousness and being, manifested in sex, will diffuse itself and eventually allow the complete development of self and human culture. We return to this solution shortly.

Our other essayist is the Right Honourable the Viscount Brentford, Sir William Joynson Hicks. For those working in aesthetic terms, his 'Do We Need a Censor?', published in 1929 soon after his departure from the office of Home Secretary, will doubtless be dismissed as a bureaucratic justification for a philistine policy repressing artistic freedom (see, for instance, Edward D. McDonald's 'Introduction' in Lawrence, 1936, p. xvi). But we shall read the text positively as a summary of practice followed in a complex transitional period in the policing of pornography.

Brentford defends the existing procedures by which pornography is regulated as a harmful substance. Those 'whose minds are open to immoral influence' (Brentford, 1929, p. 11) are now mainly the young, although harms to adults are implied, for instance in connection with the international postal traffic in obscene materials:

> Those who object to all forms of censorship cannot, I imagine, realise the extent of the traffic which goes on in filthy literature, and still more filthy photographs. In the course of my administration at the Home Office I had to place an embargo on pictures coming into this country of such a character that, whatever artistic merit they might possess, I am quite sure that not one hundred people in the country would be prepared to support or even excuse them. I know, from the examination of letters passing to certain shops on the continent, the nature of the traffic, the kind of person who indulges in it, and the harm that is done in consequence: is the Executive to allow this evil to go unchecked? (p. 12)

This 'executive' concern was with policing readily identifiable obscene and indecent materials and their various distributions, including importation of printed matter.[5] Despite claims to the contrary, a vendetta against serious literature was not the order of the day. At the same time, however, Brentford records a new problem for obscenity regulation, which is evident in reactions to legal proceedings against a small number of books and in the charge that he had tried 'to establish a dictatorship in the realm of literature and morals' and to ban works which in the world of letters were held to have literary merit (p. 5). He acknowledges that a case has been constructed, through the press, literary circles and other enterprises such as the World League for Sexual Reform (comprising sexologists, psychologists, authors and public figures), against the policing of literary and artistic works relating to sexuality. Significantly, he concedes that serious works about sex may have artistic merit. This, however, does not solve the problem, as he notes with reference to an unnamed literary work:

> The merits of the book may be as great as its admirers claim – and I confess I found it to contain much that, from a purely literary standpoint, excited admiration – but surely its merits were not strictly material to the issue; it was the demerits of the book which I was asked by the publishers to consider – not whether it possessed something of greatness, but whether it would tend to corrupt and deprave the public mind. (p. 19)

The object of 'corrupt and deprave', the 'public mind', is less specific than earlier legal references to vulnerable classes of individuals. But it makes the point that literary works on sex, however well-intentioned, can and do have a circulation and use that is not just literary. As feminists would later argue, literature's merit is rendered 'immaterial' by what appears, on balance, to be its demerit. Placing restrictions on a certain artistic style of sexual writing – specifically, on its public circulation – is simply seen as the lesser of two evils, compared with tolerating a known medical and moral harm.

This ranking of criteria is to be reversed by the time of the Obscene Publications Act of 1959 (see Chapter 5 below). By then, the spread of aesthetic education could perhaps be counted on to have produced a comparatively generalised ability among readers to recognise literary merit and in some measure to oversee their own reading of sexual fiction. In the first decades of our century, however, it was not at all evident that an aesthetic schooling of the sensibility had provided for the population at large a viable alternative to the medical-legal regulation of pornography and obscenity.[6]

It is noteworthy that Brentford does not argue to introduce new obscenity laws or strengthen existing ones. He holds that the law 'in its application to frankly pornographic matter has well served its purpose' (p. 11). He defends the Home Secretary's powers to violate the confidentiality of His Majesty's mail, by referring to the scale of the traffic in 'vicious publications' imported through the post (pp. 12–13). He supports the status quo, in which there is no official vetting of books on publication. Questionable books are sent to the Home Office with a complaint from the public that they are obscene, or with a publisher's request for advice whether there are grounds for thinking the publication would constitute, or has constituted, an infringement of the law (p. 15). Brentford states that there is a censorship of stage plays, under the separate jurisdiction of the Lord Chamberlain (p. 8), and a voluntary censorship of films, but that 'there is in England no censorship of books' in the sense of 'a scrutiny by some central authority of the whole output' in order to impose some standard (p. 9). He maintains that juridical regulation is generally less appropriate than executive consultation and self-regulation within the book trade – a task, we can recall, that figures like Dickens needed no persuasion to undertake. And, against Lawrence's painting of him as a literary censor, Brentford argues that to create a censor of books by a government department would be 'most undesirable' (p. 10).

We see, then, that in the regulatory field there existed, on the one hand, a range of police measures including powers of search and seizure, summary application of tests for obscenity, interception of mail, customs control and cooperation with other governments to control the traffic in pornography. On the other hand, in relation to works with a degree of serious artistic intent, there was advice on publication, publishers' self-regulation, the discretion of booksellers, the possibility of complaint, a degree of tolerance and, very rarely, prosecution for obscenity. Of course, some serious artistic and literary works were seized by police, but their regulation still generally involved various players. *The Rainbow*, for example, was the cause of a police summons which its publishers did not oppose (*The Times*, 15 November 1915, in Draper (1970), pp. 102–3). We are thus reminded that the regulation of pornography and obscenity involved a mix of agencies, procedures and jurisdictions – administrative, judicial, commercial and ethical – which were not bound together by any single force such as a Puritanical will to repress sex and impede enlightenment, but which directed the distribution of various types of publication to different audiences according to limited goals and imperatives. Within this context, the tensions between serious literature and obscenity law in the late nineteenth and early twentieth centuries, where they occurred, do not signify that the former was at last winning through to show the truth of sex. Rather, they indicate that educative literature was branching out into an aesthetic use of erotica, appropriating elements of pornography for consumption by a coterie which formed only an insignificant fraction within the legal, administrative and still partly medical typology of audiences.

Our discussion of these two *Criterion* pieces shows how anachronistic is the assumption that literary aesthetics was a neutral and universal knowledge of the truth of sex which could have solved the problem of pornography (as an effect caused by the repression of sex) if only the law had dared open its eyes. Literary erotics comprised a specific and limited distribution of literate techniques and ethical culture. It was the method used by the members of a coterie to read themselves into distinction. Lawrence could afford himself the luxury of condemning as 'pornographic' the majority of English writings from *Jane Eyre* to 'some quite popular English hymns'

(1936, p. 174) – works hardly like to trouble constables on their beat. But even if legal administrators had wished to use the criterion promoted by Lawrence – the aestheticising of sex – to decide the regulation of pornography, they could not have done so effectively, for it was far too specialised to gain any general purchase.

HIDE AND SEEK

By the early twentieth century, then, new relations were forming between literature, pornography and the sexual 'sciences'. The introduction of the erotic and perverse into the educative novel allowed certain individuals and groups to carry out aesthetic self-culture through the cultivation of a sexuality that – or so they told themselves – was repressed, fugitive and the key to personal identity. Providing a new facility to eroticise body and conscience, and forming a circuit between the sexologies and pornography, serious sexual literature comprised an optional – primarily ethical – mechanism for organising sexual identity even as it also constituted a new object of policing, since it could be harmful for some readers.

These complexities provide evidence for the argument that serious sexual literature has had no essential function such as representing the truth of sex, but has played an uneven and contingent role in forming and regulating sexualities. This argument may be pursued by considering in greater detail the two sets of conditions which allowed literary and sexual organisations of the self to converge: a particular interaction between literature and sexology, and a literary appropriation of pornography.

In relation to the first of these, a major precondition of the sexualisation of serious literature was the success of sexual medicine in making health, understood in sexual terms, central to the new norms of management of personal life. We recall from Foucault (1979, pp. 65–6) that the nineteenth-century medical organisation of sexuality postulated that sex was an 'inexhaustible and polymorphous' causal power and that there was 'a latency intrinsic to sexuality'. Given the former, sex could be and was entertained as the cause of almost any species of physical and moral problem. Sexual causes and effects were thought to manifest fundamental processes which could be charted through the temporal stages of an individual life. It became possible to individuate persons with reference to norms of healthy sexual development and deviations from them. This medical individualisation, Foucault argues, implanted perversions. In contrast to an earlier classification of sexual transgressions in terms of acts, in which a binary opposition of licit and illicit was adequate, these new knowledges focussed on the nature of the being of the actors, creating new types of personality requiring to be investigated, measured and understood (pp. 36–49). So, for example, in contrast to the sodomite once defined primarily by his illicit act, the nineteenth-century homosexual came to be identified as a complex personality with 'a past, a case history, and a childhood', and a problematic future, a being with a specific character to be fathomed by being identified with a certain inversion of the masculine and the feminine (p. 43). The implantation of perversions thus intensified and consolidated multiple sexualities, such that the medical schemata of sexual kinds were at once mechanisms of knowledge or classification and types of practice, forms which came to be lived out by individuals (p. 48).

If the causal powers of sex were ubiquitous, they were also obscure, since they promised to reveal a self whose truth was directly proportional to its reclusiveness. The medical-moral expert emerged as one who could bring to light that which was hidden in the individual and comprehend the mysterious workings of latent sexual natures. In the secularisation of confession which Foucault identifies (pp. 53–73), sex became the deep and elusive cause which must be spoken – in all the detail it may be necessary to hear – by the individual who is the object of medical and moral concern. This strategy of confession constituted sex as the always partly hidden problem within the self which must be turned over and over. Confessional medicine intensified the interest of the very sensations, thoughts, acts and desires which it sought to know and regulate. If this form of speaking about sex was therapeutic, it was also pathogenic. It complicated and deepened the meanings which sexual problems could have. Even in fostering a desire for self-improvement, sexual medicine made for volatile sensibilities. This is reflected in concerns such as the fear that 'over-mothering' would bring out a latent homosexuality in the sons of middle-class families. Exposure to sexual-medical influences made it possible for individuals to internalise various norms and feel new kinds of anxiety, alarm, pain, guilt, failure and embarrassment, and to engage in new kinds of introspection. The pages of William Acton's *The Functions and Disorders of the Reproductive Organs in Childhood, Youth, Adult Age, and Advanced Life* (1865), for instance, give an insight into this pathogenic dimension of Victorian medicine. Appealing to colleagues to humanise their practice by considering the physiological, emotional and moral issues of sex, Acton publishes his work precisely in order to exert 'some good and practical influence on public health and public morals' (Preface). Yet the cases, anecdotes, testimonials and advice on cures which he publishes show that his male patients and readers could literally worry themselves sick in ways that would not have been possible before the medical intensification of concerns with masturbation and similar problems such as marital excess and hypochondriacal feelings about sex (pp. 69–81, 102–15).

Sexual medicine enjoyed a significant popular print dissemination in the Victorian period.[7] Books, manuals, pamphlets and lectures played a major role in laicising sexual-medical knowledges and forms of judgement. In particular, the concerns of sexual medicine became part of the 'habitus' of middle-class reading households. Individuals were sensitised to the problem and value of their own and others' health, within a framework of relations between parent and child, and wife and husband. For instance, in the dense web of causes and effects, individuals were alerted not only to the harmful effects of masturbation but also the unconscious possible causes of this apparent evil – a flawed upbringing? an inner compulsion? a bad diet or regimen? – such that the whole fabric of everyday life could be brought under careful scrutiny (Acton, 1865, pp. 1–75). The confessional arrangement of sexual medicine did not rely solely on spoken exchanges. Individuals were encouraged to read the signs of the body for themselves, to seek and find in its bearing, gestures and appearance so many indices of a state of health and of personal and social aptitude. Literature on masturbation, for instance, urged parents to police the activity, not necessarily by extracting verbal confessions but by recognising the signs of its presence and establishing a watchful and supposedly therapeutic environment. In *Man's Strength and Woman's Beauty*, P. H. Chevasse, MD, writes that 'the confirmed masturbator' bears the impress of nature's penalty 'in his manner and upon his face' (1879, p. 392). Similarly, in *The Science of a New Life*, John Cowan, MD, cites another writer, Lallemand, on the effects of self-abuse, in a subsection entitled 'Signs in the boy, girl or man, that he who runs may read':

> [T]he slow and progressive derangement of his or her health, the diminished energy of application, the languid movement, the stooping gait, the desertion of social games, the solitary walk, late rising, livid and sunken eye, and many other symptoms, will fix the attention of every intelligent and competent guardian of youth.

(1970[1874], p. 362)

In general, then, the techniques of secular confession and observation comprised a style of physical and moral self-management to be exercised within middle-class domestic life. The literary production and consumption of a writer like D. H. Lawrence, with all its minute observation of sexualities, would have been impossible had this broader, hermeneutic 'discursifying' of sex and 'consciencising' of persons not occurred in popular sexual medicine.

The second major factor which made serious sexual literature possible was a highly localised transformation of sexual knowledges into aesthetic practice, involving a new application of the Romantic dialectic of thought and feeling (and its avatars such as mind and body, morality and the senses, norm and experience). 'Lawrentian' writing and reading were made possible by a programme of aesthetic self-fashioning which was the elite province of an upper middle-class coterie. We can illustrate this through the works of the Victorian social and sexual reformer, Edward Carpenter. Others have analysed his writings and politics, and Emile Delavenay (1971) has traced connections between Carpenter and Lawrence. Sheila Rowbotham analyses Carpenter's project as a sexual personal politics linked to a tradition of ethical or romantic socialism (Rowbotham and Weeks, 1977, pp. 25–138) and Chushichi Tsuzuki (1980, p. 3) describes that politics as best suited to a 'local socialist body or such small community'. Through his public addresses, books and pamphlets, and by maintaining an open intellectual household at Millthorpe, Carpenter advocated a 'simplification of life' and established himself as a charismatic mentor figure. Though he tended not to become an adherent to particular party platforms or sectarian organisations, his interests were related to progressive political movements, including Fabianism and feminism, and he drew his audience from advanced socialist and literary circles (cf. Delavenay, pp. 85–9). The relevant point for us is that his species of 'political' idealism was based on a practical endeavour to achieve a certain intensification and stylisation of personal existence. His project is a paradigmatic case of the aesthetic incorporation of sexual disciplines.

Carpenter's writings propagate that technique of dialectical self-shaping which derived from the Romantic practice of culture already described in Chapter 2 above. They are permeated by the strategy of distinguishing and reconciling opposites such as thoughts and feeling, morality and sensuousness, in order to perfect one's ethical being. They embody a Romantic historicism in which phylogeny imitates ontogeny. In the history of 'Man', there is a first stage in which 'the knower, the knowledge and the thing known are still undifferentiated' (1907, p. 54). Instinct is wedded to intelligence, art expresses the whole being, and social life is not yet ruptured by the rise of the ego. As it was for Matthew Arnold, this stage is embodied above all in Hellenic civilisation. Resolutely faithful to his Romantic models, Carpenter proceeds to trace the second stage of this cultural history in which the original unified consciousness is disrupted by the advent of self-consciousness; the subject and the object of knowledge are divided such that knowledge itself is reduced to abstract 'thought' cast adrift from feeling and immediate experience. Art suffers in this dissociation and grows away from Nature and from actual life. Even within this second stage, though, identified as usual with the long present, the third is anticipated as an integral state of being and knowledge which is the condition of a culture superior to the lost edenic state precisely because it has emerged through the diversifying experience of disunity (1907, Chapter IV, 'The Three Stages of Consciousness').

This aesthetic paradigm is *sexualised* in Carpenter's work. To achieve self-perfection, one must free oneself from purely rational consciousness by accepting the reality of sensuous and bodily experience. At the same time, one must strive to ensure that this experience never becomes merely sensual but is kept in touch with – and so renews – the capacity for intelligent and moral reflection (1907, Chapters V and VI, 'The Self and its Affiliations'). Precisely because sexual feelings are so deeply implicated in life they must be brought into harmony with the rest of human experience. Not until sexual love is 'checked and brought into conflict with the other parts of his being' does the whole nature of 'man' – sexual and moral – rise into consciousness (1905, p. 11) in that process which Carpenter calls love's 'coming-of-age'.

The sexual 'sciences' and the confessional tactics of self-knowledge operating within them provide new ways in which individuals like Carpenter can identify and seek to reconcile opposing tendencies within the self. Amongst Carpenter's many adaptations of biological, physiological and psychological theories, the sexualising of the aesthetic is evident in his use of an almost Fourierist model called the 'Great Sympathetic', elaborated by the moral physiologist Davey in 1858 (Carpenter, 1907, pp. 113–17). In this model, the dialectical topography of Romantic aesthetics is provided with bodily coordinates. There is an organic seat of the emotions in the 'nervous' or 'ganglionic' centres, including the solar plexus. Complete emotional sensibility requires the interaction of the organic with the conscious and reflex systems, the latter being located in the brain and in the spinal cord and medulla respectively. Carpenter cites Davey's notion that the Great Sympathetic exercised an 'architectural power, presiding over the formation and life of the body and the organs – a power to which even the brain and spinal cord were subordinate' (1907, pp. 113–4). He speculates that first the motor and then the mental capacities have come to overlie the foundation of organic and emotional life. Modern man has become dominated by mental consciousness, which means one must anticipate a time when the deeper nervous powers, having passed into 'the region of subconsciousness' (p. 116), will be restored in a dynamic fulfilment of all human faculties. Exactly the same sexualisation of the dialectic and use of moral physiology is to provide the framework for Lawrence, including his criticism of Freudian psychoanalysis for ignoring the true nature of the unconscious as a vital, organic region of experience which underlies all conscious thought and feeling. According to Lawrence, the unconscious is

> that active spontaneity which rouses in each individual organism at the moment of fusion of the parent nuclei, and which, in polarized connection with the external universe, gradually evolves or elaborates its own individual psyche and corpus, bringing both mind and body forth from itself.
>
> (Lawrence, 1971, p. 242)

The nuclei of the nerve centres are 'centres of spontaneous consciousness' (p. 242). Imbalances of the self occur if the will is in discord with the sympathetic centres or if mental impulses destroy spontaneity and the dynamic connection with others (p. 248).

A further feature of this aesthetic construction of sexuality is that the dialectic is mapped onto the polarity of masculine and feminine. Definitions of sexual difference derived from sexual knowledges as diverse as reproductive biology and moral physiology provide aesthetic discourse with the potential to identify the distinction between the masculine and the feminine with that between the rational and the affective. So, for instance, developing the theme that the body grows from a cell in which male and female are originally one and which contains all the possibilities of the self, including the division between male and female tendencies and their ultimate reconciliation, Carpenter pictures sexual intercourse as an exercise in dialectics, important not just for procreation but for physical and spiritual regeneration:

> [I]n truth it is probable, I think . . . that the spermatozoa pass through the tissues and affect the general body of the female, as well as that the male absorbs minutest cells from the female; and that generally, even without the actual Sex-act, there is an interchange of vital and ethereal elements – so that it might be said there is a kind of generation taking place within each of the persons concerned . . .
>
> (Carpenter, 1905, p. 27)

In similar terms, Lawrence writes in *Fantasia of the Unconscious* (1971, pp. 31–3) that with the 'hard physiological fact' of the fusion of the 'father nucleus' and the 'mother nucleus' is produced the new individual cell which is immediately a new self, retaining the polarity of male and female defined through the play of will and sympathy, power and ductility. This theme of a dialectical sexual aesthetics was supported – with some attempt at popularisation in the field of sex reform – by various others writing before and during Lawrence's own career. The evolution of human 'culture', it was assumed, would allow the superior union of men and women to occur through the reconciliation of essential masculine and feminine differences in which each individual would find self-realisation: any attempt to make women the equal of men as they 'merely' are in the present would therefore be premature, according to some writers at least (for example, Charles Leland, *The Alternate Sex*, 1904).

In this kind of discourse, 'sex' was subsumed into an aesthetic practice of self-culture. From the works of Havelock Ellis on primary, secondary and tertiary sexual characteristics (1929) to publications like Otto Weininger's *Sex and Character* (1906), there is an overlap of physiological and moral categories and a major identification of aesthetic oppositions such as reason and emotion with a male/female characterology. In this context, Carpenter's life and work are exemplary of the way in which certain highly-educated coteries attempted to fabricate an ethos through the sexological transformation of aesthetic self-culture.

For such groups, appreciation of the arts is a means of integrating intellectual and sensual being. According to Carpenter (1912, pp. 207ff), creativity is the fusion of masculine and feminine traits as revealed in, for example, the works of Michelangelo. This notion is reproduced by Lawrence in such writings as 'Study of Thomas Hardy' (1936, pp. 398–516) in terms highly reminiscent – as Delavenay points out (1971, pp. 205–15) – of Carpenter's argument that literature, including the novel, must revitalise the moral life by exploring the complex polarities and creative androgynous potential of sexual being.[8]

Before Lawrence even began to write, the apparatus of sexual aesthetics was assembled as the condition of his doing so. A Romantic cultivation of the self had absorbed sexual norms, producing a new personage we might call the sexual aesthete. The dialectic offered a way of developing and mastering the self through an aesthetic stylisation of sex. In Carpenter's view, as subsequently in Lawrence's, the social harms or dangers of sex could be overcome by the diffusion of this cultural ideal. The key to a 'free and gracious public life' is the purification and refinement of the moral nature, a work of conscience which needs no external guide (Carpenter, 1905, p. 23). We can see why, for the *cognoscenti*, sexual content came to be appropriated not as something super-added to the aesthetic but as something inseparable from the form of a creative work and the activity in which the writer or reader problematised sexuality through it.

The other major factor which made it possible for literary-aesthetic and sexual-medical organisations of the self to converge was the literary appropriation of pornography. We have already noted the role of early-modern pornography as literary device of self-interrogation and excitation, and the directly auto-erotic formation of the conscience and body associated with the use of nineteenth-century perverse (medicalised) pornography. It was the apparatus of Romantic aesthetics which allowed serious literature to enter an exchange with the genre of confessional pornography. In this process, on the one hand, literary aesthetics annexed various techniques of pornographic writing and their auto-erotic potential, thus issuing a challenge to explore supposedly repressed sexualities. Sexual excitation was considered necessary in order to tap dimensions of experience lying beyond the reach of norms and inhibitions. On the other hand, literary aesthetics employed a critical and moralising strategy, by submitting the erotic materials to aesthetic interpretation and judgement. In so doing, it transformed the techniques of pornography by combining them with literary devices used in the serious novel. This balancing act depended on the dialectical ability of the writer and reader – that is, the ability to treat auto-erotic excitation as a necessary moment of de-repression and at the same time to reconcile it with the intellectual and moral imperatives of educative literature.

The literary techniques which transformed and were in turn modified by this appropriation of pornography included complex characterisation and psychological narrative, hermeneutic problematisation, poetic or symbolic deepening, and thematic reflection. Literature drew from pornography the stylistic resources of confessional dialogue and eroticising physical description, including the device of presenting sexual experiences and sensations in detail, and the use of vernacular and obscene language to refer to bodies and acts. It preserved their auto-erotic interest while modifying it aesthetically in the direction of poetic introspection, complex motivation and sustained inquiry into the enigmatic nature of sex – a generic transmutation present in the merest description of a lover's swoon before a rainbow (Lawrence, 1949, p. 299).

The educative novel, of course, also borrows techniques from sources other than pornography. So, for instance, the devices of poetic or metaphoric deepening are drawn in part from a specialised nineteenth-century tradition of the erotic lyric, where a confessional interest in sexuality was already subject to the dialectic mediation of Romantic aesthetics. This tradition included the verse of Swinburne and Wilde and, in more populist mode, Whitman's often homoerotic poetic affirmations. We may record Carpenter's imitation of Whitman in his *Towards Democracy* (1896) and

Lawrence's proselytising for a Whitmanesque free verse of 'the immediate, instant self' (1936, p. 222). Lawrence is able to apply devices of lyric writing to the work of psychological characterisation in the novel in a way that allows poetic intensification of sexual experiences (cf. *Lady Chatterley's Lover*, 1961, pp. 138–9).

In general, then, Romantic aesthetics permitted a new use of literature: the appropriately trained writer and reader could engage in a sexualisation of the dialectic, and a 'dialecticisation' of sex. Writing and reading erotica became a means for individuals to organise a new and special relation to their self, one which required them to identify, differentiate, intensify and harmonise the sensuous and the moral-reflective faculties. Given that within this demanding exercise of conscience one must be alert to the ever-present dangers of falling into a relation to one's own being that is either too sensual and morally inert or too cerebral and heavily moralised, it is unsurprising that Lawrence was critical not only of pornographers but also of fellow aesthetes like Swinburne. Here was a game, at once self-forming and self-serving, that few of the literati could resist playing. If, on one side, the body of pornography is too basely sensual, on the other side poor 'Swinburne's "white thighs" are purely mental' (Lawrence, 1936, p. 552). In either instance, the discerning of a non-dialectical relation to sex in others is a sign that the beholder, Lawrence, must strive the harder to reconcile the opposed tendencies within himself. It was now the task of the novelist to reconcile 'a theory of being and knowing' with a 'living sense of being' (p. 479).

Lawrence's novels show in some detail the literary appropriation of sexual medicine and pornography. These works reinforce the relation already forged in popular medical knowledges between sexual acts or desires and personalities. In particular they sustain the erotic and excitatory imagery of perversions elaborated in medical and confessional pornography, frequently presenting perverse tendencies at the heart of so-called normal sexuality as that which must be confronted in order fully to know and understand the complex nature of the self. The novels mediate perverse and erotic elements aesthetically. Erotic writing is offered as a means of becoming open to the sensuous potentiality of the self, but the senses must in turn be brought into a revitalising relation with the whole of one's experience. At the same time, the aesthetic dialectic is sexualised. For example, the division of the ethical substance is played out by exploring the imagery of sexual difference, including a conception of sexual inversion that is now used to project and reconcile opposing tendencies within the self. Failures to reconcile the inner tendencies are identified with forms of illness and associated with physiological and erotogenic symptoms. Images of pathology are also used in an apparently positive form, that is, to suggest mental

Literary Erotics 111

and sensual tendencies which must be acknowledged and overcome if the self is to be made whole.

Lawrence's novels aesthetically transform the medicalised Victorian middle-class family and its cast of characters described by Foucault (1979, pp. 103–22). Women's bodies are sexualised, oriented either towards hysteria, frigidity, denial of vitality by intellectual self-consciousness, such that they are seen as castrating in their relation to men; or towards conductivity of emotion, intuitive being, mysterious fecundity and a potential for life through acceptance of the phallus. Men's bodies and minds are sexualised correspondingly, being subject on the one hand to sensual and mental excess, forms of wilfulness and impotence; and on the other to release from egoism through the polarity of masculine and feminine, allowing 'man' and 'woman' to emerge into their own supposedly essential being. These characterisations support narratives of sickness and cure. Readers are asked to identify with situations in which, beginning from a state of moral and physiological fragility, characters find spiritual regeneration in sexual vitality and harmony; otherwise they intellectualise and sicken, plunging in an auto-erotic spiral towards frigidity, impotence or disintegration.

Critics have often commented on the Oedipal pattern of *Sons and Lovers* (first published in 1913), authenticating it with notions of authorial experience. Such a pattern can also be seen in more historical terms, however, as part of the specialised technique of the psycho-aesthetic construction of the self. The narrative turns on the difficulties of understanding one's own desire, passing through incestuous drives towards other possible expressions. It sets up the tension between idealising sex, and failing to relate sensual awakenings to the needs and possibilities of the whole self. Paul's relation to Miriam presents the problem of abstract intimacy, of being 'too fierce in our what they call purity . . . a sort of dirtiness' (1948, p. 343); it is 'such a matter of the soul, all thought and weary struggle into consciousness' (p. 213). His relation with Clara shows the opposite problem. Despite the significance of erotic experience, gradually the passion becomes spiritless, 'some mechanical effort spoilt their loving, or, when they had splendid moments, they had them separately, and not so satisfactorily' (p. 443). In this early novel by Lawrence we already see how the narrative carries an argument that subjectivity must be incomplete, with the individual always caught up in a process of growth and yet possible sickness and perversion found within the polarities of sexual being.

The Rainbow (1949, first published in 1915) and *Women in Love* (1960, first published in 1921) are similar improvisations on the dialectical formation of the self. The former invokes a myth of organic personal and communal life, in the marriage of Tom and Lydia, against which to measure a dissociation of consciousness and experience evident in the following generations. This division is known, and may be healed, through the oppositions of the feminine and the masculine, as depicted in the relation of Ursula and Anton. The characterisation of Ursula shows how pornographic-medical elements are mobilised in presenting a narrative of aesthetic and moral growth. It includes, for instance, imagery of female 'sexual inversion'. The relationship with Winifred appropriates and adapts the pornographic theme of the novice and her teacher. This wrong turn of the body and mind is incorporated as a necessary false dawn of Ursula's awakening, in which it is made clear that independent female intellectual activity is barren and perverse: 'Winifred Inger was also interested in the Women's Movement' (1949, p. 343). This characterisation also includes the cathartic violence and pleasure of physically venting frustration in terms deriving from the literature of flagellation – in the beating of the 'rat-like' boy (pp. 397–9).

In *Women in Love*, the danger of women becoming merely intellectual is embodied in Hermione, in a satire of so-called Bloomsbury affectation. Hermione is presented as suffering 'a horrible sickness of dissolution' within the body and soul (1960, p. 103), as a hysteric in whom the perversion of all capacity for spontaneity leads to a kind of insanity and threat of castration which is seen in her physical attack on Birkin (pp. 116–19). The relation of Gudrun and Gerald is one in which the partners fail to balance the various elements of the sexual personality and so become self-willed and destructive. The potential of mutuality is demonstrated in the relation of Ursula and Birkin. Here, 'masculine' intellectual potency is modified between and within the characters by 'feminine' inwardness, permitting the androgynous transcendence of difference ('floods of ineffable darkness and ineffable riches' from a 'source deeper than the phallic source' (p. 354)). This representation does not exclude moments of consoling homoerotic heroism for men, as encountered in the wrestling scene between Birkin and Gerald (pp. 300–11). Broadly, the imagery of masculine and feminine oppositions repeats the eroticisation of the body already discussed in relation to Carpenter, as when Lawrence writes of 'a new current of passional electrical energy . . . released from the darkest poles of the body and established in perfect circuit' between the lovers (p. 353).

Lady Chatterley's Lover (1961, first published in 1928), Lawrence's most pornographic novel, works with the now familiar combinatory of pathologies. The feminine is defined as a sexual essence which, if repressed, makes women sick. Masculine identity is seen to have been rendered cerebral and impotent. Clifford is representative of those ruined boys through whom Lawrence depicts mental self-consciousness as perverse and destructive, making its victim a castrato. These terms provide the logic for a narrative lesson: the woman must free the true 'female' in herself through sexual sojourns, letting go the social 'person' (1961, p. 126). The meaning of sex, it is insisted, cannot be grasped by those flirting with it as a fashionable idea, since this imprisons men and women in their separate egos, as in Connie's first sexual encounters on the Continent (cf. pp. 5–9). Connie's maturation includes her awakening to the phallic potency of Mellors whose characterisation brings into play the pornographic image of the supersexed male. The argument is contained isotopically in Chapter 10, in a trio of sexual acts. On the first occasion, Mellors achieves orgasm and is blind to Connie's numbness. On the second, there is growing responsiveness on her part, but a residue of mental resistance, and a separateness in his pleasure. On the third, she is released from self-consciousness by the 'unconscious' force of passion. Mellors' taking of her by surprise is valorised because it is associated with an epiphanal quality in the experience. The real female is said to emerge, not 'Lady Chatterley' but 'Connie'. Again, the book adapts pornographic elements such as the dialogic relation of initiator and novice, and the mock-pastoral convention according to which a virile lower-class hero finds out the nymph in an aristocratic 'Lady'.

We may show in a little more detail how the pathological and perverse inform this novel. The imagery of fixation, including infantile regression and male hysteria, is used to complete the portrayal of Clifford's impotence. His auto-erotic intimacy with his nurse, Mrs Bolton, is presented as the ultimate stage of his ethical decay. On the other hand, if Connie is to discover the truth of sex she must do so through trial and error, passing through various dangerous psycho-sexual stages. For instance, clitoral orgasm is presented as stubborn gratification in which she resists mutuality, a sign that she is too active and the man too passive, as in her relation with Michaelis. Lawrence's association of clitorally-oriented intercourse with female masturbation is evident here. In an improvisation on existing erotogenic zonings of the body, the clitoris is pathologised through metaphoric identification with the beak of a bird. The instrument that gratifies the wilful sexuality of the woman can only injure her lover. This independent and perverse sexuality must be tamed by the gamekeeper if the true 'female' is to be set free.

A culminating act in Connie's relation with Mellors is anal intercourse. How are we to classify such a scene? In one sense, it is yet another sodomitic scene in perverse, 'turkish' pornography, with a distinct sense of sport in breaking taboos. At the same time, it is the first explicit scene of anal sex in the serious novel. The appeal to 'sheer sensuality' is supposed 'to purify and quicken the mind' (p. 259) and revitalise physical and spiritual life. The excitatory writing is taken to be necessary in order to gain access to new depths of being, while the erotic interest is poetically heightened by projecting and resolving through it the metaphysical tensions identified with the relations of male and female. The act is used to signify the upsurge of the most hidden unspoken desire and the final purging of female resistance. Even in this 'phallic hunting out' of 'the last and deepest recess of organic shame' (p. 259), the myth of androgyny persists: there is no clitoris here. Curiously, anal intercourse is both an esoteric metaphor and a conjugal technique. The reconciliation of the Romantically-divided self in a purifying erotic epiphany transcends the merely social use of sex in the getting of children. Supposedly, in this liberation from all conventional repression of the sexual drive, the masculine and feminine are fully realised and the difference between them is transcended in a new and finally completed form of subjectivity.

While we have focussed on how serious educative literature borrows from sexual medicine and pornography, it is also worth noting that it draws on other areas such as psychoanalysis. We recall that, for Freud (1977, pp. 45–87), if the normal psycho-sexual 'life' can be constituted, this is because it is knowable through so many points of contact with the perversions. The latter are deviations of the sexual aim which either extend anatomically beyond the regions of the body designed for sexual use, or are fixed in a relation to the sexual object which should be passed through on the way to discovering a final sexual aim (pp. 61–2). The perverse, the neurotic and the normal are classes of sexual life, outcomes of a development: the 'disposition to perversions' itself forms 'a part of what passes as the normal constitution' (p. 86). The 'life' is seen as an always more or less problematic movement through various stages which involve impulses or wishes that may be repressed and yet remain cathectic. Of interest here, in relation to literary characterology, is the question of whether 'a special relation holds between the perverse disposition and the particular form of illness adopted'. Freud retains the possibility that the perversions exist in relation to 'psychoneurotic constitutions' which might be distinguished according to 'the innate preponderance of one or the other of the erotogenic zones or one or the other of the component instincts' (p. 86). While the extent to which Freud's own conception of a dialectical relation between drive and norm is indebted to Romantic aesthetics is clearly a broader question, psychoanalytic discourse can be seen to lend psychological and physical coordinates to contemporary literary erotics.

In fact Freud's identification of fixation at the anal stage with the formation of a particular character type is typical of the 'implanting' strategies whereby an act in the sexual repertoire is turned into the profound and indelible sign of a pathological personality – one in which the secret of anal erotism is seen to persist as a never fully repressed element in the organisation and transformation of desire (see especially Freud, 1977, pp. 295–302). For its part, Lawrence's counter-valorisation of this character trait as the repressed truth (that is, true because repressed) of a higher sexuality is nothing new either. It is another case of the pornographic inversion of a medical characterology – one that makes a sexological image of regression over into an image of liberating and norm-breaking transgression and places the attendant charge of perverse pleasure and self-discovery at the service of aesthetic self-cultivation.

In all of these instances we should not lose sight of the fact that it is the novel's manner of addressing and enrolling an imagined reader – who is sometimes the real reader – that is crucial. The deployment of biblio-erotic technique in the educative novel is the means by which competent readers are forced to relate to themselves as subjects of repressed desires and pleasures. This is the central element of the pact formed between the writers and readers of serious erotic literature. What follows from it is the practice in which readers control and stylise their always newly-discovered sexual selves according to the reconciliatory imperatives of aesthetic self-culture where they have the capacity to do so. The rhetorical organisation of such literature is thus designed to induct readers into a certain aesthetic-erotic experimenting with the self. It is integral to the effect of the anal-erotic episode in *Lady Chatterley's Lover*, for example, that its description is highly metaphoric, recondite and suggestive. This is what involves the reader in the confessional stratagem of attributing the truth of sex to that which is most hidden; to that which must therefore be acknowledged and brought to light in oneself. Literary criticism in this context can be little more than an acting out of this stratagem. It is entirely appropriate, then, that the first literary critical publication of the dark secret of *Lady Chatterley's Lover* should have been entitled '*Regina* v. *Penguin Books Ltd*: An Undisclosed Element in the Case' (Sparrow, 1966, pp. 40–58).

A FURTHER CHAPTER IN LITERARY EROTICS

At this point we can make explicit the difference between our historical analysis of pornography and post-modernist accounts informed by psychoanalytic and Marxian currents. Stephen Heath's (1982) *The Sexual Fix* is representative of such accounts. Heath writes that 'sexuality' is a cultural system through which the meaning of 'sex' (acts and relations) and associated forms of personal identity have been produced in the nineteenth and twentieth centuries. Knowledges such as sexual medicine, sexology, psychology and psychoanalysis have been central to that system:

> [S]exuality is without the importance ascribed to it in our contemporary society (Western capitalist); it is without that importance because it does not exist as such, because there is no such thing as sexuality; what we have experienced and are experiencing is the fabrication of a 'sexuality', the construction of something called 'sexuality' through a set of representations – images, discourses, ways of picturing and describing – that propose and confirm, that make up this sexuality to which we are then referred and held in our lives, a whole *sexual fix* precisely; the much-vaunted 'liberation' of sexuality, our triumphant emergence from the 'dark ages', is thus not a liberation but a myth, an ideology, the definition of a new mode of conformity (that can be understood, moreover, in relation to the capitalist system, the production of a commodity 'sexuality').
>
> (Heath, 1982, pp. 2–3)

At the same time, argues Heath, to say that sexuality does not exist as such is not to deny the reality and complexity of the sexual dimension in contemporary Western culture. It is, rather, to indicate the possibility of displacing its present limited construction as 'sexuality' and changing the problematic forms of social relations the latter term involves (pp. 3–4). For Heath, literature overlaps with the social knowledges and practices – including pornography – which operate in the system of 'sexuality'. So, for instance, sexual writing in the novel supports and is supported by 'the novelistic' – Heath's term for the dispersed forms of narrative and character construction operating within those social knowledges (Chapter VII). The work of Lawrence contributes in a major way to the 'gaining ground' of 'sexuality' (p. 125).

The problem with this account is that it explains the function of literature and other knowledges through a single, general logic of representation, even though 'representation' indicates not a reflection of the real but a construction of meaning for a subject. Heath argues that novelistic sexual narrative appears to open into the truth of experience and make self-realisation possible, but that in fact it is highly normative and forecloses the possibilities of experience. It acts out a cycle of tension and release, a progression towards orgasm, in a ritual and fundamentally insecure attempt to deny an underlying male lack. Dominant literary and sexological writing involves a phallic fantasy through which the threat of female difference is

Literary Erotics 117

apparently denied by projecting the female as existing for and through the pleasure of the male whose identity thus seems to be confirmed. Complicit with other empiricisms of sexual knowledge, literature thus represses and reproduces the very anxiety which generates it, creating a sexual 'fix' in the dual sense that the possibilities of subjective identity are narrowed down into set masculine and feminine forms, and that this drama is repeated compulsively. This ideological function is present in any instance of the system of sexuality, and within literature operates in an historical continuum through such different works as those of Dickens and Lawrence (see especially Heath's Chapter VII). Literature is thus seen as having an essential relation to sexuality. It is the theatre in which the subject of consciousness experiences an illusory fullness of being. This subject unconsciously opts out of the play of sexual difference whose prolongation is the bliss of deferred identity: the endless anticlimax of selfhood. The progressive liberation envisioned by Heath is described thus:

> The end of oppression is a recasting of social relations that leaves men and women free, outside of any commodification of the sexual, removed from any of the violence and alienation of circulation and exchange as agents of sex and orgasm, away from any definition as a sexual identity, the identity of a sex, being fixed to this or that image, this or that norm, to this thing 'sexuality'. (p. 152)

Literary experimentation is assumed to offer the possibility of un-fixing the categories of language and hence the representations of 'male' and 'female' and the very principle of sexual identity.[9]

Heath's account is representative of a form of poststructuralist theory which has been made possible only by the historical wedding of literature and sexual knowledges officiated over by Romantic aesthetics. In the opposition between fixed sexual identity and undifferentiated or deferred identity (or between the phallus as principle of representational closure and a feminine principle of otherness or excess), and in the 'play of signification' achieved by oscillating between or eluding previously defined identifications of sexuality, we find yet another variation upon the dialectical polarisation of masculine and feminine, mental and pulsional being, norm and desire, which we have already discussed. This more recent specialised use of the dialectic is supposed to provide a liberatory teleology for the subject who must ultimately transcend the ideological experience of sexual difference, uncovering through literature the hidden flux of sexual being.

In *reproducing* this technique of aesthetic subject-formation, postmodernist theorising such as Heath's begs the question of whether literature has any necessary or fundamental relation to sexuality. Our analysis shows that serious literature has had a much more contingent relation to sexuality than is allowed for in this type of account. This is why we have displaced the usual concern with whether some particular instance of 'erotic literature' gives a true or false, an open or closed representation of sex by *describing* the conditions that have made a particular 'literary erotics' possible. Only under specific historical and cultural circumstances was one literary school able to take over a repertoire of erotic forms of writing – the techniques of biblio-erotics – and establish a new conduit for disciplines of sexuality. This event depended on no general 'ideological' mechanism of subject-formation, but on specific (medical, pornographic) conscience-forming uses of literacy, and on the historical aestheticisation of sexuality achieved when certain experimental groups succeeded in integrating the techniques of confession and those of literary self-cultivation. In arguing that the erotic novel became a textbook for disseminating norms of the sexual person, we use 'norm' not to oppose it to 'experience' or 'drive' as occurs within dialectical argument, but to re-situate the aesthetic dialectic itself as biblio-erotic ritual for actually organising an individual's relation to his or her self – one that is far from outmoded.

RULES OF THE GAME

The ethical function of serious sexual literature established in the late nineteenth and early twentieth centuries can be further specified by drawing a contrast with a historically linked use of literacy. In *The Use of Pleasure* (1986), Foucault distinguishes between *morality*, as a general rule or code of behaviour, and *ethics*, as the way in which individuals constitute themselves in practice as moral subjects. To show that there may be different ethical practices of life operating in relation to the same general moral code Foucault gives the example of conjugal fidelity (pp. 25–32). Practising fidelity can entail different ways of determining the ethical substance, that is, nominating some part of the self over which to become one's own steward. So for example one might act out of respect for personal obligations, or in order to attain mastery over one's desires. Then there are different modes of taking individual responsibility in relation to a moral code: one might be moved to act as a member of a community, as heir to a spiritual tradition, or in order to offer an exemplary personal life. Differences occur also in the form of work performed on the self: for instance, fidelity might mean an abrupt renunciation of pleasures or a long vigil over all conceivable movements of desire. Finally there are different ways of establishing the goal of moral actions: fidelity may be given its importance within a project of self-discipline, as a means of self-purification assuring spiritual salvation, and so on. By participating in these variable modes of conduct, individuals become more than simply the ciphers of a code, they become subjects of moral action.

Our point of contrast with Lawrentian writings is found in a mid-Victorian type of manual, which disseminated specialised knowledges (sexual medicine, biology, moral physiology, psychology) amongst middle-class reading families, and promoted a capacity for heath-consciousness in relation to sex and norms of domestic management, childbearing, childrearing, diet and hygiene.[10] Without ignoring important differences between individual texts, it is evident that the definition of conjugal fidelity was central to the writers of these manuals and their readers, and was related to an ethic of self-restraint.[11] For those approaching sexual medicine in the same way as Marcus (1964) and Gay (1984), such writings might seem symptomatic of the dark night of Victorian morality, shrouding and distorting human sexuality. However, these publications can be viewed more positively as part of a programme for shaping and managing the personal life. Part of this programme was a norm of fidelity which allows us to relativise the conception of love and fidelity which Lawrence would propose as leading to a fundamental truth of sex.

If we confine ourselves to this definition of fidelity in the Victorian manuals, we see that the singling-out of the husband-wife relation bore directly on individuals' willingness to manage the physical and emotional 'substance' of their own sexuality. Addressed specifically as wives, husbands, or as individuals contemplating marriage, readers were asked to become the physicians of their own sexual soul, responsible for understanding the laws which govern the physical and moral life. Only through the wise conduct of partners would the 'scientific' knowledge of sexuality bear fruit in the lives of individuals. The kind of work on the self called for was a personal commitment, a continuous care in preparing for marriage, choosing a partner, and building a relationship. In terms of purposes, fidelity was seen as an ongoing labour of love necessary for physical and moral health, such that it was not strange to speak of sexual restraint as paving the way towards a perfect unity of the couple. In Cowan's *The Science of a New Life*, for instance, individuals are urged to monitor 'every-day thoughts, words and actions' (Cowan, [1874] 1970, p. 46) in order to purify their own character and understand that of others. Cautionary tales and character-sketches are used to encourage examination of desires and motives, and many techniques described to cultivate reciprocity. For instance, while there is a 'law' of choice (Chapter III), this can only be made good if individuals prepare themselves by avoiding unhealthy habits ranging from carelessness in diet to amativeness or self-abuse which ruins partners for marriage (Chapter IV). Similarly, certain forms of thought, speech, feeling and behaviour are to be fostered in a domestically organised space of mutuality: partners should learn to make 'a full and open confession' to one another if anything occurs 'that appears in the remotest way to disturb the harmony of married life' (p. 395); a wife should not cultivate a confidante; a newly-wed couple should exclude relatives from living in the household in order to establish their own relationship (p. 400); and so on.

Significant here is the fact that knowledge of erotic techniques in the husband-wife relation is not seen as necessary in order to achieve the goal of 'perfect sexual love' (p. 48). For Cowan, it is continence which creates the true bond. This view belongs within a broader framework in which the physical and the moral are interrelated in a delicate economy of vital forces. The individual's health depends on establishing harmony of body, mind and soul in relation to 'Nature's laws' (p. 49). Within this economy, the smallest physical or moral disturbance can affect the whole self. Sickness of body and mind follows from 'ignorance of organic laws' (p. 107). Yielding to sexual appetite, for example, drains the individual's powers and causes physical ailments, nervous debility and moral decay (pp. 95–107). Masturbation and excessive coition are seen as abuses of the sexual system, a system in which two principles of the life-force are involved:

> First, the semen, which is elaborately secreted from the highest active principle of the blood of the man, and which is capable of giving life to a new being, and which, of a necessity, if re-absorbed into the blood of the individual, is capable, not of giving, but of renewing life. The second principle involved is that of the nervous system. In the exercise of coition through the abnormal development of amativeness, a great quantity of the nervous fluid of the brain is used up. This nervous fluid, when used in legitimate directions, is in a great measure supplied or vitalized by the re-absorbed semen, or rather the cells secreted from the testicle before the zoa-sperms are developed. This being so, the exercise of amativeness uses up the very life-power of the individual, and in doing this the life-force of the system is greatly lowered and weakened, laying the body open to all manner of diseases, contagious, inflammatory and chronic, insuring an existence weak and sickly, a life a great and miserable failure, and a death early and painful. (p. 101)

For Cowan, then, the storing of (at this point male) vital fluids through self-discipline reinforced the whole physical and moral constitution (cf. Elton

Boyd, MD, 1877). Some other writers maintained that denial of all sexual passion was unwise and that its careful expression was necessary to health (Acton, 1865, pp. 106–28; Fowler, 1870, pp. 637–706). This difference was only one of degree. There was general agreement that sexual excess was potentially destructive. According to Cowan, such excess caused a loss of nervous vital power to be communicated 'through the medium of the great sympathetic system of nerves' to all muscular departments of the body and the brain which coordinates them (p. 105). This excess violates physiological laws and can result even in sterility: only through sensible restraint can proper mutuality and healthy reproduction be assured in marriage (cf. pp. 368–77).

Turning now to 'Lawrentian' writing, it is evident that the vision of fidelity which it presents is identified with a supposedly repressed potential for erotic experience. The perfecting of love and of the self requires individuals to explore this potential dialectically and seek within themselves a vital reconciliation between sensuous and moral faculties. Two points should be made to put the difference between our two instances in perspective. First, although the Lawrentian celebration of pleasure may seem to be diametrically opposed to the law of continence found in the earlier work, it is in fact made possible by and is simply a variant of the economy of the medically sexualised and pathologised body. Whereas for Cowan, undue intensity of the sexual act is dangerous (p. 369), for Lawrence it is by *not* intensifying sexual acts that one misuses the vital forces and runs the risk of physiological and psychological damage. Moreover, Lawrence's pathologising comments on masturbation display his continued reliance on the medical-moral stigmatisation of improper sexual intensities. Second, this erotic supplement is itself a specific norm. The incitement to make erotic mutuality the spiritual hearth of marriage is a late refinement in the formation of middle-class families around a core of affective relationships between husbands and wives. These points can be developed by observing how in the later nineteenth and early twentieth centuries forms of sexology, closely related to literature, renegotiated what was to count as health and fulfilment in marriage.

Foremost among these writers was Havelock Ellis, who identified eroticism as a specific *capacity* of the self. In *The Objects of Marriage*, he criticises the view that 'continence is the only alternative to the animal end of marriage', as one which 'ignores the liberating and harmonising influences, giving wholesome balance and sanity to the whole organism, imparted by a sexual union which is the outcome of the psychic as well as the physical needs' (n.d., pp. 8–9). The need to balance forces within an economy of the body is still there, but now entails recognising that physical sex activity 'may prove the stimulus and liberator of our finest and most exalted activities'. Discovery of eroticism is crucial to the self yet must be kept in balance with all the creative faculties. For the individual who learns to make wise use of pleasures, 'a deeper spiritual unity is achieved than can possibly be derived from continence in or out of marriage'.

The differences between Cowan and Ellis show how mobile has been the distinction between the use and abuse of sexual capacities. What remains constant is the sense that any activity delineated in obedience to this sexological distinction becomes a matter of the conscientious management of sex, that vital but fragile substance of the self. In Ellis' scheme one must still keep vigil over one's desires, albeit for a new reason: physical and psychical fulfilment might be missed in the very place where it is freshly promised. This kind of liberatory project thus comprises a sharply altered norm and a novel threshold of expectations, bringing its own pathogenic concerns with performance. It is not only apparently perverse subjects who are identifiable as specific temperamental types: sexology dwells amongst the pleasures of the 'normal' couple where it establishes the 'erotic personality' (Ellis, 1922, Chapter IV). This personality is supposed to possess the potential for full development of all the faculties according to the familiar aesthetic dialectic – emotional and intellectual, physical and psychical. It is trapped neither by instinctual need nor conventional moralisation. This dialectical construct is synonymous with what, in a further invocation of Romantic aesthetics, Ellis calls the 'play function' of sex:

> Play is primarily the instinctive work of the brain, but it is brain activity united in the subtlest way to bodily activity. In the play function of sex two forms of activity, physical and psychic, are most exquisitely and variously and harmoniously blended. (1922, p. 132)[12]

As a second example of 'scientific' texts on erotic love, we refer to Theodore Van de Velde's work, influential in marriage counselling for several decades after being translated into English in the 1920s and early 1930s.[13] In these eclectic writings, notions of unconscious processes, aggressive and hostile drives, bisexuality and the like borrowed from psychoanalysis are combined with essentialist notions of masculine and feminine differences drawn from moral physiology. In *Sex Hostility in Marriage* (1931, pp. 41–78), we read that feminine characteristics include constriction of the conscious mind, expansion of the subconscious mind, dominant emotional capacity, innate vulnerability, variability of feelings and a need for violent stimuli, qualities supposed to have an organic physiological basis definable from the moment of penetration of the ovum by the sperm. Masculine characteristics include rationality, logical thought, objective judgement, egocentricity and a form of kinetic energy which complements female potential energy and elasticity (pp. 29–40, 80–92). The woman's submissive, emotional nature is to be moulded by the man who realises her 'sensitiveness and plasticity', her 'maternal instinct' and 'intuitive understanding of the significance of the sexual act and its results' (pp. 270–1). Eroticism is a form of insurance, uniting the woman with the man who has given her the 'love life' (p. 271). The perfecting of pleasure, including 'body *and* psyche, soul *and* senses', is in turn the 'best guarantee for the fidelity of the man' and prevents the dominance of mental life which inwardly threatens masculinity (pp. 271–2). The pattern is of course very similar to that found in *Lady Chatterley's Lover*, where the man excites the woman's supposedly intuitive understanding of sex and her 'maternal instinct' which (in contrast to the earlier medical works we have discussed) is linked to erotic intensification (Lawrence, 1961, pp. 117–20, 140–1).

Van de Velde assumes that happiness can only be attained by accepting and maximising feminine and masculine differences and by confronting the drives not just of attraction but also of repulsion within heterosexuality (p. 291). Thus hostility in marriage 'is a "disease" to which everyone is more or less exposed' (p. 278). In its milder forms it is part of 'the normal development of the marriage organism, but is capable in its more serious aspects of destroying this organism' and indeed of causing 'real disease' (p. 278). This kind of text thus perpetuates well into the twentieth century the notion that there is a precarious economy of the sexual body and mind, involving pathologies and cures (the latter now identified as mutual erotic expression) which sexual 'science' mirrors to the 'normal' couple in their own domain. What has changed from the medicine of writers such as Cowan and Blackwell is the emphasis placed on particular elements within that economy. A reversal has occurred whereby for Van de Velde (or Ellis or Lawrence) it is the absence or neglect of eroticism which is damaging to individual well-being and marital relations. Invoking his communications with 'mental specialists', Van de Velde warns that unsatisfied married sexual life has 'fatal consequences' for the 'mental equilibrium and mental health' (1931, p. 269). The 'law of asceticism' is now referred to as unnatural (p. 270n.): ideal marriage must give sexual passions 'their full rein' though without infringing on 'the natural moral law' (p. 270). The distance from the works of Cowan or Blackwell can be measured in the following statement:

Even although a marriage, based on feelings of love for one's neighbour, on insight and understanding, adaptability and goodwill, and on union and community of interests, may be a marriage without antagonism, even a harmonious marriage – it is still not a marriage in the full meaning of the word. It requires, in addition to all this, in addition to the love as described by *St Paul, sexual love*. There is no true marriage without erotic love, and no ideal marriage unless the practice of sexual love approach perfection. (1931, p. 268)

If it was deemed essential for this kind of 'science' to explore erotic meaning fully, so it was also for a certain kind of literature.[14] For Lawrence and Van de Velde who, in writing, respectively, *Lady Chatterley's Lover* and *Ideal Marriage: Its Physiology and Technique* can both be viewed as marriage reformers, the so-called suppression of the erotic impulse destroys the vital forces just as surely as excess wasted the vital fluids in the view of Victorian physicians. What counts as fidelity has shifted. Being truly married now requires embracing the need to know the secret pleasure of sexual acts. Of course, no one-to-one influence between writers is assumed here. The purpose of the comparison is to map a broader field of exchanges between literary and 'scientific' works which allowed them to relay to their writers and readers particular norms of self-problematisation and self-formation. Between an erotic literature and a literary erotics no sharp line can be drawn.

The new practice of literary erotics thus made aesthetic capital out of the investments of knowledge and pleasure in sex which were already developing in neighbouring fields. Under these circumstances, 'literature' and 'sexuality' happened to converge. There is, however, no necessary relation between them. A 'D. H. Lawrence' emerges from the contingent linking of sexual and literary technologies peculiar to modern Western cultures, but not every culture has to have one.

Literary erotics provided the means whereby those individuals equipped with the appropriate cultural abilities could construct themselves, through a detailed, continuous problematising of pleasures, as the subjects of their own sexuality. The key strategies which it entailed, the sexualisation of a dialectical work on the self and the transformation of sexual knowledge and pleasure into an aesthetic form of 'play', can be thought of as techniques of the body and practices of the self – to borrow key terms from Marcel Mauss's (1973) anthropology of the body and Foucault's (1986) history of the soul. That is, they are ways of modelling physical, mental and psychological attributes which are informed by specific cultural techniques and social practices.

Seen in this light, literary erotics is a technical and highly specialised organisation of the body and conscience. Forms of conscience, as personal modes of monitoring conduct, depend upon and vary with definite social relations and techniques (Hirst and Woolley, 1982, pp. 136–7). The literary erotics whose emergence we have traced had no exclusive rights over conscience-formation in questions of sexuality. For instance, campaigners for 'companionate marriage', contemporaries of Lawrence and Van de Velde, advocated attitudinal and institutional reforms which would allow a deliberate 'compromise' of psychological and sexual needs with economic ones (allowing an alternative to celibacy, the use of birth control and divorce by mutual consent). They envisaged a form of marital companionship based on calculations of the material security of partners in terms which would have been anathema to Lawrence, who placed a transcendent value on sexual bonding (see, for example, Judge Ben B. Lindsey, 1928, and J. A. Goldsmid, 1934). The 'Lawrentian' forming of conscience was different from that promoted in household sexual medicine which did not valorise eroticism. Blackwell had argued against the twin assumptions that wives who have reservations about how they are expected to experience pleasure must possess – according to the type-casting of the frigid woman – 'no sexual passion', and that women are 'more tyrannically governed than men by impulses of sex' because of their physiological and maternal nature (1894, pp. 1, 44–53). Even in writers such as Cowan, who were not apparently identified with feminism, there was a concern with rights and spaces, accompanied by medical arguments that play down the importance of sexual passion and gratification: a wife was not to be obligated by a husband's demands.[15]

Nor did the Lawrentian aestheticising of sex go uncontested. As early as the 1920s Florence Seabury called into question the characterology used by Lawrence. The Lawrence of *Sons and Lovers*, she says, is 'decidedly neurotic in his fear of the ultimate absorption of man. Woman he describes perpetually as a great magnetic womb, fecund, powerful, engulfing. Man he sees as a pitiful struggling creature, ultimately devoured by fierce maternal force' (Seabury, 1925, p. 227). For Seabury, the novelist's representations of male and female difference derive from cultural, literary and psychological stereotypes which operate more generally to enforce particular roles in marriage, including the definition of women 'in relation' to men, and the assumed tendency of 'Woman' towards affectivity as opposed to rationality. Sylvia Kopold (1925) criticises the ideal of comparative variability of the sexes, an idea much used by Lawrence and Ellis, according to which the male is prone to extremes of intelligence and genius, and the female is associated with intuitive stability, average rational powers and the like. She relates perceived male/female differences of this kind to different social trainings, expectations and environments, arguing against founding educational or political objectives on such notions. While she does not refer specifically to literature, her criticisms make clear the limits and partiality of the sexological knowledges at work in the Lawrentian model of self-fashioning.

Yet in the decades that followed, Lawrence's project would come to stand as an exemplary work of sexual self-discovery and aesthetic self-cultivation. We shall conclude this chapter by analysing how literary sexual ethics became something more than an uncommon pursuit.

INTO THE CLASSROOM

We have established that using sexual literature to work on the self was initially an art of living refined by a small minority of writers and readers. Contrary to the view that writers like Lawrence had to create the public taste through which they would ultimately win appropriate recognition (Beal, 1961, pp. 11–24; West, 1950, Chapter 10), contemporary forms of literary journalism made it possible for them to find a limited public for their specialised adaptation of popular sexual-medical and pornographic materials. A minor industry of small journals and magazines supported esoteric literary and intellectual movements in the late nineteenth and early twentieth centuries. Such publications helped form and maintain an upper middle-class audience with a strong sense of itself as a 'circle' distinguished from middle-class culture by personal taste and social mannerism (such as the forms of dress and speech associated with the Bloomsbury group) and by a relative indifference to general public acceptance (Dorothy Baisch, 1950).[16] These publications were in turn dependent on the milieu of the university arts faculties, which in some cases provided their home and in most cases supervised the aesthetic training of their readers and writers.[17] The *bellettristic* audience existing for the circle of writers to which Lawrence belonged was already conversant with sexology, sexual medicine, psychology, and issues of sex reform and ethics. Lawrence read and reviewed works of sexual 'science' such as writings by the psychiatrist, Dr Trigant Burrow (Lawrence, 1936, pp. 377–82), just as experts in sexology and related fields made use of literary forms – as is evident in Van de Velde's mixing of Goethe and 'genetics'. Indeed, within these particular circuits of intellectual exchange, no major distinction seems to have been marked between literary and other modes of serious writing on sex, since these were all considered to give access to the central questions and had similar uses as means of inquiring into the self.[18]

It was only in this context of an intellectual subculture that Lawrence could carry out the iterative work of posing problems for other published writings, formulate solutions and so create a sense of progress by using literature to investigate sexuality. Thus the novels of John Galsworthy, initially read as social satires and comedies of manners, were tested and found pallid by applying the dialectical-erotic method of reading (Lawrence, 1936, pp. 539–50). Lawrence argues that Galsworthy attempts to treat his characters ironically by showing them as merely 'social' beings, 'parasites upon the thought, the feelings, the whole body of life of really living individuals' (p. 543), whose own revolt reduces sex to a pose. However, according to Lawrence, the form of Galsworthy's writing is itself flawed. Sexual emotion is reduced to sentimentalism, 'the working off on yourself of feelings you haven't really got' (p. 545). Thought is cut off from sensuous awareness, reducing sex to a clever idea on the part of both the novelist and, potentially, the reader. In Lawrence's view, serious literary works could thus commit the same sin as pornography, namely didacticism – idealising the body for the sake of social ideologies while covertly goading it into auto-erotic excitement. The challenge was thus to bring literature into line with the individual's own whole – sensuous *and* intellectual – experience of sexuality. Of course, the dialectical technique could support an aesthetic work on the self without requiring univocal judgements. Many readers exercised themselves over whether Lawrence's own writings succeeded in giving harmonious form to his explorations of sexuality (see for example John Middleton Murry (1932), and the reviews of and tributes to Lawrence by Murry, T. S. Eliot, Edwin Muir, E. M. Forster and others in Draper (ed.) 1970). But this concern underlines the crucial point: initially, Lawrentian writings could make their way in the world courtesy only of a 'small public of the minority' (Lawrence, 1936, p. 186).

Left to their own devices, those who engaged in literary erotics could continue almost indefinitely to operate within their chosen and marginal practice of self-culture. That this is so can be seen from the Lawrentian discourse sustained through the 1930s and beyond by writers such as Frieda Lawrence (1934), John Middleton Murry (1932), Anais Nin (1964), Aldous Huxley (1971) and Lawrence Durrell (1959).[19] In the early 1930s, Henry Miller began writing a book on Lawrence whose work he saw as immensely inspiring (Miller, 1985, pp. 11–24). In this book, published some fifty years after it was begun, Miller predictably speaks of obscenity as the means of recovering a lost vitality, a vitality he identifies with male erotic power and its dark sensuality, and with a female otherness which cannot be grasped through any mere ideology of intellectual and social equality (pp. 188–90). The radically obscene force of literature, Miller assures us, strikes against repressive morality and law which still try to make our language betray the truths of sexual experience (p. 176). No matter how 'passionate' this kind of appraisal might be, however, of its own accord it could have made little impact on the broader social and legal regulation of sexuality.

The purpose of Lawrentian literature was not, as has often been assumed, to spread cultural values broadly and democratically but to sustain a personalist project of cultural distinction (in the sense proposed by Bourdieu, 1984). The aesthetic use of sexual literature was a way of cultivating a prestigious taste and distinguishing oneself not only from popular entertainments, but from middle-class tastes and manners such as those associated by Lawrence with the novels of Galsworthy. These other forms could be deemed to fail, in their own ways, to realise sex, that is they could be deemed to be insufficiently dialectical. In this differentiation and distinction there is a confirmation of what Foucault signals as a shift in middle-class concerns with sex that occurred from the late nineteenth century. Initially this social stratum was distinguished by acquiring a specific, sexual body, a 'class' body signifying 'health, hygiene, descent and race' (Foucault, 1979, p. 124). Once all other social sectors were provided with a sexual body, bourgeois distinction would be measured 'not by the "sexual" quality of the body, but by the intensity of its repression' (p. 129). In the elite practice of literary erotics, the problematic of repression was reproduced in order to achieve a dialectical expression of true sexuality.

If this art of knowing and shaping the self through using the techniques of literary erotics was still a localised pursuit amongst the intelligentsia in the first decades of the twentieth century, the situation was gradually changing. These techniques of literary sexual ethics were about to undergo a more general distribution. They would do so, however, not as the cultural manifestation of the dialectic but as part of an eminently institutional process in which they were transformed into mechanisms of popular education. The governmental use of literature in popular education is analysed in Hunter (1988, see especially Chapters 4 and 7); we need identify here only those factors which permitted a new and greatly expanded role for the technique of self-fashioning elaborated in modern literary erotics.

The aesthetic use of literature and criticism developed in Romantic self-culture was, in the early and middle decades of the twentieth century, grafted onto the practices of moral formation already operating in the popular school and teacher training. Since the mid-nineteenth century, these practices had been characterised by an exchange between goals of social regulation and strategies fostering self-expression on the part of the pupil. The environment of the popular school was constructed in such a way as to bring the children's real-life interests, sentiments and conducts into the classroom, where their expression would be guided by norms of personal development and welfare. In this space of 'supervised freedom' (Hunter, 1988, p. 115), the normalising procedure of moral correction was also an individualising one, through which the child was able to be equipped with cultural attributes. It was in this context that the discipline of 'English' emerged. Constituting a special pedagogy, English promoted self-expression through reading and writing and at the same time made this process a basis for re-shaping the inner life of the child according to norms publicised by contemporary psychological and social knowledges. The lynchpin of English as a pedagogy was the relation in which the teacher was formed as an exemplary figure for the student, at once sympathetic and distant, combining encouragement and surveillance.

Inducted into the practice of reading taken over from the specialised Romantic tradition of dialectical criticism, the college-trained teacher could encourage and participate in the pupil's affective responses, while allowing these to be reflected upon and tested against the formal organisation of the work being read. The text became both a free space in which personal responses could be elicited, and a powerful instrument for intervening in and reshaping the sensibility exposed by those responses. The technique of dialectical reading, once applied by the individual Romantic aesthete to mould the self, now became the support for an institutionalised pedagogic relation between teacher and student.

These conditions allowed literary erotics a second mode of existence. No longer the province of a voluntary (adult) practice, the ethical inquiry into sexual literature became part of the curriculum, where it apparently offered a way of taking English even further into the real-life interests of the young student. Of course, this use of literature did not tap some natural propensity towards self-expression. Rather, it disseminated through a new channel and on a new scale an aesthetic capacity to make sexuality central to the supervised construction of personal identity. Within this pedagogic use of literature, individuals learn to mediate sexual representations dialectically. On the one hand, readers are encouraged to identify with the text, and hear it speaking to their own feelings and curiosities. On the other, they are brought to appreciate the text's formal mediations of experience, so that their immediate responses are reflectively deepened and modified.

This pedagogic strategy is at work in many critical texts on Lawrence and similar writers by the 1950s. It is evident in, for example, Dorothy van Ghent's chapter on *Sons and Lovers* in *The English Novel* (1953), a book which combines critical essays with a section on 'Problems for Study and Discussion'. Van Ghent demonstrates how to read the novel dialectically. Thus, the loose structure of the work is to be appreciated as evidence of its openness to experience. The novel is said to explore – without excessive refinement and subtlety of technique – what the reader may recognise as 'real problems in life' (p. 245), including the 'organic disturbance' of sexual polarities and relationships, and the dissociation of intellectual and social life from 'the natural life-directed condition' of human experience (p. 247). At the same time, however, it must be appreciated that the personal and autobiographical meaning is dramatically realised by the novel's narrative and poetic form. Van Ghent describes Lawrence's task as follows:

> He must make us aware – sensitively aware, not merely conceptually aware – of the profound life force whose rhythms the natural creature obeys; and he must make us aware of the terminal individuality – the absolute 'otherness' or 'outsideness' – that is the natural form of things and of the uncorrupted person. We must be made aware of these through the *feelings* of his people, for only in feeling have the biological life force and the sense of identity, either the identity of self of others, any immediacy of reality. He seeks the objective equivalent of feeling in the image. As Francis Fergusson says, Lawrence's imagination was so concrete that he seems not 'to distinguish between the reality and the metaphor or symbol which makes it plain to us'. But the most valid symbols are the most concrete realities. Lawrence's great gift for the symbolic image was a function of his sensitivity to and passion for the meaning of real things – for the individual expression that real things have. In other words, his gift for the image arose directly from his vision of life as infinitely creative of individual identities, each whole and separate and to be reverenced as such.
>
> (pp. 247–8, footnote omitted)

We see the key elements of Romantic dialectics reiterated here: the meaning of the work must be realised sensuously and not just conceptually. Creative form and vision must arise directly out of an experience of the concrete reality whose inner meaning they reveal. Within this framework, the reader is called upon at once to identify with the feelings and problems portrayed and – under the teacher's watchful eye – to interpret these critically and aesthetically. This eliciting of affective response and corrective reflection can be seen in the study-guide questions which accompany the essay:

> CHAPTER 7. Do you find in the passage, early in the chapter, describing the swinging in the barn, that the swinging itself provides an image expressive of the emotional drives with which this chapter ('Lad-and-

Girl Love') is concerned and expressive also of the kind of values with which Lawrence is fundamentally occupied? . . . Freud suggests that children's love for swinging is an early erotic expression. How far would you say that Lawrence realizes all these associations in the very simple and natural childhood incident of the swinging in the barn? (pp. 457–8)

CHAPTER 11 . . . Why does the affair with Miriam bring Paul only "the sense of failure and of death"? What part in this failure is played by Miriam's own idiosyncracies of sensibility, and what part is played by Paul's attachment to his mother? (p. 460)

CHAPTER 12 . . . How is the scene of the love-making of Paul and Clara in the field expressive of Lawrence's positive attitude toward values? Compare this scene with that in the woods where Paul and Miriam make love (Chapter 11): is there any difference in the use of the darkness symbol? (p. 461)

In this aesthetic alternation of identification and detachment, it is made explicit that 'the critical approach to literature as a search for the principle of form in the work' is also implicitly 'a search for form in the self' ('Dedication').[20]

The same pedagogic imperative works through the criticism of F. R. Leavis.[21] Lawrence's life and work is projected by Leavis as an ideal unity of sensibility and intelligence:

There is no profound emotional disorder in Lawrence, no obdurate major disharmony; intelligence in him can be, as it is, the servant of the whole integrated psyche. It is the representative in consciousness of the complex need of the whole being, and is not thwarted or disabled by inner contradictions in him, whether we have him as artist, critic or expositor. It is intensely active in his creative writing: we have on the one hand the technical originality of the creations, and on the other their organic wholeness and vitality.

(Leavis, 1955, p. 27)

It is through the work of practical criticism that the reader learns to negotiate immediate responses with the text's 'organic wholeness' (p. 27), including the interplay of characters, events, images and the formal and sensuous qualities of the language itself. That the search for form in the text is also a patterning of the self is evident from Leavis' discussion (pp. 70–?) of *Lady Chatterley's Lover*. The question of the text's success or failure is not a matter of 'judgement' – a fact to be known about the book in itself; it is a means to shape the sensibility of the reader. According to Leavis, this novel shows a didactic tendency in Lawrence. Even though the work reflects a 'strong, vital instinct for health' (p. 71) and cleanses the language and hence physical experience which social custom has made obscene, it insists too wilfully on its purpose and thus fails to realise fully its vision:

> [T]he willed insistence on the words and facts must, it seems to me, whatever the intention, have something unacceptable, something offensive, about it; it offends, surely, against Lawrence's own canons – against the spirit of his creativity and against the moral and emotional ethic that he in essence stands for. (p. 70)

Of course, in Leavis' account the book's partial failure does not mean for a moment that it should in any formal sense be treated as 'obscene'. Rather, it is up to readers to recognise the problem of its offensiveness and come to terms with it for and in themselves. It is they who must measure the gap between the vision and the realisation, and find the right balance of sensuous immediacy and moral reflection.

This art of sexual-aesthetic reading may therefore be treated as a specialised ethos, but one which the reader, like the writer, seems to discover in the forms of an unfulfilled self, provided the dialectical method is correctly followed. Reading a book such as *Lady Chatterley's Lover* aesthetically becomes an exercise in which certain individuals learn to manage their own relation to erotica. It is in relation to this practice that the categories of form-content unity, authorial intention and literary value gain their force in dealing with sexual materials. Within the aesthetic framework, even the apparent failures of a text become part of a greater organic whole, because the dialectical practice of writing and reading builds in the possibility of always working towards a more fully achieved form of understanding.[22]

The same general strategy is found – perhaps surprisingly – in the tradition of Marxist literary criticism represented by Raymond Williams. In *The English Novel from Dickens to Lawrence* (1984), Williams is as indebted as Leavis to Romantic historicism, despite a greater sociological emphasis on the conditions of literary production. Supposedly, while it is rooted in immediate historical and class realities, literature is also that transcendent representation of experience and human possibility which reunifies art and life, self and society, against the fragmentation caused by industrial mechanisation. Most importantly, the key to Williams' understanding of literature is the technique of dialectical reading which continues to operate as a pedagogical norm. The reader is invited to approach Lawrence's work as 'a series of advances and deadlocks, and then renewed advance' (p. 170), in which triumphs and failures are of equal importance. Hence *Lady Chatterley's Lover* is presented as a work which challenges the reader to participate in the always unfinished task of reconciling the impulse towards form with the impulse towards experience in both literature and the self:

> *Lady Chatterley's Lover* hasn't the scale, the sustenance, of the earlier novels. In its single and powerful dimension it is still isolated, still reduced, from the form that had once seemed possible. But it is a positive flow again, a recovery of energy, a reaching past rigidities, and as such very moving. That he was still to the end reaching out, reaching out as a novelist, is profoundly encouraging. It is what we remember and stick to in and through the difficulties – common difficulties – which his development of the novel, his unfinished development, show [*sic*] us so clearly. Because it isn't after all an end with Lawrence. It is where in our time we have had to begin.

> (Williams, 1984, p. 184)

In the light of the historical discontinuity which we have indicated between 'elite' and 'governmental' distributions of sexual literature, what are we to make of the fact that Lawrence himself wrote on the topic of education in the schools? Joy and Raymond Williams (1973) see in Lawrence a prescient figure, discovering 'for the most part on his own' (p. 13) the central problems in making the education system more humane. According to them, Lawrence sees through the limited existing forms of instruction to a true form of education: he understands the need to connect formal learning to the deepest personal awareness in which affective and intellectual capacities are harmonised, and to foster individuals' own sense of being by integrating their real life interests within the learning process (p. 7). This biographic narrative is itself organised within the terms of the dialectical opposition of the didactic and the aesthetic. We might speculate that Lawrence's own interests were themselves influenced by the teacher training system to which he was exposed, with its well-established emphasis on re-articulating the real-life interests of the child. Certainly, the terms in which Lawrence writes of popular education are entirely aesthetic. His 'educational' writings are in fact extemporisings within the marginal art of self-culture. So, for instance, Lawrence writes that the elementary school system must give each person the 'opportunity to come to his own intrinsic fullness of being' (Williams and Williams (eds), p. 136). The means of doing so is to explore the natural and spontaneous impulses of the child, allow self-expression to occur through play, and balance these impulses with responsiveness to the affective centre of others and awareness of the life of the mind (pp. 120–94). The realisation of the individual's potential will be made possible simply by the dialectical reconciliation of mental learning with physical and spontaneous intelligence (p. 138), the interaction of the emotional and volitional polarities of individual being (pp. 145–64), and the mutuality of masculine and feminine impulses within the self and within relationships (pp. 194–203). It is only because the techniques of aesthetic criticism and self-criticism underwent a pedagogic reconstruction and distribution as devices of moral training – and not because of some prophetic power of Lawrence the individual – that such statements can in retrospect be celebrated as exemplary.

In summary, then, the educational importance which sexual literature has acquired in the twentieth century is the outcome of a process in which an aesthetic technique of self-shaping was adapted and adopted as a practical method of moral training within the governmental sphere. Initially, serious sexual literature (which encompassed various genres and crossed boundaries between novelistic, poetic, philosophical, medical and 'scientific' writing) had a self-formative function for an intellectual minority in the late nineteenth and early twentieth centuries, prior to any formal institutional dissemination. Subsequently the techniques of writing and reading associated with that function became caught up in a very different and widespread pedagogic distribution. Of course this distribution dealt with matters other than the use of sexually oriented writing, but it eventually gave a key role to the literary-critical study of serious sexual literature, especially the novel. In the 1908 *Report from the Joint Select Committee on Lotteries and Indecent Advertisements*, no educationist had argued that access to sexual literature was necessary if the moral training of pupils and their teachers was to be completed. Not many decades later, the educational study of literature became a significant means by which a capacity for individuals to manage their own sexuality, including their relation to erotica, was distributed through the official teacher-training system. As we shall see in the next chapter, this pedagogic deployment of a formerly esoteric literary erotics made it possible for the aesthetic construction of sexuality to operate as a new 'infra-legal' norm in deciding the regulation of pornography.

5 Twentieth-Century English Obscenity Law

TRANSITIONS AND UNCERTAINTIES

Given the unpredictable exchanges that occurred within the pornographic field from the late nineteenth to the early twentieth centuries, it will be no surprise that a central theme of this chapter is the historical contingency of the treatment of art, literary art in particular, in twentieth-century English obscenity law. Against the mobile background of the never completely formalised relations between the law of obscenity and the social policing of pornography, and of the migration of specialist pornography's themes and figures into the circuits of a more generally disseminated educative fiction in the guise of ethical techniques for (sexual) self-improvement, our plan is to review the English Obscene Publications Act of 1959 and the 1960 case in which the new statute was to have received its definitive construction, *Regina* v. *Penguin Books Ltd.*, popularly known as the trial of *Lady Chatterley's Lover*. This statute and this trial – the latter held at London's Old Bailey in October 1960 – are windows on to the uneven regulatory field within which modern obscenity law has operated.

A principal theme of our discussion of the *Hicklin* judgement was the evident certainty with which the court of Queen's Bench handled the matter of obscenity. This certainty was a function of the relatively stable pattern presented by the mid-nineteenth century pornographic field. On one side, pornography was routinely delineated by a set of measures designed both to police the moral and physical well-being of the popular classes and to regulate (while in effect intensifying and differentiating by age and gender) the sexuality of middle-class family members. It is true, as shown in police comments cited in Chapter 3, that depending on the circumstances and purposes of its publication and sale, and on the cultural attributes of its audience, the obscenity – and therefore the regulatory treatment – of the same work could vary. But this variation was handled as a working norm, not a cause for constant and profound uncertainty as to the nature of obscenity. Nor, importantly, was it a sign of middle-class hypocrisy. It simply meant – as literary theory is only now claiming to have discovered – that a book is not the same across different contexts of consumption and use.

On the other side, novelistic literature flowed with no apparent difficulty through differentiated audience channels and book-trade networks which legal – as well as social and commercial – regulation had established and maintained. Here it is worth recalling that we are dealing less with the enunciation of a prohibition than the delineation of different channels of dissemination. For our purposes, three interacting sectors of this system are of particular importance.

Occupying the centre space – sometimes serialised in literary and 'improving' journals targetted on the different members of the middle class household and addressing the gamut of social issues and problems – were the educative novels of Eliot, Dickens, Thackeray, Collins, the Brontes, Trollope and other writers now considered minor. The general absence of references to sex in these novels – or its presence only in forms requiring a relatively specialised sensibility to disinter – is clear enough. On one flank of this central channel of dissemination was the highly specialised and esoteric private circulation of 'curious' pornography. Often published by subscription, this closed circulation coupled the closetted pursuit of the rare perversity to the bibliophile enthusiasm for the rare publication.[1] While addressed exclusively to a minority market of wealthy men, this channel nonetheless witnessed the consolidation of a distinct pornographic literature in English. On the other flank of the educative mainstream channel flowed the popular pornography of the street corner. This comprised the residue of ancient bawdy broadsheets, French and Egyptian postcards, lithographs, 'selections' from the classics in penny part-editions, the whole pile moved along by cheap printing and a sub-booktrade network of itinerant pedlars, street hawkers and booksellers centered in Holywell Street in London and other popular sites.

This picture is of course schematic. In the category of educative and improving novelistic literature were women novelists and writers of romances, their works being the object of something like a generic contract between these authors and their specific readership. Along the axis of gender further distinctions of audiences could be drawn, extending into the category of useful publications which included books and pamphlets dealing with sexual medicine and serving as the means of equipping middle-class families – women in particular – with the means to manage the sexualities of the married couple and of the child through advice on physiological, moral, hygienic and dietary matters. Such publications – of which the writings of Drs Elizabeth Blackwell and John Cowan are examples – relied upon a degree of educated interest and of technical literacy amongst wives and mothers, although husbands and fathers, as well as children, were also addressed.

These audiences and these channels of communication evidently overlapped. Nevertheless, this triple division of the literary field remained relatively stable through the nineteenth century. Indeed, the outcry and prosecutions that could follow cases of peddling popular pornography in the precincts of boarding schools or the criticism of the bowdlerising of early classics for the broader educative market testify to the strength of these established boundaries of circulation.[2]

By the beginning of the twentieth century, however, this earlier organisation was becoming unstable. The new instability was due to the unexpected mutation within the literary field itself, as described in the previous chapter. A heady cocktail and novel cultural alliance of ethics, sexuality, literature and pornography emerged. In advanced circles, persons were formed for whom the right use of sex could now involve the most directly erotic, indeed the perverse, since this constituted – when transposed into aesthetic terms – the challenge to be faced and avowed if one was to sublimate the full truth that could now be attached so uniquely to one's sex. The history and logic of this specialised cultural practice were outlined in the previous chapter: the truest sex (and self) is the most hidden. An exemplary literary demonstration of this logic is involved, we suggested, in the depiction of anal intercourse in the sixteenth chapter of *Lady Chatterley's Lover*. Those equipped with the requisite ethical and aesthetic training were able – and required – to recognise and read that perverse incident in a way that for them transposed the sexual into quite another register. Lawrence's readers thus undertook a specific 'practice of the self' by working through a sequence of sexual acts with an increasing flow of biblio-erotic pleasure but also with a growing mastery of how to deploy this pleasure as the guiding norm for a guilt-free sexuality and a complete knowledge of one's self.

Readers possessed of these skills – the ability to reconcile the pulsions of the body and the moral imperatives of reasons – were not, however, of the social groups routinely touched by the policing of the streets. Rather, they were the 'little band' of whom Lawrence had spoken. What then is to be made of the fact that in 1960 Penguin Books printed and warehoused an initial run of 200 000 paperback copies of *Lady Chatterley's Lover*? This is a question we shall attempt to answer later. To do so we first need to trace the manner in which the sexualising of educative literature threw up a quite new and unpredicted regulatory problem: how was the law to treat the 'higher uses' of this eroticised material by a minority? This problem, variously formulated, surfaces as a juridical and jurisprudential dilemma at successively higher stages of action in the legal network.

It was not only that in the early twentieth century erotic writing and reading became an essential instrument for a specialist technique of self-shaping. This technique, together with the culturally distinctive and thus prestigious persona that was its artefact and objective, acquired a growing audience in the emergent group of teachers and popular intellectuals as well as a vehicle of dissemination in the university and college arts faculties. Newly eroticised, like Van de Velde's 'ideal marriage', the educative novel now began to cross the nineteenth-century boundary to initiate an unforeseen and uncertain exchange between the formerly disjunct circuits of popular obscenity and of the minority genre of specialist pornography.

Confronted with this mutation of the cultural field which it regulates but of which it is also part, obscenity law retreated from its earlier certainty. That certainty had been fitting in circumstances where an unquestioned boundary could be drawn between 'filth' and 'literature' or between the 'perverse' and the 'educative', since these categories were clearly and materially embodied in different circuits of distribution within the overall topography of nineteenth-century literate culture. Now, however, pornographic elements which formerly circulated within the restricted but tolerated private sphere and which, whenever they might appear in public or street literature were proper and legitimate targets of policing, began to appear in potentially large-circulation novels of aesthetic and ethical education. This is the origin of the characteristic dilemma and preoccupation of twentieth-century obscenity law: how to distinguish between art and pornography when these appear together inside mainstream educative culture?

In fact the regulatory field too was to undergo an important mutation. As argued in previous chapters, the policing of the pornographic field had been organised around the notion of a social pathology and its distinctive medical norm: the moral and physical harm caused to vulnerable persons by exposure to obscene writings and images. Both obscenity law and the other policing agencies were oriented to this norm. Without it being a perfect or complete transition, a shift occurred from a regime of regulation based on the policing of a social pathology to a regime of regulation organised around an aesthetic norm.

There are undeniable signs of this shift in the text of the Obscene Publications Act of 1959. The signs are also there to see in the arguments advanced by twentieth-century liberal proponents of obscenity law reform (whose case we consider in the next chapter). With the benefit of hindsight, it is clear what was always missing in the reformers' programme to shift the regulation of obscene publication from law to private moral judgement: an entire population possessed of the ability to use erotica in an appropriately aesthetic manner and into whose own hands the regulation of pornography could thus simply pass. This lack, perhaps, was at least intuited by courts and legislators. As a result, the policing of pornography as a social harm remains on the agenda in this last decade of the twentieth century, if not always as a blanket principle, at least as an express concern relating to the

Twentieth-Century English Obscenity Law

protection of certain categories of person from certain categories of work in certain circumstances.

Our argument should now be clear. If in a variety of ways twentieth-century obscenity law has recognised the distinctive claims of art and aesthetic values, such recognition has remained uneven. If an 'aesthetic moment' occurred around the 1960s – partly commemorated by the Obscene Publications Act 1959 and more completely by the trial of *Lady Chatterley's Lover* – today there are campaigns to withdraw from art a generalised legal immunity.[3]

How were aesthetic objectives and norms able to surface inside obscenity law? To answer this question, we must again draw on the history of the interactions between law and police, remaining mindful of the distinction between police-force work with its uses of informal and formal warnings, confiscations and other summary measures and, on the other hand, the array of regulatory and management tactics deployed independently of purely judicial mechanisms, in particular the aesthetic educative programmes whose objective is to equip individuals to be ethically self-regulating in matters of sex. A primary objective will be to discuss the relation between the law's attempt to draw absolute distinctions between the licit and the illicit and a programme for the pedagogic regulation of pornography, a programme operating an educative distribution of aesthetic norms and wedded thereby to a tactic of variable policing.

Instability is built into the 1959 Act by its historical coordinates. Here is a statute which allows for a work to be obscene yet aesthetic and, because it is aesthetic, legally publishable on the instrumentalist grounds that the publication of works of literary merit is in the public good. In short, a work can be criminally obscene yet publishable in the public good. This is not only a conceptual instability. From a practical or procedural perspective, the arrangement established by the Act depends on a hybrid framework of adjudication combining *juries* – the commonsense experience of the community decides upon obscenity – and *experts* – a policing according to specialist knowledge of aesthetic values.

The 1908 *Report from the Joint Select Committee on Lotteries and Indecent Advertisement* had recommended a new consolidated obscenity statute providing complete exemption from prosecution for books with literary merit and repute. Along with this automatic exemption for serious literature, the 1908 Report called for summary jurisdiction for mass-produced and distributed obscenity. This call is intelligible only in circumstances where a distinction between literature and obscene publication remains largely self-evident.

Seven years after the Report was tabled, Lawrence's novel *The Rainbow* faced prosecution under the Obscene Publications Act of 1857. The Bow

Street magistrate considering the case did not simply recognise the novel as something other than an obscene publication. On the contrary, he recognised that the publication met the legal criteria then operative for defining what counted as an obscene publication, and expressed his concern that a company like Methuen 'should have allowed their reputation to be soiled as it had been by the publication of this work' (*The Times*, 15 November 1915). It counted for nothing that Lawrence himself held to an equally clear distinction between literature and pornography that would have drawn the boundary somewhere else; nor – more importantly – that Lawrence himself concurred in finding pornography morally and physically harmful.

The 1915 episode contributed to the construction of Lawrence as the exemplary victim of English obscenity law and hero of art's struggle against that law. In the light of the preceding chapter, however, the picture is anything but straightforward. Lawrence's works in fact *reactivate* the imagery of pornography, but now transposing it to an aesthetic register where it becomes the occasion and the means of an ethical challenge to establish a correct reconciliatory relation between the desire of the body and the imperatives of reason.

As always in our study of pornography, the essential question concerns distribution: how were works of Lawrence disseminated? In 1929, Lawrence's *Pansies* was published by Martin Secker. Following an 'open post' discovery of the work in manuscript, and action by the Home Office, the Director of Public Prosecutions suggested removal of fourteen of the poems. The publisher complied. Also in 1929, an exhibition of Lawrence's pictures at the Warren Gallery occasioned the interest of the Metropolitan Police. A destruction order was duly sought from the Marlborough Street Magistrates:

> Mr Muskett [he had testified to the 1908 Joint Select Committee] appeared for the Crown and St John Hutchinson and John Maude for the defendants, Mr and Mrs Philip Trotter, lessees of the gallery. St John Hutchinson maintained that the pictures were works of art. To prove this, he hoped to call Sir William Orpen, Mr Augustus John, Mr G. Philpot, and possibly Mr Agnew, Professor Blair, Professor Gleadowe and Mr Rothenstein.

(St John-Stevas, 1956, p. 105)

What follows in St John-Stevas' report is a typically *ad hominem* innuendo of the sort that proliferates in censorship histories of obscenity law:

Mr Mead, the magistrate, aged eighty-two, was not impressed by the distinction of these potential witnesses and excluded them from the court. 'It is utterly immaterial', he said, 'whether they are works of art. That is a collateral question which I have not to decide. The most splendidly painted picture in the Universe might be obscene'. On the defendants promising to close the exhibition the case was dismissed with five guineas costs being awarded against them. (p. 105)

The magistrate concerned himself with the question of whether or not an obscene publication had occurred and, if so, where. To do this, he applied an established police test for the recognition of obscenity (is 'the hair . . . clearly shown on the private parts', to recall the words of Chief Inspector Drew (1908 Report, p. 40)). The hair was indeed there for all to see, thus the issue was decided. The very use of this 'police' test was itself conditioned by the public and visual character of the exhibition; that is, by the possibility of an undifferentiated access, one which meant that the pictures forfeited the protective 'special audience' categories made available by relative or circumstantial obscenity. For this reason, once this act of obscene publication had been established as a matter of fact, there was no cause to make space in the proceedings for debate on a quite different order of problem: the character of the representations themselves and, more specifically, whether they were art or not.

There is one element in this case that suggests a possible alteration of the norm-based correctional function just described. This is the defence strategy to call expert witnesses to testify that the pictures were works of art. While these witnesses could not in the event be called to testify, their presence in the court was a sign that the network of norms, disciplines and institutions which organised obscenity law was changing. The ascension of the aesthetic into the legal domain points to a future eclipsing of the truths of sexual medicine and moral psychology as the organising grounds of the legal regulation of pornography. The seven 'expert witnesses' convened to testify that Lawrence's pictures were works of art were not there to say that the paintings were not obscene. Their evidence was to be that, obscene or not, they 'furthered the interests of art' and thus served the public good (Rolph, 1969, p. 83). Despite the possibility of a retrospective colouring by a liberal reformer such as C. H. Rolph, in a formulation such as this there is a sign that the hierarchy of disciplines informing the character of legal judgement might alter if concern for the presence of art could override questions of social harm and take the centre stage. Of course, in 1929, this was no more than the sign of a far-off change. The medical-moral test (the 'tendency to deprave and corrupt') was and would remain in place, while statutory recognition of the admissibility of expert evidence on literary merit was still thirty years away.[4]

The case of Lawrence's pictures thus reveals both continuities and transformations in the legal regulation of obscenity at the beginning of this century. Continuities, in that – still caught between a 'public' metaphorics of dangerous substances and places and a 'private' pathologisation of the sexual body – publicly accessible erotic displays remained a recognisable social harm. Transformations, in that – redeployed as part of an aesthetic practice of self-cultivation – the same erotica were in the process of acquiring educative and ethical functions and, thereby, pedagogical defenders in the forms of literary experts and teachers. Moving at a tangent across the existing boundaries of the pornographic and the educative, establishing new relations between the harmful and the aesthetic, Lawrence's work is indicative of the unstable space into which in 1959 a new Obscene Publications Act emerged.

THE OBSCENE PUBLICATIONS ACT 1959

The historical ambivalence of the Obscene Publications Act of 1959 has already been noted. By retaining the 'tendency to deprave and corrupt' test, albeit in a somewhat qualified form, the Act perpetuates the nineteenth-century mechanism which made deviation from a medical-moral norm a legally sanctionable social harm. Yet even as it does this, the Act also recognises the new relations between sexuality and serious or educative literature by making statutory provision for literary and aesthetic merit to override obscenity. This provision is deemed to protect the public good. Expert testimony is allowed on the matter of literary merit, but not on the matter of the obscenity of the publication in question, this being for the jury alone to decide.

The legislation is thus characterised by an unstable interaction between the residues of sexual medicine and moral psychology and, on the other hand, the norms of aesthetic education. This is not the picture of a neat supercession of the former by the latter, but of a rather messy tension between continuity and change. Nevertheless, with the Obscene Publications Act 1959 – which, significantly, Sir Alan Herbert wished to name the Defence of Literature Act – law about obscenity was for the first time set on a statutory basis, thus demonstrating the resolve of a Parliament moved, by the pressures of liberal reform, to put limits on the common law principle by which English judges could use the law of obscene libel to punish actions

Twentieth-Century English Obscenity Law

which they found contrary to public morality. In this sense it was the end of an episode in English legal history beginning with Curll's case in 1727. There is a certain pleasure at the notion of a statute whose aim was to protect literary works from prosecution for obscenity being instrumental in curbing the common law's traditional role of preserving public morality. More important, however, is the need to describe the hybrid character of the 1959 Act, a character which indicates something of the internal variations and discontinuities of the regulatory field of obscenity law, divided between a traditional socio-medical policing and a newer aesthetic and pedagogic norm of self-regulation. As commentators have observed, when taken together, retention of the 'tendency to deprave and corrupt' test (section 1) and inclusion of a new aesthetic test to determine whether publication of the work is in the public good (section 4) make for historical doubling and theoretical incoherence. Reviewing the law in the late 1970s, the Williams Committee found

> a widespread sympathy for the idea that works of literary or artistic merit should not be liable to suppression, but many witnesses were uneasy about the way the [1959] Act tries to bring this about. Needless to say, many pointed out to us the assumption embodied in the present law, which they found extraordinary, that there could be a work which tended to deprave and corrupt those who read it, but that, at the same time, it was for the public good that the work be published – as though it was for the public good that readers be depraved and corrupted, so long as it was by art.
>
> (Williams Report, 1979, p. 15)

Others have slated the lawmakers for their alleged failure to express in legislation the 'true' view of pornography and the 'proper' – that is, the aesthetic – mode of regulating it:

> During the legislative gestation of section 1 a carefully elaborated concept of obscenity was wrecked by a misguided affection for a nineteenth-century formula. The new section 1 was an abortion: it contained one aspect of aesthetic value (the dominant effect on likely readers) but not the other (the intrinsic merit). The value of a work was to be considered from two perspectives, at two artificially but rigidly separated stages, and courts were debarred from assessing merit when deciding an article's effect on its likely readers. Instead of one clause enabling a court to weigh all aspects of the publication in one decision, the two-tier approach

set up an illogical and unworkable dichotomy between 'obscenity' and 'artistic merit'. The first stage defined obscenity by reference to the dominant effect of actual publication on the minds of likely readers, and the second required a balance of that supposedly harmful effect against the intrinsic merit of the work, irrespective of the circumstances of publication. A book's contribution to literature was not a factor in assessing its obscenity, but rather a 'justification' for the publication of a provenly obscene book. The result was a half-baked decision on 'obscenity' under section 1, and then a halfbaked decision on 'public good' under section 4, followed by acute judicial indigestion as both commodities were swallowed at once. The rigid distinction between 'section 2 [*sic*] effect' and 'section 4 intrinsic merit' committed the law to an intellectual confusion which contributed more than anything else to its uncertain and unacceptable operation for the next two decades.

(Robertson, 1979, p. 163)

Rather than mere 'intellectual confusion', the co-presence of the two different 'tests' – the medical-moral test for a social harm and the aesthetic test for literary merit – is the sign that this law was constructed across two different yet historically overlapping specifications of pornography.

From these two specifications emerged two quite different approaches to the regulation of pornography. The central issue is to determine how – compared with the earlier medical and moral test – the new aesthetic test for obscenity negotiates the relation between law and norm. This relation is pivotal for any reconstruction of the history of the role of obscenity law in the regulation of pornography. In Chapter 3, we underscored how law and police functioned jointly, but not identically, as regulatory apparatuses which understood themselves to be based on a medical norm – the moral and physical harm known to be caused by the exposure of the vulnerable person to obscene material. This norm – transposed into specifically legal form in the 'tendency to deprave and corrupt' test – cannot be reduced to an archaic 'nineteenth-century formula'. The test is the product of a complex but unplanned overlapping of the normative and the legal. In the first instance, this involved a balancing of the law's relatively undifferentiated application of the medical-moral norm with that norm's more local and variable applications in the routine policing of the streets.[5] However, the 'deprave and corrupt' test also signals the persistence of the nineteenth-century mode of regulating pornography by a medical, moral and hygienic differentiation and management of individuals and populations in their different locales. In short, rather than with a 'formula', we are dealing with a network of specialist knowledges, the institutions and agencies through which they have been operationalised, and the forms of life which they have made possible.

Can something similar be said of the aesthetic test which gained statutory existence in the 1959 Act? If so, this would help explain why even in its new and partly aesthetic orientation the law retains its older component of harm and condemnation, but with the important difference that harm is now defined in aesthetic terms as the damage done by 'failed art' to ethically immature persons. With such a definition, the nineteenth-century medical-moral sciences give way to the aesthetic, educative and therapeutic disciplines which, as we shall show, have constituted the mid-twentieth-century infra-legal domain to which obscenity law has turned for support.

There is a further qualification. When an aesthetically-oriented commentator such as Robertson (1979) assumes that legal judgement should be based on 'the intrinsic merit' of the work, is he not in fact seeking to transmute – into the generality of a law – a local norm which finds its application in the self-fashioning practised in advanced aesthetic circles when those equipped with the necessary skills read sexual descriptions as ethical recipes? Whether or not this is so, the move from the medical to the aesthetic framework is likely to prove a move from one normative domain to another, not an escape from norm-based judgement altogether.

The aesthetic test which the 1959 statute introduced into English obscenity law has four key provisions: that the work shall be taken as a whole; that it shall be considered relative to its effects on its likely readers; that a public good defence is available for works deemed obscene in fact; and that the mechanism of trial by jury is foregrounded.

The Work Taken As A Whole

[A]n article shall be deemed to be obscene if its effect or (where the article comprises two or more distinct items) the effect of any one of its items is, if taken as a whole, such as to tend to deprave and corrupt.

(Obscene Publications Act 1959, Section 1 (1))

Before 1959, convictions could be secured by citing isolated purple passages out of the context established by the work as a whole. This tactic had about it something of the instrumental certainty of the 'pubic hair' criterion, since the mere appearance of a four-letter word or a single reference to sexual acts could damn a work. Thus in a 1928 appeal to Quarter Sessions by the publishers of *The Well of Loneliness*, Sir Thomas Inskip for the Crown alleged that the 'whole book, as to ninety-nine hundredths of it may be beyond criticism, yet one passage may make it a work which ought to be destroyed as obscene' (in St John-Stevas, 1956, pp. 102–3).

The new requirement in the 1959 Act that the effect of the work be considered only as a whole certainly derived from moves to protect literature from such selective quotation. The first draft of the Bill in fact required the Court to consider 'the general character and dominant effect' of the work. Concern with the essential unity of literary texts, that is with the work taken as a whole, was a longstanding feature of Romantic aesthetics concurrently being reactivated by the New Criticism. It was not, therefore, a simple widening of the scope of evidence that was in question; it was the admission of a new kind of expertise to the ritual of judgement.

The Work Considered Relative To Its Effects On Its Likely Readers

[P]ersons who are likely, having regard to all relevant circumstances, to read, see or hear the matter contained in it . . .

(Obscene Publications Act 1959, Section 1 (1))

With the new statute, arguments that a work was inherently obscene became statutorily inadmissible since obscenity was now recognised to be relative to a definite category of persons, that is 'persons who are likely . . . to read' the article. For Robertson (1979, p. 55), the 'need to ascertain the target audience in prosecutions under the 1959 Act effects the most important shift in emphasis from the common-law definition, which looked not to the likely readership, but to the impact of the article on the most vulnerable members of society'. In fact something of a modern myth is at work here. In Chapter 3, we argued that obscenity has been relative *from the start*. As for the nineteenth-century pornographic field, the fact of different channels of dissemination, different sites of sale, was taken to be relevant to the issue of the obscenity or otherwise of publications. Moreover, by virtue of price or mode of marketing, potentially obscene works could be deemed *not* to be directed at the 'most vulnerable'. As such, they were in effect declared non-harmful relative to their specific destinations and circumstances of use. In other words, 'most vulnerable' carried both an inclusive and an exclusive sense. Sensitivity to the differentiation of cultural milieus and their populations was not, therefore, lacking in the nineteenth-century policing of pornography. In 1868 the *Hicklin* judgement had recognised the differential organisation of legal-cultural space, *The Confessional Unmasked* being 'sold at the corners of streets'. Or again, to repeat the exemplary police opinion expressed in 1900 on the circumstances of circulation of the *Heptameron*: 'If it had been in a library to which students had access, no one would deny that the book was properly there and properly kept for a proper use'.

A Defence Of Public Good, Providing For Expert Evidence To Be Given On Artistic, Literary And Scientific Merit.

(1) A person shall not be convicted of an offence against Section Two of this Act, and an order for forfeiture shall not be made under the foregoing section, if it is proved that publication of the article in question is justified as being for the public good on the ground that it is in the interests of science, literature, art or learning, or of other objects of general concern.

(2) It is hereby declared that the opinion of experts as to the literary, artistic, scientific or other merits of an article may be admitted in any proceedings under this Act either to establish or to negative the said ground.

(Obscene Publications Act 1959, Section 4)

The dual requirement that a work be considered as a whole and relative to its likely readers is the concrete mode in which an aesthetic criterion establishes itself within obscenity law. With the provision for a defence of public good and for expert literary testimony, this new deployment of aesthetic norms confirmed its juridical standing.[6] This was a striking advance for aesthetic pedagogy into territory previously held by the moral-medical disciplines.

There had been earlier signs of movement in this direction. However, back in 1928, the prosecution of Jonathan Cape for publication of *The Well of Loneliness* gave warning that expert testimony was admissible only where artistic merit is concerned. On the prior question of whether the prosecuted work has a tendency to deprave and corrupt, expert evidence is not admitted, at least in theory, since this is the question of fact that only the magistrate or jury can decide. According to the 1959 Act, it is for expert witnesses to tell a jury that the work before them – once its obscenity has been established – is highly valued by the literary establishment, if such is the case. Socio-psychological researches into the effects of pornography on readers – for instance research showing or disproving correlations between exposure to sexual writing and criminal behaviour, or research arguing for some form of therapeutic benefit – have typically been excluded from both the legal determination of fact and the public good determination. Matters are thus arranged so as to preserve the jury's role in deciding the question to which Section 1 of the Act is directed: does the work have a tendency to deprave and corrupt a certain category of reader? Psychological and sociological researches into pornography's alleged causal powers – or lack thereof – have served to sustain the debate, not to terminate it, as we shall see in later chapters.

The Role Of The Jury

The 1959 Act foregrounds the function of the jury in obscenity trials. What for the Obscene Publications Act of 1857 was a point of distant recourse – the ceremony of trial by jury – moved to centre stage in the mid-twentieth-century legislation, bringing with it an archaic ritual for staging community judgement. The mix of contemporary aesthetic expertise and jury trial ceremonial is a sign of the patchwork character of obscenity law in general and of the 1959 Act in particular.

For some, the jury is the appropriate agent to decide obscenity cases, given that the matter is one of the community standards. For others, such a preference is anachronistic, as indeed is the whole conceptual edifice of the 1959 Act with its reliance – through the jury mechanism – on vague entities such as 'community standards' and folk beliefs which can neither rationally know nor themselves be rationally known: 'At the outset, one is faced with an archaic statutory definition, perhaps even an archaic basic concept, and a cumbersome law which prevents the reception of evidence which would undercut the very basis of the provisions themselves' (Bates, 1978, p. 264). The tension between jury and expert underscores the point hat obscenity law has been stretched, in historical terms, across the distance between law and norm. In the nineteenth century the norm in question is medical and moral in character. For the 1959 Act, the norm towards which part of the law is oriented is aesthetic, even though the older medical-moral norm is not yet fully displaced.

THE TRIAL OF *LADY CHATTERLEY'S LOVER*

Though both were 'test cases', the 1960 prosecution involving D. H. Lawrence's *Lady Chatterley's Lover* displays certain differences from the nineteenth-century case concerning *The Confessional Unmasked*.[7] First, the more recent case involves a serious literary work. Second, in 1960, the court's attention was directed centrally to the issue of the redeeming aesthetic character of the work in question. In *Hicklin*, the concern was whether or not an act of obscene publication could be said to have taken place, given the publisher's and seller's 'good intentions'. Third, the Penguin case received the full ceremonial of trial by jury. Obscenity was to be the focal point of a national ritual in which the community would be invoked – juridically – to speak on the limits of sexual expression in that national culture.

These differences are in part related to the exchange which had taken place between the genre of the educative novel and that of pornographic fiction, and to the subsequent deployment of erotic writing for pedagogic uses. Between the time of *Hicklin* and that of *Regina* v. *Penguin Books Ltd.*, the character of novelistic truth and its use in the education of the self had radically altered. It is therefore worth recalling the medical and pornographic origins of Lawrence's literary personages, including his sodomitic lovers, and the aestheticisation of such figures for the purposes of a specialised ethical exercise. The law too, at least to an extent, had prepared itself to deal with this new mode of serious educative literature. The preamble to the 1959 Act explicitly records as one of its three objectives: 'to provide for the protection of literature'. This objective is to be realised by the provisions just discussed: the work is to be considered as a whole; the work is to be considered in relation to its likely readership; a public good defence can be offered – based on testimony by literary experts – which, if successful, would override the fact of the work's obscenity.

Our account of *Regina* v. *Penguin Books Ltd.* will stand somewhat apart from the predominant approach to the trial.[8] This treats Penguin Books' acquittal as a landmark in the liberalisation of literary representation of sexuality, a 'turning point in the fight for literary freedom' (Robertson, 1979, p. 128). As such, the trial has been celebrated as a sign of the maturation of British Society, a triumph of the jury system and the (British) vox populi (Morpurgo, 1979, pp. 318–9). Given this approach, the trial has become the object of anniversary celebrations, including a dramatised reconstruction for television. However, this happy approach has not been shared by another, predominantly feminist, viewpoint. Indeed, as we shall show in Chapter 7, many feminists have seen the processes and judgements of obscenity law as legitimating and protecting sexist representations of women – including the male tradition of erotic and emancipatory writing within which Lawrence's works have been canonised, and where only sexist (rather than sexual) representations have been formed. For our part, neither celebrating nor denouncing obscenity law, we shall attempt to describe its shifting coordinates as these are revealed in the 1960 trial, paying particular attention to the aestheticisation of the law, and to the tensions which result for the specification of obscenity.

One new coordinate, as we have seen, is the requirement that the work be 'taken as a whole' and not in de-contextualised extracts. With this requirement, the court becomes the site of competing readings of the work, and must draw the boundary of pornography and literature by determining the character of the publication as a whole. This is a far cry from identifying deviations – the public display of pubic hair or the public utterance of taboo words – from a known and well-practised medical-moral norm. Just where such a boundary could be set had become uncertain, above all in the circumstance where a publisher would print, and be ready to distribute, 200 000 copies of a work such as *Lady Chatterley's Lover*. According to a Penguin spokesperson, it seems that the 'classic' status which had posthumously descended on Lawrence, the fact that the work contained no words that had not been previously and freely published, and the becoming law of a Bill explicitly for the protection of literature led the company to suspect nothing by way of imminent prosecution (Morpurgo, 1979, pp. 316–17).

As to the procedural guidelines that organised the trial, the provisions of the 1959 Act meant that it was for the prosecution to prove the work obscene, and for the defence to prove that – even if obscene – the work has a redeeming literary merit which justifies its publication as being in the public good. As to the level of proof required, Gerald Gardiner for the defence put it as follows:

> [W]here the Prosecution has to establish something in a criminal case the burden which rests on them is to satisfy a Jury beyond reasonable doubt: *where the Defence have to discharge some burden of proof it is a lesser burden, it is the burden of satisfying a Jury on a mere balance of probabilities.*
>
> (Rolph, 1961, p. 175)

The two issues of obscenity and public good thus required different standards of proof. The 1960 trial also departed from the order of speech usual in criminal trials, allowing the defence to open before the jury retired to read the book, rather than having heard only the prosecution's opening and presentation of supporting evidence. This pattern has been followed in subsequent obscenity trials.

There were also important rulings on evidence. To an extent, these rulings defined the scope of the expert testimony on the 'literary, artistic, scientific or other merits' of the article. In the strict sense, the Act allowed expert testimony only on these 'merits'. In practice, the conduct of the experts led the judge, Mr Justice Byrne, to attempt some general points on conditions for evidence about the public good and about the obscenity of the work in question:

[E]vidence can be called, quite plainly, by the defendant – expert evidence as to the literary merits of the book – but those witnesses cannot be asked to solve the question as to whether publication of the book is justified as being for the public good. That is a question for the Jury and not a question for witnesses to determine. (p. 112)

The Judge further ruled that the experts could not testify on the matter of whether or not the work was obscene, that is, whether the book had 'a tendency to deprave and corrupt . . . those persons who are likely, having regard to all relevant circumstances, to read, see or hear' the matter contained in it. That too was an issue which the jury had to determine for itself. Further limitation was on the scope of expert testimony: experts could not advise on the calculation to be made when literary merit is balanced against obscenity. Expert testimony is therefore inadmissible on the comparative obscenity of the work in question. Reference to other works found obscene is not allowed, nor to the intention of the author not to write an obscene work. On the other hand, expert evidence on other works and authorial intention is permissible provided that it relates to literary merit. In short, as the Judge indicates in his summing-up, the evidence of obscenity is 'the book itself', not the testimony of experts (p. 202).

The logic of these rulings is clear enough, and certainly they provide a formal definition of the limitations of the expert testimony and of the area of the jury's responsibility. In practice, the judge failed to impose these limitations. Given the terms of then current literary critical discourse and the apparent urge of those who spoke as literary experts to speak of everything, this failure was perhaps inevitable. Less so was Mr Justice Byrne's failure to impose a two-stage judgement, as required by the Act, whereby first a decision is reached as to the obscenity of the work, the matter of its possible literary merit only then being made an issue of determination by the court.

Evident difficulty confronts a jury which has to judge the character of a work as a whole representation and classify it as obscene and suppressible or obscene but publishable in the public good, all the time adjusting the precise placement of the boundary between pornography and art. Little wonder that the court became a literary seminar where aesthetic pedagogy takes on the full weight of the judicial ritual: 'Long passages were read out . . . in a court which was hushed by the sheer strength, previously unrecognised by many now listening, of Lawrence's writing' (p. 84). This is not an activity for which the jury is necessarily equipped, yet it is the jury that must negotiate the exchange between norm and law, without ceasing to speak for the community who condemn and punish, or exculpate.

The aestheticisation of obscenity law can be directly traced from the forms of argument preferred by the 'thirty-five distinguished men and women of letters, moral theologians, teachers, publishers, editors and critics' called by the defence (p. 4). Some but by no means all of the experts could claim an institutional status by formal membership of an accredited 'corps' of academic specialists; others lacked an institutional guarantee of this sort. Aided by the judge's failure to insist upon a strict prior determination of the work's obscenity, their testimony – supposedly on the literary merit of *Lady Chatterley's Lover* – slipped irresistibly into assertions of its non-obscenity.

It is appropriate to ask just what is the specialist 'knowledge' that we call literary expertise. Indeed, although habitually depicted as a buffoon by liberal celebrants of the case (Rolph, 1961; Morpurgo, 1979; Robertson, 1979), the Prosecuting Counsel, Mr Griffith-Jones, posed the question of what such experts 'know' in a way that was not buffoonish. His cross-examination of Anne Scott-James makes the point:

'Please don't think that I am being rude about this. You run, do you not, or are responsible for, the ladies' page in some newspaper?' – 'No.'
'Or were?' – 'Some time ago, yes. Ladies' page is not the phrase we use now. It is very old fashioned; it has not been used since 1927.'
'Fashion page?' – 'Women's page, not fashion.'
'Called?' – 'It was called "Anne Scott-James's Page".'
'Is that what you run now?' – 'No, I am a freelance writer now.'
'Still on that type of subject?' – 'Writing about family problems and children, mostly, and controversial topics of the hour.'
'I only have this question – as I say, please don't think I am intending to be rude, but evidence as to the literary merit of this book is confined to experts – I only wondered, do you claim any particular qualifications to be a literary expert?' – 'I think I do, yes.'
'What?' – 'Of a popular kind.'
'What?' – 'Well, I was a classical scholar at Somerville College, Oxford.'
'Not every classical scholar at Somerville College, Oxford, is a literary expert?' – 'No. It isn't a negligible qualification though.'
'I couldn't agree with you more . . . ' – 'I was brought up in a very literary family.'
'But apart from the qualifications you have mentioned, you have no other

qualification such as might put you in the category of a literary expert?'
– 'Not the same as a reviewer has, no.'

(Rolph, 1961, pp. 102–3)

So, what is it that allows an Anne Scott-James to speak as an 'expert' on literature? How can Cecil Day-Lewis, speaking as a 'literary expert', comment on what an 'averagely sexed woman' is like (p. 134)? What equips a twenty-year old Cambridge English graduate, just beginning her first novel, to comment on 'industrial civilisation' (p. 150)? What precisely qualifies a witness to know that *Lady Chatterley's Lover* demonstrates 'all that makes sex human' (p. 172)? Many other such formulations could be cited, all the while with the reminder that those statements were made under the relatively strict and formal conditions for expert evidence as to literary merit given under Section 4 of the Obscene Publications Act of 1959.[9] And even where the expert has the credential of an academic post in a university department of English, we cannot help wondering just what it is that allows a literary critic – Raymond Williams – not only to be asked but also unhesitatingly to answer a question such as the following: 'It has been said that these descriptions are always emphasizing pleasure, satisfaction and sensuality. Do you agree that that is wrong, in a true sexual relationship between two people on a permanent basis?' (p. 117). When aesthetics and literary criticism were in effect being granted statutory standing as legally recognised expertise by the 1959 Act, it is unlikely that questions were asked as to the precise content of and qualifications in this 'knowledge'. It is even more unlikely that they could have been answered. What was envisaged was doubtless someone able to furnish objective and authoritative evidence as to the standing and merit of a work, not a band of individuals who without a moment's hesitation would testify as expert on the 'deadness' of industrial civilisation and on the 'sensibility' of the 'averagely sexed woman'.[10]

We must remember the novelty of the circumstances of the 1960 trial, in which considerable expectations of a new cultural order were invested by many of those involved. With the admission of the testimony of literary experts, together with the full ritual of trial by jury, the courtroom became the site of a definitive contest between competing claims to know the nature and effects not only of obscenity but also of works of literary merit. What the court in fact received was not a set of statements drawing on an expert knowledge. It was, rather, a vivid practical demonstration of how to be a full-blown aesthetic personality, a demonstration of the use of aesthetic *techniques* of ethical self-fashioning, including a stunning capacity to poetically deepen any sexual description, however pornographic.

A battery of interpretive procedures was deployed by the witnesses. First, there was placement of the work in the authorial *œuvre*. While Section 2(4) of the 1959 Act specifically excludes evidence for or against the work in question that makes reference to other obscene publications, it was ruled in *Penguin Books* that on the matter of literary merit other works could be referred to as evidence. Thus the literary experts had recourse to the syllogistic procedure of citing other works by Lawrence, establishing a Lawrence *œuvre*, then placing *Lady Chatterley's Lover* in it. Raymond Williams, for example, testified that *Lady Chatterley's Lover* 'is one of Lawrence's four major works, the others being the three novels *Sons and Lovers, The Rainbow* and *Women in Love*. I think *Lady Chatterley's Lover* is clearly a book of that substance and would be ranked with those other three' (Rolph, 1961, p. 133). This representation of a Lawrence literary *œuvre* and the placement therein of *Lady Chatterley's Lover* appears to have functioned successfully as a means of retrieving the novel from an alternative obscene Lawrence *œuvre* of banned works and damaging anecdotes about the author's personal life. This cultural ploy had already found its commercial counterpart in Penguin Books' plan to publish the paperback edition of *Lady Chatterley's Lover*, along with the other Lawrence novel – *Women in Love* – not previously issued by them, in the form of a Lawrence 'million': ten titles each printed in 100 000 copies. Publication of these titles on this scale is, in demographic terms, an index of the vastly expanded educative and curricular use of such literature.[11]

Second, the work was placed in the canon of great literature. This procedure involved invoking or constructing a canon of the major works and authors of English literature as the proper setting for the Lawrence *œuvre*, now including *Lady Chatterley's Lover*. During the trial, the jury – through the mediation of work in questions – thus found itself in the presence of the *Bible, The Canterbury Tales, Hamlet, Paradise Lost* and *Ulysses*. In the sphere of authorial signatures, Lawrence was joined to Hardy, George Eliot, Austen and Fielding (Rolph, 1961, p. 67); Hardy again, and Conrad (p. 75); Bunyan and Blake (p. 99); Galsworthy and Bennett (p. 136); Woolf, Joyce, Conrad again, and Forster (p. 139). Alongside the litany of signatures, another procedure involved the representation of a patriotic cultural 'tradition' into which Lawrence and his novel could be placed. For Richard Hoggart (pp. 99–100) 'the tradition of British puritanism' does service, although of course without the slightest reference to the complicity of Puritanism and the intensification of personal and erotic concerns to which we have referred. That these canonical allocations have no universal truth is demonstrated by the quite different canon in which the same novel gets placed in histories of obscenity, not in the class of works signed 'Lawrence', nor in the great 'tradition of British puritanism' but alongside other obscene publications: *Venus in the Cloister, The Lustful Turk, The Confessional Unmasked, Lady Bumtickler's Revels, The Quintessence of Birch Discipline*, and so on. The content of the canon appears to vary with the purpose of the canonisation (Saunders, 1982).

A third procedure involved the investment of authorial intention. The question of intention has exercised both legal and literary fields. We have already noted the limited conditions under which the 1959 Act admits evidence of authorial intention. In fact, a retrospective calculation of likely effect is the crucial factor. Once the effect of the work – a tendency to deprave and corrupt the persons who are 'likely . . . to read, see or hear the matter contained in it' – is established as fact, the intention to produce that effect is necessarily inferred. In the case of obscene publication, a limit is thus set to the usual requirement in criminal law to establish intent or *mens rea* as a crucial component of the crime (Smith and Hogan, 1972, pp. 569–72). Furthermore, this limit is set by a legal calculation of the socio-ethical effect of the work's dissemination which is quite unconcerned with the originary state of the author's soul or sensibility. In other words, criminal liability for obscene publication is a determinate artefact of legal reasoning; it neither derives from nor coincides with the literary hermeneutic procedures used to generate authorial intentionality as this is commonly understood in the sphere of literary studies.

Given the centrality in literary critical practice of the argument from authorial intention, the literary experts fail to surprise us by their reflex recourse to accounts of Lawrence's intention. Judge and Prosecution proved unable to curtail statements of this sort: 'neither in intention or effect is this book depraving' (Rolph, 1961, p. 64). Though inadmissible, such statements were a staple means of claiming the work for literature by investing sexual depictions with an authorial intention to have them serve a variety of laudable moral and aesthetic purposes, for example to assist 'the redemption of the individual, and hence of society, by what Lawrence calls "reciprocity of tenderness"' (p. 129). The imponderable relation between a calculation based on authorial intention and one based on social effects was left for the jury to decide.

Fourth, there was the procedure of poetic deepening, or allegorisation. The performance of allegorical readings allowed the experts to say what Lawrence really said in the novel. By allegorisation, depictions of sex were cleansed of any depraving and corrupting tendency and rewritten in terms of immaculate moral purpose. Rebecca West thus demonstrated to the court how to recognise thirteen detailed descriptions of sex as moments in 'a return of the soul to the more intense life' (Rolph, 1961, p. 67), this demonstration being sealed by reference to a founding intention whereby *Lady Chatterley's Lover* was said to have been 'designed from the first as an allegory'. The Prosecution in closing gave the following account of this procedure:

> Miss Rebecca West . . . was asked about the book and gave, you remember, a number of rather long answers to the questions that were put to her . . . 'The idea that the story is padding cannot be true; as a matter of fact the book has that story because it was designed from the start as an allegory. Behind the book the allegory which he intended was that here was a culture that has become sterile and unhelpful to man's deepest needs, and he wanted to have the whole of civilization realizing that it was not living fully enough, that it would be exploited in various ways if it did not try to get down to the springs of its being and live more fully, and bring its spiritual gifts into play. The baronet and his impotence are a symbol of the impotent culture of his time, and the love affair with the gamekeeper was a calling, a return of the soul to the more intense life that he felt when people had had a different culture, such as the cultural basis of religious faith.' I have no doubt [commented Griffith-Jones] that with the learning and reading that lies behind Miss Rebecca West she is capable of reading all that into this book, but I ask you, is that typical of the effect that this book will have upon the average reader, and all the more, the average young reader? Are they really going to see an allegory in the thing?
>
> (Rolph, 1961, pp. 188–9)

These questions too are for the jury to determine. But are there limits to such allegorisation? Or could no sexual depiction resist this aesthetico-ethical procedure of interpretation? Could such poetic deepening be attached to the specific depiction of the episode of anal intercourse between Mellors and Connie Chatterley? The Prosecution recognised the episode as perverse and obscene, and read it out (p. 195), but the act was not directly named. Rolph observes that 'this unexpected and totally unheralded innuendo visibly shocked some members of the Jury' (p. 195). Would the literal naming of what might still have registered as a perversion have triggered that not entirely superseded machinery founded on the medical-moral norm and preserved in the 'tendency to deprave and corrupt' test for obscenity? None of the expert witnesses demonstrated how to read a description of anal intercourse as an exercise in ethical self-completion. The courtroom, it seems, was not yet a sufficiently aestheticised locale for this to be done with composure.

The exculpatory allegorising skill in question is, of course, the property of a special category of persons, and not evenly distributed across that general community for which the jury speaks. Once the 1960 case was won – but perhaps only then – even those liberals who celebrated the decision to acquit Penguin Books as a triumph of the *vox populi* can be found proposing that obscenity cases 'should be tried only by ascertainably literate jurors', and asserting that 'since the introduction of "expert evidence" in obscenity trials it has certainly become apparent that an ordinary jury is not the best tribunal to determine the future of English Literature' (Rolph, 1969, p. 11). The proposal by John Calder, publisher of *Last Exit to Brooklyn* which was condemned at the Old Bailey in 1967, is particularly notable, given the pedagogical dissemination of the aesthetic use of pornography:

> In the new climate in which publishers and writers now find themselves, where highly complex literary concepts will be argued out in criminal courts, it is essential that the framers of the Obscene Publications Act should bring in a new provision that enables juries to be selected from those who have at least A-levels in their education and can show that they are capable of reading and understanding the book they have to judge.
>
> (in Rolph, 1969, p. 111)

Such notions of a 'special' jury and a 'special' literacy – both of course to be formed by the aesthetic discipline we have described – directly underscore the relative character of obscenity as recognised in the provision in section 1(1) of the 1959 Act concerning the 'likely' readerships of works in question. In keeping with this provision, in the 1960 trial, the Prosecution attempted to construct a particular readership for the work, referring to the 'average reader' and – more specifically – to the 'average young reader'. These categories lean backwards towards *Hicklin* but also forwards towards notions of 'variable obscenity' which we shall consider in Chapters 6 and 7. The grounds signalled for this tactic were Penguin Books' popular pricing (at 3s 6d) and massive print run in paperback. The Defence follows much the same tack, but trying to evade the problem of the moral vulnerability of the likely mass audience unskilled in ethical allegorisation of sexual descriptions. The reputation of Penguin as publisher of works of value at prices all literate persons could afford is emphasized:

> [I]n a work published at 3s. 6., you are to consider the question in relation to the general public and not some particular section. It is of importance that you should remember the former definition – and I mention this because again this is one of the things read out to you in opening – the

former definition which in addition to the words 'deprave or corrupt those into whose hands the work may fall', used the words 'and whose minds are open to such immoral influences'. Those words have been expressly and carefully omitted by Parliament from the new Statutory definition, so we are not to consider some particular type of person or particular group, but the general public.

(Rolph, 1961, pp. 176–7)

A problem arises here. The 'persons likely' clause of Section 1(1) was added as a limiting condition to assist in the protection of literary works. Certainly this is how commentators, for example Robertson (1979, pp. 54–9), have considered it. A clue to the Defence thinking is provided, however, by Rolph's editorial footnote to the passage cited: 'Neither the Judge nor Mr Griffith-Jones made any reference to this ingenious interpretation which, by logical extension would enable all the more esoteric obscenities to be sold at the lowest possible prices' (Rolph, 1961, p. 177n.). The logic in question would seem to be commercial.

In *Regina* v. *Penguin Books Ltd.* the success of the several literary procedures employed by the Defence witnesses cannot be inferred from the fact of acquittal, since it was not made clear whether the work was found to be not obscene, or found obscene but redeemed by literary merit. In fact, by the following decade, this distinction was itself on the way to becoming unthinkable. In 1979, the Williams Report would propose that the boundary between art and pornography be drawn in such a fashion that any *written* work, whatsoever its contents, would be immune from criminal prosecution, the whole regulatory apparatus having shifted such that it would in large part no longer involve the criminal law. Such proposals – exposed further in the next chapter – are additional signs that the medical-moral machinery established in the nineteenth century is losing power. In its place arises the aesthetic-pedagogical approach to the policing of pornography.

As an application of the Obscene Publications Act of 1959, the 1960 trial of *Lady Chatterley's Lover* shows this aestheticisation of the law under way. An aesthetic specification of obscenity now confronts the jury. But this new specification awkwardly overlaps the older – more habitual and commonsense – medical-moral specification of obscenity as a social harm directly threatening the vulnerable and, in consequence, as something to be punished rather than managed or treated. The 1959 Act and 1960 trial are properly described as hybrid and transitional cultural arrangements because they embody the tension between a hygienic and an aesthetic approach to the policing of pornography.

POLICED BY ART

In the next chapter we shall consider reformist arguments that the law should not concern itself with pornography, since what an individual reads and watches is properly a moral not a legal matter, a private not a public affair. The emergence of such arguments, in which what we have termed aesthetic pedagogy takes on the role of handling pornography without need of juridical buttressing, might seem to indicate a pure gain to aesthetics, as if the tension and ambivalence of the 1959 Act were well on the way to resolution. However, the exit of erotic expression from the field of legal regulation is not quite so straightforward.

In Chapter 3 we suggested that obscenity law's channelling of esoteric specialist pornography was a constitutive factor in the nineteenth-century literary field. In effect, the law contributed directly to the threshold which Lawrence – along with so many subsequent avantgarde aesthetes – claimed to transgress in the name of art, sex and truth. If erotic writing is decriminalised, no latter-day Lawrence could repeat that gesture. As the criminal law approaches a point of announcing its indifference to whatever writers write, because nothing written would meet the new 'non-art' or 'failed art' criterion demarcating literature from pornography, will avantgardes – mindless of the new role of aesthetic norms – continue to proclaim that all authentic literature is transgressive of law?

There is a further problem in assuming a pure gain to aesthetics and an absolute reduction of regulation. A theme of our later chapters is the ethical and disciplinary character of the aesthetic. It is precisely this, after all, which is demonstrated by witness after witness instructing the court in *Regina* v. *Penguin Books Ltd* on how to discipline the self by confronting the secret truth of sex and how to discipline sex by remembering, for instance, the 'tradition of British puritanism'. In this sense, the trial presented a powerful gallery of aesthetic disciplinarians, equipped with the techniques which we have catalogued. At stake is the capacity of the aesthetic to take on the infra-legal role of police, previously borne by moral medicine, but working now through pedagogy and therapy. Rather than the exit of the law from a space which it should never have occupied in the first place and the consequent emancipation of sexual expression from all regulation, there has been a mutation of the pornographic field towards regulation – legal and extra-legal – in accordance with an aesthetic disciplinary norm.

From this vantage point, the English Obscene Publications Act of 1959 does not appear a piece of *flawed* legislation. Its evident tension – the keeping of the medical norm expressed in the 'deprave and corrupt' test *and* the incorporation of the aesthetic norm embodied in the public good defence – are indicative not of logical contradiction and conceptual error but of the historically mixed character of the modern pornographic field.

POSTSCRIPT

Penguin Books has just reissued a Thirtieth Anniversary Commemorative Edition of C. H. Rolph's edited transcript of the 'trial of Lady Chatterley', adorned with a selection of cartoons and a new Foreword by Geoffrey Robertson (Rolph, 1990). For us this is a timely chance; for Robertson, a timeless truth. Nothing, it would seem, has changed in three decades of intense debate about pornography. The feminist denunciation of Lawrence as pornographer and campaigns for renewed recognition of pornography as capable of causing social harm might as well not have happened ('The damage that gets attributed to books is caused only by the actions of the people who try to suppress them', p. xxii). They leave no trace on the monolith of philosophical liberalism and the truth of 'literary emancipation'. An olympian moral certitude thus lets Robertson harness together an array of different social issues – homosexuality, abortion, free expression and, of course, Salman Rushdie's resistance to the decree of death by the late Ayatollah Khomeini for 'blasphemy' against Islam – in a global and undifferentiated opposition to 'censorship'.

Thirty years of retrospection have allowed Robertson some distance on the event of *Regina* v. *Penguin Books Ltd*, although what he proposes is not descriptive revision but partisan endorsement and applause. The trial has become an exemplary triumph, one to cement into the forensic canon. He would have us see in Gardiner's advocacy 'the best of modern barristering' (p. viii) while 'it would be a good test for students of advocacy to consider how they would have handled the brief for the Crown' (p. xi). Aside from these pedagogical retrievals and the usual smug mockery of the person of Mr Griffith-Jones – he alone is singled out for a charge of sexism – the only interesting shift discernible in Robertson's review is his apparent disenchantment with the jury system. Unlike the Penguin partisans of 1960 for whom the British jury was the *vox populi* through which History itself had spoken, this 1990 liberal has doubts about the capacity of juries to set public standards given, for instance, their very patchy record on protecting freedom of literary expression and their proven readiness not always to acquit in trials for obscenity.

Such patchiness – a corollary, we would suggest, of the uneven distribution of the cultural ability to perform aesthetic readings of sexually descriptive literature – earns Robertson's displeasure. Arch-liberal that he is, he claims to see through to the 'fundamental' opposition of 'literary emancipation' and 'censorship'. It is symptomatic of such a view that something even worse than the merely unreliable jury has appeared, namely the 'state' censor:

> What is most noticeable about this past decade is that the new breed of statutory censors who sit on the British Board of Film and Video Classification and the Broadcasting Standards Commission are establishment pillars who bear no resemblance to the jurors who acquitted the likes of *Lady Chatterley* and *Linda Lovelace*. Juries are no longer trusted to 'set public standards' – they have erred too often on the side of freedom of expression.
>
> (Robertson, 1990, p. xxi)

In the following chapters we shall see that the liberal conviction of a single great choice between the wholly free self-regulating individual conscience and the censorious police state is anything but an idiosyncrasy of Geoffrey Robertson. For the present, however, we hope to have shown that *Regina* v. *Penguin Books Ltd*, like the Obscene Publications Act of 1959, was more complex, contingent and interesting than is suggested by the triumphant liberal claim that the 1960 verdict was 'the first breach in the repressive dam of establishment hypocrisy' (p. xiv).

6 The Limits of Law Reform

THE REFORMING IMPULSE

The three decades following the 1959 Obscene Publications Act and the United States Supreme Court's *Roth* judgement of 1957 have witnessed major committees of enquiry into obscenity laws in both England and the United States, a welter of academic and jurisprudential argument for law reform, and – in the United States at least – some important changes to the law of obscenity. These decades have also been marked by growing uncertainty and division amongst those groups seeking reform. The programme to abolish the legal regulation of erotic literature, while allowing a restricted 'private' consumption of pornography, was an unambiguously good cause for liberals and radicals during the 1960s. But by the time the Williams Committee began to hear evidence in 1977 this was no longer the case. The liberal consensus on the harmless or beneficial nature of erotic representations had been undermined by the feminist exposure of the gender-specificity of their consumption and its undesirable consequences for women.

Today this split in the campaign to reform the law confronts us in the form of an impassable debate over whether the dissemination of erotic representations is 'harmful' or not. On one side of this dispute we find the depleted battalions of philosophical liberalism and liberal jurisprudence whose argument is that, because erotica causes no demonstrable harm to others, its consumption is a matter of private moral judgement outside the scope of the criminal law.[1] The opposing side is far less unified. The claim that (certain kinds of) erotica are the source of real harms, and should therefore be legally suppressible, runs through a variety of feminist, 'moralist', and conservative jurisprudential positions – albeit in widely differing versions.

Clearly, what is not in dispute here is the so-called 'harm condition' itself; that is, the principle formulated by Mill that the limits to the social coercion of individuals should be set by the condition of whether their actions are likely to cause harm to others. It is the argument of this chapter, however, that the harm condition cannot provide a general ground for reforming obscenity law, in either of the directions contended for.

The thesis supporting this argument will come as no surprise, given the perspective of the preceding chapters: the question of whether pornography is harmful or not is a thoroughly practical question, a matter inseparable from the historical disposition of a network of administrative calculations,

The Limits of Law Reform

ethical practices, aesthetic devices, social knowledges and disciplines. In Chapter 5 we argued that obscenity law is itself part of this network. Hence we must be sceptical of attempts to found the reform of obscenity law in a rational analysis lying beyond the network in which that law is practised; for example, in a philosophical or empirical analysis of the question of pornography's harms. In fact all such attempts are futile, given the inescapably practical and historical determination of the question of harm. It is this determination that sets the scope and limits of law reform.

In order to provide a *prima facie* justification for this way of proceeding it is necessary to scrutinise again the confidence with which philosophical and jurisprudential liberalism has assailed the existing law. This assault, it will be recalled, is directed at the *Hicklin* judgement and its qualified restatement in the 1959 Act. In its brief to report on law and policy on obscenity and film censorship, the Williams Committee provides a representative summary of the liberal critique:

> The implication of the *deprave* and *corrupt* test and of the judicial comments on it is clearly that for an article to be found obscene a court should be satisfied that it is likely to have some kind of deleterious effect on an individual even if the nature of the effect is hard to specify . . . It is on the basis of claiming those deleterious effects that the law is supposed to work. It is much less clear, however, that that is how the law works in practice. We noted the comments of Lord Wilberforce in *DPP v. Whyte* that although the words 'deprave and corrupt' appeared in Chief Justice Cockburn's formula they had in fact been largely disregarded in common law obscenity cases: the courts simply considered whether the publication was obscene in some everyday sense and the tendency to deprave and corrupt was presumed. Lord Wilberforce went on to say that the Obscene Publications Act 1959 had changed all this. However, we gained the clear impression from the evidence we received that much of the time the law has continued to work as Lord Wilberforce said it worked before 1959.
>
> (Williams Report, 1979, p. 10)

Williams goes on to locate the 'error' in the failure of *Hicklin* to discriminate between what is harmful and what is morally offensive: '[I]t is one thing to claim that a publication tends to deprave and corrupt, and a different thing to claim that it offends against current standards of what is acceptable' (p. 11). It is to this slippage between the truly harmful and the merely offensive that Williams traces the alleged moralism and paternalism of the law, its willingness to use the susceptibilities of the most vulnerable in order to legally impose a particular morality on the community at large. The same philosophical mistake is also blamed for the law's more recent failures and inconsistencies arising, so it is argued, from the attempt to apply an incoherent statute – the Obscene Publications Act 1959.

Parameters for reform of the existing law are derived fairly directly from this philosophical analysis. After arguing that the harm of obscenity cannot be demonstrated on independent (psychological and sociological) grounds (Chapter 6), Williams claims that it is the fact that some people are morally offended by it that causes them to object to the obscene. Offensiveness as an autonomous object of social regulation – or perhaps as a lesser species of the harm principle – warrants only the administrative restriction of access to pornography, not its criminal suppression (Chapter 7).

Offensiveness is in turn construed with the help of a particular concept of representation. Erotic publications which are offensive are so by virtue of the manner in which they represent 'real sex'. Finally, this offensive manner of erotic representation is itself specified with the help of the psycho-aesthetic differentiation of art from pornography (Chapter 8). Erotic representations are offensive when they transmit real sex in a transparent manner, without the distancing and cooling mediation of ideas, and with the single intention of sexual arousal. It is this non-aesthetic transparency of a class of erotic representations – together with their capacity to manifest properly private acts in public – that makes them offensive. Indeed, the Report contends (p. 99), it makes pornography strictly analogous to soliciting, which the Wolfenden Committee on prostitution and homosexuality had earlier proscribed as the limit of its liberalisation of private sexual conduct.

> Pornography crosses the line between private and public since it makes available in the form, for instance, of a photograph, some sexual act of a private kind and makes it available for a voyeuristic interest... The basic point that pornography involves by its nature some violation of lines between public and private is compounded when pornography not only exists for private consumption, but is publicly displayed. The original violation is then forced on the attention of those who have not even volunteered to be voyeurs. They are thus forced or importuned to see things which they do not think should be seen, and images are thrust into their mind which they reject. Whatever may be true of the willing consumer, pornography is straightforwardly offensive to those who do not want to take it in.
>
> (Williams Report, 1979, p. 97)

The Limits of Law Reform 165

It is here, at the level of publicly displayed 'photographic' pornography, that liberalism has established the threshold of offensiveness. Across this controlled border previously illegal materials will be permitted to migrate to the bedroom, the closed-front adult book-shop and the restricted-access cinema.

It is not difficult to detect the three intersecting coordinates that govern the liberal analysis of the law and programme for its reform. The first of these coordinates is provided by the *harm condition* itself. In a rhetorical manoeuvre which stakes the claim of philosophical liberalism to the territory of jurisprudence, Mill's harm principle has been invoked to impose on court-made obscenity law a general ethical and political limit to its intervention in individual conduct. If the consumption of obscene publications causes no harm to others then it is beyond legal prohibition; however, a lesser version of the harm principle might restrict the scope of this consumption if it proves to be offensive to others.

The second coordinate is the *privacy or autonomy of individual moral judgement*. Where the freedom of the individual conscience stops, there and only there, at the limit set by the harm condition, the law (and other forms of social coercion) begins. The individual's conduct should only be constrained by rational argument and persuasion, according to a deeply embedded doctrine that social progress is ultimately dependent on the free reasoning subject. It is for this reason that philosophical liberalism and liberal jurisprudence privilege individual rights and freedoms, whenever they come into conflict with the policing of crime, health, manners and decency introduced by nineteenth-century governmental liberalism.

The third coordinate is a concept of *representation*, ultimately derived from Romantic aesthetics and psychology. If obscenity is not actually harmful that is because it consists of ideas and representations. What people object to as obscenity – so the argument goes – is in fact aesthetically deficient erotic representation, in other words pornography. A representation is deficient either because it transmits real sex in a direct and unmediated manner ('naive') or because it displaces real sex altogether with a tendentious and overwrought erotic fantasy ('sentimental'). In either case, apparently, the absence of the appropriate reconciliation of experience and fantasy, drive and norm, allows pornography to breach the line between private and public, coerce the imagination of the reasoning subject – transforming him into the Williams Report's 'unwilling voyeur' – and thereby open itself to restriction as offensive (although remaining immune from criminal prohibition).

On the basis of these three coordinates the liberal reform campaign has theorised the alleged failure of *Hicklin*-based law and given birth to a variety of proposals for replacing the crime of obscene publication with some system of restricted access to 'explicit' pornography. It is important to observe, however, that what the liberal campaign has produced is not a single set of statements about obscenity but a discursive domain inside which a variety of (sometimes conflicting) statements about pornography can be made. This is the domain in which the legality of pornography is routinely discussed in terms of its fit with the harm condition, the moral autonomy or privacy of the reasoning subject, and its problematic qualification as a class of aesthetically deficient erotic representations.

The scope and power of this domain is such that many feminist arguments fall within it, despite their ostensible anti-liberalism. For example, in arguing for a new type of legal regulation of pornography, Andrea Dworkin (1981) and Susanne Kappeler (1986) invoke the harm condition – metaphorically equating pornography with rape – as a general ground of legal intervention. They also specify pornography as an aesthetically deficient representation of real sex – one whose 'didactic' subservience to male fantasy overwhelms the experience of sex and leads to the objectification and subordination of women. And if on this basis they seek to restrict the scope of male freedom, this is only to enlarge the freedom of women. The following remarks are representative:

> The reproduction of women in images makes woman-images ever more exotic and remote – remote from any real experience of women. Women starve themselves to death in an attempt to force their bodies to correspond to the surreal body-shapes designed by the fashion designers. They kill their own experience in an attempt to conform to existences imaged for them. The images and ideals are getting ever more exotic and remote.
>
> (Kappeler, 1986, pp. 79–8)

Our concern with the liberal analysis of obscenity law is, therefore, not so much with any particular version of it as with the field of intelligibility in which its various versions have appeared.

REAL LIBERALISM

To bring ourselves up against the limits of this domain of discourse we can briefly consider a case brought before the High Court of Australia in 1956, on appeal from the Supreme Court of Queensland. In *Transport Publishing Co.* v. *The Literature Board of Review*, the Queensland Literature Board of Review had prohibited the appellant company (and a group of similar companies) from distributing a series of periodical 'love comics' – variously entitled *Real Love, Romance Story, Real Story, Real Romances* and *Love Experiences* – on the grounds that they were objectionable within the terms of the Objectionable Literature Act 1954 (Q). The case is significant for us because this Act embodies a modified version of the *Hicklin* test, construing 'objectionable' in the following way:

> In relation to literature or any part of any literature, regard being had to the nature thereof, the persons, classes of persons, and age groups to or amongst whom that literature is or is intended to be or is likely to be distributed and the tendency of that literature or part to deprave or corrupt any such persons (notwithstanding that persons in other classes or age groups may not be similarly affected thereby), objectionable for that it –
> (i) Unduly emphasises matters of sex, horror, crime, cruelty or violence; or (ii) Is blasphemous, indecent, obscene, or likely to be injurious to morality; or (iii) Is likely to encourage depravity, public disorder, or any indictable offence; or (iv) Is otherwise calculated to injure the citizens of this State.
>
> (*Transport Publishing Co* v. *The Literature Board of Review*, p. 111)

We might expect this case to display the moralism and paternalism presumed to flow from *Hicklin*'s 'confusion' of harm with offensiveness or, perhaps, the beginnings of the inconsistent judgements of jurists attempting to evade the confusion without a clear alternative.

In fact neither of these deficiencies is apparent in the decision of the High Court. The Court found by a majority of three to two that the publications were not objectionable within the meaning of the Act. But if in the judgement of the dissenting minority we fail to find the moralistic conversion of personal offence to social harm, then neither in the majority judgement in favour of the appellant company do we find any uncertainty regarding the appropriateness of the *Hicklin*-based law. The relation between the two opposed judgements does not obey the historical analysis projected by liberalism. As in most cases based on *Hicklin*, the issue that divided the minority and majority opinions was not the nature of the publications *per se* (about which they were in broad agreement) but the nature of the likely audience, in particular its susceptibility to erotic corruption and depravity.

Consider in this regard, the remarks in dissent of Justice McTiernan who, in specifying the nature of the likely audience, reproduced Justice Mansfield's summary of the evidence heard on this matter before the Full Court of Queensland:

Mansfield S. P. J. made a sufficient and correct view of this evidence, which I adopt. 'The evidence of the witnesses who swore affidavits and who were cross-examined at the hearing' (I enclose their names in brackets), 'leads me to the conclusion that the persons, classes of persons, and age group amongst whom the subject literature is or is likely to be distributed consist of the following – 1. A group of unstable female adolescents (Dr Stafford). 2. Adolescent girls between fourteen and eighteen years of age who have been committed to the Salvation Army Girls Industrial Home at Brisbane, most of whom were committed for offences of a sexual nature, and particularly those who were below average intelligence, emotionally unstable or irresponsible (Matron Gedes). 3. A group of psychopathic adolescent girls, corresponding to group No. 1 (Dr Matchett). 4. Normal persons, both adolescents and adults, of average intelligence (Dr McGeorge). 5. Females 'in their late teens' or any age, actually, above that, married women and the 'not so young', excluding middle aged women (Allen Thomas Stacey). 6. Senior office girl class, many of whom are married women (Aubrey Imrie Panton). 7. Young men aged twenty years or upwards, of average intelligence and education (John Wallace Metcalfe)'. (p. 123)

No doubt such a list appears quaint enough at this distance. Still, what we find here is not some ideological *ignus fatus* under whose cover a purely moral affront is attempting to impose itself as law in the guise of a calculation of social harms. Instead, we catch a glimpse of that infra-legal network of specialist institutions and knowledges which had long ago carved up the space of the city into areas of social danger, peopled them with vulnerable (and dangerous) problem populations, and entered into a remarkable historical exchange with the law. This was an exchange in which the law could be called in to help manage the residual failures of social policing, while itself drawing special 'social' knowledges and techniques from this regulatory sphere. As we saw in Chapter 3, it was in this specific historical context – particularly in the exchange between legal regulation and the medical policing of problem populations – that the category of moral harms entered the judicial sphere, not in some access of moralism and paternalism that mistook moral umbrage for harm.

What, then, is the relation between Justice McTiernan's defence of the quasi-medical proscription of the love comics as a specifiable social pathology and the majority's overruling of this judgement? The majority certainly leave us in no doubt as to their low opinion of the publications. However, this is expressed not in the language of medical policing but in the unmistakable pedagogical idiom of literary criticism:

> The theme of them all nearly is love, courtship and marriage. Virtue never falters and right triumphs. Matrimony is the proper end and if you are not told that happiness ensues it is the constant assumption. They are, of course, intended for feminine readers. (p. 116)

As a result, say the majority justices:

> What they contain is an affront to the intelligence of the reader but hardly a real threat to her morals. The stories are extremely silly, the letter press is stupid, the drawings are artless and crude and the situations absurd. But we are not concerned with the damage done to the intellect or for that matter to the eyesight of the readers of these foolish periodicals. (p. 118)

This shift from the medical to the pedagogical is, however, carried out *within* the *Hicklin* framework, through the provision of an alternative – non-pathological – audience typology. This was derived from the evidence of two newsagents.

> The shop of one was opposite a suburban school. According to him he sold up to six a week of each title of the publications now in question, and they were bought by adult females whose age was from the late 'teens to thirty-five years, and not by schoolgirls. The other newsagent carried on business in the city of Brisbane. He sold six a week of each title (the number supplied) to customers he described as married women and the senior office girl type. (p. 118)

On this basis, the Court decided not only that the likely audience consisted of ordinary members of society, but also that the effect of the publications on this audience could not be the subject of expert testimony – this effect being a matter for the 'triers of fact', judge or jury. The decision was given the force of a dictum.

> Ordinary human nature, that of people at large, is not a subject of proof by evidence, whether supposedly expert or not. But particular descriptions of persons may conceivably form the subject of study and of special knowledge. Before opinion evidence may be given upon the characteristics, responses or behaviour of any special category of persons, it must be shown that they form a subject of special study or knowledge and only the opinions of one qualified by special training or experience may be received. Evidence of his opinion must be confined to matters which are the subject of his special study or knowledge. (p. 112)

In this manner the pathological typology of abnormally susceptible audiences was ushered from the court-room, along with the testimony of the custodial psychiatrists, matrons and doctors. In the vacated space we see the emergence of a new threshold for the problem of erotic representations, one which is less concerned with its pathological effects on problem populations than with its pedagogical effects on 'people at large'. Needless to say, this was also a threshold for the admission of new forms of regulatory expertise to the courtroom. Following the medical we have the aesthetic 'police'.

What do we learn from this little judicial drama? First, as we have already observed, the correlation of moral delinquency and social harm, characteristic of the initial organisation of obscenity law, is not a philosophical mistake made by those rushing to impose their own morality as law. This correlation was the product of a whole network of norms, institutions and special knowledges in which the conduct, demeanour and sentiments of urban populations – as well as their health, literacy and domestic economy – had been brought within the scope of corrective regulation. It was within the quasi-medical organisation of this governmental network that pornography had first surfaced as a medical and moral harm – an agent of social pathology, like gambling and drinking – and the *Hicklin* test had become possible.

Second, the High Court's move to reject the pathological audience typology and the configuration of expertise characteristic of this initial phase – to replace the most vulnerable with the average audience – does not signify the collapse of the *Hicklin* framework. Rather, it is carried out *within* this framework but through a new specification of the classes of persons relative to which the tendency to deprave and corrupt must be measured. The move from more to less vulnerable audiences (and vice versa) is in fact entirely characteristic of *Hicklin* law, reflecting the imperative that the effects of obscenity be calculated relative to particular normatively specified populations. This move in no way signifies the law's incipient acknowledgement of the autonomy of individual moral judgement.

Third, despite the Court's proscription of expert testimony on them, the new categories of 'ordinary human nature' and 'people at large' do not point to a non-specific audience of morally free individuals. In fact the new and more general 'likely audience' is composed of a determinate class of individuals – 'married women', 'the senior office girl type' – whose pedagogical formation is deemed less than complete and thus problematic. While this condition may not be a problem as far as love comics are concerned, where a more dedicated biblio-eroticism is involved the psycho-literary immaturity of this audience may give rise to new types of harm. We

The Limits of Law Reform

can suggest, then, that far from signifying the incipient departure of the law from the moral sphere, the move to a broader and less corruptible audience is indicative of a transition from a medical to a pedagogical and aesthetic regulation of pornography. In short, the liberalism of the judgement is governmental not philosophical.

The argument thus far should be construed neither as a defence of the timeless legal rationality of the *Hicklin* framework nor as a denial of the evident instability of modern obscenity law. It does imply, however, that the problems currently besetting *Hicklin* are not due to some fundamental categorial error in that law. If we are right about this, then changes to the law cannot take the form of a philosophical rectification – typically a rational recognition of the difference between law and morality – of the sort proposed by philosophical liberalism. But neither can such changes be justified by appeal to the real harm done by pornography. *Transport Publishing Co.* v. *The Literature Board of Review* – and, arguably, the *Roth* decision and the 1959 Obscene Publications Act – indicate that the law is changing neither in order to rectify an old error nor to acknowledge a new truth, but as a result of a new configuration of the infra-legal field surrounding obscenity law.

Let us suggest, as a hypothesis to guide discussion, that the shift in question is between two strategies of regulation: from a strategy organised around the quasi-medical policing of socially pathological problem populations, to one governed by the pedagogical formation of the sensibility of the population at large. Taking note of the role of popular literary education and (non-pathologising) psychological counselling in this new strategy, and recalling from our discussion of Lawrence the increasing deployment of erotic representations *within* the institutions of moral formation, we can begin to grasp the scope of the changes that obscenity law is responding to. If pornography is losing its status as a social harm and is acquiring that of an offensive assault on the sensibility, this is not due to a sudden recognition that erotic representations are harmless and hence should be placed beyond legal regulation. It is a result of the ambivalent role (morally formative if appropriated through the correct pedagogical channels but deleterious otherwise) that these representations have come to play in what is in fact a new (pedagogical) organisation of the regulatory sphere.

This hypothesis makes sense of the ambivalence of many proposed liberalisations of the law which, despite their claims that pornography is merely offensive and can be harmlessly consumed in private, nonetheless establish strict thresholds of access to it based on criteria of sexual maturity. But is also enables us to put a series of questions to the whole framework of philosophical liberalism in which law reform is based on the notions of harm, moral autonomy, and representation.

1. If what is to count as the harm of pornography can only be determined relative to a particular historical network of regulatory knowledges and institutions – a network that includes obscenity law itself – how can harm function as a general and independent criterion for limiting the scope of legal coercion?
2. Can the individual moral sensibility have some sort of intrinsic autonomy or privilege in relation to forms of social regulation and organisation if the pedagogical formation of this same sensibility is one of the objects of the latter?
3. Can the problem of erotic representations be understood in terms of the manner in which they represent 'real sex' if their effects vary with their uses in the practices and institutions of sensibility formation?

These questions will guide the next steps of our discussion.

HARM, MORAL AUTONOMY, AND REPRESENTATION

The alignment of these three elements of the liberal programme is well illustrated in the 1979 *Report of the Committee on Obscenity and Film Censorship* (the Williams Report). If (as is more or less taken for granted by the Report) obscene publications cause no specifiable harms, then, it is argued, we have a clear limit to the extent of legal regulation in this area. On the other side of this border, individual moral judgement regarding erotic representations should be free and unconstrained: the reason being that it would be wrong to enforce a particular socially approved moral code when we cannot tell in advance which of the available moral positions might point in the direction of full human development (Williams Report, 1979, pp. 50– 60). All erotic representations capable of carrying moral ideas or of aesthetically expressing moral opinions should, therefore, be protected from legal interference. This view leads Williams to recommend, as we have already noted, the complete lifting of restrictions on publications consisting solely of the written word. Some erotic representations, however, neither carry nor express ideas or values, being merely 'photographic' transmissions of real sex acts fulfilling the single intention of sexual arousal. While not actually harmful and hence open to legal suppression, these representations are nonetheless offensive insofar so they are public windows on to private acts, which makes them a nuisance like soliciting. Hence they should be restricted to a volunteer adult audience consuming them in private (pp. 100–2). The boundary between law and morality – between erotic representations liable to restriction and those suitable for public dissemination – is thus set by a specific (aesthetic) conception of pornography as 'transparent' sexual representation. This transparency, the Report assumes, will be registered in the offended sensibility of the 'reasonable person' unwillingly encountering pornography in a public place.

The most striking and problematic feature of the liberal programme is its apparent removal of pornography from its role in the historical deployment of sexuality and the formation of the erotic self. This removal is attempted by constant appeal to the responses and judgements of an unspecified human subjectivity. Few have gone further in this regard than Joel Feinberg, who, in laying down 'the moral limits of the criminal law', removes obscenity from the sexual sphere altogether. Obscenity cannot be identified with sexually arousing reading matter because, apparently, sexual excitement is an unambiguously good thing. Through a largely etymological argument, Feinberg (1985, pp. 97–126) claims that the judgement of obscenity originates in the feelings of distaste and discomfort aroused by (non-erotic) vulgarity and repellent phenomena ('yukkiness'). Because pornography is not necessarily vulgar or repellent, then, says Feinberg (pp. 139–40), it is not generally obscene. In fact those who find it so are the victims of their own distorted moral sensibilities. Only pornography that is vulgar and repellent· in addition to being sexually arousing should therefore be liable to restriction under an offensiveness statute.

Setting aside the inaccuracy of Feinberg's etymology (the Oxford English Dictionary records 'Offensive to modesty or decency; expressing or suggesting lewd thoughts' as a meaning for 'obscene' dating from the sixteenth century), the most problematic feature of his attempt to de-eroticise obscenity is its ostensible appeal to the non-specific responses of a general human subject. Pornography is not necessarily offensive, according to Feinberg, because the response of the normal person to the sexual arousal that it induces is – or should be – that of healthy unalloyed pleasure. The optimism of this line of argument is matched only by its vacuity. Not only does it erase the gender-specificity of the 'response of pornography', it also begs the question as to the latter's offensiveness (or harmfulness) by arbitrarily privileging a particular kind of response – uncomplicated erotic pleasure – as normal.

The arbitrariness of the attempt to set the threshold of offence (or harm) by appealing to a given normal response is made all the more clear by the fact that different specifications of normality jostle against one another even within the framework of philosophical liberalism. In descending from the philosophy of law to levels of analysis where it stumbles onto the actual forms of reasoning involved in legal regulation, liberal optimism regarding normal 'human' sexuality begins to disintegrate. According to Lockhart and McClure's influential 'Censorship of Obscenity: The Developing Constitutional Standards', for example, the normal response to pornography is anything but robust pleasure:

> For hard-core pornography appeals to the sexually immature because it feeds their craving for erotic fantasy; to the normal, sexually mature person it is repulsive, not attractive.
>
> (Lockhart and McClure, 1960, pp. 72–3)

Lockhart and McClure's normally repelled person is thus the same person whose reactions to pornography Feinberg regards as abnormal and hence as inappropriate for setting the threshold of harm or offensiveness.

To complete the confusion, the Williams Report attempts to combine the two contradictory specifications of the normal response in a single complex figure. On the one hand the Report argues that normal people find pornography offensive because it transmits properly private sexual activity into the public domain and 'makes it available for a voyeuristic interest':

> For those who are not disposed, as willing consumers, to make scenes of pornography into objects of their own fantasy, those scenes have a special and saddening ugliness. In people who are particularly resistant to such fantasy, either in general, or as involving objects such as these, anger, disturbance and oppression will be the reactions.
>
> (Williams Report, 1979, pp. 97–8)

On the other hand, because of the nature of the projected scenes, the involuntary spectator can, as it were, begin to take pleasure in them against his own will:

> The exact relation of pornographic material to the consumer and to his fantasies is a subtle manner. Even when it is taken up into fantasy, pornography often retain an assaulting quality – there is a sense in which it can be found offensive even while it is being enjoyed. In other cases, the sense of offensiveness evaporates for the consumer who involves himself in the images offered by photographs or films, or develops his own fantasy from the written word. (p. 97)

At this point the attempt to draw a general line between law and morality by appealing to a normally offended response reaches the end of its tether.

The Limits of Law Reform

Likewise the appeal to the unified subject of such a response dissolves in the contradiction of a pornography that gives offence 'even while it is being enjoyed'.

In other words, the attempt to use the harm condition to set a general limit to the legal regulation of conduct breaks down under its own weight. The ostensible appeals to the responses of a subject who might or might not be harmed or offended by pornography are in fact covert legislative specifications of what is to *count* as harmful or offensive (or normal and enjoyable), using a variety of unacknowledged criteria.

It is possible to suggest, at this point, that the judgement of harm or offence is in fact inseparable from specific forms of ethical and social calculation, which are themselves typically embedded in normative programmes of ethical and social organisation.[2] Ernest Nagel puts the matter in this way:

> [T]he point needs stressing that though in a given society certain kinds of conduct seem unquestionably harmful, [or, we might add, unquestionably harmless] the classification of such conduct as harmful may, and frequently does, involve far-reaching assumptions about the public weal – assumptions which may be modified for a variety of reasons, and which may not be operative in other societies. This is evident when we reflect that even in our society not all actions resulting in physical injury to others, or in depriving others of their possessions, are held to be harmful in the sense here relevant. Thus the infliction of physical injury on others in duels or feuds currently counts as action that is harmful, but the infliction of such injury is not so regarded when it occurs in boxing contests, in acts of self-defence, or in many though not in all surgical operations. Moral assumptions and considerations of social policy surely control this classification of such conduct; and there have been societies in which those actions have been classified differently.
>
> (Nagel, 1969, pp. 143–4)

As a result, argues Nagel, all attempts to set general limits to the social and legal regulation of individual conduct – that is, limits independent of the specific and often variable forms for calculating harm or offence – must fail. All such attempts will involve covert and often conflicting appeals to particular specifications of what is to count as harmful, like those made by Feinberg and Williams. Moreover, these specifications derive from the very forms of social, ethical and legal regulation whose moral limits philosophical liberalism purports to adjudicate. We can agree with Nagel, therefore, that 'there appear to be no determinate and fixed limits to the scope of justifiable legal regulation of conduct'. In answer to the first of the questions asked, we can propose that the harm condition cannot set general moral or philosophical limits to the legal regulation of obscenity. Indeed, it seems that what is to count as harm (or offensiveness) in this area will be determined *within* the regulatory network of which the law is a part.

What consequences does this have for the second element of the liberal framework that we have questioned – the element of *individual moral autonomy or privacy*? Clearly, if there is no general way of calculating the harm or offensiveness of pornography, then there is no universal or fundamental domain of conscience in which individuals should be free to exercise their moral judgement over pornography. (As we shall see in a moment, there may well be discretionary areas of a quite different sort.)

The first casualty of this relativising of the moral domain is the liberal slogan that the activities of 'consenting adults in private' should be free of legal constraint. As Beverley Brown (1980, pp. 10–11) has pointed out, 'privacy' is an ambiguous term in liberal discourse and in the Williams Report in particular. It embraces the sense of conduct that is private because it takes place behind closed doors, as well as the quite different domain of moral judgement which is private in the sense of being beyond public (legal, social) regulation. The only thing that holds these two domains of privacy together is yet a third form of privacy, the privacy of sexual conduct. According to Williams it is the manner in which pornography projects the bedroom into the street that offends us, simultaneously breaching architectural privacy and the privacy (autonomy) of our moral judgement, which is subjected to an eroticising coercion. Conversely, the space that is behind closed doors should be free for us to exercise individual moral judgement regarding erotic representations. And, indeed, this is the space of the adult bookshop, whose closed front marks the line between law and morality drawn in the Williams Report.

This neat alignment of architectural and moral privacy starts to come adrift, however, as soon as we ask how we are to tell *which* erotic representations are the ones that transparently or pornographically project private sex into the public domain. And it should be remembered that during the 1960s and 1970s this was the crucial question for those seeking to free erotic art from legal regulation. We have seen that the Williams Report attempts to solve this problem by invoking the psycho-aesthetic specification of pornography. Pornography differs from art either because, in lacking the mediation of aesthetic intention, it assaults us with raw sexual experience or because, being dominated by the single intention of sexual arousal, it subordinates the complexity of experience to the tyranny of fantasy. It is this dual aesthetic failure, the Report argues, that makes some erotic representations into transparent projections of private sex and, allegedly, causes the offended response. Erotic art on the other hand, no matter how hot, always allows scope for the cooling power of the reader's or viewer's judgement and places the obstacles of realism in the path of runaway fantasy.

It should be clear, however, that this aesthetic discrimination of erotic representations – which presumes a reader or viewer equipped with the capacity to achieve aesthetic distance in relation to erotic experience and to balance the complexity of this experience against the single-mindedness of sexual fantasy – is far from being a general human capacity. Rather, it is an instance of the highly sophisticated and specialised dialectical skill which we have described in Chapters 2 and 4. In other words, in demarcating the point at which erotic representations become offensive, the attempt to establish a fixed domain of moral autonomy (privacy) is jeopardised by the specialised and hence variable character of the capacity for discrimination. Given the variable distribution of this discriminatory capacity or skill, it seems unlikely either that it will be able to constitute a general threshold for moral privacy, or that such a threshold could conveniently coincide with the architectural privacy of the closed bedroom or bookshop.

Appealing to the figure of the 'reasonable person' as the legal reagent will not by itself solve this problem, for obvious reasons. It is the virtue of Lockhart and McClure's analysis that it faces this issue – which they call the problem of the audience – head on. If the response to erotic representation varies with the kind of person responding, then, they argue, the legal test for obscenity must itself be a variable one. Moreover, they go so far as to link variation in response not to purely random individual differences in taste but to the socially organised patterns of consumption associated with particular channels of communication:

> The existence of substantial variations in audience appeal within every channel of communication is well known but often overlooked by those who state that material must be tested for obscenity by the standard of the average, normal, or ordinary person. Under variable obscenity the concept of the average or normal person has little place. Instead, variable obscenity requires first a determination of the audience to which the material is primarily directed, and then, as the standard for testing the material, the postulation of a hypothetical person typical of that audience.

(Lockhart and McClure, 1960, pp. 78–9)

This postulation of a sliding audience scale relative to which the judgement of obscenity would itself vary is a substantial improvement on the appeal to the 'reasonable person', even if it is strongly reminiscent of the typology of vulnerable audiences characteristic of the reviled *Hicklin* framework. It should be clear, however, that the move to a threshold for obscenity that varies with the cultural level of the audience undermines the liberal attempt to establish a protected sphere of privacy or individual moral autonomy. And, indeed, it must be said that Lockhart and McClure are far less concerned to defend such a sphere than either Feinberg or the Williams Report.

Their chief concern is to discriminate those erotic representations that qualify for protection under the Freedom of Speech Amendment to the United States Constitution. It is to this end that they make the test of 'appeal to prurient interest' vary with the categories of their audience taxonomy. We shall return in the next chapter to the complex matter of constitutional rights. For the present what is important is to recognise that because the chief division of this taxonomy – the division between 'sexually mature' and 'sexually immature' audiences – is in fact determined by the psychoaesthetic differentiation of art from pornography, Lockhart and McClure's variable space of constitutionally protected erotica threatens to ossify into a fixed Williams-like domain of private moral autonomy.

Like the Williams Report, Lockhart and McClure invoke the psychoaesthetic specification of pornography in an attempt to establish a water-tight correlation between type of material and type of response, or audience type. Pornography, they say – invoking D. H. Lawrence and the Kronhausens – appeals to the sexually immature because it offers materials for autoerotic fantasy unmediated by a sense of social norms or the complexity of experience. Erotic art, on the other hand, appeals to the sexually mature because it provides materials enabling them to bring fantasy up against the recalcitrant details of sexual and personal life and to subject sexual experience to the balancing and shaping force of aesthetic intention. But at this point Lockhart and McClure's attempt to establish a variable threshold for protectible erotica necessarily confronts the same obstacle as the Williams Report's attempt to fix a more determinate threshold for the sphere of individual moral freedoms: namely, the fact that the aesthetic discrimination of erotic art from pornography, a discrimination on which these would-be thresholds are based, is in reality a specialised cultural capacity or ability whose social distribution is far from universal.

This is what undermines Lockhart and McClure's (1960, pp. 72–3) confident judgement that 'hard-core pornography appeals to the sexually immature because it feeds their craving for erotic fantasy; to the normal, sexually mature person it is repulsive, not attractive'. In fact, Lockhart and

The Limits of Law Reform

McClure themselves seem to acknowledge that responses to pornography are far murkier than this neatly etched psycho-aesthetic differentiation of audience types allows for:

> If it is true that the common man knows little and cares less about literary qualities, what is to be done with material of substantial aesthetic value that the common man peruses for his own private titillation, oblivious of its artistry? (p. 72)

Here – in the gap between the 'normal sexually mature person' who responds to erotic art via the controlled aesthetic dialectic of fantasy and norm, and the 'common man' oblivious to everything in it save that which serves his own 'titillation' – the attempt to correlate materials and persons and thereby define the scope of legal intervention falls to pieces. The best that Lockhart and McClure can do with this recalcitrant common man, whose biblio-erotic practices open such a breach in their audience categories, is to call on the stern rebuke of F. H. Bradley:

> [M]ost of the time the failure [to achieve an aesthetic appropriation of erotic art] is in ourselves; but when this happens it is not art's failure. There may be some who can't appreciate art, and perhaps they should stay away from it. But what is not tolerable is that stunted natures should set up their defects as a standard.
>
> (Bradley, in Lockhart and McClure, 1960, p. 72)

But this only succeeds in making it quite clear that the aesthetic discrimination of erotic representations, far from being a general capacity for moral judgement independent of social regulation, is in fact being deployed as a normative ethical ability at the behest of a specific (pedagogical) form of regulation. The 'normal sexually mature person' who responds to erotic representations with an exacting and correct reconciliation of sensuous heat and intellectual detachment is anything but the 'ordinary man', precisely because this person is the exemplar for what the ordinary man *should be*.

We can thus answer our second question by concluding that moral judgement has no general or given form in the individual behind which social and legal regulation might retreat in order to allow the free private circulation of erotic representations. Instead, it seems that the aesthetic discrimination of pornography is a specialised ethical practice deployed as a norm of ability and a form of conduct inside a definite pedagogical form of social regulation. Access to erotic representations cannot therefore have the form of a civil or legal right deriving from the presumption of a general individual moral autonomy. It remains a regulated conduct, contingent on the acquisition of normative ethical abilities and varying in scope as the socially regulated pedagogical distribution of these abilities itself varies. Moral autonomy, we can suggest, is not based on a general faculty for reason. Nor can it be made to coincide with the space behind closed doors – contingent as it is on the practical and variable social distribution of special ethical techniques and skills. In this light Lockhart and McClure's variable test for obscenity might well be defensible. It cannot, of course, be defended as a general test establishing the threshold of moral freedom. But it may well be accepted as a specific normative mechanism for determining when the regulation of erotic images can, depending on the ethical qualification of the audience, be *transferred* from the legal to the pedagogical apparatus.

What do the preceding remarks imply for the third question that we addressed to the programme of philosophical liberalism – the question concerning the concept of *representation* that it employs? It will be recalled that the liberal strategy for reforming obscenity law assumes that pornography is defined by its representational relation to 'real sex'. Pornography is specified in terms of the manner in which it portrays real sexuality in ideas or images. There are a number of reasons for this privileging of the concept of representation in philosophical liberalism.

First, it appears to provide a secure basis for the operation of the harm condition. After all, the argument goes, no one has ever been actually harmed by ideas or images. If these are what erotic representation consists of, then there is no justification for its legal suppression. Second, representation provides an appropriate and uniform ontology for the presumptive domain of free moral judgement. This is the domain in which the subject's rational scrutiny of ideas can supposedly only reach the truth in the absence of extrinsic constraint and coercion. An erotica consisting of ideas and aesthetic expressions of sex is therefore an appropriate object for the free exercise of moral judgement. Third, the concept of representation allows philosophical liberalism to fill the formal space of moral judgement with a particular ethico-sexual content. This occurs because it is assumed that (normal) real sex is an unqualified good – an important focus for individual identity and a legitimate source of human happiness and pleasure. If this is so then erotic representations which do no more than portray real sex in ideas are also a *prima facie* good.

Pushed as far as it will go – as it is by Feinberg – this argument issues in a call for the deregulation of erotic representations, because all they do is reactivate real sexual desire and pleasure in the sphere of ideas. Those offended by erotica are precisely those whose own real sexuality is deficient. They are, says Feinberg (1985, p. 140), 'people with prudish moral sensibilities who get trapped between their own salaciousness and shame'. The more typical liberal position, however, is represented here by the Williams Report. While assuming that sex is good and that so (therefore) is its representation, the Report argues that certain kinds of erotic representation – that is, those that transmit real sex too transparently or leave it at the mercy of an unconstrained auto-erotic fantasy – are (psycho-aesthetically) inappropriate to their subject matter and therefore open themselves to regulation. Indeed, these pornographic representations acquire such erotic force that they may forfeit their status as representations altogether. They tend to coerce the imaginations of their viewers, and thereby threaten to cross Mill's line of reasonable persuasion and re-enter the domain of harms, albeit in the milder form of offensiveness.

It is not difficult to make out the philosophical conception of the subject lying behind this specification of pornography as the (psycho-aesthetically) inappropriate representation of real sex. The philosophically conceived subject is after all the subject of consciousness or representations. This is the subject that is immune to the putative harms of erotic representations simply because they are representations. And it is this subject that possesses moral and rational faculties able to judge these representations, except where their inappropriateness to their object invests them with an erotic force that pushes them outside the sphere of representation altogether. But it is this very generality of the subject of representation – with its presumed faculties of reason and moral judgment – that we have begun to call into question. Our analysis of the historical contingency of harms and the practical variability of the ethical capacity deemed appropriate for consuming erotic representations is inimical to this philosophical conception of the subject.

Nor should we be too surprised if the general concept of representation invoked by the liberal programme is susceptible to evidence of similar sorts of historical contingency and variability. The difficulty of maintaining such a concept is apparent in the Williams Report. On the one hand, given that it construes the offensiveness of pornography in terms of the latter's capacity for transparently projecting real sex acts into the public domain, the Report equates offensiveness with the representational function of pornography:

> The term 'pornography' always refers to a book, verse, painting, photograph, film, or some such thing – what in general may be called a representation. Even if it is associated with sex or cruelty, an object

which is not a representation – exotic underwear, for example – cannot sensibly be said to be pornographic (though it could possibly be obscene).

(Williams Report, 1979, p. 103)

On the other hand, erotic objects that are clearly not representational in the required sense, are elsewhere deemed to be objects falling within the definition of restricted matter: 'Restriction will apply not only to publications, but to 8 mm films etc; also, the kind of sex hardware to be found in many sexshops would we think be equally covered by the definition' (p. 125). In the ambiguous space between the 'exotic underwear' that is not a representation and is therefore not offensive, and the 'sex hardware' that is similarly non-representational but for some reason fails to evade offensiveness, we can detect a deep instability in the concept of representation. This incoherence points us towards the fact that erotic representations (books, videotapes) are typically found alongside a range of other activities and objects (fantasising, underwear, intoxicants, sex aids) used in a variety of erotic and eroticising practices. In other words, the non-representational offensiveness of the sex hardware suggests that the problematic character of erotic representations is not to be looked for in their representational function but in their *use*, as eroticising devices.

This hypothesis is amply confirmed if we recall the manner in which the (putative) representational inappropriateness of pornography to its object is specified within the liberal framework. Pornographic transparency or explicitness is specified in terms of a dual failure to achieve the correct aesthetic disposition; that is, the disposition in which raw sensuous experience is shaped by ideas and the single-mindedness of erotic fantasy is diversified by an access of experiential complexity. In short, the offensiveness of pornography is a function of its failure to be erotic art.

As we have seen in earlier chapters, the infra-legal knowledge operative in this specification is the discourse of Romantic aesthetics. The central idea that a work of art can never be pornographic – because its erotic parts are never merely erotic but always integrated into a more complex and detached aesthetic whole – is a function of the imperative that art must achieve the reconciliation of experience and ideas, content and form. The role of the Romantic dialectic in detaching the erotic from the pornographic is clear enough in Jean Paul's remark:

For instance: that a work of art as such can never be immoral – any more than a flower or the whole of creation – and that any partial immorality,

The Limits of Law Reform 183

like any partial lapse of taste, is resolved into its opposite by the spirit of the whole, stood less in need of proof yesterday than it did the day before yesterday.

(Jean Paul, in Witte, 1975, p. 361)

It soon becomes apparent, however, that this aesthetic dialectic has as its focus not the representational relation between *art and reality* but a relationship of a quite different order which is generally understood in Romantic terms. The nature of this other focus was long ago made clear by Schiller in a set of remarks in his *On the Aesthetic Education of Man* concerning the relation between the work of *art and its reader*.

> But it is by no means always a proof of formlessness in the work of art itself if it makes its effect solely through its contents; *this may just as often be evidence of a lack of form in him who judges it*. If he is either too tensed or too relaxed, if he is used to apprehending either exclusively with the intellect or exclusively with the senses, he will, even in the case of the most successfully realized whole, attend only to the parts, and in the presence of the most beauteous form respond only to the matter. Receptive only to the raw material, he has first to destroy the aesthetic organisation of a work before he can take pleasure in it, and laboriously scratch away until he has uncovered all those individual details which the master, with infinite skill, had caused to disappear in the harmony of the whole. The interest he takes in it is quite simply either a moral or a material interest; but what precisely it ought to be, namely aesthetic, that it certainly is not. Such readers will enjoy a serious and moving poem as though it were a sermon, a naive or humorous one as though it were an intoxicating drink.

(Schiller, 1795, pp. 157–9, our emphasis)

In other words, this aesthetic is not concerned with the representational relation of art to its object but with the ethical relation of the individual to his or her self, something which can be picked out for attention through a specific practice of reading.

In Chapter 4 we saw that the activity of aesthetic reading is organised around a recipe for dividing the 'ethical substance' into intellectual and sensuous drives and a practice of modifying each against the other. The object is to shape a self that reconciles and transcends the poles of moralism ('too tensed') and sensuousness ('too relaxed'). This practice of aesthetic reading and viewing is thus an ethical practice for specifying and shaping one's relation to one's self. In Schiller's dual stigmatisation of readers who are alternatively moralised or intoxicated by their inappropriate use of literature, we can see the historical emergence of the normative audience typology through which liberalism seeks to specify pornography. The aesthetic reading of literature thus has the form of an ethical test or discipline associated with the mastery of a special 'practice of the self'. And the imperative to achieve the aesthetic integration of erotic material – for example, Schiller's (1795, p. 109) wish to balance his sensuous and intellectual interests in the statue of a Greek goddess – must be seen in this context.

It should now be clear that the inappropriateness which liberalism ascribes to some erotic representations is attributable not to their representational relation to 'real sex' but to the ethical disposition of those who use such representations for either moralising or excitatory purposes. Consequently, pornography concerns not one's relation to the sex that it represents but one's ethical relation to representations of sex. Pornography is not a representation of real sex but a real practice of sex using representations.

Ethics here is not identifiable with a moral code or framework through which the subject of consciousness judges erotic representations. Rather, we must understand the ethics of the Romantic aesthetic in terms of that specific set of techniques and practices through which the individual uses erotic representations to problematise the self and subject it to the paired forces of desire and norm, concupiscence and judgement. As we saw in our discussion of Lawrence, far from casting pornography out of the literary field, this highly technical aesthetic-ethical practice is the key to admitting it – as the source of the erotic fantasies and experiences that must be confronted and tamed by an art whose access to sexual truth and pleasure they nonetheless guarantee.

If something like the preceding reconstruction of the concept of erotic representation is correct, then the threshold of pornographic offensiveness cannot have a general form determined by the criterion of representational inappropriateness. This remark applies with equal force whether the reality that pornography is supposed to represent is that of a liberated erotic mutuality, or a repressed women's experience. The concept of pornographic transparency or explicitness in fact signifies a 'failure' of the dialectical shaping of the self, typically through an indulgence of autoerotic fantasy. Hence this concept only makes sense relative to the specific ethical techniques and practice – or ethos – in which this capacity for ethical self shaping is formed and maintained. Needless to say this special capacity is far from universal; its social availability and importance is contingent on its practical (pedagogical) distribution. For this reason, it can be accorded no epistemological privilege in relation to other (medical, social) regulatory deployments of erotic representation.

It is possible to suggest, then, that the framework of harm, moral autonomy and representation – on which the liberal programme depends but which has also played an important role in feminist counter-arguments – is inadequate for understanding the network of social, ethical and legal institutions responsible for the regulated circulation of erotic representations. In the first place, the harm condition cannot establish universal moral limits to legal coercion – nor indeed provide a general moral basis for such coercion. This is because what is to count as a harm is contingent on specific and variable forms of calculation and social regulation, among which we find obscenity law itself. The judgement of harm cannot be made independently of the specific domains of intelligibility formed by the practical deployment of such forms of calculation and regulation.

Second, it seems we cannot legislate for a sphere of deregulated access to erotic representations on the presumption of a given individual capacity for free moral judgement. The (psycho-aesthetic) discrimination of pornography, which liberalism imports to establish the threshold of private consumption, turns out to be a specialised and more or less restricted ethical ability. This ability is itself dependent on the regulated mastery of a definite ethical technique and practice and varies with their practical-historical distribution. The question of at what points and to what degree the law might withdraw from the regulatory field cannot, therefore, be settled in advance of practical assessments of the social distribution of ethical competence. A wider dissemination of the aesthetic capacity for self-direction may well now be in progress. However, such a change does not signify the deregulation of the moral sphere. It indicates a mutation inside the regulatory field, from a legal-medical to a legal-pedagogical configuration.

Third, a threshold for restrictable publications which is organised around a distinction between art and pornography cannot have a determinate form based on the latter's alleged inappropriateness as a representation of 'real sex'. The inappropriateness of erotic representations, we discovered, was not epistemological and general, but ethical and contingent; that is, contingent on the variable distribution and mastery of the ethical technique and practice that determine what counts as an appropriate relation to and use of such representations. As the offspring of this Romantic practice, the psycho-aesthetic threshold for pornographic transparency has no epistemological privilege in relation to other thresholds, but itself remains dependent on the social distribution of a particular cultural competence.

If the foregoing analysis is correct, then the difficulties confronting the legal regulation of obscenity cannot be understood in terms of the 'confusion' or 'paternalism' of the law. Nor can they be resolved through an exemplary process of rectification and reform founded on a general theoretical analysis of harm, moral autonomy and representation. Obscenity law is not founded in an all-purpose subject of consciousness whose susceptibility to harm or offensiveness can be universally calculated, whose inherent moral capacity sets limits to legal regulation and constraint, and whose sexual being is transgressed by an inappropriate representation. Instead, as we have argued, the thresholds, procedures and effects of obscenity law are determined by its place in the network of communicational, ethical, and governmental institutions in which the circulation of erotic representations takes place.

In other words, we are suggesting that this field – together with notions of its reform or transformation – is without foundation in the human subject, whether the latter is construed as liberalism's free moral reasoner or in terms of an unfulfilled women's sexuality. The pornographic field is governed neither by the reasoning subject nor by 'women's experience'. Approaches to its reform should therefore recognise the field as organised by a shifting network of administrative calculations, ethical disciplines, economic incentives and regulatory institutions relative to which particular forms of reasoning and experience become possible. The action of obscenity regulation and the scope for its reform are contingent on the historical configurations of this network, and on the forms of assessment which these make possible.

HISTORY LESSONS FOR LAW REFORMERS

In this chapter, our primary concern is to show why the attempt to render law transparent to the truth of human sexuality and to the principle of privacy, through a fundamental reconstruction of the obscenity statutes, remains impractical and unrealisable. In this demonstration, we have returned more than once to the fact of the historical variability of the sphere of biblio-erotics. One aim in doing so has been to show that in the shaping of western sexuality the most intense effects of eroticisation have been confined – paradoxically, given the supposedly unfettered sexuality of the popular classes – to those sectors of the population most highly-educated in the techniques of sexual self-mastery. In the light of this variability, we have undertaken an historical reconstruction of the shifting forms of obscenity law within the regulatory field concerned with pornography. In this final section, we shall outline certain lessons, learned from that reconstruction, which apply to programmes for the reform of obscenity law. Our delimiting of the categories of autonomous moral subjectivity and of aesthetic representation finds a further application here, in relation to liberal-philosophical projects of deregulation that seek once and for all to dissociate law from morality by expelling the former from the sexual areas of life. These projects typically envisage law only as an intrusion into the given and sacrosanct sexual freedom of individuals.

Despite what the censorship historians say, the entrance of the law into the sphere of biblio-erotics did not occur in one fell swoop at the beginning of the eighteenth century, when an ascendent Puritanism deployed the common law to repress a previously unconstrained expression of sexuality. Not only were Puritan techniques of ethical intensification far more ambivalently related to the expression of desire than this concept of repression allows for, but also, in the creation of the crime of obscene publication, the steps by which the law entered the field were too small, faltering and contingent to be attributed to any epochal 'spirit'. Obscene publication became a crime only when an unforeseen expansion of the government sphere – dependent on a new identification of morality with public order – coincided with the demographic expansion of the ethical sphere. In its turn, this latter expansion was dependent on the printed dissemination of 'ethicising' literature and on an unforeseen widening of the consumption of ambivalently moralising eroticising books. This was the threshold of juridification for pornography. The law's entrance was not the sign of an intensification of Puritan repression, the first fatal intrusion of the criminal law into a sphere of morality that properly belonged to the individual conscience.

From the outset, then, obscenity regulation has not marked an exemplary border between law and conscience but the historical relation between governmental techniques and the cultural techniques of conscience-formation. The example of *Curll* already points to why it is impossible to understand the regulation of the field in terms of a timeless division between a public domain of legal regulation and a private sphere of individual moral autonomy. The private formation of the individual's ethical relation to his or her self, as desiring subject, was itself contingent on the public dissemination of books as a commodity.

Nor is the fact that the law was very little used during the eighteenth century a reflection of some fundamental confusion in its relation to morality – an early uncertainty over whether obscenity actually harms or merely offends – that might later be rectified in an exemplary rationalising gesture by reformers. It is simply a historical indication that the overlap of the techniques of government and the techniques of ethics registered by the new law was initially relatively unimportant.

That obscenity law should subsequently have come to cover a wide regulatory spectrum – from police regulation through minor laws regulating street trading to the full majesty of the criminal law and jury trial – is not a sign of moral inconsistency in need of rational reconstruction. It too simply indicates that, as far as pornography is concerned, the object of governmental regulation has been the circulation of a particular cultural commodity, a commodity bearing the (biblio-erotic) techniques responsible for a specific practice of the self as a desiring subject.

The emergence of the modern configuration of the pornographic field was, as we proposed in Chapter 3, largely a nineteenth-century development, and once again dependent on a particular transformation in the techniques of government. In the decision to punish Curll for breaking the King's peace and corrupting the morality of the King's subjects by placing him in the pillory, we witness a late instance of the exercise of power through the public display of the sovereign's might to the crowd. By the beginning of the nineteenth century, power was increasingly exercised through a network of less conspicuous institutions – medical, pedagogic, assistantial. These were not organised around the direct public display of sovereign power before the disorderly crowd. Their logic was provided by a whole series of less visible disciplinary techniques working below the threshold of the law. These operated at the level of the individual, but the individual was now envisaged as member of a population whose moral and physical condition was the concern or 'problem' of various medical, educative and demographic knowledges and institutions.

According to Foucault (1979, pp. 33–4, 103–4), it was through this network of disciplinary institutions that the 'confessional' techniques of ethical self-problematisation underwent their own remarkable redeployment, transformation and diversification. In their migration through the new institutions of public health, popular education, family reform and population management, the ambivalent techniques for 'revealing' oneself as a desiring subject acquired new objects. They re-surfaced in a variety of new forms: as medical techniques for managing an ever-present pathological sexuality; as pedagogical techniques for eliciting and normalising the sexuality of school-children; and as medical educative strategies targetted on the family. In this play of watchfulness and confession, a whole series of problematic sexualities would appear and multiply, leading to increased sexual attentiveness and a further intensification of eroticism in family existences.

Needless to say, this multiplication was not without consequences for the circulation of erotic representations and biblio-erotic techniques. First, it was the thresholds set by the new governmental institutions that were

The Limits of Law Reform 189

responsible for the forms in which pornography surfaced as a social problem during the nineteenth century. The explanation in terms of general and trans-historical concepts of repression – moral or economic – is quite misplaced. The eighteenth-century juridical notion of corruption of public morals by an obscene libel was thoroughly reconstructed when the harms of pornography became calculable in terms of the norms, knowledges and objectives of the medical, pedagogical and demographic deployment of sexuality. It was in this new cultural-legal environment that the *Hicklin* framework became possible. If *Hicklin* made the crime of obscene publication relative to a classification of vulnerable populations and dangerous places, this was not due to the rise of a moralistic Victorian paternalism. It was the straightforward outcome of the manner in which erotic representations crossed the thresholds of the new institutions whose management of problem populations extended to the policing and welfare of their sexuality.

Second, pornography was anything but a passive agent in this process. Pornography had emerged at the margins of the religious and ethical techniques responsible for forming the relation to the self as the subject of desire. The historical pattern in which the transmission of these techniques through the printed book had permitted the erotic destabilisation of the play between norm and desire was repeated in the new context. In the more recent medical, pedagogical and familial organisations of sexuality, the pornographic book operated as a destabilising relay point. Through it, the already unstable relation between normative problematisation and erotic intensification could be tipped in favour of a desire whose pleasure derives from its subversion of the pedagogical process and its transgression of the sexual order of the family. Nineteenth-century pornography – with its characterology of insatiable perverts, precocious schoolchildren and debauching teachers and parents – is thus not the revenge of the drives against the repressive force of the institutions of sexual regulation. It is an optional practice of sexuality that arose when the ambivalent techniques of sexual formation deployed in these institutions were redeployed and revalorised through the destabilising medium of the book.

This deep mutual dependency of pornography and the social regulation of sexuality has made the policing of obscenity laws both a sophisticated and an unstable area of our judicial systems. If pornography did indeed represent the return of a repressed sexuality after its banishing by morality, then – whether one applauded or bewailed this return – there would be no difficulty in proposing its unconstrained circulation or, alternatively, its prohibition. However, far from signifying the return of a banished sexuality, pornography represents a communicational relay *within* a set of institutions that operate through the regulated *intensification* of sexuality. The problem with pornography is not that it represents a sexuality which medical, pedagogical and familial institutions are busy denying, but that it permits the controlled techniques of sexual incitation used in these institutions to be relayed to milieus where they are put to different and eroticising uses.

These uses are not altogether different, however. For this reason, the regulation of pornography cannot be based on a single general division between the licit and the illicit. Instead, it has been historically organised by a set of medical and educative norms that allow the regulation of erotic representations to vary with the circumstances of their use and the 'maturity' of their specific audiences. We can now see why obscenity law and – more importantly – its reform cannot take as their object the complete extirpation (or complete deregulation) of pornography. We also see why the role of obscenity law has typically been to provide legal buttressing for medical, pedagogical or other systems for managing the consumption of erotic representations.

Equally liable to evaporation in the face of the historical facts is the allegedly fundamental distinction between 'literature' and 'pornography'. It is this distinction which – according to the liberal reform programme – the law chose to ignore in its haste to enforce a particular moral point of view. However, as we have noted, far from being timeless and fundamental, this distinction only emerged gradually during the nineteenth century, with the dissemination of a specialised Romantic aesthetic. This aesthetic provided the dialectic between sensuousness and morality, content and form, relative to which certain works could be stigmatised as pornographic for their failure to integrate sexual detail and moral structure, erotic fantasy and experiential complexity. By contrast, the field of eighteenth-century publishing had simply not been organised by an exemplary division between the aesthetic and the non-aesthetic. This was because an audience equipped with the aesthetic taste and ethical technique for consuming published literature in this specialised manner had not yet emerged.

Nor was the emergence of such an audience universal in the nineteenth century. We have noted the tripartite division of nineteenth-century English literate culture: an esoteric 'pornography of perversions' directed at a minority of middle-class men; a mainstream of educative novels directed at the bourgeois household; a popular bawdy of the streets. This division cannot be understood via the aesthetic model. Rather, it must be described in terms of the differential circulation of specific types of publication to particular audiences – audience types increasingly shaped and differentiated by the new medical, pedagogical and familial institutions that formed

The Limits of Law Reform

the emerging 'social' sphere. Nineteenth-century obscenity law – which, as we have argued, needed to contain no exemption for erotic art or literature, since it was chiefly engaged in a medical policing of street pornography – cannot be criticised for failing to embody the distinction between literature and pornography which liberal reform takes as a fundamental truth. The historical and ethical space in which this distinction was to become routine, intelligible and policeable was still in the process of forming.

If the aesthetic exemption has since emerged as a crucial element of obscenity law and its reform, and if the novel of erotic education has emerged as a staple commodity of the literary field and the book trade, these changes were in part determined by the long march to dominance of Romantic ethics and aesthetics. It was this advance which permitted the 'confessional' relation to the desiring self to be recast in the form of a dialectical exercise, in which the imperative to reveal the smallest movements of desire was a function of their normative prescription. In this exercise the point of acknowledging desire is not to open for inspection the shameful secret of human nature – a desire which threatens the individual's spiritual composure and physical health unless kept in check. Rather it is to allow desire to enter into an equal partnership with morality and the intellect: to acknowledge that if sensuous experience has to be shaped by moral ideas in order to free 'man' from its unconscious immediacy, then these ideas must themselves be pliable to the force of desire if they are to avoid repressing pleasure and warmth beneath the cold weight of abstraction.

While remaining parasitic on the logic of the confessional apparatus – which implants desire in the individual who seeks to organise his thought and feelings around its hidden presence – the Romantic dialectic thus codifies the individual's relation to the desiring self by treating it as the other half of a still (and perhaps always) incomplete being. For those who master it, this sophisticated exercise permits a modification in which the flesh ceases to be what one is forced to acknowledge despite one's self, becoming instead that which one actively avows in order to more fully become one's self.

Are we justified in seeing in this technical modification the source of the more liberal attitude to sex that emerged in advanced circles – the increasingly aestheticised stratum of the educated middle class – towards the end of the nineteenth century? In any event, there seems little doubt that the Romantic dialectic opened a space where sexuality would enter the educative novel as a condition of the latter's organic adequacy to what was then coming to count as the 'full' range of experience. Needless to say, the sexuality that stepped forward to fill this role was anything but some long suppressed human essence. Instead, the Romantic dialectic opened a door to the specific range of sexualities that had been positively created by nineteenth-century medical, pedagogical and familial problematisations, relayed through the eroticising circuit of the bourgeois pornography of perversions, and now finding a way back into the sphere of regulated public culture. Through this door – at first somewhat shyly, in the manner of Lawrence's discreet sodomites and Nabokov's aesthetic and witty paedophiles, and then more flagrantly in the form of Miller's insatiable bohemians and Burroughs' hallucinogenic fetishists, coprophags and necrophiles – the whole sorry characterology of the nineteenth-century deployment of sexuality stepped out into the educative novel.

We are in no danger of overlooking the eroticising effects of this migration. What we are less likely to observe, however, is the manner in which the old sexual personae underwent a pedagogical change in their new environment. They were in fact transformed by the Romantic dialectic into so many opportunities and occasions for members of an ethical elite to practice facing up to their sexuality and achieving its aesthetic sublimation.

Although the Romantic aesthetic provides an important clue to the form of the modern pornographic field, we must not lose sight of the fact that for most of the nineteenth century it remained the esoteric ethical practice of a social minority. No logic inherent in 'history' or 'man' dictated that the new dialectical erotics should become anything more than it was in the 1880s and 1890s – the caste practice of those small erotic-aesthetic coteries associated with the names of Edward Carpenter, Havelock Ellis, Walt Whitman and D. H. Lawrence. The central condition for the aesthetic transformation of the pornographic field is to be found elsewhere, in the emergence of popular education.

The popular school became perhaps the principal scene for that disciplinary strategy according to which the social attributes of populations could be governed via an administration of individualising ethical techniques. In this context, literacy was not only an attribute whose statistical distribution could be used to measure the cultural level of population; it was also a normative ethical skill whose mastery allowed individuals to measure the degree to which they had succeeded in improving their self. It is the fact that print literacy permitted a rapid assimilation of information while remaining deeply embedded in the techniques of ethical self formation that marks its importance for the pornographic field. A population that cannot read cannot be 'corrupted' by eroticising books: but then, neither can a population that is not equipped for and habituated to the use of reading as a definite means of gaining access to, and shaping, a self.

As we observed in Chapter 4, the emergence of a popular education system organised around techniques of moral supervision allowed the Ro-

The Limits of Law Reform

mantic dialectic itself to be transformed and redeployed as a disciplinary technique. In this system, the esoteric relation to the self produced by the aesthetic dialectic was gradually grafted onto the teacher's supervisory relation to the student. As a result, for the first time the formerly virtuoso exercise of dividing and reconciling sensuousness and reason, fantasy and norm, found application as a pedagogical task of behaviour for much larger groups. This governmental re-deployment of the Romantic aesthetic meant the appearance of a new type of literary and ethical education. Whole populations could now be routinely required to discover their sexuality in the newly erotic characterology of the educative novel, while learning how to play it off against a variety of medical, pedagogical and familial norms. What is more, in schools and universities they were examined on their success in these endeavours.

The emergence of a literary erotics based in a dialectical stylisation of the desiring self and the gradual deployment of this exercise as a pedagogical discipline have been centrally responsible for the modern re-organisation of the pornographic field. And in these intersecting developments lie two historical lessons for would-be law reformers.

First, by allowing the auto-erotics of nineteenth-century pornography and the pedagogical action of the social novel to exchange functions in the novel of erotic education – and by expanding the audience possessing the ethical capacity required for the latter's consumption – these changes set the scene for the great literary show trials of the twentieth century. The trials involving works of Radclyffe Hall, Lawrence, Joyce, Miller and Burroughs have typically been commemorated as the attempts of a desperate moralism to repress the exploration of human sexuality carried out by the aesthetic vanguard on behalf of all of us. In the light of the preceding historical analysis, however, these events are more adequately understood in terms of the surfacing of pornographic auto-erotics inside the educative novel; that is, in a novel whose mass circulation forced it into the hands of everybody and thus across the thresholds of obscenity set by the medical and pedagogical policing of populations.

Second, the social expansion of the educational apparatus has been accompanied by a shift from the medical to the pedagogical management of sexuality. Not only has this shift moved regulation away from the pathological and towards a focus on personality formation and self-improvement, it has also provided regulation with a new form and goal: the dialectical reconciliation of erotic representations and social norms in an appropriately aestheticised biblio-erotics. These are the circumstances – not some fundamental rectification of an earlier moralism – that explain the recent shift from a preoccupation with the harms caused by obscenity, to a preoccupation with the offense that pornography might give by virtue of its (or its consumer's) aesthetic incompleteness.

Drawing a distinction between art and pornography, as we have argued, cannot provide a universally valid line marking the point at which the individual conscience is to be freed from regulation. It cannot do this because the capacity to make this distinction is itself a highly normative ability dependent on thresholds of ethical-erotic 'maturity' decided within the pedagogic regulation of sensibility. The idea that the task of law reform is to redeem the law from moralism by showing it how to withdraw from the sphere of conscience – together with the idea that the threshold of conscience can be set in terms of the aesthetic appropriateness of erotic art to true sex – should therefore be set free to wander in the higher and most speculative reaches of philosophical liberalism. In their place we have offered a more historical and practical understanding of the direction taken by recent changes to obscenity law. This direction has been set by the pedagogical transformation of the management of sexuality. As a result of this transformation, the law is acquiring the function of administering a variable access to erotic representations, an access calculated according to the aesthetic and ethical maturity of particular audience types.

In this context, the liberal reformer's attempt to set apart a fixed domain of individual conscience, moral freedom and private consumption, an attempt based on a fundamental distinction between art and pornography, becomes unintelligible. The 'offensiveness' registered by the aesthetic assessment of pornography is in fact, as we have shown, an ethical inappropriateness dependent on what is taken to be an unbalanced use of pornography by 'immature' audiences. The immunity of certain erotic representations from legal or administrative restriction – that is, their status as 'erotic art' – can, therefore, never be absolute or universal since it must vary with the distribution of the ethical technique that permits an audience to aesthetically integrate and sublimate the pornographic elements of these representations. The variable test for obscenity proposed by Lockhart and McClure and used in some American jurisdictions is in this sense quite defensible. What needs to be kept in mind, however, is that the requisite thresholds for audience maturity are not facts to be registered by the law, but norms of erotico-ethical competence that the law helps maintain and administer.

In the event, the withering away of pornography promised by the more open aesthetic avowing of sexuality has not occurred. Quite the reverse: the era of Lawrence and Miller, Burroughs and Bataille, has witnessed an expanded dissemination of pornography and a multiplication of its forms. The reason for the failure of the derepressive hypothesis lies, we would

The Limits of Law Reform

suggest, in the fact that pornography is not a product of repression in the first place, but an autonomous practice of sexuality – a biblio-erotics. Lawrence's lyrical use of obscenity did not herald the imminent purification of the field of erotic representations. It was a sign of that unpredicted surfacing of pornography in the educative novel for which popular education would provide an unstable – because not yet aesthetically equipped – mass audience. Through the channel provided by the pedagogical deployment of the new literary erotics, an unplanned exchange was set up between the literate, masculine pornography of perversions and an increasingly photographic popular pornography. From this exchange have issued two of the most important changes in the modern pornographic field.

On the one hand, it has conditioned the emergence of the genre of 'respectable' soft pornographic magazines and novellas, mixing easily consumable erotic photography with literary essays and stories and directed at a vastly expanded audience network that remains, nonetheless, predominantly masculine. On the other hand, this exchange has also made possible the migration of the esoteric forms of sexual self-identification, characteristic of the pornography of perversions, to the popular market. Hence the proliferation of specialised magazines directed at the exotic sexualities of a predominantly masculine network of micro-audiences. These works wear the label of hard-core pornography.

At one level, then, the distinction between art and pornography laid down in the celebrated literary trials of the mid-century was made redundant even as it was being decided. In the unstable zone of exchanges which the educative erotic novel opened up between esoteric and popular pornography, it is the distinction between hard and soft-core pornography that has become critical for law and social policy. At another level, however, the aesthetic discrimination has acquired remarkable importance of another kind, having being taken up by Western judiciaries as the key to distinguishing hard from soft – restrictable from non-restrictable – pornography. In other words, with the shift in infra-legal regulation from a medical to a pedagogical register, the aesthetic criterion has become central to the legal-pedagogical administration of erotic representations.

This governmental re-deployment of the erotic and ethical threshold sets limits to and governs the direction of law reform. We develop this theme in the next chapter, but may observe here that the limits are clearly visible in the cases of *Mishkin* v. *New York* and *Ginzburg* v. *United States* heard on appeal before the US Supreme Court in 1966. The convictions of Mishkin and Ginzburg were upheld, but it is the manner in which the Court functioned as the site for a particular process of social deliberation and judgement which is of interest.

On the one hand, the liberal strategy of deregulation is passionately advocated by the dissenting judges. They speak indignantly of the 'three-year sentence imposed on Mishkin and the five-year sentence imposed on Ginzburg for expressing views above sex'. And, citing Krafft-Ebing's *Psychopathia Sexualis* as authority, they summarise the testimony of witnessing priests, psychologists and literary critics in the following terms:

> Some of the tracts for which these publishers go to prison concern normal sex, some homosexuality, some the masochistic yearning that is probably present in everyone and dominant in some. Masochism is a desire to be punished or subdued. In the broad frame of reference the desire may be expressed in the longing to be whipped and lashed, bound and gagged, and cruelly treated. Why is it unlawful to cater to the needs of this group? They are, to be sure, somewhat offbeat, nonconformist, and odd. But we are not in the realm of criminal conduct, only ideas and tastes. Some like Chopin, others like 'rock and roll'. Some are 'normal', some are masochistic, some deviant in other respects such as the homosexual. Another group also represented here translates mundane articles into sexual symbols. This group, like those embracing masochism, are anathema to the so-called stable majority. But why is freedom of the press and expression denied them? Are they to be barred from communicating in symbolisms important to them? When the Court today speaks of 'social value', does it mean a 'value' to the majority? Why is not a minority 'value' cognizable? The masochistic group is one; the deviant group is another. Is it not important that members of those groups communicate with each other? Why is communication by the 'written word' forbidden? If we were wise enough, we might know that communication may have greater therapeutical value than any sermon that those of the 'normal' community can offer.
>
> (*Ginzburg* v. *United States*, p. 489)

In this use of sexology to demonstrate the harmless nature of pornography, to place it in the domain of representation and individual moral judgement and to claim an emancipatory and de-repressive therapeutic value for it, we find the main elements of the philosophical liberal programme.

On the other hand, in *Mishkin* v. *New York*, the concurring majority, whose judgement hinged on the way in which Mishkin commissioned his books and targetted their audiences, was concerned with a different use of sexological literature:

The Limits of Law Reform

No substantial claim is made that the books depicting sexually deviant practices are devoid of prurient appeal to sexually deviant groups. The evidence fully establishes that these books were specifically conceived and marketed for such groups. Appellant instructed his authors and artists to prepare the books expressly to induce their purchase by persons who would probably be sexually stimulated by them. It was for this reason that appellant 'wanted an emphasis on beatings and fetishism and clothing – irregular clothing, and that sort of thing, and again sex scenes between women; always sex scenes had to be very strong'. And to be certain that authors fulfilled his purpose, appellant furnished them with such source materials as Caprio, Variations in Sexual Behaviour, and Krafft-Ebing, Psychopathia Sexualis.

(*Mishkin* v. *New York*, pp. 509–10)

The deep historical reciprocity in Western confession-based technologies between the knowledge of sexuality and the pleasure gained from it renders this second use of Krafft-Ebing no less exemplary than the first. It is a representative instance of those larger historical processes in which pornography transposed the already ambivalent sexologies into the erotic register, and in which the expansion of popular literary education has been accompanied by a proliferation of specialised pornographies and audiences.

It is meaningless to propose to deregulate the circulation of erotic representations once they cross the thresholds of aesthetic sensibility and therapeutic sexuality. The forms in which it is possible to become conscious of sexuality and to achieve its therapeutic expression are themselves already artefacts of a regulated circulation of erotic representations. It is in this context that the court in *Mishkin* in fact extends the regulatory domain first announced in *Hicklin* by making obscenity relative to the level of development of the audience's erotic sensibility ('sexual maturity'), as revealed by book commissioning guidelines and marketing procedures.

For the same sorts of reason, however, it is equally meaningless to propose to tighten obscenity law on the basis of pornography's misrepresentation of women's sexuality. Erotic representations are not governed by some notional true sexuality but by their role in the pedagogic management of an array of historically determinate sexualities. However, as we shall see in the final two chapters, given the gender specificity of pornographic audiences, this by no means rules out the possibility of making the erotic sensibility of 'men' a specific target in the regulatory field.

7 United States Obscenity Law

LIBERALISM, PHILOSOPHICAL AND GOVERNMENTAL

The philosophical categories used by liberal jurisprudence for understanding the regulation of pornography, as we have now shown, have their historical limits. Attempts to reform the law on the basis of these categories – the general mechanism of the harm condition, the distinction between morality and law, and the aesthetic idea of representation – meet a series of obstacles. Individuals 'experience' pornography, we have argued, not as universal moral subjects but as the bearers of specific ethical competences or abilities, purposively but unevenly distributed in populations through governmental pedagogies. The fact that pornography has historically formed part of a masculine auto-erotics further undermines the attempt to separate morality from law through appeal to a universal subject of moral judgement. Finally, the prospect that sexological knowledges might allow a detached view of pornography starts to look less rosy once the confessional-incitatory structure of these knowledges becomes clear. In this chapter we develop the consequences of these observations for the category of individual 'rights'.

This involves shifting our jurisdictional focus to the United States of America where centre stage is occupied by a certain philosophical conception of rights, the main assumptions of which are that rights of expression are the intrinsic possession of the individual, whose essence is given independently of social institutions or the state, and that the proper role of law is to 'represent' the rights of the individual, including his or her independence of thought and conscience. Even though the law is assumed to have this ideally representational function, the subject of rights is imagined to exist in a constant torsion with a sovereign power in that the law, like other instruments of government, is also ultimately a vehicle of state interests.

It is possible to rework this conception by re-examining the relationship between *philosophical liberalism* and the practices of *liberal government*. We can begin by asking: What happens to the notion of rights once its foundation – the individual moral subject – loses its autonomous and transcendental character as a result of the historicising analysis that we have been pursuing? To open up this question, let us ask another: What are we to make of the fact that in the United States the regulation of pornography is powerfully inflected by questions of constitutional rights, questions which do not arise in English law? A key factor in the legal regulation of pornography in the United States, in contrast to England, is the existence of a Bill of Rights, in particular the First Amendment to the Constitution, which states: 'Congress shall make no law . . . abridging the freedom of speech or of the press'.[1] This Amendment has been accepted within judicial processes as applying to the states, and to any form of governmental action, not only legislative statutes (*Gitlow* v. *New York* (1925)). Many commentators have assumed that this constitutional mandate does something which – according to our analysis of various contexts thus far – is impossible: namely, ground the law and its application in the recognition of a given moral right. The First Amendment is frequently referred to as a transcendent guarantee of the right of expression, affording protection against any attempt by the state to encroach upon the privacy of free thought and individual conscience. From this point of view, the guideline to follow on obscenity law reform seems clear: remember the individual's inherent right to liberty of expression, determine if and where the law infringes upon that right, and remove the infringement so as to restore the right to free self-expression.

Within the context of constitutional rights of expression, the assumptions of liberal jurisprudence issue in what has been termed First Amendment 'absolutism'. This position is perhaps never represented in its pure form, since even its most enthusiastic advocates acknowledge some exceptions to the constitutional protection of speech. These exceptions include acts of speech or press which are deemed to inflict injury (libel), disturb the public peace, constitute a criminal conspiracy, create a 'clear and present danger' that some proscribed action will result from the utterance, or to be obscene.[2] The words of the famous Justice Holmes from 1919 are often cited on this matter: 'the 1st Amendment . . . cannot have been, and obviously was not, intended to give immunity for every possible use of language' (*Frohwerk* v. *United States* (1919), p. 206). At first, the legal policing of obscenity was not taken to pose any constitutional question in relation to the freedom of speech. First Amendment absolutism in relation to obscenity is a relatively recent phenomenon. It was made possible, we have suggested, by the widescale pedagogic dissemination of those aesthetic, psychological and sexological norms which allow the personal use of sexual materials to be valorised as a domain of intellectual and emotional expression, one which individuals feel they should be free to explore and organise for themselves. In the wake of that dissemination, since the middle of the twentieth century, First Amendment 'absolutists' have been able to insist that it is essential to hold the line against the apparently ever-present danger that governmental and political interests will infringe the individual's fundamental right of free expression in relation to sexual materials.

As we saw in the preceding chapter, philosophical liberalism attempts to protect individual rights by invoking the harm condition as a general criterion for their legitimate exercise. So, for example, David A. J. Richards argues that, whatever its historical origins, the First Amendment represents a moral theory, namely, 'the greatest equal liberty of communication compatible with a like liberty for all' (1980, pp. 100–1). Hence, it seems, constitutional rights involve a familiar balancing act. They include 'both a right to communicate and a right to be the object of communication' (p. 101). One's right of expression must be adjusted to the right of others to choose whether to be constructed as an audience. Sexuality is seen to be an important content of 'expression', no matter whether one is dealing with serious art and literature or pornography. However, it is acknowledged, harms may flow from pornography if subjects lack developed powers of rational choice. Richards thus accepts that protection is justified for minors and that 'time, place and manner' restrictions (affecting distribution and display but not the content of works) are tolerable to prevent materials being foisted upon unconsenting adults (p. 121). However, the law should not interfere with acts of expression which cause no harm to others. Attempts to regulate the contents of communications by law are said to be incompatible with the principle of equal liberty (pp. 101–2). Echoing some of the classic formulations of nineteenth-century philosophical liberalism, Richards claims that we can never be sure of knowing what the truth is, and the most likely way of approximating it and preserving a democratic society is to maintain a free marketplace of ideas (cf. Haiman, 1981, p. 7). For Richards, the First Amendment rests on a moral basis that cannot be reduced to 'a utilitarian calculus of the political usefulness of a debate on divergent points of view':

> Rather, the First Amendment rests more fundamentally on the moral liberties of expression, conscience and thought; these liberties are fundamental conditions of the integrity and competence of a person in mastering his or her life and expressing this mastery to others. The freedom to determine the contents of one's communications is fundamental to this mastery. Without this freedom, one lacks a basic ingredient of self-determination. (p. 120)

The freedom to decide upon the 'sexual' content of those communications which one creates or receives is, according to Richards, an essential part of this more general freedom of expression (p. 120). In a familiar argument, obscenity law is treated as a desperate but doomed attempt to give a repressive morality legal force – to deny the true understanding of the varieties of sexual experience and 'the human capacity to master one's sexual life in the light of independent judgement' (p. 120). This denial has supposedly been acted out in the Supreme Court's obscenity decisions, especially in a series of cases in 1973, including *Miller* v. *California* in which the obscenity standard was reformulated. According to Richards, these decisions incorrectly treated obscenity as falling outside First Amendment protection and endorsed a particular moral and political view at the expense of other views and capacities for experience, under the guise of making a morally neutral legal judgement (pp. 111–121). The error can only be redressed by recognising that pornography should, like other forms of expression, be protected under the First Amendment, and by bringing state prohibitions or regulations of communications into line with the principle of greatest equal liberty (p. 113).[3]

A position verging on First Amendment absolutism is identifiable also in certain opinions formulated in the courts, it having been contended that the judiciary has a duty to uphold an essential principle of justice embodied in that Amendment if it is not to endorse the only apparent alternative, censorship. This position has been adopted by some members of the Supreme Court, in particular by Justices Black and Douglas. In his concurring opinion in *Smith* v. *California* (1959), for example, Mr Justice Black states:

> Certainly the First Amendment's language leaves no room for inference that abridgements of speech and press can be made just because they are slight. That Amendment provides, in simple words, that 'Congress shall make no law . . . abridging the freedom of speech, or of the press'. I read 'no law . . . abridging' to mean *no law abridging*. The First Amendment, which is the supreme law of the land, has thus fixed its own value on freedom of speech and press by putting these freedoms wholly 'beyond the reach' of *federal* power to abridge. No other provision of the Constitution purports to dilute the scope of these unequivocal commands of the First Amendment. Consequently, I do not believe that any federal agencies, including Congress and this Court, have power or authority to subordinate speech and press to what they think are more important interests.
>
> (pp. 157–9, footnote omitted)

A similar theme is expressed by Mr Justice Douglas in his dissenting opinion in *Paris Adult Theatre 1* v. *Slaton* (1973):

When man was first in the jungle he took care of himself. When he entered a societal group, controls were necessarily imposed. But our society – unlike most in the world – presupposes that freedom and liberty are in a frame of reference that makes the individual, not government, the keeper of his tastes, beliefs, and ideas. That is the philosophy of the First Amendment; and it is the article of faith that sets us apart from most nations in the world. (p. 73)

Such views have been influential in the judicial regulation of pornography but not, as we shall see, determinative.[4]

One of the most thoroughgoing attempts to put the tenets of philosophical liberalism into practice in the governmental sphere within the USA is made in *The Report of the Commission on Obscenity and Pornography*, presented to the President and Congress in 1970. The Commission was chaired by William B. Lockhart, whose jurisprudential contributions on obscenity law, coauthored with Robert C. McClure, we discussed in the previous chapter.[5] The Commission's central recommendation contains an argument for deregulating sexual materials in recognition of a right to expression that is given with the individual and limited only by the harm condition: 'In general outline, the Commission recommends that federal, state and local legislation should not seek to interfere with the right of adults who wish to do so to read, obtain, or view explicit sexual materials' (p. 57).[6] In the Lockhart Report, the individual's intrinsic right of expression is identified with the adult's entitlement to read or see explicit sexual materials (p. 58). The production and circulation of such materials are in turn seen as orienting themselves towards the exercise of that right, deriving from it their own legitimacy. First Amendment guarantees are thus taken as properly extending beyond the individual expression or reception of meaning to encompass technological practices and commercial relations of communication. It follows, for the Commission, that just as laws forbidding adults from obtaining, reading or viewing sexual materials of their choice should be repealed, so, too, should laws prohibiting the sale, distribution and exhibition of obscene materials (pp. 62, 75–6). It is assumed that the principle of rational choice embodied in the individual is replicated at a general level of social communication where the mechanism of 'the competition of ideas in a free market place' (p. 56) will ensure that the production, distribution and use of sexual materials will ultimately be unproblematic because self-regulating. The Report states that the 'spirit and letter of our Constitution tell us that government should not seek to interfere' with the rights of free speech and press which include 'the right of each individual to determine for himself what books he wishes to read and what pictures or films he wishes to see' *and* 'the right of writers, publishers, and booksellers to serve the diverse interests of the public', unless a 'clear threat of harm' dictates otherwise (p. 60). If government is to avoid '[c]oercion, repression and censorship' (pp. 56–7), it must deregulate the use of sexual materials while controlling their sale to the young and their presentation to unconsenting adults (pp. 76–9). The Report's recommendations are supported by two interrelated arguments, both of which we have encountered in other settings. It is said that there is no evidence to show that exposure to explicit sexual materials is harmful in the sense of adversely affecting character, attitudes or conducts, or leading to anti-social or criminal behaviour (pp. 61, 169–309). It is also claimed that the 'problem' of pornography and obscenity is in fact *created* by over-regulating the field of sexuality and that it 'stems from the inability or reluctance of people in our society to be open and direct in dealing with sexual matters' (p. 53). Supposedly, this psychological incapacity gives sex a magical, 'non-natural quality', warps the expression of sexuality, and makes difficult the task of 'teaching children and adolescents to become fully and adequately functioning sexual adults' (p. 53). Pornography becomes a problem, it is suggested, because it confronts people with their own fears, representing to them directly the 'danger and unpleasantness' which they associate with sex (p. 312). In other words, pornography has become the scapegoat for Americans' 'confusion and ambivalence about sexuality' (p. 311).

For these reasons, obscenity law is seen as a category mistake, to be rectified by 'a massive sex education effort' (p. 54) as a counterpart to the strategy of deregulation. This project should involve government, schools, families, churches, health practices, citizens' groups and the media, working with people of all age groups and in all sectors of society (pp. 54–7), the aim being to create healthy attitudes towards sexuality, provide a sound foundation for the basic social institutions of marriage and family, and achieve 'an acceptance of sex as a normal and natural part of life and of oneself as a sexual being' (p. 54). Once created, this informed relation towards human sexuality would reduce interest in pornography – referred to several times in the Report as nothing more serious than an inferior 'source of information about sexual behaviour' (p. 312), to which people turn when more open and honest forms of knowledge are not made available. This sex education project would provide a 'powerful positive approach' (p. 55) to the problem of pornography and obscenity, in contrast to the distorted regime of representations associated with the failure 'to talk openly and directly about sex' (p. 53) and the negative and counter-productive role played by the law. There is of course a utopian element in the manner in which the Commission pins its faith on a fundamental human capacity for full and balanced sexual self-realisation. But the combining of legal deregulation with a stepping-up of pedagogic regulation suggests that liberal jurisprudence in fact takes a more pragmatic view of the free reasoning subject then its philosophical rhetoric allows.

Dispassionate attention to the problems underlying the Lockhart Report's approach has perhaps been preempted as a result of its contemptuous rejection by a conservative political administration.[7] Nonetheless, these problems are severe. Because they stem from the assumptions of philosophical liberalism, we can identify them summarily by recalling the main findings of the preceding chapter. First, philosophical liberalism cannot provide a rational basis for law reform by neutrally arbitrating the question of whether pornography is harmful, because what is 'harmful' depends on the particular historical circumstances in which pornography is problematised and the particular intellectual, ethical and regulatory means used to problematise it. The defence of pornography as a basically harmless, if distorted, representation of sex is not separable from the Report's activation of certain sexological and psychological norms which (as we shall see in the final chapter) have come under attack in other contexts for condoning discriminatory and harmful sexual interests, attitudes and behaviours. Second, the capacity to come to terms with sexual materials 'through individual resolutions of personal confrontations with human experience' (p. 62), which for the Report provides the ground for a general deregulation, represents a level of ethical competence not universally distributed throughout the population. Third, the knowledges of sex which inform the Report place it in an ambiguous relation to the pleasures and entertainments it investigates. The Commission assumes that if accurate information is disseminated, sexual enlightenment will follow. While such a recommendation may seem naively to overlook the problem of pathological responses to sexual materials, in fact it reproduces the confessional strategy whose medical, sexological and psychological role in forming auto-erotic sexuality is already familiar to us from historical analysis of the pornographic field. Urging recourse to a process of information-giving as the panacea for all evils of sexual ignorance, the Report insists on establishing sex as something which all must learn has been repressed, hence as something to be attended to ever more conscientiously within the family and community.[8] It thus confirms a suspicion raised in the preceding chapter: that such arguments for legal *deregulation* are typically covert and confused arguments for a (pedagogic) *reregulation* of pornography, dependent on unacknowledged 'governmental' assumptions.

The beliefs about the person expressed in philosophical liberalism are less 'absolute' than they might appear. In fact, they are themselves already part of a governmental process which sustains yet also – precisely because the implementation of such beliefs always appeals to some particular set of pedagogically constructed personal abilities – sets limits to them. So, for instance, the harm condition accepted within philosophical liberalism depends upon being spelled out in practice, and as soon as this occurs rights of expression are limited according to differential intellectual and ethical capacities which certain 'receivers' of materials are presumed to have. We can thus insist that the Lockhart Report's delineation of rights of expression and communication does not transcend the regulatory field in which particular cultural norms and ethical techniques are disseminated; particularly the techniques of confession and de-repression in which individuals are supposed to learn that these rights contain personal truths misrecognised thus far by the law but now to be fearlessly avowed. The gaze of philosophical liberalism might be raised above the horizon of history, but its feet are stuck in the more messy historical clay overseen by its governmental twin.

In the framework of our historical and positive account, how may rights of expression be re-defined? We identify here three interlocking themes which inform the following sections' more detailed treatment of the management of rights of speech and press in the pornographic field.

The Positivity Of Legal Rights And Means

We shall analyse rights not as intrinsic moral properties of the individual which are simply recognised by the law, but as 'interests' created by specifically legal means. Rights are constructed through legislative and judicial procedures of decision-making. Seen in this way, rights – like liabilities – are devices for regulating conducts, devices which in some measure individuals are able to see themselves as 'owning'. Establishing a course of relief, action, or duty of forbearance, rights are ascribed to persons for specific not general purposes. Only by dint of particular forms of legislative and judicial definition operative within 'juridified' cultures do individuals become specified as legal personalities *capable* of 'possessing' rights. As to the regulation of pornography, the individual – far from being treated as the unified source of general moral capacities and rights – is ascribed through legislative and judicial decision-making procedures particular capacities to pursue particular interests in the production, circulation or use of sexual materials.

The Overlap Of Legal Rights With Extra-Legal Norms and Objectives

This emphasis on the positive effect of legal processes does not mean that legislative and judicial decision-making depends upon entirely mechanical and self-enclosed processes of legal reasoning. The construction and delimitation of rights bring into play extra-legal norms and objectives. These wider considerations do not emanate from the essential rights and attributes of the subject as these are conceived in philosophical liberalism; rather, rights are relative to certain purposes of legislation and administration which are themselves informed by 'socially determined policy objectives' (Hirst, 1980, pp. 96, 104). In the regulation of pornography, the legal administration of rights of speech and press takes into account both governmental interests in maintaining the level of free expression, involving access to highly diverse uses of media, *and* governmental and community interests in minimising the harms that may be associated with pornography for certain groups.

Rights such as those granted in free expression are thus key forms in which various extra-legal norms and objectives may be empowered at law. They are important means of settling disputes when questions of the validity or interpretation of statutes arise (Hirst, p. 97), as frequently occurs in relation to the constitutionality of obscenity laws in the United States, or when definition is required of the scope of action available to parties pursuing particular interests in or actions against pornography. Despite the philosophical ideal of a pure or absolute form of right, legal rights may be contradictory: the specification of rights of expression involves a balancing act between competing claims and interests in the regulation of pornography. In other words, rights are not anterior to the mechanisms adopted to solve practical problems; as attributes of legal personality they relate to a plurality of objectives and are not 'all of a piece' (Cousins, 1980, p. 119). Because they are created for particular purposes, legal rights are limited in their reach – in contrast to the image of universal and inalienable rights publicised by philosophical liberalism. In fact, we should not expect social problems identified in the production and circulation of pornography to be solved purely by the legal administration of rights and liabilities; this administration depends for its effect partly upon extra-legal formations of personal capacities, knowledges and conducts.

Rights Of Expression Permit Exchange Between Different Modes Of Regulating Pornography

Rights such as the right of free expression are regulatory – but also personally formative – mechanisms which provide competent individuals with a certain leeway to organise their own conducts. The legal and governmental mechanisms which construct and delimit rights of expression therefore play a positive role in the patterning of personal and institutional capacities. In other words, the nature and function of rights of expression in the pornographic field cannot properly be grasped by the terms of the philosophical-liberal model opposing state to individual subject and law to morality.

Philosophical arguments for deregulating the moral domain in favour of an essential right of free expression can in fact be relativised by being recontextualised as part of a broader practice whereby government supports the wide-scale dissemination of techniques of self-management. Far from being absolutely antithetical to one another, the liberal and the governmental have intertwined, philosophical liberalism contributing a justificatory rhetoric to the historical adjustment in which medical and moral policing has been replaced by a sophisticated strategy of self-government. This reciprocity, unsanctioned by the canons of political philosophy, has been dependent on pedagogic technologies which promote amongst individuals within large sectors of the population the desire and disposition – consonant with politically developed public objectives – to be self-governing.

The legal administration of rights in speech and press thus allows the more interventionist kinds of regulation to target those forms of conduct which cannot adequately be managed by the mechanisms of self-government.[9] Rights in speech and press, depending on pedagogic, aesthetic and ethical modes of self-formation and self-management, are delimited in the law's administration of obscenity as a historical category which varies according to different distributions of capacities, interests and levels of maturity.

Legal systems within the liberal state support a variety of mechanisms, ranging from the most directive forms of policing to the most discretionary processes of self-government, allowing the lines between them to be continuously re-adjusted according to calculations of public policy. In the field of pornography and obscenity, the emphasis has shifted historically between mechanisms of legal sanction and pedagogic administration of psychological and aesthetic disciplines for forming sensibility and managing the self. In this context, the right to free expression is no intrinsic property of the individual which the law must represent against intrusive state interests, but a normative technique for negotiating the relations between juridical policing and self-regulation. In relation to sexual materials, this right is a regulatory device typical of the practices of liberal government. Its administration involves an exchange whereby the law – opening into systems of prohibition and sanction, surveillance and summary jurisdiction – helps manage those problem conducts which welfare and education cannot handle.

At the same time, from these infra-legal domains the law draws norms by which to distinguish between the proscribed and the permitted and – in the constitutional context – between the proscribed and the protected. The liberal governmental regulation of obscenity thus relies centrally on the administrative, procedural and intellectual technologies of the law whose operation sets limits to the actions both of individual and state (or other collective) interests seeking to work through them. In other words, the administration of rights in the field of pornography and obscenity is carried out through a variety of permissions, obligations and restrictions to negotiate the mobile line between regulation by law and regulation by self.

JUDICIALLY CALCULATED RIGHTS: FROM MEDICAL POLICING TO PEDAGOGIC MANAGEMENT

With these revisions in mind, we embark on a more detailed reconsideration of the institutional administration of rights in speech and press with regard to the regulation of pornography in the United States. We can summarise these revisions in the proposition that in the institutions concerned, rights are operationalised as a mechanism for balancing the tactics of policing with forms of self-management.

The array of governmental mechanisms includes legislation (penal codes and statutes), the courts and various law enforcement agencies. These mechanisms which neither flow uniformly from the philosophical notion of right nor, despite the claims of libertarians, from the will of some centre of power, indicate that the regulation of pornography operates through varied and legally adjudicated forms of authority and decision-making. These forms require negotiations of social norms and policy objectives.

The network of federal, state and municipal legislation covers numerous activities including the producing and publishing or broadcasting of obscene works in various media; distributing such works through sale or loan; advertising and exhibiting sexual materials, using the mails, delivery services and other methods of transportation and communication; customs procedure and the importation of obscene materials; and so on.[10] Obscenity legislation is subject to constitutional constraints and is thus influenced by the Supreme Court's obscenity standards. Statutes assign a wide range of tasks to various kinds of law enforcement agencies, while limiting their powers in specific ways. So, for example, these tasks include the promulgating of regulations in accordance with federal statutes, regulations whose constitutional validity is in turn subject to judicial appeal and review.[11]

State and federal courts deal with actions which may infringe laws. They also contribute to the formation of laws by providing standards for determining obscenity and by considering the constitutionality of particular items of legislation brought before them. If, as in *American Booksellers*

Association v. *Hudnut* (1984) which we discuss in the next chapter, a court decides that under Article III of the Constitution a 'case or controversy' exists, a law, even though it has not yet been applied, is considered 'ripe for adjudication' of the constitutional issue. This intensive practice of constitutional validation may seem to make obscenity law in the United States quite distinct from the English common law system, particularly since – while there are landmark obscenity cases in the United States – there is in that country no precise equivalent to the ceremonial English show trial before judge and jury, the major constitutional decisions being made by the Supreme Court. However, in practice constitutional rights are deployed in a way that makes the workings of United States law on obscenity comparable to those of English common law. This deployment of rights depends not solely on the prior existence of constitutional principles, but on the historically conditioned and exacting interpretation of such principles. Rather than a 'representation' of the individual's given right of expression, the work of judicial interpretation and decision in relation to obscenity is a specialised process of constitutional 'calculation'. In this process rights are administered in relation to determinate objectives of government as these are measured through specifically legal forms of reasoning, establishing the context for an exchange between legal and infra-legal disciplines. Adopting particular cultural, governmental and pedagogic norms, legislatures and courts recognise the need for certain forms of self-regulation; at the same time, they relay into the domain of police a responsibility for dealing with various kinds of conduct deemed too difficult to manage in a self-regulatory mode.

The constitutional calculations made in the courts entail the judicial formulation and application of normative standards, comparable with the common law construction of criteria for regulating obscene publication. Indeed, the United States law continues to overlap extensively with English common law on obscenity from which it derived. The *Hicklin* test, with its embodied medical-moral norm, held sway in the United States for more or less the same period as in England.[12] Moreover, psychological and aesthetic criteria made major inroads into judicial calculations in the United States by the mid-twentieth century, just as they did in England. Nonetheless, a significant difference obtains between the legal administration of obscenity in the two countries: in the United States, the question of whether obscenity is something which the state should regulate becomes a specific issue in the courts, rather than in parliament. Is the emergence of this issue in the courts a sign that at last the law is coming to realise that as an instrument of state it should not trespass upon the domain of fundamental moral rights?

The question of whether obscenity law is constitutionally valid in relation to the First Amendment is posed squarely for the first time in the Supreme Court, in *Roth* v. *United States* (1957).[13] The Court notes that it had always assumed obscenity could legitimately be regulated by law (p. 481). While Roth contends that obscenity is 'expression not excepted from the sweep of the provision of the First Amendment' protecting speech and press, the Court rules that obscenity is 'not expression protected by the First Amendment' (p. 492). The Court's deliberations are consonant with longer-term judicial calculations allowing the administration of obscenity to respond to changing social norms and policy objectives. It does not resolve the problem of whether obscenity laws are constitutional by attempting to define once and for all the object being regulated; neither does it treat the appellant as a moral subject possessing an intrinsic right to expression. Rather, it enunciates standards which are – predictably – normative, and which allow obscenity to continue to be regulated as a variable category.[14]

The test which prevailed as the *Roth* standard from 1957 to 1973 drew upon criteria already established in the courts and was in turn amplified in subsequent opinions (*Jacobellis* v. *Ohio* (1964) and *A Book Named 'John Cleland's Memoirs of a Woman of Pleasure'* v. *Attorney General of the Commonwealth of Massachusetts* (1966)). According to this test (*The Supreme Court Obscenity Decisions*, p. 8), to be obscene, material had to:

(a) be patently offensive to contemporary community standards, going substantially beyond customary limits of candour, and
(b) appeal to the prurient interest of the average person, and
(c) be utterly without redeeming social value.

The categories of 'community standards', 'the average person', 'prurience' and 'social value' serve to ascribe rights to or withhold them from legal personalities. They are devices for allowing the threshold between legal policing and self-management to be negotiated in the calculation of these rights. We can trace this process of negotiation by focussing on the way in which medical notions of harm are by the time of *Roth* giving way to psycho-aesthetic notions of value and maturity.

In *Roth*, the Court alleges (incorrectly) that under the *Hicklin* test obscenity was judged by 'the effect of isolated passages upon the most susceptible persons' (p. 489). It is stated that this test now 'might well encompass material legitimately treating with sex and so it must be rejected as unconstitutionally restrictive of the freedoms of speech and press' (p. 489). Various court decisions have already rejected this standard, replacing it with the test of 'whether to the average person, applying contemporary community standards, the dominant theme of the material taken as a whole appeals to prurient interest' (p. 489). We recognise in this test of 'prurience' the emerging aesthetic emphasis on individuals' ability to mediate and order their own sexual interests and to balance the excitations of erotica with an aesthetic appreciation of the work as a whole. This test displaces the earlier medical policing which was concerned with the pathological effects which pornography – even in fragments – might have in the wrong hands. *Roth* is therefore symptomatic of a transition in legal regulation from a regime of medical policing to one of (pedagogically) managed pleasure. In *Roth*, the Court reiterates elements of sexological and aesthetic discourses, stating in truly Lawrentian style that sex is a 'great and mysterious motive force in human life', a 'subject of absorbing interest to mankind through the ages' and 'one of the vital problems of human interests and public concern' (p. 487). It is in such transcendent terms that works dealing with sex may now be seen to have 'value'. Constitutional safeguards, it is said, must exist for works which have a degree of value, even 'the slightest redeeming social importance' as statements of ideas (p. 484).

However, the Court also draws a line between this valuable interest in sex and obscenity. Without attempting to define obscenity other than as 'material which deals with sex in a manner appealing to prurient interest' (p. 487), the Court indicates in a completely routine way that there exists a class of such materials bereft of social value. Thus the judgement of prurient interest places a limit of sorts on the deregulation of access to sexual representations. The Court rejects the claim that obscenity laws violate the free speech provisions of the Constitution in seeking to punish sexual 'thoughts' which are not related to any anti-social 'conducts'. It does so by implicitly accepting the validity of governmental concerns with checking the harms of obscenity, concerns which run through previous statutes, policies and decisions.[15] In thus combining a norm of aesthetic and sexological value with a norm justifying state interests in minimising harms, the Courts allows the balance between self-management and legal policing to be maintained and adjusted.

In adopting aesthetic criteria, the courts at the same time perpetuate a welfarist concern with obscenity as a variable and potentially harmful phenomenon. To amplify this point we turn to a New York District Court trial of 1959 in which a publisher and distributor take action to restrain the enforcement of a Post Office Department decision that a novel, *Lady Chatterley's Lover*, is obscene and therefore non-mailable, or to have the statute itself declared unconstitutional (*Grove Press, Inc.* v. *Christenberry*). The Court identifies the novel as a work of literature, entitled to the protections guaranteed to freedoms of speech and press by the First Amendment (p. 503), holding that the book does not appeal to prurient interest and does have literary merit (pp. 499–502). As in the English trial of the same novel, this merit is established in terms borrowed directly from Romantic literary criticism. *Lady Chatterley's Lover* is said to be a serious literary work in its 'theme', in which sexual representations are open to symbolic interpretation, and in its use of 'character', 'plot', 'situation' and style ('fine writing and . . . descriptive passages of rare beauty') (pp. 488, 500). Even if it is assumed that some passages 'taken in isolation tend to arouse shameful, morbid and lustful sexual desires in the average reader', they are integral to 'the development of theme, plot and character' (p. 500). Here it is evident that the legal criterion according to which the work must be judged 'as a whole' derives from a literary critical conception of the unity that distinguishes the true work of art. Most courts (according to Judge Frank in his concurring opinion in *United States* v. *Roth* p. 825) do not consider the intention of the author, publisher or distributor independently of the effect which a work which is found to be obscene has on those who read or view it. However, it is worth noting that in *Grove Press* the author's intention, understood in aesthetic terms, is taken as relevant: the sincerity with which this intention is 'expressed in the manner' in which the book is written has a great deal to do with deciding the question of literary and intellectual 'merit' (p. 502). Lawrence's 'A Propos of *Lady Chatterley's Lover*' and 'Pornography and Obscenity' and his claim that pornography, unlike literature, tries 'to insult sex, to do dirt on it', are cited approvingly (pp. 500–1) by the judge to support the view that the novel is not 'dirt for dirt's sake'.

This canonising work of citation is a measure of the extent to which the aesthetic practice of writing, reading and shaping the sexual self – once the esoteric ethic of a refined few – has by the later 1950s been sufficiently widely distributed to allow for a legal relaxing of policing in favour of pedagogy. Indeed, the logic of the court's decision is explicitly distributional . Detailed reference is made to the institutional arrangements of publication, dissemination and reception which distinguish the literary from the pornographic: 'A work of literature published and distributed through normal channels by a reputable publisher stands on quite a different footing from hard core pornography furtively sold for the purpose of profiting by the titillation of the dirty minded' (p. 503). The Court notes that the advertising and promotional materials treat the novel as serious literature without any attempt 'to pander to the lewd and lascivious minded for profit', that the book is distributed 'through leading bookstores throughout the country' and that it is treated seriously by the press (pp. 497, 502). These references show that the aesthetic discipline is admitted as both a critical lexicon or technique of reading now able to be applied to erotic literature and as the guarantee of a legitimate practice of production and distribution.[16]

From *Roth* and *Grove Press* we thus see that the emergence of the question whether obscenity laws are constitutionally valid, together with new decisions allowing considerable latitude in the circulation of serious sexual literature, need not be treated as moves to deregulate the use of erotica in recognition of a general moral right of expression. Rather, these cases exemplify a shift from one form of regulation, medical policing, towards another which operates through the widescale but always less than universal distribution of psychological, aesthetic and sexological techniques for schooling the pleasures.

The Supreme Court's obscenity standards have, of course, continued to be modified. The general test which has prevailed since 1973 was formulated in *Miller* v. *California*, in which for the first time since *Roth* the Court arrived at standards acceptable to the majority of its members. In the *Miller* test, obscenity is determined according to the following criteria:

(a) whether the average person, applying contemporary community standards, would find that the work, taken as a whole, appeals to the prurient interest, and
(b) whether the work depicts or describes, in a patently offensive way, sexual conduct specifically defined by the applicable state law, and
(c) whether the work, taken as a whole, lacks serious literary, artistic, political or scientific value.

(*Miller* v. *California*, p. 24)

Miller differs from *Roth* in the following regards: the tastes of the average person have shifted from the position of object of the obscenity test to that of its legal reagent; those states wishing to ban obscenity under *Miller* are required to define the sorts of depicted conducts which are proscribed; and obscenity has become material without 'serious' value rather than being 'utterly without redeeming social value'. More important than these differences, however, is a commonality: the Supreme Court standards continue to operate not as legal definitions but as variable operational norms. In *Miller*, reference to 'community' standards and 'literary, artistic' or other value indicates that the categories of prurience, offensiveness and value continue to allow the legal threshold of obscenity to float in relation to a normative distribution of capacities and interests among audiences. The examples given of proscribed conducts indicate that the distinction between hard-core and soft-core pornography has begun to displace that between art and pornography as the main distinction for establishing whether materials are entitled to protection under the First Amendment. The hard-soft distinction, however, still works in aesthetic terms, allowing soft-core materials to be regulated mainly through the exercise of personal and commercial discretion. While the application of this distinction has expanded the types of materials entitled to constitutional protection, the *Miller* test nonetheless continues to permit proscription of materials and conducts in which certain governmental responsibilities, such as preventing harms, are judged to outweigh rights of free expression.

For philosophical liberals, the hand of censorship is still seen to be working through the *Miller* changes. Richards (1980, pp. 111–12) claims that *Miller* allows reliance on local obscenity standards and hence 'a variety of constitutionally permissible restrictions' such that a person's First Amendment rights can be constrained 'without appeal to a national standard'. However, the Supreme Court standards, allowing the forms of regulation to be modulated in relation to the variability of audience capacities and interests, are perhaps a more flexible and subtle instrument of regulation than such criticism allows. The jury application of local standards which *Miller* (pp. 30–1) permits may mean that the standards will vary with the educational and cultural dispositions of specific regions, leading to a systemic pluralism (cf. *People* v. *Wiseman* (1983), and *Staten* v. *State* (1985)). Similarly, in applying the *Miller* test, courts have allowed 'prurience' to be judged relative to some clearly defined sexual interest of a group referred to as 'deviant', provided there is evidence that the material in question is designed for and primarily disseminated to such a group (cf. *State* v. *Summers* (1985)). That there is continuing ambivalence and variation in the management of obscenity is underlined by the fact that the provision of community standards may be used to restrict the access of such groups to specialised forms of erotica. It has also been possible in the courts to interpret 'community standards' as a populations's perception of 'what is generally acceptable in the community considering the intended and probable recipients of the materials' (*Saliba* v. *State* (1985), p. 1186).[17]

In some instances, the administration of obscenity as a variable category has entailed adapting a prevailing standard for specific purposes, while preserving the main formulations. In *Ginsberg* v. *State of New York* (1968), where the Supreme Court formally approved the mechanism of variable obscenity, which had been operating *avant la lettre* in United States as in English regulations, it was held that the prevailing *Roth* standard could be adapted to allow an assessment of obscenity relative to minors in terms of its specific appeal to them. Calculations of the variable nature of obscenity depend on taking cognisance of particular norms: in *Ginsberg* the norm is 'the ethical and moral development of youth' which might be harmed in a way not necessarily proven scientifically but nonetheless requiring to be policed socially (p. 641). Similarly, the courts have held that government has a surpassing interest in preventing the sexual exploitation and abuse of children in the production of pornography. In *New York* v. *Ferber* (1982) the Supreme Court explicitly went beyond *Miller* by upholding a statute prohibiting persons from distributing child pornography, regardless of claims of 'value', stating:

> When a class of material . . . bears so heavily and pervasively on the welfare of children engaged in its production, we think the balance of competing interests is clearly struck and that it is permissible to consider these materials as without the protection of the First Amendment. (p. 3358)

Special standards for juvenile obscenity have in fact been provided in many statutes and have been upheld in broad principle in the courts (*M. S. News Co* v. *Casado* (1983); *Upper Midwest Booksellers* v. *City of Minneapolis* (1985)).

From the standpoint of philosophical liberalism, the regime of management confirmed in *Roth* and *Miller* has discriminated against the fundamental right of individual judgement and expression. Richards thus maintains that the criteria of prurience, offensiveness and community standards translate moral fears into proscriptions against 'harms' which are more imaginary than real, and that the test of value allows arbitrary and unconstitutional prohibitions on particular kinds of meaning. The legal decisions and controls which the prevailing standards represent are 'profoundly political and violate the ideal of neutral principles of constitutional adjudication' (p. 119). Here the idea that the law fails to represent naturally given rights of the individual combines with the idea that the law directly transmits a political and ideological will. This philosophical notion that constitutional adjudication degenerates into 'mis-representation', and that the law fails to recognise an intrinsic moral right because of distorting political interests, may be contrasted with our own description of the 'constitutional calculations' of obscenity law. By this we mean the use of definite judicial categories and procedures to decide, in the light of certain norms and policy considerations, which are the appropriate formal jurisdictions to activate and which the appropriate interrelations between legal regulation and self-regulation to empower in the pornographic field.[18]

DIFFERENCES AND LIMITS

We turn now to the legal administration of rights in connection with the various law enforcement agencies in the United States. In the light of our discussion thus far, we would expect that in relation to policing practices, rights and interests in pornography will be organised, delimited and modified by particular legislative and judicial means, according to public policy objectives, in an exchange between summary regulation and pedagogic management. As we saw in a different historical context in Chapter 3 when discussing the 1908 *Report from the Joint Select Committee on Lotteries and Indecent Advertisements*, the policing of pornography involves a dense network of agencies which have different kinds of authority and modes of operation. In the United States, the relevant law enforcement agencies include local, state and federal police, the Customs Bureau, the Post Office Department and the Federal Communications Commission. The jurisdictions of these agencies may overlap, as they do in the policing of major producers and distributors of erotica operating in different states and through multiple channels, but as the Lockhart Report states (p. 394), there is 'no systematic cooperation' between them. The powers and operations of these agencies are supported, and delimited, by legislative and judicial calculations of Americans' rights and interests in relation to pornography.[19] The judicial balancing of summary procedures with constitutional rights which this involves may be illustrated with reference to the procedures of routine policing.

This balancing is seen in a general division of responsibilities between types of personnel. While police officers administer 'questions of law', the determination of what meets the standards of prurient interest and patent offensiveness raises 'questions of fact' which cannot receive a single definitive answer and require case by case judicial decisions in the light of relevant community standards. Routine policing involves a system of warrants (judicial referrals) in which agents have powers of search and pre-trial seizure of materials which is presumptively obscene.[20] Provision exists for material to be destroyed in order to avoid criminal prosecution for obscenity. When it comes to whether the material in question is actually obscene, the decision can only be made by the trier of fact. In the courts, this is the role of a judge, magistrate or jury. In routine police work, it is the task of the judicial officer (magistrate or judge) issuing the search warrant to make an initial determination whether there is probable cause to believe the material in question is obscene (see, for example, *Ross* v. *State* (1984)). This decision is to be made on the basis of facts stated in the relevant police affidavit. The police statement must not be merely conclusory. It must describe the materials with sufficient particularity to enable the judicial officer to focus searchingly and independently on the question of obscenity in the light of the prevailing Supreme Court test (see, for instance, *Commonwealth* v. *Dane Entertainment Services, Inc. (No. 1)* (1983)). The trier of fact's decision must be made under the prevailing judicial standards for obscenity which are embodied in constitutionally valid legislation. These formalised arrangements are seen as a safeguard of due process, ensuring that police do not become 'censors' by suppressing materials independently of an appropriate judicial and constitutional test for obscenity.[21]

Other procedural limitations on policing, marking an intersection with forms and rights of self-regulation, include the conditions of *scienter* and prior restraint. Under the *scienter* requirement established for obscenity in *Smith* v. *California* (1959), a defendant may not be punished for a violation unless he or she is proven to have committed the violation knowingly (cf. the Lockhart Report, p. 376). This requirement is intended to avoid placing a prior restraint on the publication and dissemination of constitutionally protected material. Inhibition of protected expression might occur if persons can be held criminally liable for dealing in material whose contents they do not know and so decide to limit the materials they possess for sale or similar purposes to those which they have inspected. The definition of 'knowing' has included both direct knowledge of the character of the materials and reason to believe further inspection of them is warranted (see, for example, *Commonwealth* v. *Stock* (1985)). The effect of this requirement is that for an action to become an obscenity violation it must include the element of *mens rea*.[22]

This requirement for the element of prior knowledge in the definition of the crime – relating as it does to certain commercial and moral rights and interests – allows us to make a further argument against the recurring philosophical liberal criticism that obscenity law infringes on First Amendment rights because its definition is vague, subjective and too arbitrary to allow consistency in the policing of sexual materials. The Lockhart Report contends (p. 59) that the *Roth* criteria are 'vague and highly subjective aesthetic, psychological and moral tests'. They do not, it is said, provide meaningful guidance for law enforcement officials or the courts, and so produce erroneous decisions and interfere with constitutionally protected materials (cf. *Paris Adult Theatre I* v. *Slaton*, Mr Justice Brennan dissenting, pp. 73–114). Supposedly, this subjectivity and vagueness also make it impossible for publishers, distributors, retailers and others to know in advance whether they will be charged with a criminal offence for purveying a particular work. This may lead to over-cautiousness on their part and have a damaging effect on free expression and the free market in ideas (Lockhart Report, pp. 45–6).

However, the *scienter* requirement works precisely to afford a measure of constitutional protection to purveyors of sexual materials, while limiting their ability to have recourse to the right of free expression. It is a defence for booksellers to claim that, having not inspected their entire stock, they did not know that it contained pornographic works; but this defence implies that what *counts* as pornographic is indeed known routinely. In other words, this mechanism shows that the policing of pornography cannot be dismissed as a clumsy infringement of an inherent right to expression. On the contrary, in regulating obscenity the police and courts are usually dealing with more or less 'known' quantities – that is, specific forms of production of materials, channels of distribution and categories of consumer. This holds for the range of statutes we cite in the following paragraphs covering diverse law enforcement agencies, which include the *scienter* condition or, as in the case of radio communication, are understood to imply it – *United States* v. *Smith* (1972). To adapt Mr Justice Stewart's comment on the problem of defining obscenity – 'I know it when I see it' (*Jacobellis* v. *Ohio* (1964), p. 197) – judicial agents and police may know or presume to know obscenity when they see it because there is a trade whose agents usually know obscenity whether they actually see it or not. It is held in the courts that absolute precision is not necessary in statutory definitions of obscenity, and that in order to satisfy due process requirements it is necessary only for the language used to provide what was described in another context in *United States* v. *Petrillo* (1946, p. 8) as 'sufficiently definite warning as to the proscribed conduct when measured by common understanding and practices'. From these specifications, we see that due process and judicially administered procedural limitations cannot adequately be understood through reference to a given right of expression that is automatically compromised by the presence of state interests. In practice, rights and interests are objects of calculations made in terms of social norms and policy objectives, in order to regulate more or less readily recognisable practices, or what Mr Justice Brennan referred to as the 'calculated purveyance' of pornography (*Mishkin* v. *State of New York* (1966), p. 512). [23]

If we turn to the other law enforcement bodies, we see similar interactions with judicial agents.[24] The Customs Statute prohibits all persons from importing obscene articles into the United States.[25] Procedures followed by the Customs Bureau allow for random inspection of imported items, and any matter discovered which the Bureau believes to be obscene is subject to seizure and forfeiture by customs officers. Such matter must be referred to the United States attorney of the relevant district who arranges for a district court adjudication, made according to prevailing constitutional standards, of the question of whether the material is obscene, and only then may an article declared obscene be destroyed.[26]

The basic mail statute prohibits the use of the mails for sending or delivering obscene materials.[27] The United States Postal Inspection Service has the power to investigate suspected violations of statutes, although (according to the Lockhart Report, p. 389) the Justice Department may also initiate proceedings and has done so especially in relation to pandering – that is, the 'business of purveying graphic or textual matter openly advertised to appeal to the erotic interest' of potential customers (*Ginzburg* v. *United States* (1966), p. 467). To a large extent, postal regulation works through administrative procedures rather than relying on prosecution. These procedures include the denial of second-class mailing privileges, declarations of non-mailability, and procedures of prevention and suppression, including the provision of lists of persons desiring to receive no sexually-oriented advertising mail.[28] Statutes and legal judgements demarcate responsibilities here, in a way similar to that just discussed in relation to police warrants, such that any final decision on whether an article is obscene is (as we saw in *Grove Press*) a matter specifically for judicial resolution according to prevailing obscenity standards.

The Federal Communications Commission investigates violations of the federal statute which prohibits the use of obscene, indecent or profane language by means of radio communication.[29] It is of interest that in 1970 the Lockhart Report implied that the Commission was not actively regulating obscene or indecent broadcasting (neither independently monitoring stations in order to detect violations nor as a rule imposing penalties on broadcasters or amateur operators unless as a result of citizens' complaints). However, by 1986 the use of such means of communications as cable and satellite television and the telephone to transmit obscenity has come to be regarded as a serious problem. The Hudson Report (pp. 562–82) recommends that Congress review the laws to allow agencies such as the Federal Communications Commission to control these activities more effectively. Such a reversal shows how calculations of the nature and effects of obscenity have continued to shift, often suddenly, in response to changing uses of technology, forms of distribution and audience dispositions.

In line with our general redefinition of the category of rights, these examples of judicial and police processes show that to understand the practical availability of rights of expression in the regulation of pornography, the philosophically conceived right of expression needs to be disaggregated into the miscellany of statuses, entitlements, obligations and types of agency, located at the level of either the regulating or the regulated bodies. Rights of expression here have differentiated forms and limits dependent on the law's calculation of governmental interests in regulating various eroticising uses of media and in negotiating relations between summary regulation and self-management. To spell out this 'disaggregation', three points can be extrapolated from the materials presented above, in keeping with our emphasis on the positivity of legal means, the overlap of legal process and public policy objectives, and the exchange between different modes of regulating pornography.

First, in the regulation of pornography and obscenity the individual is not the unified origin of some essential right, but may be invested with legal attributes appropriate for pursuing particular interests. In practice, the myriad statutes and cases relating to obscenity in the United States show that rights of speech and press in relation to pornography are invested in persons performing such different roles as those of publisher, importer, distributor, writer, film-maker, videotape producer, translator, advertiser, broadcaster, librarian, exhibitor and consumer. These individuals pursue such diverse activities as producing, recording, transporting, mailing, importing, carrying, transmitting, selling, lending, projecting, buying, receiving, renting, reading and viewing numerous kinds of sexual materials, as well as employing certain categories of personnel and conducting certain types of businesses. In regulating obscenity, the courts are not attempting to reconcile the actions of policing with some all-purpose right to free expression which individuals possess; they are deciding whether persons are entitled to specific economic and moral rights in the light of governmental and welfare interests in regulating pornography.

Second, the law resolves competing or in some cases contradictory rights and interests. It does so in terms of particular norms and policy considerations which it can recognise and adopt. Despite the privileged place accorded in liberal jurisprudence to the individual's right to read or see what he or she chooses to consume, in practice no particular right of speech and publication is held to transcend all other rights and interests. In the legal regulation of pornography, rights of expression are maintained for specific purposes and are negotiated against other rights and interests. So, for example, rights of booksellers, book distributors and publishers to deal in sexually explicit materials which are not considered 'obscene as to adults' encounter restrictions on the *display* of such materials in business or commercial districts where minors are likely to be exposed to view them – restrictions which are considered constitutionally valid because of a policy of protecting minors even though booksellers might engage in self-censorship because of them (cf. *American Booksellers Association, Inc.* v. *Rendell* (1984)).

Further evidence of the way in which the law mediates different interests through its consideration of extra-legal norms is furnished by the fact that the same individual may occupy different and possibly contradictory statuses. Thus the rights of *adults* to have access to sexually explicit materials are not simply identical with the rights of *parents* to exercise their own discretion in directing their children's upbringing, including their relation to sexual materials. The latter rights are tempered by judicial recognition of a governmental interest in the welfare of minors and hence in managing problems posed by child pornography, commercial display, and the use of media in the household – including independent access of minors to pornography on cable television (that is, in the very space in which a parent may wish to exercise an adult right to receive pornographic messages).[30]

To identify this legal construction, delimitation and mediation of rights in another way, rights of expression in sexual materials do not originate in an essential moral right but are built up alongside other legally constructible rights and liabilities inseparable from public policy considerations. The question of whether a particular course of action can be made a right of expression is decided in the context of both already established rights of expression and other layers of rights and liabilities. Hence the question of whether pornography counts as speech – that is, as a constitutionally protected use of a medium outweighing any identified governmental interests in restricting its free performance and circulation – is a practical and variable question.

That this is so is reflected in the fact that there are preconditions and limits on access to a protected right of expression in pornography. The circumstances under which individuals or groups are entitled to invoke First Amendment rights to support a particular type of action or relief are a matter of legislative determination and, in contested cases or challenges to the legislation's constitutionality, judicial deliberation. Courts have thus held that an element of 'expression' associated with a practice cannot be used to extend constitutional protection to conducts otherwise proscribed, such as obscenity and prostitution. In *Arcara* v. *Cloud Book, Inc* (1986), it was ruled that the attempt to gain protection for illegal activities by associating them with the domain of 'expression' (in this case, by selling books on premises used for prostitution) was invalid. Once limits have been set on the protecting of certain activities as 'speech', there can follow constraints on attempts to use other rights to overcome those limits. In *Commonwealth* v. *Stock* (pp. 316–7), it was held that the right to enter a business contract does not entail the right to require that distributors or retailers take for resale any materials of an obscene nature. These instances underscore the fact that it is the law which decides whether the behaviour in question is of a kind to which rights of expression attach.

Third, the fact that within the legislative, judicial and policing networks concerned with the regulation of pornography, rights of expression are variable entitlements confirms that such rights are mechanisms which allow the boundary between law and policing to be maintained or adjusted. This means that if the circumstances under which rights may be mobilised are a matter of judicial decision, so, too, are questions of the scope of particular rights. This may be illustrated by looking at the way in which the right of privacy – a relatively new right, now in the process of rapid expansion – has come to intersect with the regulation of pornography.[31]

In the nineteenth century the policing of obscenity and indecent materials was mainly concerned with supervising the streets and places of popular entertainment. In those circumstances, the consumption of erotica in the home, in the form of gentlemen's pornography for instance, was not a major issue. There was no question of passionately defending the individual's 'privacy' and keeping the door shut against the state, nor of arguing that the law should be reformed to respect a universal right of individuals to use pornography privately. A legal notion of a 'privacy' exercised in the use of book sex was not then available. By the mid-twentieth century, the idea of the right to cultivate one's sexual self through the auto-erotic use of various sexual media has become a major theme in the liberatory project of deregulation. As noted in Chapter 6, philosophical liberalism conveniently conflates an architectural space of privacy with the assumed autonomy of the subject of consciousness. The right to choose for oneself what to read, write or view by way of sexual materials becomes fused with the spatial right of privacy, which can then be treated in turn as flowing from the natural definition of the individual as self-possessed subject.

The legal use of the category of privacy is, however, dependent on particular social relations, spatial arrangements and norms of conduct, not on the putative moral autonomy of individuals left to their own devices. In United States law, a right in the private use of obscenity was specifically recognised in *Stanley* v. *Georgia* (1969). Now, on the issue of whether the appellant has 'the right to read or observe what he pleases – the right to satisfy his intellectual and emotional needs in the privacy of dhis own home' (p. 565), there is no doubt that the Supreme Court rhetorically equates the privacy of a place with the privacy or individuality of thought. It holds that the mere categorisation of the materials in question as obscene does not justify state inquiry into what the individual possesses and reads:

> Whatever may be the justifications for other statutes regulating obscenity, we do not think that they reach into the privacy of one's own home. If the First Amendment means anything, it means that a State has no business telling a man, sitting alone in his own house, what books he may read or what films he may watch. Our whole constitutional heritage rebels at the thought of giving government the power to control men's minds. (pp. 565–6).

However, this decision does not introduce an unlimited privacy right deriving from the inviolate personality of the individual. We have already observed that with regard to domestic privacy the same individual may be the bearer of incompatible rights attached to the legal personas of 'adult' and 'parent'. In fact, the construction of the right in *Stanley* is a highly specific judicial adjustment of the line between policing and self-management, made possible by the judicial adoption of an aesthetic, infra-legal norm. This judicial definition of a right turns on an idea of privacy in which aesthetic regulation is equated with a capacity of more or less civilised behaviour; protection is not implied for problem behaviours which may come to the attention of the police and in relation to which private spaces might begin to look less sacrosanct. The type of action or relief recognised does not provide a general base on which other rights claimed in relation to privacy will necessarily be granted. As we observed, constitutional rights are specific and bounded, and the recognition of one does not spread, rhizome-like, to form others on the ground of some all-inclusive moral right. The entitlement granted in *Stanley* is conditional on 'possession' by the individual of obscene material for his own use 'in his home' (p. 568).

The Lockhart Report points out that some lower federal courts gave a degree of recognition to correlative rights in distribution, importation, mailing and exhibition, soon after this ruling was made. However, this direction was not followed by the Supreme Court, whose decisions have shown that the right to private use is not readily transferable to other contexts. The Court distinguished explicitly between the public distribution of obscene materials and possession in the home (p. 567) and made no suggestion that the privacy right could be extended by linking it to places other than the home, or to the notion that there is a private space which persons carry with them wherever they might go. Further it refused to accept that certain social relations of confidence deserving of protection might provide an acceptable basis for privacy rights more generally.[32] In *United States* v. *Orito* (1973), the Court rejects the idea that 'some zone of constitutionally protected privacy follows [obscene] material when it is moved outside the home area protected by *Stanley*' (pp. 141–2). In this and several other cases, attempts to argue that the right of private possession entails a correlative right to sell, receive, import, transport or distribute obscene material, were unsuccessful.[33]

The fact that an individual may have the right to possess but not receive obscene materials, perhaps inconsistent from a philosophical point of view, makes sense when it is remembered that rights in the use of erotica are determined in relation to interests in regulating conducts associated with the circulation of possibly harmful materials. It is also worth noting that there are constraints on individuals' abilities to invoke privacy rights in conjunction with forms of 'conduct' just as there are in relation to the exercise of rights of 'speech'. So, for example, in *Swann* v. *State* (1981) it is held that an art outraging public decency – an act noticed by police on commercial premises – is not protected by a privacy interest related to the use of a confined film booth for viewing pornography. From judicial considerations of the policing of pornography outside the home, in locations such as adult bookstores with viewing facilities, clubs, cinemas and theatres, we see that 'privacy' is not a right to make use of a given space at will which is granted legally in recognition of the inherent attributes ('consciousness', 'rationality', 'inviolate personality') of the individual. On the contrary, in delineating the private and the public, the law is authorising different mechanisms (here self-management and there policing) for regulating specific types of behaviour associated with the circulation of sexual materials in differentiated social spaces.

In the regulation of pornography, rights of expression and privacy are categories through which individuals are, to a degree, made responsible for managing their own conducts in relation to sexual materials. Our disaggregation of rights of expression shows that the balance between strategies of regulation and deregulation is a matter of complex and continuous assessment. The idea of an essential individual right in the use of sexual materials as 'expression', and the accompanying theme of legal and social reform to be achieved through derepression, cannot guide legal calculation beyond a certain point in dealing with competing interests, different uses of materials and different specifications of pornography's effects on character and conduct. Of course, philosophical and aesthetic norms have come into play in the legal interpretation of constitutional rights. However, when they do so, the recognition of rights takes place according to definite and limited legal calculations, deeply informed by the interests of government and self-government.

RIGHTS OF THE ETHICALLY COMPETENT

We have seen that in the regulation of pornography, not only is the construction of rights of expression historically contingent, but the rights so constructed are variable. In other words, rights are relative to the availability of certain capacities for self-regulation, and to the legal buttressing of different channels of distribution. The definition of a right of private possession of obscenity marks the legal adoption of a pedagogically distributed aesthetic norm which literally has become domesticated (the individual has

United States Obscenity Law 225

the right 'to satisfy his intellectual and emotional needs in the [peaceful] privacy of his own home'). However, some 'private' practices of sex using pornographic representations have also posed problems within the domain of policing. That 'privacy' may be viewed as a space in which sexual media are used in ways linked with problem behaviours can be seen from the submission made in 1969 to the Presidential Commission on Pornography and Obscenity by the Director of the FBI, J. Edgar Hoover, and the police 'case studies' which follow it in the dissenting report of Commissioner Charles H. Keating, Jr (the Lockhart Report, pp. 632–54). Many of these case studies register a private or group use of pornography by men and adolescent males as a means of excitation in committing anti-social acts and crimes of sexual violence particularly against women and girls. On the basis of a frequency of association established through police observation, as against the forms of proof of causality required by certain branches of social science, Hoover argues that the key issue before the Commission should be the 'relationship' of pornography and obscenity to anti-social behaviour and the recommendation of effective and constitutional means of controlling the traffic in those materials (pp. 633–4). He gives the following example of common forms of police evidence:

> [I]n one case of a rape of a 12-year-old girl by a 20-year-old boy (*sic*), a girlie magazine belonging to the suspect was left at the scene of the attack and was identified by the victim as being in the youth's presence at the time of the attack. The presence of the girlie magazine in the possession of the rapist at the time of the attack is sufficient to warrant notice as a statistic giving evidence of the 'relationship' of obscenity to anti-social behaviour and bearing on the 'rationality' of [obscenity] legislation. (pp. 635–6)

Hoover is not the most acceptable angel to have on one's side. In this book, though, we have often asked readers to reconsider rejected sources, and such police documentation indicates that governmental responsibilities in controlling harms associated with uses of pornography may be compelling even in a context of extensive pedagogic management of sexualities. We can also note that the Hudson Report, taking a different approach from the majority in the Lockhart Report, argues that certain problems associated with the use of evidence provided by 'clinical' professionals on the effects of exposure of pornography (such as the problem of statistical generalisation on the basis of experimental samples) diminish if demographic evidence is taken into account (p. 315). Significantly, the mechanism of this wider observation is again the provision of evidence from law enforcement personnel. While it is acknowledged that such data is less 'scientific' than some other kinds of evidence, it is seen as able to produce 'some positive statistical correlation between the prevalence of some type of material and some harmful act':

> For example, we have heard much evidence from law enforcement personnel that a disproportionate number of sex offenders were found to have large quantities of pornographic materials in their residences. Pornographic material was found on the premises more, in the opinion of the witnesses, than one would expect to find it in the residences of a random sample of the population as a whole, in the residences of a random sample of non-offenders of the same sex, age, and socioeconomic status, or in the residences of a random sample of offenders whose offenses were not sex offenses. To the extent that we believe these witnesses, then there is a correlation between pornographic materials and sex offenses. (p. 316)

Despite their apparent vulnerability to scientific critique, such correlations have been the stock-in-trade of governmental calculation and intervention since the early nineteenth century, when the collection of social statistics was irrevocably tied to the agencies and objectives of social policing. The idea that it is possible to reject such action-oriented knowledges by appealing to non-normative statistical descriptions is, in our view, certainly utopian and possibly meaningless. For this reason we are not uncomfortable with the overlap between police-statistical correlations of pornography with criminal behaviour and our own thesis that pornography is not a type of representation but a type of behaviour using representations. The reference to links between use of pornography and sex offences is comparable to the use of pornography as a script to be emulated in real-life situations involving physical and psychological harms to women.[34] In the Hudson Report, the way in which the circulation, 'possession' and use of pornography show up – through the use of statistical evidence – as a social problem requiring regulation, is related to normative concerns with uses of sexual media in patterns of conduct, not to the goal of establishing an objective 'truth'. This report thus demonstrates that governmental interests and policy objectives in regulating pornography persist, and that the key problem is considered to be not whether the pursuit of such interests offends the First Amendment, but *where* the adjustable threshold is to be established between ethical self-regulation and juridical policing.

In placing a limit on the 'absolutist' view that even the hardest-core pornographic item is a communicative act whose distribution and use 'is within the First Amendment's coverage', the Hudson Report accepts that the fundamental direction of the Supreme Court in *Roth* and *Miller* is correct (cf. pp. 263–4). Like the judicial calculation of rights and interests, the logic of its recommendations is distributional. The right of expression is specific and is limited to the production, dissemination and use of materials which surpass 'some admittedly low threshold of cognitive appeal, whether that appeal be emotive, intellectual, aesthetic, or informational' (p. 264). While lines are not easy to draw, most hard-core material falls below 'this minimal threshold of cognitive or similar appeal' (pp. 264–5). The 'marketplace of ideas' is not evoked as the democratic scene on which the universal potential for self-expression will be realised. Even though hard-core material might be seen as containing some characteristics of expression serious enough to merit constitutional protection if it appeared in a different context and was presented in a different way, there is no doubt that the commercial trade in such material is in fact 'directed virtually exclusively at sexual arousal' (pp. 265–6). In other words, as observed above, pornography is a trade in 'known' quantities, distributions and uses. The use of hard-core materials, in the Report's view, is less a matter of speech than of conduct:

> The manner of presentation and distribution of most standard pornography confirms the view that at bottom the predominant use of such materials is a masturbatory aid. We do not say that there is anything necessarily wrong with that for that reason. But once the predominant use, and the appeal to that predominant use, becomes apparent, what emerges is that much of what this material involves is not so much portrayal of sex, or discussion of sex, but simply sex itself. As sex itself, the arguments for or against restriction are serious, but they are arguments properly removed from the First Amendment questions that surround primarily materials whose overwhelming use is not as a short-term masturbatory aid. (p. 266)

From this point of view, the acceptance of a constitutional right to 'expression' in the use of sexual materials is thus limited to those channels and populations in which what we have called 'aesthetic' techniques of production and use are distributed and maintained. The governmental distinction made in the Report between those uses of erotica which can be managed as 'speech' through processes of self-regulation and those which need to be regulated through legal intervention and policing clearly overlaps with our account of the limited ethical and political options for regulating pornography. There has been no access (nor, it seems, will there be) to a position in which one can automatically invoke constitutional guarantees covering free speech in order to gain protection for the conducts associated with the production and use of sexual materials. The Report adds that, of course, 'using a picture of sex as a masturbatory aid is different from the simple act of masturbation, or any other form of sex' (p. 267), and that the very use of words and images requires some attention to First Amendment questions. However, it continues, standard pornographic material in its 'standard context of distribution and use' is 'so far removed from any of the central purposes of the First Amendment, and so close to so much of the rest of the sex industry' that affording such material constitutional protection seems 'highly attenuated' (p. 267).

In the foreseeable future, there will be further decisions on what kinds of sexual materials and related conducts will be proscribed, permitted or protected. Moreover, we will see a process of continuous adjustment to the boundary between self-regulation and regulation by law. Philosophical liberalism is itself attached to the system of pedagogical management which comprises one of the two major available strategies – along with legal policing – which are available for regulating sexualities and the uses of erotica. Decision-making in this field of regulation cannot be founded in universalising distinctions between sex and its representation, conduct and speech, or the private domain of the moral subject of rights and the public realm of state controls. Rights and interests in pornography will continue to be constructed and mediated variably by means of norm-based legal and governmental calculations. Yet it would be unreasonable to expect that philosophical liberalism – even confronted by the assemblage of evidence of the bounded purposiveness of the rights in question – will meekly evacuate the field, leaving the work of decision-making to less sweeping and more particularised criteria. Too much has come to be at stake; for some nothing less than the belief that 'our "liberation" is in the balance', as Foucault (1979, p. 159) ironically concludes. Even discredited, philosophical liberalism persists, not least because – unbeknowns to its adherents – its deregulatory rhetoric is embedded in the regulatory strategies of its governmental twin.

8 Feminism and Law Reform

No one who enters the debate over pornography gets out unscathed, neither do we expect to be exceptions in this regard. Our historical studies have indicated that the fields in which pornography is discussed are in principle incapable of giving rise to a single unified truth of pornography, in relation to which all individuals could be expected to adjust their thought and conduct. As an eroticising device, a target of medical-pedagogical programmes, a tradable commodity, an aesthetic category, an object of feminist and governmental reform campaigns, a legal problem – pornography has taken shape differently in different departments of existence. Let those who think that these different constructions of pornography can be reconciled in one overarching philosophical or moral judgement deal with the fact that two centuries of dispute have brought us no closer to this goal. In these studies we have therefore taken the disputes as permanent and philosophically irresolvable. Each of the departments mentioned deploys norms, techniques, conducts and forms of personhood in relation to which pornography can be produced, used, judged, appreciated, pathologised, regulated, and so on. But neither individually nor collectively are they capable of supporting a judgement that might be true of pornography in general, because the norms of judgement reach no further than the sphere in which they are actually deployed.

The one apparent exception is the sphere formed by the institutions of law and government which can, under certain historical circumstances, adjudicate the contending claims advanced by the other departments. This is not really an exception, however. The law does not attempt such adjudication in the name of a philosophical judgement of pornography. In other words, its judgements are neither formal nor empirical as these terms are understood in the epistemological disciplines. Rather, legal judgements are processual, ceremonial, and based on categories informed by specific purposes – the regulation of trade or morality, the proscription of certain behaviours, the facilitation of others. This technical and purposive mode of judgement, coupled with the fact that the law is amongst other things an institution for settling disputes, is what allows the law to adjudicate in the case of pornography, through the historical category of obscenity. The law adjudicates on pornography not through a universally true judgement but by maintaining a quite narrow set of procedures, categories and purposes that permits a judgement to take place and to be seen to have taken place. The law is the final court of appeal in the dispute and its judgement is binding by virtue of this institutional finality.

We are quite comfortable with this view and role of the law. It is of course compatible with our view of obscenity law as a set of juridical procedures and categories that have been developing in tandem with the governmental 'policing' of modern populations since the early eighteenth century. Moreover, this view of legal judgement – as binding in its social finality – informed our rejection of liberalism's attempt to found and rectify obscenity law in a philosophical analysis of harm. What is to count as harmful, we argued, cannot be decided in advance of the procedures and categories of obscenity law itself and the governmental (medical, pedagogical) programmes with which it is aligned. It will be recalled that at that point we rejected the project to draw a universal boundary between law and morality based on the philosophical distinction between harmful conducts and harmless representations. It became clear that this latter distinction could not be drawn in a uniform and *a priori* manner by presupposing a subject of consciousness able to exercise judgement through given intellectual and moral faculties. And we showed to the contrary that the law in fact draws this distinction in a variable fashion; that it does so relative to medical and pedagogical goals for the conduct of individuals as social types; and that it treats capacities for moral judgement not as given in the faculties of the subject but as acquired ethical abilities or competences, differentially distributed according to age, gender, educational level and social situation.

Feminism is surely right in rejecting the liberal notion of a universal rational subject as the basis of political and social action, although perhaps overly optimistic in thinking that reason is divided along gender lines only, and that the problems associated with constructions of pornography can be solved by removing the distorting effects of patriarchal interest. If the judgements of the law's 'reasonable man' are not the transparent expression of a universal reason, then neither are they duplicitous or botched attempts at such expression – mere distortions of reason open to rectification through exposure of the (patriarchal) 'interests' supposed to inform them. The limits of legal reason are far more varied and far less escapable than any such account can allow. This is because the 'reasonable man' is not the (true or distorted) foundation of legal judgement but a purely retrospective construct, its form and content changing constantly and routinely with changes in the objectives of legal regulation and the forms of calculation informing these objectives.

Our rejection of the project of philosophical liberalism signifies a choice between two different intellectual styles and approaches: the philosophical-aesthetic and the legal-governmental. Under other circumstances it would be possible to explore the historical determination and reality of this dichotomy. Reinhart Koselleck, for example, traces its emergence to the religious butchery and social chaos of the seventeenth century. It was then, in those particular historical circumstances, that legal and political intellectuals detached sovereignty and law from absolute notions of morality and justice and subjected them to a pragmatic and positive reformulation in terms of the needs of the state and the security and well-being of its citizens. These were the circumstances in which philosophical and, later, aesthetic intellectuals defined themselves oppositionally, through the project of subjecting 'positive' law and politics to a higher moral critique – in the name of universal history and its subject.[1] For present purposes, however, it is enough to note that it was just such an attempt to subject positive law to a higher moral critique that was called into question in our critical discussion of philosophical liberalism. That discussion was conditioned by our recognition that the governmental objectives embodied in obscenity law set the parameters within which socially binding judgments on pornography can actually be achieved.

The manner in which our style of analysis problematises philosophical liberalism should, therefore, be reasonably clear. What is perhaps not quite so clear is the coldness of the comfort that it brings to the most widely promulgated feminist analysis of pornography and obscenity law. It is the uncertainty of our relation to this latter analysis that we wish to discuss in these concluding remarks.

It is arguable that the most consistent attempt to translate feminist critique into law reform – the project of Andrea Dworkin and Catharine MacKinnon – is characterised by a blurring of philosophical-aesthetic and legal-governmental objectives, similar to that which undermines the liberal project. If this is so, then we should expect the Dworkin-Mackinnon project to be divided by a radical ambivalence: between the imperative to make feminist objectives socially binding by reformulating them within the categories, procedures and purposes of the law; and the attempt to reconstruct the law from a higher moral position, in the name of universal history and its repressed feminine subject.

Dworkin and MacKinnon drafted a model anti-pornography ordinance and liaised with local government bodies interested in incorporating it in their codes relating to human relations and equal opportunity. A version of this ordinance was passed in Indianapolis in 1984.[2] How does the Indianapolis ordinance (hereafter the Ordinance) enunciate the case against pornography? It defines pornography as a 'practice of exploitation and subordination based on sex which differentially harms women'. It seeks to 'prevent and prohibit' all discriminatory practices of sexual subordination and exploitation operating through pornography (598 F. Supp., p. 1320). The means to do so is to declare pornography unlawful because discriminatory. The Ordinance also provides forms of relief and redress against a range of pornographic practices: trafficking in pornography, that is, the production, sale, exhibition or display of pornography; coercion into a pornographic performance; forcing pornography on a person 'in any place of employment, in education, in a home, or in any public place'; and assault or physical attack due to pornography (pp. 1321–2). The mechanisms for obtaining relief are complaint by persons claiming to be aggrieved by such practices, or by members of a designated board who have reasonable cause to believe that a violation of the law has occurred. In relation to trafficking, a type of class action is provided whereby 'any woman may file a complaint as a woman acting against the subordination of women and any man, child or transsexual may file a complaint but must prove injury in the same way that a woman is injured in order to obtain relief' (pp. 1322–3).

A complaint sets in train an investigation aimed at conciliation and persuasion in relation to the alleged discriminatory practice. If the complaint is not satisfactorily resolved through informal proceedings, the Complaint Adjudication Committee may hold a public hearing. If the complaint is sustained, the relevant party may be ordered to discontinue the unlawful practice and to undertake certain affirmative action including restoration of the complainant's losses incurred as a result of the discriminatory treatment. Provisions for appeal are made. Finally, if it is found that a person engaged in discriminatory practice has failed to correct or eliminate it, the board may file a complaint in the Marion County circuit or superior court for injunctive relief and other affirmative relief or orders 'designed to put into effect the purposes of the ordinance' (pp. 1322–5).

Key themes of a broader feminist critique of pornography reverberate in the finding that is incorporated into the Ordinance:

> Pornography is a discriminatory practice based on sex which denies women equal opportunities in society. Pornography is central in creating and maintaining sex as a basis for discrimination. Pornography is a systematic practice of exploitation and subordination based on sex which differentially harms women. The bigotry and contempt it promotes, with the acts of aggression it fosters, harms women's opportunities for equality of rights in employment, education, access to and use of public accommodations, and acquisition of real property; promote rape, battery, child abuse, kidnapping and prostitution and inhibit just enforcement of laws against such acts; and contribute significantly to restricting women

in particular from full exercise of citizenship and participation in public life, including in neighbourhoods. (p. 1320)

In line with wider feminist arguments, this finding treats pornography not as some self-enclosed world of representations having no tangible effects in real life but as a 'practice' of sex discrimination. Pornography is a harmful type of behaviour because it reduces the status of women by treating them as 'sexual', where the meaning of this term is wholly imposed by men for their own gratification. In the Ordinance, pornography is identified with various ways of 'presenting' women: as sexual objects who enjoy pain and humiliation, or experience sexual pleasure in being raped; as bodies in bondage, cut up, bruised, physically hurt, fragmented, severed, or in other scenarios of sexual violence and inferiority; as being penetrated by animals; as sexually available for domination, possession, use and the like (p. 1320). This mix of instances is placed under the rubric of 'graphic sexually explicit subordination' of women (although the same ways of presenting men, children or transsexuals are also said to constitute pornography for the purposes of the legislation).

There is a clear difference between the feminist arguments on which the Ordinance rests and the First Amendment absolutist position on pornography examined in the previous chapter. The emphasis has shifted from defending a supposedly inherent right of expression to attacking an insidious form of power. Specifically, it is argued, the pseudo-right of expression relating to pornography should be displaced by recognising the right of women not to be discriminated against on the grounds of sex, a right invoked under the Fourteenth Amendment. On this account, the abstractness of obscenity and also of free expression as *concepts* is said to have allowed pornographic speech – which is in fact a discriminatory conduct – to be passed off as everyone's speech, a universal value to be protected. Obscenity law, it is said, thus protects the speech of men which 'silences the speech of women', and fends off consideration of the actual harmful conducts involved in pornography. Since the defence of pornography is to male supremacy what its critique is to feminism (MacKinnon, 1987, p. 146), there is little chance of genuine and profound reform being achieved by working within the compromised logic of existing obscenity law and First Amendment 'principles'.

In fact, two quite different political and intellectual styles organise this mix of elements and the argument of the Ordinance. On the one hand, the Ordinance specifies the harm of pornography in legal and governmental terms, as an impediment to women's full participation in civic and economic life. Here the operative term is *discrimination*, and harm is construed as an infringement of civil rights, in turn constructed in terms of governmental objectives associated with equity, efficiency, participation and equality of opportunity.

On the other hand, the harm of pornography is also specified in philosophical and aesthetic terms, as an impediment to the full realisation of women's being. In this regard the key term is *objectification*, and pornography is conceived as a premature fixing of an ideal mode of being in an alien form, the alien form and purposes of the male psyche. The lineage of this conception in Romantic aesthetics and philosophy will be evident from earlier discussion and is clearly signalled in the claims that pornography commodifies, fragments, fetishises and alienates women's bodies.[3] It is this conception that lends a dramatic ambivalence to feminist characterisations of the pornographically represented body as cut up, fragmented, distorted, bound, and so on. Such characterisations hover between an aesthetic repugnance fastidious enough to be applicable to all instrumentalised representation, and a fantasmagoria in which metaphor slides into fact, the Hegelian fragmentation of being finding its lurid correlative in the actual dismemberment of bodies.

Needless to say, we have no interest in the game of accusing and convicting Dworkin and MacKinnon of a philosophical confusion. The ambivalence in question is far more important than that and is historically rather than conceptually rooted. It arises from a radical instability in the forms in which intellectuals may *conduct themselves* in relation to positive law and government. Part of the problem is that there is no way to translate between the philosophical-aesthetic conception of pornography as objectification and the actual operations of legal and governmental institutions. The former conception is a prisoner of the aesthetic dialectic in which a completely developed (women's) being is unfolded from the successive mutual modifications of mind and body, intellect and emotion, the ideal and the real. The law operates quite differently with men, women and children; it constructs their attributes retroactively, in terms of definite and limited legal and governmental norms, objectives and programmes.

What is more, the aesthetic dialectic is actually a means of *withdrawing* from the legal-governmental field and of orienting oneself to another set of concerns: those of the self conceived as the problematic interface of the two sides of the dialectic. In fact, the dialectic is an ethical weapon directed against positive law and government. It aims to problematise their normative regulation of conduct and attributes by picturing 'complete' human development as the dialectical neutralisation of all positive norms and the recovery of 'wholeness' from the fragments. But these of course are precisely the terms in which pornography itself is problematised. For those under the sway of the dialectic, then, obscenity law is just as problematic as pornography, and for the same reasons. The definite and limited (positive) character of legal norms and objectives is treated as a fragmentation of a more complex and organic sphere of women's development (and oppression), it being necessary for society to be totally transformed if full being is to be realised. Once this point has been reached we can be sure that the project to reform the law has given way to an endeavour of an altogether different kind: aesthetic critique and self-refinement.

If our diagnosis of this ambivalence is correct, then there is clearly a danger that the important attempt to construct the harm of pornography as an infringement of civil rights may be swamped by aesthetically conceived rights and harms (the right not to have one's being objectified and misrepresented) whose limitlessness puts them beyond legal claim and redress. More specifically, if the Dworkin-MacKinnon project is indeed torn between legal-governmental and philosophical-aesthetic objectives, we should expect to see it give rise to two interrelated tendencies: first, a tendency to subordinate obscenity law to philosophical and aesthetic critique – to problematise its norms, categories and objectives by showing their inability to realise complete (non-objectified) being; second, the tendency of lawyers to reject the proposed legal enactment of aesthetic imperatives as non-constructable within the technical and normative framework of the law. There is no shortage of evidence for both these tendencies.

Consider in this regard the following remarks by Catharine MacKinnon:

> Feminism doubts whether the average person gender-neutral exists: has more questions about the content and process of defining what community standards are than it does about deviations from them; wonders why prurience counts but powerlessness does not and why sensibilities are better protected from offense than women are from exploitation; defines sexuality, and thus its violation and expropriation, more broadly than does state law; and questions why a body of law that has not in practice been able to tell rape from intercourse should, without further guidance, be entrusted with telling pornography from anything less. Taking the work 'as a whole' ignores that which the victims of pornography have long known: legitimate settings diminish the perception of injury done to those whose trivialization and objectification they contextualize. Besides, and this is a heavy one, if a woman is subjected, why should it matter that the work has other value? Maybe what redeems the work's value is what enhances its injury to women, not to mention that existing standards of literature, art, science, and politics, examined in a feminist light, are remarkably consonant with pornography's mode, meaning, and

message. And finally – first and foremost, actually – although the subject of these materials is overwhelmingly women, their contents made up of women's bodies, our invisibility has been such, our equation as a sex *with* sex has been such, that the law of obscenity has never even considered pornography a women's issue. (1987, pp. 174–5)

Here feminism is constituted as the higher philosophical and moral prospective from which it is possible to condemn the arbitrariness of the law's categories; the narrowness of its regulatory ambit; its gender blindness; and the absurdity of its attempt to differentiate culture from pornography when – 'examined in a feminist light' – culture itself is pornographic.[4] Indeed, so high is the moral and philosophical ground from which this critique is directed that it risks losing sight of its actual target. It is hardly surprising that the legal categories of prurience and offensiveness 'fail' when they are set a task – the representation of women's invisible being – that only makes sense within the domain of aesthetics.

We are thus given an invitation we may or may not wish to accept: to convert obscenity law into an occasion for aesthetic critique. And the alternative we are offered is to remain with such categories as prurience and offensiveness through which American law has been reconstructing obscenity and defining a programme for the variable pedagogical policing of problem sensibilities. No doubt the extent to which specifically masculine sensibilities to pornography can be affected by such a programme remains an open question, but are we ready to dismiss the question – and the reform opportunities it may afford – by opting instead for the promise of a total aesthetic transformation of masculine being?

With this choice in mind, let us return to the solution proposed in the Ordinance to the perceived problem of sexist bias in the law: the linking of the feminist critique of pornography as objectification of women to the legal-governmental category of a civil right of women, under the Fourteenth Amendment, not to be discriminated against on the grounds of sex.[5] The drafters of the Ordinance deliberately go beyond existing standards in order to make 'pornography', not just 'obscenity', unlawful. They do not attempt to couch the restrictions on pornography in terms of community standards, offensiveness or prurience, nor do they allow for consideration of the literary, artistic or other value of an otherwise 'pornographic' work. The restrictions of the Ordinance would thus extend to soft-core pornography and other materials deemed to be demeaning to women, even though they need not be 'obscene' in the present legal sense (598 F. Supp., pp. 1331–2). The scale of these changes indicates what MacKinnon (1987, p. 195) refers to as an attempt to create an 'affirmative access' to speech for those to whom it has been denied.

There is no denying the uncompromising clarity of this vision. By virtue of a major theoretical intervention, there would be a general jettisoning of the heterogeneous array of thresholds and distinctions which have emerged as the means of achieving and administering a variable dissemination of materials according to legal and pedagogical judgements about kinds of use and kinds of user. As we have demonstrated, legal distinctions between art and pornography or between soft and hard-core inhere neither in sexuality or writing nor in their putative human subject. Rather, they are the particular *instruments* on which a variable obscenity and its administration depend. To abandon them in favour of a global and undifferentiated concept of pornography at the very least must raise the question of the *means* whereby, in practice, distinctions could be drawn between different writings about sex and different uses of such writings. Whatever the preferred thresholds might be, what cultural competences would be required in order to recognise them? Would courts and judges become the agents of what would be essentially an aesthetic judgement?

The courts' reluctance to embark on wholesale change has been taken by some feminists as confirmation that constitutional process has already institutionalised and consecrated a male will to power. Referring to the Supreme Court's affirmation of the decision in *Hudnut*, MacKinnon thus claims that the law continues to make pornography 'available in private while decrying it in public' (1987, p. 211). And Kappeler sees the rejection of the Minneapolis ordinance by liberals and sections of the media as part of a wider defence of patriarchal power, protecting the privileges of men purveying and using pornography and so perpetuating women's oppression (1986, pp. 11–17).[6]

Given the profound ambivalence between principled commitment to an aesthetic conception of recovering the wholeness of women's repressed being and pragmatic embracing of positive legal mechanisms – in this case the constitutional apparatus protecting US citizens against infringements of their civil rights – it is not surprising the law cannot construct an equivalence between the feminist definition of pornography as objectification, and an all-purpose right not to be discriminated against. But is a decision not to validate such a right necessarily to be seen as a failure to recognise and redress the sexist bias of obscenity law?

In relation to this question it is appropriate to recall the manner in which the law recognises and resolves the often intractable disputes and problems presented to it. We can take as an example the process of judicial decision-making in this particular case. In doing so, we shall refer to the constitutional calculation of rights in the District Court (598 F. Supp., 1984), although the same general line of reasoning is followed in the Court of Appeals. The District Court sees the litigation as requiring it 'to weigh and resolve the conflict between the First Amendment guarantees of free speech, on the one hand, and the Fourteenth Amendment right to be free from sex-based discrimination on the other hand' (p. 1327), and to establish whether the Ordinance has an unconstitutionally 'chilling effect' on the right to free speech (p. 1328). It is thus a matter of deciding between two legal options. And in fact the Court decides that the state's interest in prohibiting sex discrimination created by pornography as the sexually explicit, graphically depicted subordination of women is not so compelling as to outweigh the constitutionally protected interest of free speech (p. 1326).[7]

Constitutional analysis of the Ordinance is then said to require determination of the following three issues:

> [F]irst, the Court must determine whether the Ordinance imposes restraints on speech or behaviour (content versus conduct); if the Ordinance is found to regulate speech, the Court must next determine whether the subject speech is protected or not protected under the First Amendment; if the speech which is regulated by this Ordinance is protected speech under the Constitution, the court must then decide whether the regulation is constitutionally permissible as being based on a compelling state interest justifying the removal of such speech from First Amendment protections. (pp. 1329–30)

On the first of these issues, the defendants' premise is that the Ordinance regulates conduct, not speech. They find an analogy for this distinction in the fact that the courts have held that advocacy of a racial segregation doctrine is protected speech under the First Amendment, while segregation itself is not constitutionally protected behaviour (p. 1330). For this analogy to work, it must be accepted that pornography is not only a form of statement or doctrine but also embodies – in its sex discrimination – an equivalent to the category of conduct referred to in the area of racial segregation. The defendants claim that 'the production, dissemination, and use of sexually explicit words and pictures *is* the actual subordination of women' and so constitutes a harmful action, a form of regulable behaviour, not an expression of ideas entitled to First Amendment protection (p. 1330). However, the Court sees this claim as ambiguous and ultimately unacceptable: pornography is acknowledged in the Ordinance to involve 'words and pictures', and although pornography 'conditions society to subordinate women', the means by which the Ordinance seeks to combat this discrimination is 'through the regulation of speech' (pp. 1330–1).

Having found that the Ordinance seeks to regulate speech not conduct, the Court states that pornography as defined therein cannot be held to fall within one of the established categories of speech unprotected by the First Amendment. It rejects the defendant's claim that since pornography is 'nothing more than the infliction of injury on women', it comprises a form of what were identified in *Chaplinsky* as 'fighting words' which can legitimately be regulated because by their very utterance they 'inflict injury or tend to incite an immediate breach of the peace' (p. 1331). The fact that the Ordinance 'sweeps beyond' unprotected obscenity (p. 1326) would normally be enough for it to be overturned as unconstitutional, but the defendants argue that this case raises a new issue for the Court and that while the Ordinance regulates protected speech it does so in a constitutionally permissible fashion (p. 1332).

For all their sweeping character, these claims and counterclaims are in fact conducted *within* the instituted technical procedures of the legal sphere. For instance, and quite predictably, there is the mode of argument from precedent. The defendants claim that the legal category of obscenity has not been the only basis for regulating sexually explicit materials and conducts or for distinguishing the protected from the unprotected, and that the existing variations on *Miller* should be extended to include the newly-defined class of discrimination as a form of unprotected materials (pp. 1332–5). They cite a trio of precedents to make this point, arguing firstly that the interests of protecting women from sex-based discrimination are as compelling and fundamental as those upheld in *New York* v. *Ferber* (1982) for the benefit of children (p. 1332–4). In that case, it was ruled that a state interest in 'safeguarding the physical and psychological well-being of a minor' outweighs the interest in upholding guarantees of free speech for child pornography, even despite any literary or other value which the material in question may be deemed to possess. In *Hudnut*, however, the Court holds that the *Ferber* rationale for going beyond *Miller* applies only to minors. The governmental interest in protecting children is not 'readily transferrable to adult women as a class' because the latter 'do not, as a matter of public policy or applicable law, stand in need of the same type of protection which has long been afforded to children'.[8]

The Court also holds that the second case invoked by the defendants, *FCC* v. *Pacifica Foundation* (1978), is not controlling in the present case (p. 1334). In *Pacifica*, the Supreme Court held that broadcast offensive speech was not entitled to protection. Because the broadcast media have established 'a uniquely pervasive presence' in the lives of Americans, such speech may infringe on the individual's right to be left alone in the privacy of the home. Moreover, broadcasting is 'uniquely accessible to children, even those too young to read'. In *Hudnut*, the Court holds that this precedent, although permitting regulation of the 'content' of speech, specifically involves problems of dissemination. Since the Ordinance does not restrict itself to regulating broadcast media nor to protecting children, the reasons used to justify restrictions in *Pacifica* cannot be called upon in this case.

The Court also rejects the precedent of *Young v. American Mini Theatres, Inc.* (1976) invoked by the defendants (pp. 1334–5). While it notes that in *Young* the Supreme Court upheld a city ordinance regulating the location of cinemas featuring erotic films, it also observes that this was a 'place' restriction, not a complete ban on the pornographic materials. The judgement concerned not the content of the films alone but a type of distribution which, it was considered, would have an effect on the character of the city's neighbourhoods of a kind which justified restrictions on the communications. However, the Indianapolis Ordinance is seen to prohibit the distribution of 'material depicting women in a sexually subordinate role, at all times, in all places and in every manner' and therefore cannot find support from such a precedent.

The argument on these precedents provides an economical and practical reminder of what is meant by obscenity as variable category and of what is involved in its legal administration. The juridical policing of sexual materials and conducts is deemed permissible only when justified by a judicial calculation of governmental interest in relation to particular norms: the welfare of minors, standards of decency in broadcasting, the character of urban spaces. The putative harm of objectification – applicable 'at all times, in all places and in every manner' – is meaningless in a system where harm is variably calculated relative to a diversity of specific social-legal objectives. In each case, what is more, the recourse to legal policing measures has to be balanced with another governmental interest in protecting speech. In its turn, protected 'speech' entails a series of rights and interests exercised by diverse agents of production, distribution and reception. In other words, despite the charge that they simply 'reflect' First Amendment absolutism by misrepresenting harmful conduct as protected speech (MacKinnon, 1987, p. 165), the courts do not enshrine a philosophical-liberal conception of rights, since in delimiting rights of expression they are dealing with the pragmatic question of how particular practices and diverse behaviours associated with pornography are to be regulated. Finally, it is only when practices such as those considered in these precedents pose problems which pedagogic and ethical strategies of management do not adequately resolve, that legal policing measures are seen to be warranted.

Since precedent does not permit the regulation by the Ordinance of otherwise protected speech, the Court then asks whether there is a compelling state interest which would justify a new exception to First Amendment guarantees (pp. 1335–7). Here the Court notes that the premise of the Ordinance is that the discrimination of pornography degrades women as a class, and so does not require specifically defined victims for most of the proscriptions introduced. The reality of this discrimination is not denied. The Court rehearses the arguments that pornography negatively affects those women who suffer the direct abuse of its production or on whom violent kinds of performance are imposed, and that exposure to pornography fosters discriminatory attitudes and behaviours, and causes in its male viewers 'an increased willingness to aggress toward women' (p. 1336). The defendants argue that just as the Supreme Court accepted as constitutional legislation which regulates obscenity as harmful to people, so too should the Court now accept legislation which regulates pornography as harmful specifically to women (pp. 1336–7).

However, the Court distinguishes between judicial and legislative functions. It says that there may be good reason to support legislative action such as the finding on which the Ordinance is based. The Court's own role is not to question the legislative finding but 'to ensure that the Ordinance accomplishes its purpose without violating constitutional standards or impinging upon constitutionally protected rights' (p. 1337). In this framework, the Court reiterates that the Ordinance seeks to regulate protected speech, and states that in its own role it 'cannot legitimately embark on judicial policy-making, carving out a new exception to the First Amendment' for this or some other interest group claiming to be victimized by 'unfair expression' (p. 1337).

Faced with this daunting series of precedential and procedural distinctions, we might well be drawn towards the seeming clarity and directness of a less differentiating and temporising mode of argument and decision-making. Yet, as previously, we would then have to ask: what would be the practical consequences of throwing these legal distinctions away? Would it be feasible to pass the policing of pornography entirely over to a domain other than the law, for instance to pedagogy or to sociology? The Court itself, in fact, acknowledges such an 'alternative' domain when it refers to the discrimination of pornography against women as a class as a 'sociological harm' diminishing the legal and social status of women (p. 1335). However, having admitted the notion of a 'social' judgement and administration of pornography, the Court moves to recognise the limits of its own competence, which reaches no further than the limits of the legal sphere. The Court thus contends that necessary or desirable changes in 'sociological patterns' (p. 1337) are not likely to be brought about by legislative dictate. This is, perhaps, the Court's way of admitting that there is no single or unified truth of pornography, and that the legal definition and management of obscenity is pursued not in some unbounded and undifferentiated space but within the confines of a jurisdiction. This delimitation of institutional competence is in keeping with our argument that the governmental pedagogies by means of which some sectors of the population have learned to problematise their own relation to erotica have not entirely replaced and cannot entirely be replaced by mechanisms of legal policing. A civil right not to be discriminated against by pornography cannot easily be superimposed as a generalised mechanism to police a pornographic field in which forms of self-regulation already play a significant role.

To argue that there are – and in the foreseeable future will need to be – limits on the scope of legal policing is not to imply that an attempt such as that made in the Ordinance to introduce a civil rights law against pornography creates a police state:

> Audiences of lawyers say it is politically naive to rely on courts to administer our pornography law our way. Then they say we should rely on existing law and existing courts for relief of any harms of pornography that they concede are real. Our civil rights law will produce a police state, they say. Then they recommend vigorous enforcement of criminal laws against rapists and batterers, whose victims are conceded to number well over half of all women. When told that they are, in effect, recommending reversing the numbers of those in and out of prisons, they say, do not rely on law at all. Now that we want a law against pornography, they say that law doesn't do anything significant anyway. Rely on the First Amendment – as if that is not a law. Forget law, educate – as if law is not educational. They say that the state is eager for the chance to suppress all sexually explicit materials. They have no explanation – these, the political sophisticates to our political naivete – for the fact that with a tool as vague and discretionary as criminal obscenity statues, this same state has stood by and watched the pornography industry double in the last ten years. Some day try solving a legal problem that has vexed legal minds for decades only to find (or, perhaps, to prove) that many people do not want it solved. And that many of these people are lawyers.
>
> (MacKinnon, 1987, pp. 222–3, footnotes omitted)

MacKinnon's account of reactions to anti-pornography legislation should also serve to distinguish our arguments from those she attributes to liberal critics. For her, despite the appearance that the law's maintenance of free speech is disinterested, the administration of obscenity law is motivated by the underlying self-interest of those holding power within the patriarchal system. However, we would reject both the notion that the law must recognise an inalienable right of the individual to be free from regulation in the moral domain *and* that it feigns to do so because in reality it expresses an ideological will to power. The issue we have raised concerning the Ordinance is not that governmental regulation of morality is tantamount to censorship. Rather, we have argued that if the ethical problems created by pornography are to be taken seriously, so too are the historical and technical means whereby the 'ethos' of pornography has been produced and may be reformed.

Some form of what the Lockhart Report refers to as 'non-legal' regulation will almost certainly continue to play a crucial role in managing the production, circulation and use of sexual materials. We have shown that to determine where the line should be drawn between legal regulation and self-management the law has had to call on normative and interested knowledges, there being no detached and objective insight into the 'truth' about pornography. When the law calls on such knowledges, it does not act in bad faith or fail to align itself with some transcendent ethical principle of social justice. Sexual aesthetics and sexology are major disciplines of the self which have come to play a role in constructing and governing sexualities; yet their deployment of confessional strategies renders them not clearly distinguishable from a predominantly male auto-erotics. Seen in this light, the *Hudnut* decision is not retrograde. On the contrary, in balancing demands for legal and administrative policing against demands for self-management, it cannot but leave open the question of what are to be appropriate norms for assessing and regulating pornography.[9]

There is no reason to assume that the present ethical forms of regulation are established once and for all. Whilst philosophical liberalism and sexual aesthetics cannot be ignored in current projects of law reform, they might still prove precarious forms of self-management, their practice being always reliant on deployments of particular norms, knowledges and media in a pornographic field which remains constitutively unstable. Evidence of this instability is provided by the marked shift on the question of harm within liberal jurisprudence over the past two decades, under the dual influence of feminist campaigns on the status of women and recurring governmental and familialist concerns with the welfare of children.[10]

Mutation, complexity and disunity continue to characterise the pornographic field. This field now includes a mix of old, modified and nascent communications technologies – print, photography, film, cable television, video, telephone, videophone, computer – whose distributions and uses call for differential regulation according to criteria of reach, age, educational levels, public decency standards and so on. It is also made up of an open-ended series of established and novel interests in criticising, appreciating, regulating, embracing or adapting particular forms of pornography. While we have concentrated in this chapter on a major feminist critique of obscenity law and pornography, other quite different claims are pressed. So, for instance, some groups identifying themselves more or less with feminist or radical cultural politics (and from whose viewpoint the Dworkin-MacKinnon project would doubtless be seen as belonging to a puritanical feminism) have adapted the pornographic repertoire as the basis for an aestheticised and supposedly transgressive and therefore true performance of the self (see, for instance, the treatments of avantgarde erotica by Elinor Fuchs (1989), Linda Montano (1989) and Kate Davy (1989)). Or again, there are various gay and lesbian celebratory uses of pornography to form and intensify sexual identity through the re-functioning of heterosexual pornography. Disregarding their divergent contents and targets, feminist, gay and lesbian pornographies share a common form, now quite familiar to us. In each case pornography structures an exchange in which knowledge of the self is identified with the auto-erotic use of sexual representations and in which pleasure is extracted from the forms of probing the 'true self' beneath its mundane forms.

There is no certainty that affirmative uses of pornography escape or solve the problem of harms. For instance, there are those who contend from their own experience that the use of pornography is destructive, inasmuch as it creates violence in the gay community (*Pornography and Sexual Violence*, pp. 65–6). Surrounded by multiple interests and changes in the pornographic field, the law could not plausibly be expected to realise a single agreed truth of pornography. It has to mediate diverse and often competing interests which may be well-established or, like child rights, still in the process of crystallising. In these circumstances, the law can do no more than continue to treat obscenity as a variable category. By calculating the effects of particular distributions in terms of different audience interests, susceptibilities, competences and patterns of conduct, the law decides where the moveable line should be drawn between legal regulation and the available forms of self-regulation, not to mention regulation by administrative devices such as constraints on public funding of the arts, or the adjudication of legal or other actions generated by the resurgence of conservative campaigns to mobilise 'public opinion' against pornography and to challenge existing aesthetic conceptions of what is to be protected.

To return to our principal example and to clarify the relation between our historical studies and the law reform project of Dworkin and MacKinnon, let us say that we would endorse one element of that project but not the other. This is not a coy reluctance to take sides. It is, rather, a direct response to the fact that the case put by Dworkin and MacKinnon rests on two incommensurate intellectual postures: one concerns objectification and a recovery of repressed being; the other concerns discrimination and an effective administration of a positive constitutional right. In the terms used in this chapter, the former involves an objective in the field of aesthetics, the latter an objective in the field of law and government. Their incommensurability, as suggested in our brief anthropology of the aesthetic personality, is historical and practical not conceptual and theoretical. For a heuristic purpose, the distinction between self-management and legal regulation can be aligned with the distinction between aesthetic and government rationales for defining and dealing with pornography.

This alignment has a definite advantage: it reminds us that however clearly the distinction might be drawn in philosophical terms, in practice there has been no stable boundary between regulation by the criminal law and self-regulation by an aesthetic pedagogy. In both the United Kingdom and the United States, obscenity law has come increasingly to regulate pornography by grounding itself on pedagogic and aesthetic norms for assessing the conduct of individuals and defining what is to count as sexually 'mature' personalities. Even so, Dworkin and MacKinnon's philosophical critique of law as failing to recognise pornography's objectification of women cannot be articulated to legal policing in the form of a civil right. While this critique may, as part of a social *campaign*, have effects on people's attitudes, conducts and manners, its aesthetic components simply cannot be made into law. However, while the law cannot give unified expression to the categories of discrimination and objectification in the form of a global civil right not to be harmed by pornography, it can indeed construct and protect more limited and specific civil rights relating to anti-discrimination objectives. In other words, we see a choice to be decided, not a synthesis to be achieved. The choice is whether to pursue the fundamental transformation of society in order to de-objectify women's being, or to pursue specifically legal and administrative action to promote certain mentalities and behaviours, and to discourage others. The second option includes developing workplace codes of conduct aimed at reducing the incidence of sexual harassment of women and de-eroticising professional relationships and decision-making.[11]

Such action may of course be deemed superficial, a mere masking of the 'fundamental' problem of domination. Between them, in their aesthetic analyses, Dworkin and MacKinnon would reject each of the options. Dworkin has argued that, given existing social and gender relations, the act of sex is the fact of domination of women by men: 'that slit which means entry into her – intercourse – appears to be the key to women's lower human status'

(Dworkin, 1987, p. 123). In her account, heterosexual mutuality can only register as a naive contradiction in terms. The evidence is, however, that even this forthrightness will not stop the fashioning of aesthetic images of human emancipation and completeness that are resolutely heterosexual, homosexual, bisexual, pansexual or nonsexual, each of which will claim in the name of a true species to judge the forms of positive law and government as constraining in more or less important respects.

As late in the piece as 1986, it was observed in the Hudson Report (p. 233) that the history of pornography had not yet been written. We hope to have made a beginning to the writing of this history, and to have learned some lessons. The form of erotic sensibility which we have described is an artefact of that particular phenomenon – book sex – whose history is a composite of definite interests and capacities, print and other media technologies, commerce, religion, government, moral and psychological medicine, relations of gender, levels of education and cultural literacy and, not least, the historical interactions of aesthetics, police and law. To attribute an essence to this contingent and mobile amalgam would be to fly in the face of plausibility and the historical evidence. Changes in arrangements for managing pornography cannot be assessed according to whether they promise the complete realisation of our sexual being. What can be achieved is better management – by the legal and ethical means actually available – of the forms of subjectivity which happen to have emerged for and among us.

Notes

2 THE PORNOGRAPHIC FIELD

1. See, however, the Postscript to Chapter 5 below.
2. At the same time, argues Marcus, the problem of pornography will ultimately be solved by the harmonious working-out of the dialectic through which individuals – and, more generally, culture itself – reach maturity: 'Pornography is, after all, nothing more than a representation of the fantasies of infantile sexual life, as these features are edited and reorganized in the masturbatory daydreams of adolescence. Every man who grows up must pass through such a phase in his existence, and I can see no reason for supposing that our society, in the history of its own life, should not have to pass though such a phase as well' (Marcus, 1964, p. 289).
3. The point is tellingly made in the concurring opinion of Chief Justice Warren, 1957, in *Roth* v. *United States:*

   > Present laws depend largely upon the effect that the materials may have upon those who receive them. It is manifest that the same object may have a different impact, varying according to the part of the community it reached. But there is more to these cases. It is not the book that is on trial; it is a person. The conduct of the defendant is the central issue, not the obscenity of a book or picture. The nature of the materials is, of course, relevant as an attribute of the defendant's conduct, but the materials are thus placed in context from which they draw colour and character. A wholly different result might be reached in a different setting.
   >
   > (*Roth* v. *United States*, p. 495)

4. The fluctuating relation between the materiality of the *body* and the ethically infused entity of the *flesh* is a sign of the degree to which the body has been penetrated and organised by variable spiritual, somatic and social techniques and imperatives. The body is as it were transformed into the flesh when, in the context of the confessional relationship, it is endlessly scrutinised for signs of the desire hidden deep within. This investigation, however, is more than just semiotic. Under the pressure of the interrogation the body provides a 'surface of emergence' for specific somatic and spiritual intensities, also identified with the flesh.
5. For the full reference to this and all other cases cited, see the Table of Cases.
6. See, for example, Kaufmann (1966), Hunter (1966), Starr (1965, 1971) and Slights (1981).
7. It is characteristic that the major collection of English and United States cases (de Grazia 1969) is introduced in these psycho-aesthetic terms and is presented as a 'censorship' history. On the problem of obscuring historical and legal distinctions by under-specifying the notion of 'censorship', see Saunders (1990).

8. Indeed, seeking to evade a conviction, Curll himself argued in the *Weekly Journal* that Henry Rhodes' 1683 edition of the work had not been prosecuted (Foxon, 1964, p. 14).
9. 'Juridification' refers to the process of transfer into a legal register of certain conducts, in this instance because they were now taken to bear on the maintenance of public order and morality.

3 NINETEENTH-CENTURY ENGLISH OBSCENITY LAW

1. Works for the theatre were already subject to statutory regulation under the Lord Chamberlain (Tribe, 1973, p. 64).
2. Routine indications of problems encountered in the summary policing of offences relating to obscene or indecent materials in the second half of the nineteenth century are found in the recurring practical inquiries on 'particular points' of statutory regulation and interpretation dealt with in the columns of the magistrates' publication, the *Justice of the Peace*. These inquiries, relating to such statutes as the Town Police Causes Act (1847), the Post Office Act (1875) and the Indecent Advertisement Act (1889), arise in relation to a series of problem behaviours for the policing of the streets, including indecent conduct, gambling, gaming, drinking, public nuisance and so forth.
3. During the parliamentary debate, Lord Brougham had in fact asked 'how did [Lord Campbell] propose to define what was an obscene publication' (*Hansard, Lords,* 25 June 1857, CXLVI, p. 329, but the Bill passed without this question being answered).
4. Alongside the criminal law concerning obscene publication there exists the civil law provision – now in disuse – whereby copyright protection is withheld from works that are found obscene. The logic behind this arrangement is that the civil courts would not intervene to protect the property in a work whose publication was against the public interest, possibly to the extent of constituting a criminal offence. This doctrine, whose historical development rests largely on a series of decisions in the court of Chancery, has in fact operated without ever generating its own test or definition of obscenity, such as was constructed for the criminal law in *Regina* v. *Hicklin*. Nor was this criminal law definition adopted by the civil courts. Phillips (1977, pp. 157–8) comments thus on the correlation between civil and criminal standards of obscenity:

> [T]he expressed assumption behind [early civil cases] was that to deprive the author of protection could hardly benefit the infringer who by his very action was committing a criminal offence (though, curiously enough, in none of the early leading cases did the successful infringer attract criminal charges). This underlying notion may still be reflected today in current judicial attitudes. It certainly would appear to be convenient to kill two birds with one stone, as it were, by making the one test satisfy both criminal and civil needs, and the law could then not stand accused of setting double standards; but there may be an objection to this, based upon the different functions of diverse laws in distinct jurisdictions.

Criminal matters, for example, are in essence disputes between state and individual as to the acceptability to the former of the deeds of the latter; the burden of proof upon the prosecutor is heavy and weighted in the individual's favour; since it is the freedom of individual action which is at stake as much as the conduct of the individual brought before the court, the law is construed in a manner which, in theory, preserves for the individual the greatest degree of freedom of speech and action compatible with the intentions of the law-makers. Contrast civil proceedings, where the matter in dispute is that of the ownership or possession of property held by one man as against some or all of his fellow men, where the rights of litigants are balanced along with a general and all-pervasive body of rules known as 'public policy', and where the burden of proof is far easier to discharge; granted, issues such as First Amendment freedom of speech may be touched upon, but they are not central to litigation. Thus where two separate jurisdictions must apply the same test of obscenity, may there not be some inherent danger in creating an anomaly by applying the same test?

5. Radzinowicz (1959) suggests that the influence of the Vice Societies was significantly limited by their tenuous relation to liberal and other political organisations.
6. The Joint Select Committee was established at the time of a dual concern: with popular gambling crazes – competitions and lotteries – conducted in the popular press, and with postcards, advertisements for contraception and abortion distributed by mail, often from abroad (for example from France, but also from Egypt, where a penny post to England had been set up). What the lotteries and the indecent publications had in common were technical means of communication – press and mail – which posed problems for the routine established policing of local streets and traditional agents of 'demoralisation', that is, local and well-known 'rogues' and 'vagabonds'. New markets and new forms of conduct were emerging which eluded the constables on the beat.
7. On the postal regulation of obscene materials, see Manchester (1983).
8. For the detail of the record, we note the following factual errors in accounts of Curll's case. Thomas (1969, p. 82) names the three judges as Raymond, Fortescue and Reynolds. The first of these names is wrong; it should be Mr Justice Probyn. The Williams Report (1979, p. 167) has the Chief Justice say that 'if it were not for the case of Read, he would see little difficulty in it'. In fact these are the words of the Attorney General prosecuting, in response to the opening by Curll's counsel, Mr Marsh. The error arises from a misreading of a vocative at the head of the concluding paragraph of the Attorney's statement ('Chief Justice, I think this is a case of very great consequence, though if it was not for the case of *The Queen* v. *Read*, I should make no great difficulty of it.') The Chief Justice is responding to this statement, so we can take the Attorney's 'Chief Justice' to refer to him, not to signal the reporter's identification of the speaker.
9. On these courts, see Chapter 8, 'The Bawdy Courts', in Hill (1964). On the state and functions of the ecclesiastical courts at the start of the eighteenth century, see Archer (1956).

10. Reynolds (1975, p. 222) warns against too much reliance on early obscenity decisions since 'the eighteenth-century legal precedents for punishment of obscene publication have politics as their basis, not close legal reasoning'. Curll had published the memoirs of John Ker, a spy in the service of Queen Anne, which reflected unfavourably on the House of Hanover. According to Reynolds (p. 221), George II intervened in the case by having Chief Justice Fortescue replaced by Francis Page, 'the "hanging judge" notorious in Pope's poems, Johnson's *Life of Savage*, and Fielding's *Tom Jones'*. With Page's appointment, the court rapidly and unanimously found in favour of punishing Curll.

4 LITERARY EROTICS

1. We use the term 'serious literature' in a value-neutral manner to refer to those works appropriated by the educated in pursuit of various kinds of cultivation.
2. References made to the question of obscenity in the columns of the *Justice of the Peace* in the early decades of the twentieth century show that for magistrates the main practical problem was still the policing of mass-produced pornography which was readily distinguishable from serious literature.
3. Of course, some serious literature did come into conflict with the police in relation to obscenity law in England in the late nineteenth century. So, for example, prosecutions were brought against Charles Bradlaugh and Annie Besant in 1877 for publishing Charles Knowlton's *The Fruits of Philosophy*, Henry Vizetelly in 1888 for publishing an English translation of Zola's *La Terre*, and George Bedborough in 1898 for selling Havelock Ellis's *Sexual Inversion* (Hyde, 1964, pp. 16–17; Ellis, 1898). However, such cases are relatively few and far between and hardly justify the view found in Robertson (1979, p. 30) that the *Hicklin* formulation was a weapon used systematically against serious literary and scientific works.
4. References are to the text reprinted in Lawrence, 1936, pp. 170–87.
5. In this period various cooperative inter-governmental attempts were made to promote international policing of the traffic in obscenity and related harmful practices. On the suppression of obscene publications, see for example, League of Nations (1928).
6. Brentford's position was shared by others involved in executive and judicial decision-making at the time. The Public Prosecutor, Edward Atkinson, replied as follows to Havelock Ellis who had sent him his essay 'The Revaluation of Obscenity', written after the unsuccessful appeal against the banning of Radclyffe Hall's *The Well of Loneliness* and suggesting that pornography in general should be deregulated since obscenity was a fundamental human impulse whose suppression is to be blamed for the pornographic betrayal of sex:

> May I respectfully suggest that you are in advance of the times in holding that education would now sufficiently protect the young from the dangers of really pornographic literature and pictures? Quite apart from the prob-

lems of literary works – I instance some of D. H. Lawrence's by way of contrast – such practical experience as I have had leads me to think that really pornographic wares still in these imperfect days need that attention of what you possibly regard as a clumsy weapon viz: the criminal law.

(Cited in Grosskurth, 1980, p. 400)

The official who makes this statement is not blind to the possible merits which literary representations of sex have for some readers, but subordinates them to medical-moral criteria in the context where capacities of reading and self-regulation remain unevenly distributed across the population as a whole.

7. The title page of Elton Boyd's 1887 reprint of *Vitality: How Wasted and Preserved* states '14th Edition of Ten Thousand'.

8. Thus Carpenter wrote:

> The redemption of Sex, the healthy and natural treatment of it in Art, is one of the greatest works any artist of today has before him to carry out ... The same with the literary artist, the poet or novelist. Notwithstanding the outlines sketched by Whitman, and less healthily by Zola and Ibsen, the world still waits for anything like a large and artistic treatment of this grand subject.
>
> (1917 [1898], p. 80)

Lawrence concludes 'Study of Thomas Hardy' thus:

> Now the principle of the Law is found strongest in Woman, and the principle of Love in Man. In every creature, the mobility, the law of change, is found exemplified in the male; the stability, the conservatism is found in the female .... It needs that a man shall know the natural law of his own being, then that he shall seek out the law of the female, with which to join himself as complement .... He must with reverence submit to the law of himself: and he must with suffering and joy know and submit to the law of the woman: and he must know that they two together are one within the Great Law, reconciled within the Great Peace. Out of this final knowledge shall come his supreme art. There shall be the art which recognizes and utters his own law; there shall be the art which recognizes his own and also the law of the woman, his neighbour, utters the glad embraces and the struggle between them, and the submission of the one; there shall be the art which knows the struggle between the two conflicting laws and knows the final reconciliation, where both are equal, two in one, complete. This is the supreme art, which yet remains to be done.
>
> (1936, pp. 514–6).

9. Thus Heath cites the poetry of Adrienne Rich to link a refusal of any fixed notions of essentially male or female language with an androgynous play of language opening onto a form of 'desire and pleasure beyond the orders, the commandments, of identity' (Heath, 1982, pp. 135–6). While liberation from normative and ideological 'sexuality' is primarily imagined as part of an ethical and political future (cf. p. 152), Heath also invokes the Romantic

theme of a unity of sexual expression and being which preceded the alienating imposition of modern Western sexual knowledges and identities: 'In previous ages ... there had at least existed the possibility of speaking sexual experience in terms distinct from regulation and the finality of an economic exchange, in terms that stray and run over in pleasure; not "spending" but "bliss" ... ' (p. 14).

10. Our main example, *The Science of a New Life* by John Cowan, MD (1970, originally published 1874) is a compendium of themes which pervade middle-class medical manuals in Britain, the United States, Australia and other countries in this period. Other relevant texts include Elizabeth Blackwell, (1894), Elton Boyd (1884), and P. H. Chevasse (1879). Further discussion of such publications is to be found in Haller and Haller (1974).

11. As Haller and Haller point out (1974, pp. 97–9), major differences on questions of marriage and sexuality can be seen between writers such as William Acton and Elizabeth Blackwell. Acton holds that women have little capacity for sexual feeling and that this is naturally ordained to prevent the exhaustion of male sexual vitality, and yet is also one cause of apparent or temporary impotence in men (1865, pp. 111–5). Against this, Blackwell states that those who deny sexual feeling to women 'confound passion and appetite' (1894, p. 49), attach sexual passion exclusively to the act of coition (p. 51) and neglect the importance in personal and social arrangements of the varying manifestations – physical, reproductive, intellectual, emotional and moral – of the sexual faculties (p. 46). She argues that apprehension of sexual congress is not a natural female trait but results for many women from painful experience of sex, brutal or awkward conjugal approaches or fear of injury from childbirth (p. 50).

12. Unlike Ellis's longer 'scientific' studies, texts such as *The Objects of Marriage* and *Little Essays of Love and Virtue* were available in cheap editions and intended for a popular readership. Ellis considered that recognising the sexual personality, which meant recognising the erotic rights of women, was a necessary part of acknowledging the more general rights of women (1922, Chapter V), although the very identification of women with the erotic was seen by many contemporary feminists as problematic (cf. Rowbotham and Weeks, 1977, p. 13).

13. On Van de Velde and similar sex reformers in the early twentieth century, see Margaret Jackson (1987) and Sheila Jeffreys (1983).

14. Lawrence records that in his early days Edward Garnett had suggested to him that it was necessary to go the whole way in describing sex and that this suggestion stayed in his mind until he wrote *Lady Chatterley's Lover* (letter to David Garnett, 24 August 1928, in H. T. Moore (ed.) (1962, Volume 2, p. 1079).

15. Cowan writes that women should have such rights as those of suffrage, property, equal participation in government, employment and education, and the right to their own person which husbands insisting on their 'marital rights' have ignored (pp. 380–1). As Rowbotham and Weeks point out (1977, p. 13), in the second half of the nineteenth century there was an overlap between social purity movements (in which writers like Cowan participated) and middle-class feminism on the issue of women's rights over their own bodies.

16. See also Paul Delaney (1978).

17. For details of the original publication and reception of Lawrence's work, see James Cowan (ed.) (1982); Draper (ed.) (1970); Roberts (ed.) (1963); and the Introduction and Appendix in Lawrence (1936).
18. To pick up some of the voices from this circle: Lawrence saw in Burrow's psychological theories an attempt akin to his own to overcome the didacticism of 'the Freudian method'; Havelock Ellis, writer of literary as well as sexological works, read some of Lawrence's novels and referred ambivalently to their insight into sexual love (Grosskurth, 1980, p. 328); while the psychoanalyst Ernest Jones, writing to Ellis, suggested that the idea of 'sensationalism' in Lawrence's novels is equivalent to his own use of the term 'autoerotism' to describe an 'essentially objectless' activity of the self (Grosskurth, p. 391).
19. Beal (1961, pp. 112–3) records the view of Diana Trilling that in the 1920s Lawrence was seen in her circles as a great liberal thinker rather than a great writer: 'we thought his metaphors were translateable into a programme for practical conduct'.
20. In a similar vein, Mark Schorer's use (1967, pp. 250–66) of Lawrence's 'The Horse Dealer's Daughter' displays the typical features of mid-century New Criticism and practical criticism, insisting on the aesthetic unity of form and content, and the need continually to adjust one's responses by rehearsing the distinction between aesthetic and didactic modes of reading and writing:

> So what does the story tell us at last? It tells us that human love, love between man and woman, is, first of all, *living* . . . that it is elemental . . . that love is *terrible* . . . and . . . that love is *crucial* . . . All this exists in the densely physical symbolic texture and movement of the story, and we must ourselves experience it through that texture and movement. To abstract it as we have just done cannot be a successful operation, but a mere pointing back to the story itself; if it could be successful, there would be no need for such stories. The meaning is the prose that carries it. (p. 266)

21. Leavis's early pieces on Lawrence, such as those appearing in the Minority Press edition of *For Continuity* (1933), originally had a limited circulation and made little general impact on educators (cf. Coombes (ed.), 1973, p. 45). References to Lawrence's work in Leavis and Thompson's *Culture and Environment* (1933), designed for use in school, university and teacher training, relate to the question of literary value and the loss of the organic community rather than to representations of sexuality. The most detailed work by Leavis assimilating Lawrence into the system of pedagogic criticism is *D. H. Lawrence: Novelist*, first published in 1955. For data on the stages of published writings about Lawrence and his work – in which differences may be discerned between the earlier specialised circulation and the pedagogic distribution which was established from the late 1940s – see Coombes (ed.) (1973) and James Cowan (ed.) (1982 and 1985).
22. The stress on the formation of the reader's own sensibility is found throughout Leavis's writings on Lawrence, including his criticism of T. S. Eliot for finding fault with the latter's work when the problem lies, supposedly, with Eliot's own failure to read the work and comprehend literature's relation to sexuality dialectically. Once the dialectical method brings literature and sexuality together, of course, radically different evaluations of creative achieve-

ment are possible. So, for instance, Vivas (1960) re-evaluates Lawrence's works in a way that is consciously less generous towards Lawrence than is Leavis's appraisal, but he does so within the same framework of dialectical criticism. More generally, the aestheticising of sexual knowledges has made it possible to disdain whole categories of discourse as inferior to 'literature' since they impose didactically and normatively upon experience, as we see in Leavis's denunciation (1933, pp. 147–8) of the work of Marie Stopes, or in Marcus's contrast (1974) between the error of sexual medicine and the truth of sexual literature.

5 TWENTIETH-CENTURY ENGLISH OBSCENITY LAW

1. Ashbee (1877) provides encyclopedic testimony to this ethos. Combining the obsessive empiricism of the bibliophile and the fervid interest of a connoisseur of the perverse, Ashbee's work is also a monument to the reciprocal relation between the techniques of knowledge and the forms of pleasure in nineteenth-century biblio-erotics.
2. In Chapter 3 we noted the concern expressed in the 1908 *Report from the Joint Select Committee on Lotteries and Indecent Advertisements* at technical forms of communication – the press and the mail – which could not be regulated by the means of policing which accompanied the three-sector organisation of the literary field described here.
3. In our closing remarks in this book, we note that programmes for the eradication of sexual harassment in the workplace have recognised that works of art cannot be granted total immunity from regulation.
4. In the 1928 prosecution of Jonathan Cape for publishing Radclyffe Hall's *The Well of Loneliness* a similar defence strategy also founded. There, Norman Birkett KC for the publishers announced his intention to call 'evidence from every conceivable walk of life which bears on the test whether the tendency of this book is to deprave and corrupt'. Havelock Ellis in fact declined to be a witness for the book. Rolph reports on the case, indulging his usual taste for speculative personal asides:

> [Birkett] added that a more distinguished body of witnesses had never before been called in a Court of Justice. Sir Charles Biron [the presiding magistrate] said he doubted whether their evidence would be admitted, and Birkett retorted that if it couldn't a magistrate was a censor of literature. Biron, who probably thought he was, said that the witnesses could not be allowed to express their opinions upon matters which were for the decision of the court.
>
> (Rolph, 1969, p. 79)

It is now accepted that Birkett erred in asking his very first witness, the literary critic Desmond MacCarthy, whether the book was in his view obscene. Certainly no evidence of literary merit was admitted from that point on, either from MacCarthy or the thirty-nine other witnesses. Rolph in fact formulates the question that, in his opinion, Birkett should have put: 'Whether

this book is obscene or not – and that of course is a matter for the learned magistrate – is its publication advantageous to the pursuit of literature?' (1969, p. 80).
5. The degree of convergence between law and police has been contingent upon cultural and historical circumstances. In the United States, for instance, there have developed close links between statutory-judicial interpretations and decisions and police and local city council measures. See Chapter 8.
6. The notion of a public good defence is sometimes traced back to a nineteenth-century source in the 'submission' attached by Sir James Fitzjames Stephen to Article 228 of his *Digest of the Criminal Law:*

> A person is justified in exhibiting disgusting objects, or publishing obscene books, papers, writing, prints, pictures, drawings or other representations if for the public good, as being necessary or advantageous to religion or morality, to the administration of justice, the pursuit of science, literature or art, or other objects of general interest; but the justification ceases if the publication is made in such a manner, to such an extent, or under such circumstances, as to exceed what the public good requires in regard to the particular matter published.
>
> (Stephen, 1877, p. 173)

In a footnote, a recognition of the variable nature of obscenity is evident:

> [T]he publication of an edition of Juvenal, Aristophanes, Swift, Defoe, Bayle's Dictionary, Rabelais, Brantôme, Boccaccio, Chaucer, etc. cannot be regarded as a crime; yet each of these books contains more or less obscenity for which it is impossible to offer any excuse whatsoever. I know not how the publication of them could be justified except by the consideration that upon the whole it is for the public good that the works of remarkable men should be published as they are, so that we may be able to form as complete an estimate as possible of their characters and of the times in which they lived. On the other hand, a collection of indecencies might be formed from any one of the authors I have mentioned, the separate publication of which would deserve severe punishment. (p. 173)

The 'separate publication' of the part-edition would, as we have suggested, have a different circuit of distribution – that of popular pornography – from that of the classic edition.
7. *Regina* v. *Penguin Books Ltd* was the first trial but the second prosecution under the new Act. The first prosecution was *Shaw* v. *DPP* (1961), in which action was taken against Shaw for the publication of *The Ladies Directory*, a collection of contact advertisements for London prostitutes. These first two prosecutions show the varied couplings which the category of obscene publication continues to produce.
8. No official transcript of the trial exists. Rolph (ed.) (1961) provides a transcript, laced with partisan observations and asides against the Prosecution, which was published as a Penguin Special, three months after the acquittal.
9. During cross-examination of Dr Robinson, Bishop of Woolwich, the Prosecution seeks clarification of the nature of the admissible expertise. The

Judge's view was that Section 4 was 'sufficiently elastic' to allow a bishop to speak as an 'expert' on literary merit (Rolph, 1961, p. 63).
10. Rolph euphorically interjects that by the time Anne Scott-James took the stand, 'there had appeared a tendency to stop treating the witnesses as literary experts, or ethical experts, or "other merits" experts, and just treat them as experts' (Rolph, 1961, p. 103).
11. In fact, as already noted, 200 000 copies of *Lady Chatterley's Lover* had been printed (Morpurgo, 1979, pp. 314–25).

6 THE LIMITS OF LAW REFORM

1. The difficulties in attaching a coherent meaning to the notion of liberalism are well known. Not only is it split between economic, political and philosophical kinds but each kind is subject to varying descriptions. We use the term *philosophical liberalism* to refer to the doctrine that political liberties and rights are grounded in the rational capacities of the individual subject, a notion variously addressed in the works of Locke, Hume and Mill. We do so in order to distinguish *governmental liberalism* which, while it may adopt 'liberal' measures – non-coercive administrative systems, rights-based jurisdictions – does so on instrumental grounds of efficiency and productivity. Some believe that governmental liberalism is ultimately grounded in philosophical liberalism's rational individual via the mechanism of democratically elected legislatures. Our reasons for rejecting this article of faith and for insisting on irreducible differences between governmental and philosophical liberalism will emerge as the chapter progresses.
2. It can be observed that the Kantian currents informing modern moral philosophy render it startlingly incapable of discussing this issue. For Kant the independence of moral judgement from all calculations of personal and social interest is what makes it moral. Yet we learn from historians of morality that both Catholic and Protestant traditions of casuistry routinely modified the absolutism of their moral imperatives after assessing the ethical abilities of their flocks and the particular circumstances in which the imperatives were to be applied. See, for instance, Kittsteiner (1988). Legal judgement can be viewed as inherently casuistical in this regard, as it is perpetually adjusting moral absolutes to historical circumstances.

7 UNITED STATES OBSCENITY LAW

1. All Amendments to which we refer, together with details of their judicial history, are to be located in the relevant Constitutional Amendments volumes of the United States Code Annotated (hereinafter USCA).
2. A common reference point on these issues is the following statement made by Mr Justice Murphy:

Notes 257

There are certain well-defined and narrowly limited classes of speech, the prevention and punishment of which have never been thought to raise any Constitutional problem. These include the lewd and obscene, the profane, the libellous, and the insulting or "fighting" words – those which by their very utterance inflict injury or tend to incite an immediate breach of the peace.

(*Chaplinsky* v. *New Hampshire* (1942), pp. 571–2)

Certain constraints may also apply to categories of commercial speech (see, for example, *Pittsburgh Press Co.* v. *Pittsburgh Commission on Human Relations* (1973)).

3. In a similar vein, Edward de Grazia and Roger Newman see in the regulation of sexual and other contents of communications in the United States the presence of a 'censorial impulse' which should alarm those who care about 'the free flow of ideas': 'Danger to the open society lurks when any group seeks to impose *its* values on the rest of the populace. At stake is the First Amendment and, ultimately, the mind of America' (1982, p. 384).

4. For an account (informed by libertarian assumptions about censorship) of positions adopted on these First Amendment questions by various members of the Supreme Court in the period from *Roth* to *Miller*, see de Grazia and Newman (1982, pp. xix–xxii, 95–139).

5. We shall refer to this document as the Lockhart Report and, where the meaning is clear from the context, the Report. At this stage, we are concerned with the majority view of the Commission. We refer later in this chapter to dissenting statements.

6. By 'explicit sexual materials', the Commission means 'the entire range of explicit sexual depictions or descriptions in books, magazines, photographs, films, statuary, and other media' including 'the most explicit descriptions or what is often referred to as 'hard-core pornography'" (p. 72, n. 2). The Commission's use of the harm condition is seen in its subsidiary recommendations: 'We recommend legislative regulations upon the sale of sexual materials to young persons who do not have the consent of their parents, and we also recommend legislation to protect persons from having sexual materials thrust upon them without their consent through the mails or through open public display' (p. 57).

7. Stanley Fleishman, for example, claims that the views both of President Nixon, reflected in this rejection, and of the Supreme Court, evident in its policy on obscenity, 'represent a radical break from basic First Amendment principles affording the broadest possible protection to books, films and other media of expression, regardless of their content' (1973, p. 19). See also de Grazia and Newman (1982, pp. 129–31).

8. So, for example, the Commission endorses various uses of explicit sexual materials in educational contexts, including the practice followed in certain medical schools of presenting materials usually classified as pornographic or obscene in order to deal openly with the sexual interest of the students themselves such that in turn they will learn to deal with the sexual interests of patients, including minors (pp. 327–9). More generally the Commission urges governmental agencies concerned with education, child health and

mental health to 'include a wider range of topics relating to human sexuality, specifically including encounters with explicit sexual materials' (p. 56).
9. Cf. Jacques Donzelot (1979) on the historical negotiations occurring between governmental pedagogies (including what he calls the 'psy' complex) promoting self-management, in which social norms become more or less internalised as personal values, and 'tutelary' administrations of problematic relations and conducts within the 'policing of families' in France.
10. Cf. the Lockhart Report, (pp. 380–94) and the *Attorney General's Commission on Pornography and Obscenity Final Report* (1986, pp. 353–403, 433–765) on obscenity laws and their enforcement. Hereafter we refer to the latter document as the Hudson Report, or where the meaning is clear in context, the Report. The Commission which produced this report was appointed in 1985 by the Attorney General of the USA, Edwin Meese.
11. See, for instance, *Carlin Communications, Inc.* v. *Federal Communications Commission* (1984) where regulations promulgated by the Federal Communications Commission to regulate the dissemination of pornographic materials by telephone are challenged.
12. Historical reviews of United States obscenity law in relation to English law are contained in the working summaries of cases such as *Roth* and in the historical sections of the Lockhart Report (pp. 348–60) and the Hudson Report (pp. 236–48).
13. This is a consolidated case in which the decision covers two appeals. Previous court cases dealing with constitutional rights in relation to obscenity had been concerned with whether particular works were obscene under certain statutes (cf. *United States* v. *One Book Entitled Ulysses by James Joyce* (1934), in which the book was found not to be obscene within the Tariff Act of 1930) and not whether statutes proscribing obscenity were themselves constitutionally defective, specifically in relation to First Amendment provisions. In *Roth*, the Court limited itself to the constitutional questions of the validity of the statutes and was not concerned with the specific facts of either case. The significance of *Roth* is that a majority of the Court agreed on the standard to determine what constitutes obscenity.
14. After *Roth*, legislatures continued to have the latitude to prohibit distributions of explicit sexual materials to children or the obtrusive presentation of such materials to unconsenting adults, in terms stricter than those applying to distributions to consenting adults which are the concern of that case.
15. The references to harms of obscenity are more explicit in the trial judge's opinion in *United States* v. *Roth* (1956), where constitutional rights are weighed up against what is referred to explicitly as the law's role in administering a 'public policy' targeting recognisable forms of 'commercialized obscenity' and 'salable pornography' (pp. 797–9).
16. From the cases documented by de Grazia (1969, pp. xvii–xxxii) it is possible to trace the emergence of literary aesthetics in jurisprudential campaigns in the United States in the 1940s and 1950s. For other significant literary trials, see *Besig* v. *United States* (1953), in which Henry Miller's *Tropic of Cancer* and *Tropic of Capricorn* are found obscene; and *Memoirs* v. *Massachusetts* (1966), in which *Fanny Hill* is found not to be obscene.
17. In *Jenkins* v. *Georgia* (1974) the Supreme Court made clear that regardless of what local community standards might be, they could not operate to establish

that a work such as the film *Carnal Knowledge* appeals to prurient interest or is patently offensive.
18. It may be appropriate here to catalogue some of the ways in which 'government and community interests' in controlling obscenity have been specified as the courts weigh them up in relation to rights of expression. These interests include minimising influences identified in psychological, moral and ethical terms as harmful to particular groups, especially minors, and checking the exploitation of persons involved in the production of pornography (cf. the Hudson Report, pp. 595–745). They also include maintaining levels of decency, public safety and the welfare of neighbourhoods. These concerns extend into controlling public nuisance and crime associated with pornography and its often zonal distribution (*Star Satellite, Inc.* v. *City of Biloxi* (1986), monitoring activities in commercial and business districts (cf. *Brown* v. *Pornography Commission of Lower Southampton Township* (1982), and regulating industrial practices including the conditions, duties and obligations of employees within retail institutions and places of exhibition (*Pack* v. *City of Cleveland* (1982)). The policing of obscenity involves using laws against criminal activities ranging from large-scale production and distribution of illicit materials to what the Hudson Report refers to as the 'cottage industry' of child pornography (Part 2, Chapter 7, and Part 4 Chapter 4). A characteristic deliberation on these kinds of interests is found in the Supreme Court's opinion, delivered by Mr Chief Justice Burger, in *Paris Adult Theatre 1* v. *Slaton* (1973). The Court holds that there are 'legitimate state interests at stake in stemming the tide of commercialized obscenity': these include 'the interest of the public in the equality (*sic*) of life and the total community environment, the tone of commerce in the great city centers, and, possibly, the public safety itself' (pp. 57–8). The Court refers (p. 59) to the Hill-Link Minority Report in the Lockhart Report and to other legal opinion for the view that there may indeed be a link between obscenity and the development of dispositions towards anti-social conduct. It acknowledges that there may not be conclusive proof that such a link exists but – in contrast to the Lockhart majority which argues that there should therefore be no restrictions on access to explicit sexual materials for consenting adults – rules (p. 61) that it is reasonable to determine 'that such a connection does or might exist' and reiterates that in *Roth* it was implicitly accepted that a legislature could act on such a conclusion to protect '*the social interest in order and morality*'.
19. The regulation of pornography also involves governmental censorship boards, industry self-regulation and education departments (cf. de Grazia and Newman (1982, pp. xv–xxii, 3–151)).
20. See 18 United States Code Annotated Section 1467(d).
21. These due process requirements are related to the Fourth Amendment guarding the right to be secure against unreasonable searches and seizures. It is often stated in the courts that since obscenity cases involve First Amendment issues they require more stringent application of Fourth Amendment safeguards than do other criminal cases (*Macon* v. *State* (1984)). Various other checks on warranty procedures are found in the courts. So, for example, police cannot delegate official functions of search and seizure to unauthorised persons. In *State* v. *Furuyama* (1981), for example, it was found that the purchase of materials selected by members of a citizens' group participating

in a 'joint effort' with an undercover police officer to gather evidence in a bookstore constituted unlawful seizure.
22. The opinion delivered in *Smith* v. *California* (p. 150) is that the existence of a *mens rea* ('guilty mind') is 'the rule of, rather than the exception to, the principles of Anglo-American criminal jurisprudence' and that elimination of the *scienter* requirement may substantially restrict the freedom of speech and of the press.
23. Mr Justice Stewart's comment has often been taken as a sign of the self-evidently subjective nature of judicial decision-making on obscenity. It is perhaps forgotten that he was making the point that court decisions since *Roth* had been constitutionally limiting obscenity to hard-core pornography and that one could recognise the latter without having to define it exhaustively. He was in no danger, then, of confusing the cause of the trial, *The Lovers* – 'a French film depicting an unhappy marriage and the wife's falling in love with an archaeologist, and including in the last reel an explicit, but fragmentary and fleeting love scene' (Jacobellis, p. 184) – with the less genteel class of hard-core pornography.
24. Several of the federal statutes which we cite in this section, relating to the various law enforcement agencies, are amongst those which the Lockhart Report recommends be repealed (p. 75). Local, state and federal policing involves a wide range of statutes, practices and policies (for instance, the Federal Bureau of Investigation has a role in relation to 18 USCA Sections 1462 and 1465 prohibiting transportation of obscene matters in interstate or foreign commerce). On the role of police departments and the FBI see the Lockhart Report (pp. 386–8, 393–4) and on problems in policing, especially 'under-enforcement', see the Hudson Report (pp. 353–381, 415–8). The latter report, in contrast to the former, recommends extensive review and updating of federal, state and local obscenity legislation and law enforcement activities (pp. 459–593).
25. See 19 USCA Section 1305 of the Tariff Act; also 18 USCA Section 1462.
26. In any such proceeding 'any party may have an appeal or the right of review as in the case of ordinary actions or suits' (19 USCA Section 1305, p. 48).
27. See 18 USCA Section 1461; also 18 USCA Section 1463 and 39 USCA Section 3006.
28. See 39 USCA Section 3010. Cf. the Lockhart Report, pp. 389–90.
29. See 18 USCA Section 1464 and 47 USCA Sections 503(b) and 510.
30. See, for example, *People* v. *Lerch* (1985); *Upper Midwest Booksellers Association* v. *City of Minneapolis* (1985); and on the question of minors' access to cable in the home see the Hudson Report, pp. 579–82.
31. On historical and legal aspects of the construction of the right of privacy in the USA, see Hixson (1987). A major text here is Samuel D. Warren and Louis D. Brandeis (1890) which established the concept of a right to privacy (as a right to be let alone) independently of existing rights of property, contract and the like.
32. In *Paris Adult Theatre 1* v. *Slaton*, the Court states: 'If obscene material unprotected by the First Amendment in itself carried with it a "penumbra" of constitutionally protected privacy, this Court would not have found it necessary to decide *Stanley* on the narrow basis of the "privacy of the home," which was hardly more than a reaffirmation that "a man's home is his

castle'"(p. 66). In an accompanying footnote, the Court reiterates that the right of possession is restricted to a place, in contrast to certain other constitutional privacy rights which are not just concerned with a particular place but with 'a protected intimate relationship' and so extend to various places (as the privacy of, for instance, family and marriage extends to the doctor's office, the hotel room or the hospital).
33. See, for instance, *United States* v. *37 Photographs* (1971); *United States* v. *Reidel* (1971).
34. Cf. the statements of those testifying in the Minneapolis public hearings (*Pornography and Sexual Violence*, especially pp. 59–77) that pornography is used by men as a device for sexual excitation and experimentation in real-life situations and relations. These uses include clients requiring prostitutes to join in often violent scenarios from pornography: 'Women were forced constantly to enact specific scenes that men had witnessed in pornography. They would direct women to copy postures and poses of things they had seen in magazines and then they would take their own pictures of the women' (p. 72, Ms Z: Prostitutes' experience of pornography).

8 FEMINISM AND LAW REFORM

1. See Reinhart Koselleck (1988). A parallel account of the emergence of technically and rationally organised forms of law and politics – although one in which the difference between state and civil society is less absolute than in Koselleck – can be found in Foucault (1981).
2. An attempt to introduce a similar ordinance in the City of Minneapolis had been unsuccessful when a Bill introducing an amendment to that city's Civil Rights Code was vetoed by the Mayor after having been passed by the relevant Council. For a transcript of the first of two ordinances thus vetoed, see *Constitutional Commentary*, Volume 2, Number 147, 1985, pp. 181–9. The transcript of the Minneapolis public hearing held in conjunction with this ordinance appears in the Everywoman publication *Pornography and Sexual Violence* (1988). Interest developed in other cities, states and countries in developing Bills along similar lines (see Seator, 1987, p. 299 including note 8; *Pornography and Sexual Violence*, pp. 4–5). A version of the Dworkin–MacKinnon ordinance was signed into law by the Mayor of Indianapolis, William H. Hudnut, on 1 May 1984 with amendments on 15 June 1984. It was promptly challenged in the courts on constitutional grounds by various parties including the American Booksellers Association, Inc. and the Association for American Publishers, Inc. – both major representatives of trade interests with elements located in but reaching well beyond Indianapolis – together with other distributional, library, retail, video-rental and reading-public interest groups or individuals. The United States District Court, S. D. Indiana, Indianapolis Division, granting that the action was a justiciable case or controversy under Article III of the Constitution, whereby plaintiffs need not be the subject of an administrative or judicial proceeding at the time the lawsuit is initiated, held that the ordinance was unconstitutional on First and Fifth Amendment grounds (*American Booksellers Association, Inc.* v. *Hudnut*,

198 F. Supp. 1316 (1984)). The decision was affirmed by the United States Court of Appeals, Seventh Circuit, (771 F. 2d 323 (1985)), whose finding was summarily affirmed by the United States Supreme Court (106 SCt 1772 (1986), rehearing denied 106 SCt 1664 (1986)).

3. In discussing the feminist ideas and goals which underlie the anti-pornography laws, Dworkin identifies pornography's subordination of women with objectification defined in a way that subsumes discrimination as dehumanisation:

> Objectification occurs when a human being, through social means, is made less than human, turned into a thing or commodity, bought and sold. When objectification occurs, a person is depersonalised, so that no individuality or integrity is available socially or in what is an extremely circumscribed privacy . . . Objectification is an injury right at the heart of discrimination: those who can be used as if they are not fully human are no longer fully human in social terms; their humanity is hurt by being diminished.
>
> (Dworkin, 1985, p. 15)

4. This critique of law builds upon the feminist idea of a continuum in which pornography both becomes a metaphor for a series of cultural and political practices determined by the same logic of misrepresentation and subordination of women's being and naturalises those practices by eroticising inequality (cf. MacKinnon, 1987, p. 171–4). For a discussion of problems involved in treating pornography as a metaphor for sex discrimination in general, see Lesley Stern (1982).

5. For a historical discussion of sex discrimination and the Fourteenth Amendment, see Morais (1988). On the expansion of interest in the United States in articulating ethical objectives on issues of sexuality and sexual politics to governmental administration of civil rights and liberties, see Kim Ezra Shienbaum (ed.) (1988).

6. Broadly speaking, we can identify two lines of argument in jurisprudential responses to the Ordinance and *Hudnut*. MacKinnon's negative view of the category of 'speech' in obscenity regulation and her belief that the *Hudnut* decision reveals the sexist bias of the law is shared by several other writers. For example, Penelope Seator argues that in *Hudnut* the courts fail to recognise the reality of pornography as sex discrimination, reinforcing harmful conducts under the guise of defending a right of free expression equally available to all. The social reality of discrimination is thus reduced to a mere idea which, according to the 'liberal, idealistic philosophy reflected in the decision' is sacrosanct under the First Amendment (1987, p. 352). The decision shows that the 'first amendment is a tool of male hegemony' (p. 352). The courts' maintenance of a distinction between obscenity and pornography is seen as a political refusal to recognise women's experience and civil rights. A status quo is thus said to be preserved in which legislation made from the male point of view is not seen as from a point of view; it is only legislation written from the point of view of those injured by pornography rather than those gaining profit, pleasure and power from it that is found to be viewpoint discrimination (p. 354).

In other responses, 'speech' in the context of pornography is not treated as a fundamentally ideological category. Some writers, acknowledging that pornography is problematic or harmful, maintain to a greater or lesser degree a negative conception of free speech as a given right of the individual, such that the Ordinance poses for them a risk of 'censorship' leading onto the slippery slope of loss of fundamental liberties (cf. James Branit, 1986) or, indeed, plays into the hands of a reactionary, antifeminist moral crusade against pornography (Lisa Duggan, 1988). Numerous liberal and feminist writers, while treating the attempt to translate the generalised idea of pornographic 'subordination' of women into law with a degree of scepticism, identify 'speech' positively with processes of educational change (cf. Winifred Sendler, 1985; Geoffrey Stone, 1986).

7. The Court also considers Fifth Amendment due process requirements including overbreadth, prior restraint and vagueness which affects the *scienter* requirement (pp. 1337–41).

8. Of course, the spirit of the Ordinance is to seek not paternalistic protection but redress against sex discrimination. However, the problem encountered in extending the principle of protecting minors to control harms flowing more generally from pornography's subordination of women indicates that the form of governmental 'protection' first associated with medical-moral norms (according to which, as we have seen, women were indeed linked with children as vulnerable subjects) has given way to more sophisticated and differentiated calculations concerning parties affected by pornography. The problems posed by an aesthetic commitment to a universal and undifferentiated subject arise in relation to a lower-level set of discriminations – by gender, age, social situation, level of education and so on – which *for some purposes* women might want to make.

9. To cite the Court of Appeals (771 F. 2d, pp. 329–30), pornography's harms demonstrate pornography's power as speech. In other words, the subordination and discrimination it creates and maintains depend on particular technologies of media sex, and if the constructions of male sexuality which these involve are to be changed, then this requires forms of intellectual and ethical mediation which, while they may be aligned with the law, are not reducible to it.

10. From this point of view, feminism is clearly the major force contending to redefine the norms operating in what the Court of Appeals refers to as the 'socializing' effects of pornography. We have already seen that the agnosticism professed in the Lockhart Report in support of deregulation does not cut much ice in more recent governmental calculations (cf. the Hudson Report, pp. 299–351). On the shift with regard to harms, see also the *Report of the Special Committee on Pornography and Prostitution: Pornography and Prostitution in Canada, Summary* (1985, pp. 11–13, 45–56) and the recent New Zealand *Report of the Ministerial Committee of Inquiry into Pornography* (1989, pp. 38–47).

11. In *Pornography and Sexual Violence* (pp. 77–9) appears the testimony of a woman employed as a plumber who objected to the display of pornography at her workplace and whose attempts – supported by affirmative rights officers – to have it removed, drew retaliations such that she sought a transfer. Administrative measures to prevent or resolve such situations are inscribed in

that part of the Ordinance which makes it actionable to force pornography on a person in employment, education, the home or public places. For such a right to be fully effective it needs to be linked to other economic and civil guarantees of employment, equity, participation and the like. Jeffrey Minson has brought to our attention the promulgation of public service regulations in Australia which include the display of offensive sexual materials in the workplace among those activities which constitute harassment, mentioning for instance 'provocative posters with a sexual connotation. Even works of art may be inappropriate on occasions' (Public Service Board, Australia, 1986, p. 3). It is suggested by William Brigman (1985, p. 501) that the 'forcing' of pornography in the work environment might be treated as a form of sexual harassment and hence as a violation of the United States Civil Rights Act of 1964. Similarly, the sensitisation which has occurred in governmental contexts to problems of prejudicial stereotyping of women, such that it is possible to register and refer to law certain of its discriminatory effects, is arguably related in some measure to campaigns criticising media and other objectification and subordination of women. This is reflected in recent legal decisions such as that made by the United States Supreme Court requiring Price Waterhouse to appoint a women employee to full partnership with back pay because its promotions review system had permitted 'negatively sexually stereotyped comments to influence partnership selection' *The Weekend Australian*, November 10–11, 1990, p. 45). We may also note here complex issues surrounding the interests and rights of those harmed in the production of pornography, one of the areas of 'forcing' with which the Ordinance is concerned. The Hudson Report (pp. 595–735) deals with preventions, penalties and remedies specifically in relation to the production of child pornography, including child abuse in this production, and the problem of welfare assistance for runaway or homeless young people.

Bibliography

Acton, William (1865) [1857] *The Functions and Disorders of the Reproductive Organs in Childhood, Youth, Adult Age and Advanced Life* (London: John Churchill and Sons) 4th edition.
Alcott, W. A. (1972) [1837] *The Young Wife; or Duties of Woman in the Marriage Relation* (New York: Arno Press).
Alcott, W. A. (1972) [1841] *The Young Husband; or Duties of Man in the Marriage Relation* (New York: Arno Press).
Andrews, W. T. (ed.) (1971) *Critics on D. H. Lawrence* (London: Allen and Unwin).
Archer, P. (1956) *The Queen's Courts* (Harmondsworth: Penguin Books).
Archbold, J. F. (1886) [1812] *Pleading and Evidence in Criminal Cases; with the Statutes, Precedents of Indictments, & C., and the evidence necessary to support them.* (By John Jervis. Twentieth edition by William Bruce.) (London: H. Sweet and Sons).
Ashbee, Henry Spencer (1962) [1877] *Bibliography of Prohibited Books* (New York: Brussel). Introduction by G. Legman.
Atkins, J. (1970) *Sex in Literature* (London: Calder and Boyars) 4 vols.
Bain, A. (1861) *On the Study of Character* (London: Parker, Son and Bowers).
Bain, A. (1868) *Mental and Moral Science* (London: Longmans, Green and Co.).
Baisch, Dorothy R. (1950) 'London Literary Circles, 1910–1920, with Special Reference to Ford Madox Ford, Ezra Pound, D. H. Lawrence and Virginia Woolf', unpublished doctoral thesis: Cornell University.
Barry, Kathleen (1979) *Female Sexual Slavery* (New York and London: New York University Press).
Bates, F. (1978) 'Pornography and the Expert Witness', *Criminal Law Review* 20, pp. 250–64.
Beal, Anthony (1961) *D. H. Lawrence* (Edinburgh and London: Oliver and Boyd).
Beal, Anthony (ed.) (1967) See D. H. Lawrence (1967)
Beale, L. J. (1851) *The Laws of Health in Relation to Mind and Body* (London: John Churchill).
Berger, Fred (ed.) (1980) *Freedom of Expression* (Belmont, California: Wadsworth Publishing Company).
Blackwell, Elizabeth (1879) *Counsel to Parents: On the Moral Education of their Children in Relation to Sex* (London: Hatchards).
Blackwell, Elizabeth (1894) [1884] *The Human Element in Sex: Being a Medical Enquiry into the Relation of Sexual Physiology to Christian Morality* (London: J. and A. Churchill).
Bloch, I. (1910) *The Sexual Life of Our Time in its Relations to Modern Civilization* (New York: Allied Book Co.).
Bold, Alan (ed.) (1982) *The Sexual Dimension in Literature* (London: Vision Press Limited and Totowa: Barnes and Noble).
Boucé, P. G. (ed.) (1982) *Sexuality in Eighteenth Century Britain* (Manchester: Manchester University Books).

Bourdieu, Pierre (1984) *Distinction: A Social Critique of the Judgement of Taste* (London: Routledge and Kegan Paul).

Boyd, Elton (1877) *Vitality: how wasted and how preserved; nervous debility, neurosthenia, diagnosis and treatment.* (Sydney: no publisher given) 14th edition.

Branit, James R. (1986) 'Reconciling Free Speech and Equality: What Justifies Censorship?', *Harvard Journal of Law and Public policy*, vol. 9, no. 2 pp. 429–60.

Brentford, The Right Hon. the Viscount (Sir William Joynson Hicks) (1929) *Do We Need a Censor?*, *The Criterion Miscellany*, Number 6 (London: Faber and Faber).

Brigman, William E. (1985) 'Pornography or Group Libel: The Indianapolis Sex Discrimination Ordinance', *Indiana Law Review*, vol. 18, no. 2, pp. 479–505.

Bristow, E. J. (1977) *Vice and Vigilance: Purity Movements in Britain Since 1700* (Dublin: Gill and Macmillan).

Brown, Beverley (1980) 'Private Faces in Public Places', *I and C*, no. 7, pp. 3–16.

Brown, Peter (1989) *The Body and Society: Men, Women and Sexual Renunciation in Early Christianity* (London: Faber and Faber).

Brownmiller, Susan (1975) *Against Our Will: Men, Women and Rape* (New York: Simon and Schuster).

Brunsdon, Charlotte (ed.) (1986) *Films for Women* (London: British Film Institute).

Burns, A. (1972) *To Deprave and Corrupt* (Technical Reports of the United States Commission on Obscenity and Pornography) (London: Davis-Poynter).

Caplan, Pat (ed.) (1987) *The Cultural Construction of Sexuality* (London: Tavistock).

Carlen, Pat and Collison, Mike (eds) (1980) *Radical Issues in Criminology* (Oxford: Martin Robertson)

Carpenter, Edward (1889) *Civilization: Its Cause and Cure and Other Essays* (London: George Allen and Unwin).

Carpenter, Edward (1896) [1883] *Towards Democracy* (London: Swan Sonnenschein).

Carpenter, Edward (1905) [1896] *Love's Coming-of-Age* (Chicago: Charles H. Kerr and Company).

Carpenter, Edward (1905) *Prisons, Police and Punishment: An Inquiry into the Causes and Treatment of Crime and Criminals* (London: Arthur C. Fifield).

Carpenter, Edward (1907) [1904] *The Art of Creation: Essays on the Self and its Powers* (London: George Allen).

Carpenter, Edward (1912) [1908] *The Intermediate Sex: A Study of Some Transitional Types of Men and Women* (London: Swan Sonnenschein).

Carpenter, Edward (1917) [1898] *Angel's Wings: A Series of Essays on Art and its Relation to Life* (London: George Allen and Unwin).

Carrithers, M., Collins, S. and Lukes, S. (eds) (1985) *The Category of Person* (Cambridge: Cambridge University Press).

Charney, Maurice (1981) *Sexual Fiction* (London: Methuen).

Chester, Gail and Dickey, Julienne (eds) (1988) *Feminism and Censorship: The Current Debate* (Bridport: Prism Press).

Chevasse, P. H. (1879) *Man's Strength and Woman's Beauty* (Melbourne: Standard Publishing Co.).

Chidley, W. J. (1977) *The Confessions of William James Chidley* (St Lucia: University of Queensland Press). Edited by S. McInerney.

Cleland, John (1985) [1748] *Fanny Hill or Memoirs of a Woman of Pleasure* (Harmondsworth: Penguin Books).

Bibliography

Colby, R. A. (1967) *Fiction With a Purpose: Major and Minor Nineteenth Century Novels* (Bloomington: Indiana University Press).

Colby, R. A. (1979) *Thackeray's Canvass of Humanity: An Author and His Public* (Columbus: Ohio State University Press).

Colby, R. A. (1984) 'Rational Amusement: Fiction vs Useful Knowledge in the Nineteenth Century', Kincaid, J. R. and Kuhn, A. J., (eds.) (1984) pp. 46–73.

Collins, Joseph (1923) *The Doctor Looks at Literature: Psychological Studies of Life and Letters* (New York: George H. Doran).

Comstock, Anthony (1883) *Traps For the Young* (New York: Funk and Wagnells).

Coombes, H. (ed.) (1973) *D. H. Lawrence: A Critical Anthology* (Harmondsworth: Penguin Books).

Colquhoun, Patrick (1801) [1797] *A Treatise on the Police of the Metropolis* (London: Printed by H. Fry). Revised and enlarged on by magistrates.

Constitutional Commentary (1985) Volume 2, Number 147.

Cousins, Mark (1980) '*Mens rea:* A Note on Sexual Difference, Criminology and the Law' in Carlen, P. and Collison, M. (eds) (1980) pp. 109–22.

Cowan, James C. (ed.) (1982, 1985) *D. H. Lawrence: An Annotated Bibliography of Writings About Him* (De Kalb, Illinois; Northern Illinois University Press) Volumes I and II.

Cowan, John, M. D. (1970) [1874] *The Science of a New Life* (New York: Source Book Press).

Davy, Kate (1989) 'Reading Past the Heterosexual Imperative: Dress Suits to Hire', *The Drama Review*, Volume 33, Number 1, pp. 153–70 (New York: New York University).

Defoe, Daniel (1965) [1719] *The Life and Adventures of Robinson Crusoe* (Harmondsworth: Penguin Books).

De Grazia, Edward (1969) *Censorship Landmarks* (New York: R. R. Bowker Co.).

De Grazia, Edward and Newman, Roger K. (1982) *Banned Films: Movies, Censors and the First Amendment* (New York: R. R. Bowker Co.).

Delaney, Paul (1978) *D. H. Lawrence's Nightmare: The Writer and his Circle in the Years of the Great War* (New York: Basic Books, Inc.).

Delavenay, Emile (1971) *D. H. Lawrence and Edward Carpenter: A Study in Edwardian Transition* (London: Heinemann).

Deleuze, G. (1971) *Sacher-Masoch: An Interpretation* (London: Faber and Faber).

Dharan, R. and Davies, C. (1978) *Censorship and Obscenity* (London: Martin Robertson).

Donzelot, Jacques (1970) *The Policing of Families* (New York: Pantheon Books).

Draper, R. P. (ed.) (1970) *D. H. Lawrence: The Critical Heritage* (London: Routledge and Kegan Paul).

Duggan, Lisa (1988) 'Censorship in the name of feminism', in Chester, G. and Dickey, J. (eds) (1988) pp. 76–86.

Durrell, Lawrence (1959) *The Black Book* (Paris: The Olympia Press).

Dworkin, Andrea (1981) *Pornography: Men Possessing Women* (New York: Perigree Books).

Dworkin, Andrea (1985) 'Against the Male Flood: Censorship, Pornography and Equality', *Harvard Women's Law Journal*, vol. 8, pp. 1–27.

Dworkin, Andrea (1987) *Intercourse* (London: Secker and Warburg).

Eisenstein, Elizabeth (1979) *The Printing Press as an Agent of Change: Communications and Cultural Transformations in Early-Modern Europe*, 2 vols. (Cambridge: Cambridge University Press).

Eliot, T. S. (1927) 'The Contemporary Novel' (excerpt) from *La Nouvelle Revue Française*, May, pp. 669–75. Reprinted in Draper, R. P., (ed.) (1970), pp. 275–7.
Ellis, Havelock (1898) *A Note on the Bedborough Trial* (London: The University Press).
Ellis, Havelock (1899) *Studies in the Psychology of Sex* – vol. 1 (Philadelphia: F. A. Davis).
Ellis, Havelock (1915) [1898] *Affirmations* (Boston and New York: Houghton Mifflin).
Ellis, Havelock (1922) *Little Essays of Love and Virtue* (New York: George H. Doron Co.).
Ellis, Havelock (1929) [1894] *Man and Woman: a study of human secondary sexual characters* (Boston and New York: Houghton and Mifflin Co.).
Ellis, Havelock (1931) *More Essays of Love and Virtue* (London: Constable and Co. Ltd.).
Ellis, Havelock (1940) *Studies in the Psychology of Sex* – vol. 2 (New York: Random House).
Ellis, Havelock (n. d.) *The Objects of Marriage: A Radical View of Sex Relationships* (Melbourne: Will Andrade). Also published in London in 1918 by the British Society for the Study of Sex Psychology.
Ernst, M. L. and Schwartz, A. U. (1964) *Censorship: The Search for the Obscene* (London: Collier – Macmillan).
Feinberg, Joel (1984) *The Moral Limits of the Criminal Law*, vol. 1: *Harm to Others* (Oxford: Oxford University Press).
Feinberg, Joel (1985) *The Moral Limits of the Criminal Law*, vol. 2: *Offense to Others* (Oxford: Oxford University Press).
Finnane, M. (1989) 'Censorship and the Child: Explaining the Comics Campaign', *Australian Historical Studies*, no. 92, pp. 220–40.
Fleishman, Stanley (1973) 'Overview' in the *Supreme Court Obscenity Decisions* (South San Diego: Greenleaf Classics), pp. 7–20.
Forster, E. M. (1970) Broadcast transcript from *The Listener*, 30 April 1930, iii, pp. 753–4. Reprinted in Draper, R. P., (ed.) (1970), pp. 343–7.
Forster, E. M. (1972) *Maurice* (Harmondsworth: Penguin Books).
Forster, E. M. (1983) [1920] 'Letter to Siegfried Sassoon' in Lago, M. and Furbank, P. N., (eds) (1983) p. 316.
Foucault, Michel (1975) 'Les Anormaux' (The A-Normals). Unpublished transcription of a series of lectures given at the Collège de France, January–March.
Foucault, Michel (1979) *The History of Sexuality*, vol. 1: *An Introduction* (London: Penguin Books).
Foucault, Michel (1981) 'Omnes et Singulation: Towards a Criticism of "Political Reason"', in S. McMurrin (ed.) *The Tanner Lectures on Human Values* (Salt Lake City: University of Utah Press).
Foucault, Michel (1986) *The History of Sexuality*, vol. 2: *The Use of Pleasure* (Harmondsworth: Viking [Penguin]).
Fowler, O. S. (1870) *Sexual Science: Including Manhood, Womanhood and their Mutual Interrelations* (Philadelphia: National Publishing Co.).
Foxon, D. (1964) *Libertine Literature in England, 1660–1745* (London: The Book Collector).

Freud, S. (1977) *On Sexuality: Three Essays on the Theory of Sexuality and Other Works* (Harmondsworth: Penguin Books).
Fryer, P. (ed.) (1970) *Forbidden Books of the Victorians* (London: The Odyssey Press). An abridgement of Ashbee's bibliography.
Fuchs, Elinor (1989) 'Staging the Obscene Body', *The Drama Review*, vol. 33, no. 1, pp. 33–58.
Gay, Peter (1984) *The Bourgeois Experience: Victoria to Freud* (Oxford: Oxford University Press), 2 vols.
Goldsmid, J. A. (1934) *Companionate Marriage* (London: William Heinemann [Medical Books Ltd.]).
Griffin, Susan (1982) *Pornography and Silence: Culture's Revenge Against Nature* (New York: Harper and Row).
Grosskurth, Phyllis (1980) *Havelock Ellis: A Biography* (London: Allen Lane).
Hagstrum, J. H. (1980) *Sex and Sensibility: Ideal and Erotic Love from Milton to Mozart* (Chicago: University of Chicago Press).
Haiman, Franklyn S. (1981) *Speech and Law in a Free Society* (Chicago and London: University of Chicago Press).
Haller, John S. Jr. and Haller, Robin M. (1974) *The Physician and Sexuality in Victorian America* (Urbana: University of Illinois Press).
Haller, W. and Haller, M. (1942) 'The Puritan Art of Love' in *Huntington Library Quarterly*, vol. 5, pp. 235–72.
Heath, Stephen (1982) *The Sexual Fix* (London: Macmillan).
Herzinger, K. A. (1982) *D. H. Lawrence and His Time, 1908–1915* (East Brunswick, New Jersey: Bucknell University Press).
Hill, C. (1964) *Society and Puritanism in Pre-Revolutionary England* (London: Secker and Warburg).
Hirst, Paul (1980) 'Law, Socialism and Rights' in Carlen, P. and Collison, M. (eds) (1980), pp. 58–105.
Hirst, Paul and Woolley, Penny (1982) *Social Relations and Human Attributes* (London: Tavistock).
Hite, Shere (1976) *The Hite Report: a nationwide study of female sexuality* (New York: Macmillan).
Hite, Shere (1981) *The Hite Report on Male Sexuality* (New York: Alfred A. Knopf).
Hixson, Richard F. (1987) *Privacy in a Public Society: Human Rights in Conflict* (New York: Oxford University Press).
Hunter, Ian (1988) *Culture and Government: The Emergence of Literary Education* (London: Macmillan).
Hunter, J. P. (1966) *The Reluctant Pilgrim, Defoe's Emblematic Method and the Quest for Form in Robinson Crusoe* (Baltimore: Johns Hopkin University Press).
Huxley, Aldous (1971) [1928] *Point Counter Point* (London: Chatto and Windus).
Hyde, H. Montgomery (1964) *A History of Pornography* (London: Heinemann).
Jackson, Margaret (1987) "Facts of Life" or the eroticisation of women's oppression?' in Caplan, P., (ed.) (1987), pp. 52–81.
Jacobs, Caryn (1984) 'Patterns of Violence: A Feminist Perspective on the Regulation of Pornography', *Harvard Women's Law Journal*, vol. 7, pp. 5–55.
Jeffreys, Sheila (1983) 'Sex reform and anti-feminism in the 1920s' in The London Feminist History Group (ed.) (1983) pp. 177–202.

Jordan, F. (1896) *Character as seen in Body and Parentage* (London: Kegan Paul; Trench and Trubner).
Jordan, F. (1901) *Moral Nerve and the Error of Literary Judgements* (London: Kegan Paul).
The Justice of the Peace, and County, Borough, Poor Law Union and Parish Law Recorder (London: Richard Shaw Bond). Established 1837.
Kappeler, Susanne (1986) *The Pornography of Representation* (Cambridge: Polity Press).
Kaufmann, U. M. (1966) *The Pilgrim's Progress and Traditions in Puritan Meditation* (New Haven, NJ: Yale University Press).
Kincaid, J. R. and Kuhn, A. J. (eds) (1984) *Victorian Literature and Society: Essays Presented to Richard D. Altick* (Columbus: Ohio State University Press).
Kinsey, A. C. et al. (1948) *Sexual Behaviour in the Human Male* (Philadelphia: Saunders).
Kirchwey, Freda (ed.) (1925) *Our Changing Morality: A Symposium* (London: Kegan, Paul, Trench, Trubner and Co.).
Kittsteiner, H. -D. (1988) 'Kant and Causistry' in Leites, E. (ed.) *Conscience and Casuistry in Early Modern Europe* (Cambridge: Cambridge University Press).
Knowlton, C. (1878) *Fruits of Philosophy: An Essay on the Population Question.* Reprinted in Rothman, D. J. and Rothman, S. M. (1972).
Kopold, Sylvia (1925) 'Where are the female geniuses' in Kirchwey, F. (ed.) (1925) pp. 107–26.
Kronhausen, E. and Kronhausen, P. (1959) *Pornography and the Law* (New York: Ballantine Books). Revised in 1964.
Koselleck, Reinhart (1988) *Critique and Crisis: Enlightenment and the Pathogenesis of Modern Society* (Oxford: New York and Hamburg: Berg).
Krafft-Ebing, R. (1951) *Aberrations of Sexual Life. The Psychopathia Sexualis* (London: Panther Books).
Kurtz, Paul (ed.) (1969) *Moral Problems in Contemporary Society* (Englewood Cliffs, New Jersey: Prentice Hall).
Lago, Mary and Furbank, P. N. (eds) (1983) *Selected Letters of E. M. Forster* (London: Collins).
Lawrence, D. H. (1929) 'Pornography and Obscenity'. The Criterion Miscellany (London: Faber and Faber).
Lawrence, D. H. (1936) *Phoenix: The Posthumous Papers of D. H. Lawrence* (London: Heinemann). Edited by Edward D. McDonald.
Lawrence, D. H. (1948) [1913] *Sons and Lovers* (Harmondsworth: Penguin Books).
Lawrence, D. H. (1949) [1915] *The Rainbow* (Harmondsworth: Penguin Books).
Lawrence, D. H. (1953) *Sex, Literature and Censorship* (New York: Twayne). Edited by Harry T. Moore.
Lawrence, D. H. (1960) [1921] *Women in Love* (Harmondsworth: Penguin Books).
Lawrence, D. H. (1961) *Lady Chatterley's Lover* (Harmondsworth: Penguin Books).
Lawrence, D. H. (1961) *A Propos of Lady Chatterley's Lover and Other Essays* (Harmondsworth: Penguin Books).
Lawrence, D. H. (1967) *Selected Literary Criticism: D. H. Lawrence* (London: Heinemann). Edited by Anthony Beal.
Lawrence, D. H. (1971) [1923] *Fantasia of the Unconscious and Psychoanalysis and the Unconscious* (Harmondsworth: Penguin Books).
Lawrence, Frieda (1934) *Not I, But the Wind . . .* (New York: The Viking Press).

Leavis, F. R. (1933) *For Continuity* (Cambridge: Gordon Fraser, The Minority Press).

Leavis, F. R. (1964) [1955] *D. H. Lawrence: Novelist* (London: Chatto and Windus).

Leavis, F. R. and Thompson, Denys (1977) [1933] *Culture and Environment: The Training of Critical Awareness* (Westport, Connecticut: Greenwood Press).

Lederer, Laura (ed.) (1980) *Take Back the Night: Women on Pornography* (New York: William Morrow and Co.).

Leland, Charles G. (1904) *The Alternate Sex or the Female Intellect in Man and the Masculine in Women* (London: Philip Wellby).

Lindsey, Ben B. (Judge) with Evans, Wainwright (1928) *The Companionate Marriage* (New York: Brentano's).

Liston, Angela A. (1985) 'Pornography and the First Amendment: The Feminist Balance', *Arizona Law Review*, vol. 27, pp. 415–35.

Lockhart, W. B. and McClure, R. C. (1954) 'Literature, the Law of Obscenity and the Constitution', *Minnesota Law Review*, vol. 38, pp. 295–395.

Lockhart, W. B. and McClure, R. C. (1960) 'Censorship of Obscenity: The Developing Constitutional Standards', *Minnesota Law Review*, vol. 45, pp. 5–121.

London Feminist History Group, The (ed.) (1983) *The Sexual Dynamics of History: Men's Power, Women's Resistance* (London: Pluto Press).

Loth, D. (1962) *The Erotic in Literature* (London: Secker and Warburg).

Maag, Marilyn J. (1985) 'The Indianapolis Pornography Ordinance: does the right to free speech outweigh pornography's harm to women?', *University of Cincinnati Law Review*, vol. 54, no. 1, pp. 249–69.

MacKinnon, Catharine A. (1982) 'Feminism, Marxism, Method and the State: An Agenda for Theory', *Signs: Journal of Women in Culture and Society*, vol. 7, no. 3, pp. 515–44.

MacKinnon, Catharine A. (1983) 'Feminism, Marxism, Method, and the State: Toward Feminist Jurisprudence', *Signs: Journal of Women in Culture and Society*, vol. 8, no. 4, pp. 635–58.

MacKinnon, Catharine A. (1987) *Feminism Unmodified: Discourses on Life and Law* (Cambridge, Massachusetts: Harvard University Press).

Manchester, Colin (1983) 'Obscenity in the Mail', *The Criminal Review*, February, pp. 64–77.

Manchester, Colin (1988) 'Lord Campbell's Act: England's First Obscenity Statute', *The Journal of Legal History*, vol. 9, no. 2, September, pp. 223–41.

Marcus, S., (1964) *The Other Victorians: A Study of Sexuality and Pornography in Mid-Nineteenth Century England* (New York: Basic Books).

Mauss, Marcel (1973) 'Techniques of the Body', *Economy and Society*, vol. 2, no. 1, pp. 70–87.

Mauss, M. (1985) 'A Category of the Human Mind: The Notion of Person; the Notion of Self' in Carrithers, M. et al (1985), pp. 1–25.

McDonald, Edward D. (1936) Introduction to Lawrence, D. H. (1936), pp. ix–xxii.

Mill, J. S. (1963) *Three Essays by J. S. Mill* (London: Oxford University Press).

Miller, Henry (1985) *The World of Lawrence: A Passionate Appreciation* (London: John Calder). Edited by Evelyn J. Hinz and John J. Teunissen.

Millot, M. and L'Ange, J. (1972) [1655] *The School of Venus* (*L'Ecole des Filles*), trans. D. Thomas (London: Panther Books).

Montano, Linda (1989) 'Summer Saint Camp', *The Drama Review*, vol. 33, no. 1, pp. 94–103.

Moore, H. T. (ed.) (1962) *The Collected Letters of D. H. Lawrence* (New York: The Viking Press) 2 vols.
Morais, Nina (1988) 'Sex Discrimination and the Fourteenth Amendment', *Yale Law Journal,* vol. 97, no. 6, pp. 1153–72.
Morpurgo, J. E. (1979) *Allen Lane, King Penguin: A Biography* (London: Hutchinson).
Muir, Edwin, (1970) 'D. H. Lawrence', *Nation,* 11th February 1925, CXX, pp. 148–50. Reprinted in Draper, R. P. (ed.) 1970, pp. 243–9.
Murry, J. M. (1932) *Son of Woman: D. H. Lawrence* (London: Jonathon Cape).
Murry, J. M. (1970) 'Review of *Women in Love*', *Nation and Atheneum,* 13 August 1921, XXIX, pp. 713–14. Reprinted in Draper, R. P. (ed.) (1970), pp. 168–72.
Nagel, Ernest (1969) 'The Enforcement of Morals' in Kurtz, Paul, (ed.) (1969) pp. 137–66.
Nehls, Edward (1957–1959) *D. H. Lawrence: A Composite Biography* (Madison: University of Wisconsin Press) 3 vols.
Newton, A. E. (1875) *The Better Way: An Appeal to Men* (New York: Wool and Holbrook).
Nin, Anais (1964) [1932] *D. H. Lawrence: An Unprofessional Study* (Chicago: The Swallow Press).
Oestreich, G. (1982) *Neostoicism and the Early Modern State* (Cambridge: Cambridge University Press).
Owen, R. D. (1859) *Moral Physiology* (London: Hollyoake and Co.). Reprinted in Rothman, D. J. and Rothman, S. M. (1972).
Paroissien, David (ed.) (1985) *Selected Letters of Charles Dickens* (Houndmills: Macmillan).
Pearsall, Ronald (1976) *Public Purity, Private Shame* (London: Weidenfeld and Nicolson).
Pepys, Samuel (1976) *The Diary of Samuel Pepys* (London: Bell and Hyman) 11 vols. Edited by R. Latham and W. Matthews.
Phillips, J. (1977) 'Copyright in Obscene Works: Some British and American Problems', *Anglo-American Law Review,* vol. 7, pp. 138–71.
Pritchett, V. S. (1970) 'Comment on expurgated edition of *Lady Chatterley's Lover*', *Fortnightly Review,* 1 April 1932, CXXXI, pp. 536–7. Reprinted in Draper, R. P. (ed.) (1970), pp. 287–8.
Public Service Board Australia (1986) *Eliminating Sexual Harassment: guidelines for sexual harassment officers and personnel officers* (Canberra: Public Service Board).
Radzinowicz, Leon (1959) *A History of English Criminal Law and its Administration from 1750,* vol. 3: *Cross-currents in the movement for the reform of the police* (London: Stevens and Sons Limited).
Rembar, Charles (1968) *The End of Obscenity: The Trials of Lady Chatterley, Tropic of Cancer and Fanny Hill* (New York: Random House).
Reynolds, Richard (1975) 'Our Misplaced Reliance on Early Obscenity Cases', *American Bar Association Journal,* February, vol. 61, pp. 220–2.
Rich, R. Ruby (1986) 'Anti-Porn: Soft Issue, Hard World' in Brunsdon, C. (ed.) (1986), pp. 31–43.
Richards, David A. J. (1980) 'The Moral Theory of Free Speech and Obscenity Law' in Berger, Fred (ed.) (1980), pp. 99–127.

Roberts, F. Warren (1963) *A Bibliography of D. H. Lawrence* (London: Rupert Hart-Davis).
Robertson, Geoffrey (1979) *Obscenity: An Account of Censorship Laws and their Enforcement in England and Wales* (London: Weidenfeld and Nicolson).
Robertson, Geoffrey (1990) 'Foreword' in Rolph, C. H. (ed.) *The Trial of Lady Chatterley: Regina v. Penguin Books Limited. The Transcript of the Trial,* revised edition (Harmondsworth: Penguin Books).
Rolph, C. H. (ed.) (1961) *Does Pornography Matter?* (Freeport, New York: Books for Libraries Press).
Rolph, C. H. (ed.) (1961) *The Trial of Lady Chatterley: Regina v. Penguin Books Limited. The Transcript of the Trial* (Harmondsworth: Penguin Books).
Rolph, C. H. (1969) *Books in the Dock* (London: André Deutsch).
Rothman, D. J. and Rothman, S. M. (1972) *Birth Control and Morality in Nineteenth Century America: Two Discussions.* (New York: Arno Press).
Rowbotham, S. and Weeks, J. (1977) *Socialism and the New Life: The Personal and Sexual Politics of Edward Carpenter and Havelock Ellis* (London: Pluto Press).
Sandler, Winifred Ann (1985) 'The Minneapolis Anti-Pornography Ordinance: a valid assertion of civil rights?', *Fordham Urban Law Journal,* vol. 13, Fall, pp. 909–46.
Saunders, D. (1982) 'The Trial of *Lady Chatterley's Lover*: Limiting Cases and Literary Canons', *Southern Review* vol. 15, pp. 161–77.
Saunders, D. (1990) 'Copyright, Obscenity and Literary History', *English Literary History,* vol. 57, no, 2, pp. 431–44.
Schorer, Mark (ed.) (1967) [1950] *The Story: A Critical Anthology* (Englewood Cliffs, New Jersey: Prentice Hall).
Schiller, F. (1967) [1795] *On the Aesthetic Education of Man* (Oxford: Clarendon Press). Edited, translated and introduced by E. Wilkinson and L. A. Willoughby.
Seabury, Florence (1925) 'Stereotypes' in Kirchwey, F., (ed.) (1925), pp. 219–31.
Seator, Penelope (1987) 'Judicial indifference to pornography's harm: *American Booksellers* v. *Hudnut* (Women's Law Forum)', *Golden Gate University Law Review,* vol. 17, pp. 297–358.
Shienbaum, Kim Ezra (ed.) (1988) *Legislating Morality: Private Choices on the Public Agenda* (Rochester, Vermont: Schenkman Books).
Slights, C. W. (1981) *The Casuistical Tradition* (Princeton, NJ: Princeton University Press).
Smith, John C. and Hogan, Brian (1972) *Criminal Law* (London: Butterworths).
Sparrow, John (1966) *Controversial Essays* (London: Faber and Faber).
St John-Stevas, Norman (1956) 'Obscenity, Literature and the Law', *Dublin Review,* vol. 230, pp. 41–56.
Starr, G. A. (1965) *Defoe and Spiritual Autobiography* (Princeton: Princeton University Press).
Starr, G. A. (1971) *Defoe and Casuistry* (Princeton: Princeton University Press).
Stephen, Sir James Fitzjames (1947) [1877] *A Digest of the Criminal Law* (London: Sweet and Maxwell). Edited by Lewis Frederick Sturge.
Stern, Lesley (1982) 'The Body as Evidence', *Screen,* vol. 23, no. 5, pp. 38–60.
Stone, Geoffrey R. (1986) 'Anti-Pornography Legislation as Viewpoint-Discrimination', *Harvard Journal of Law and Public Policy,* vol. 9, no. 2, pp. 461–80.
Supreme Court Obscenity Decisions (1973) (South San Diego: Greenleaf Classics).

Thomas, Donald (1969) *A Long Time Burning: The History of Literary Censorship in England* (London: Routledge and Kegan Paul).
Thomas, Donald (1972) 'Introduction' to *The School of Venus (L'Ecole des filles)* (London: Panther Books). Translated by Donald Thomas.
Thompson, R. (1976) *Samuel Pepys, Penny Merriments* (London: Constable).
Thompson, R. (1979) *Unfit for Modest Ears* (New Jersey: Rowman and Littlefield).
Tribe, David (1973) *Questions of Censorship* (London: George Allen and Unwin Ltd.).
Tsuzuki, Chushichi (1980) *Edward Carpenter, 1844–1929; Prophet of Human Fellowship* (Cambridge: Cambridge University Press).
Van de Velde, Theodore (1931) *Sex Hostility in Marriage* (London: William Heinemann [Medical Books]).
Van de Velde, Theodore (1934) [1928] *Ideal Marriage: Its Physiology and Technique* (London: William Heinemann [Medical Books]).
Veyne, Paul (1988) *Roman Erotic Elegy: Love Poetry and the West* (Chicago: Chicago University Press). Translated by D. Pellauer.
Van Ghent, Dorothy (1953) *The English Novel: Form and Function* (New York: Rinehart and Company).
Vivas, Eliseo (1960) *D. H. Lawrence: the Failure and the Triumph of Art* (Evanston: Northwestern University Press).
Wagner, Peter (1985) 'Introduction' to the Penguin edition of *Fanny Hill* (Harmondsworth: Penguin Books).
Warren, Samuel D. and Brandeis, Louis D. (1890) 'The Right to Privacy', *Harvard Law Review*, vol. IV, no. 5, December 15, pp. 193–220.
Weber, Max (1930) *The Protestant Ethic and the Spirit of Capitalism* (London: Allen and Unwin).
Weekend Australian, The (1990) November 10–11.
Weeks, J. (1981) *Sex, Politics and Society: The Regulation of Sexuality Since 1800* (London: Longmans).
Weininger, O. (1906) *Sex and Character* (London: William Heinemann).
West, Anthony (1950) *D. H. Lawrence* (London: Arthur Barker).
Widmer, K. and Widmer, E. (1961) *Literary Censorship: Principles, Cases, Problems* (San Francisco: Wadsworth).
Wilson, Colin (1982) 'Literature and Pornography' in Bold, Alan, (ed.) (1982) pp. 202–19.
Williams, Joy and Williams, Raymond (1973) *Lawrence on Education* (Harmondsworth: Penguin Books).
Williams, Raymond (1984) [1970] *The English Novel from Dickens to Lawrence* (London: The Hogarth Press).
Witte, W. (1975) 'The Literary Uses of Obscenity', *German Life and Letters*, vol. 28, pp. 360–73.

Table of Cases

AUSTRALIA

Transport Publishing Co. v. *Literature Board of Review* (1956) 99 C. L. R. III

UNITED KINGDOM

R. v. *Curl* (1727) 93 E. R. 849
R. v. *Delaval* (1763) 3 Burr. 1438
Director of Public Prosecutions v. *Whyte* [1972] A. C. 849; [1972] 3 All E. R. 12; [1972] 3 W. L. R. 410
R v. *Hicklin* (1868) L. R. 3Q. B. 360
R v. *Moxon* (1841) 4 St. Tr. (N. S.) 693
R v. *Penguin Books Ltd.* [1961] Crim. L. R. 176
R v. *Read* (1708) 11 Mod. Rep. 142
R v. *Sedley* (1663) 1 Sid. 168
R v. *Thomson* (1900) 64 J. P. 456

UNITED STATES

A Book Named "John Cleland's Memoirs of a Woman of Pleasure" v. *Attorney General of Massachusetts*,
383 US 413; 16 L Ed 2d I (1966)
American Booksellers Association v. *Hudnut*
598 F. Supp. 1316 (1984)
771 F. 2d 323 (1985)
106 S Ct 1772 (1986)
reh. den. 106 S Ct 1664 (1986)
American Booksellers Association Inc v. *Rendell*
481 A. 2d 919 (Pa. Super. 1984)
Arcara v. *Cloud Books, Inc*
478 US 697; 92 L Ed 2d 568 (1986)
Besig v. *United States*
208 F. 2d 142 (1953)
Brown v. *Pornography Commission of Lower Southhampton Township*
620 F. Supp. 1199 (D. C. Pa. 1985)
Carlin Communications, Inc v. *Federal Communication Commission*
749 F. 2d 113 (1984)
Chaplinsky v. *New Hampshire*
315 US 568 1942); 86 L Ed 1031 (1942)

Cologne v. *Westfarms Associates*
   469 A. 2d 1201 (Conn. 1984)
Commonwealth v. *Dane Entertainment Services, Inc (No. 1)*
   452 N. E. 2d 1126 (Mass. 1983)
Commonwealth v. *Stock*
   499 A. 2d 308 (Pa. Super. 1985)
Federal Communication Commission v. *Pacifica Foundation*
   98 S Ct 3026 (1978)
Frowherk v. *United States*
   249 US 204; 63 L Ed 561 (1919)
Ginsberg v. *State New York*
   390 US 629; 20 L Ed 2d 195 (1968)
Ginzburg v. *United States*
   383 US 463; 16 L Ed 2d 31 (1966)
Gitlow v. *New York*
   268 US 652; 69 L Ed 1138 (1925)
Grove Press v. *Christenberry*
   175 F Supp. 488 (1959)
Jacobellis v. *Ohio*
   378 US 184; 12 L Ed 2d 793 (1964)
Jenkins v. *Georgia*
   418 US 153; 41 L Ed 2d 642 (1974)
Macon v. *State*
   471 A. 2d 1090 (Md. App. 1984)
Memoirs v. *Massachusetts* (1966). See *A Book Named "John Cleland's Memoirs of a Woman of Pleasure"* v. *Attorney General of Massachusetts*.
Miller v. *California*
   413 US 15; 37 Ed 419 (1973)
Mishkin v. *State of New York*
   383 US 502; 16 L Ed 2d 56 (1966)
M. S. News Co v. *Casado*
   721 F. 2d 1281 (1983)
New York v. *Ferber*
   458 US 747; 73 L Ed 2d 1113 (1982)
Paris Adult Theatre I v. *Slaton*
   413 US 49; 37 L Ed 2d 446 (1973)
Pack v. *City of Cleveland*
   438 N. E. 2d 434 (Ohio 1982)
People v. *Lerch*
   480 N. E. 2d 1253 (Ill. App. 1 Dist. 1985)
People v. *Wiseman*
   341 N. W. 2d 494 (Mich. App 1983)
Pittsburgh Press Company v. *The Pittsburgh Commission on Human Relations*
   413 US 376; 37 L Ed 2d 669 (1975)
Ross v. *State*
   475 A. 2d 481 (Md. App. 1984)
Roth v. *United States*
   354 US 476; I L Ed 2d 1498 (1957)
Saliba v. *State*
   475 N. E. 2d 1181 (Ind. App. 2 Dist. 1985)

Table of Cases

Smith v. *California*
    361 US 147; 4 L Ed 2d 205 (1959)
Stanley v. *Georgia*
    394 US 557; 22L Ed 2d 542 (1969)
Star Satellite, Inc v. *City of Biloxi*
    779 F. 2d 1074 (1986)
State v. *Furuyama*
    637 P. 2d 1095 (Hawaii, 1981)
State v. *Summers*
    692 S. W. 2d 439 (Tenn. Cr. App. 1985)
Staten v. *State*
    686 S. W. 2d 268 (Tex. App. 14 Dist. 1985)
Swann v. *State*
    637 P. 2d 888 (Ok1. Cr. 1981)
United States v. *Orito*
    413 US 139; 37 L Ed 2d 513 (1973)
United States v. *Petrillo*
    332 US 1; 91 L Ed 1877 (1946)
United States v. *37 Photographs*
    402 US 363; 28 L Ed 2d 822 (1971)
United States v. *Reidel*
    402 US 351; 28 L Ed 2d 813 (1971)
United States v. *Roth*
    237 F. 2d 796 (1956)
United States v. *Smith*
    467 F. 2d 1126 (1972)
United States v. *One Book Entitled Ulysses by James Joyce*
    72 F. 2d 705 (1934)
Upper Midwest Booksellers Association v. *City of Minneapolis*
    780 F. 2d 1389 (8th Cir. 1985)
Young v. *American Mini Theatres, Inc.*
    427 US 50; 96 S Ct 2440; 49 L Ed 2d 310 (1976)

Table of Statutes

AUSTRALIA

Objectionable Literature Act (Queensland) 1954

UNITED KINGDOM

Customs Consolidation Act 1876
Indecent Advertisements Act 1889
Libel Act (Lord Campbell's Act) 1843
Metropolitan Police Act 1839
Obscene Publications Act 1857
Obscene Publications Act 1959
Post Office Act 1870
Post Office (Protection Act) 1875
Theatres Act 1843
Town Police Causes Act 1847
Vagrancy Publications Act 1824; 1838

UNITED STATES

Civil Rights Act (1964)
Tariff Act (1930)
U. S. C. A (Constitution of the United States Annotated, St Paul's, Minnesota: West Publishing Co.):
 Amendment 1 ⎫
 Amendment 4 ⎪
 Amendment 5 ⎬ 1987 edition
 Amendment 14 ⎭

 18 U. S. C. A. Section 1461 ⎫
 18 U. S. C. A. Section 1462 ⎪
 18 U. S. C. A. Section 1463 ⎬ 1984 edition and cumulative pocket (annual)
 18 U. S. C. A. Section 1464 ⎪
 18 U. S. C. A. Section 1465 ⎭

 19 U. S. C. A. Section 1305}   1980 edition and cumulative pocket (annual)

 39 U. S. C. A. Section 3006 ⎫
 39 U. S. C. A. Section 3010 ⎬ 1980 edition and cumulative pocket (annual)

Table of Statutes

47 U. S. C. A. Section 503(b) ⎫ 1962 edition including 1990 supplementary
47 U. S. C. A. Section 510   ⎬ pamphlet covering 1963 to 1989

Reports and Parliamentary Debates

CANADA

Report of the Special Committee on Pornography and Prostitution: Summary (1985) *Pornography and Prostitution in Canada* (Ottawa: Department of Justice/Canadian Government Printing Centre). Committee chaired by Paul Fraser.

LEAGUE OF NATIONS

Assembly documents: report of the Child Welfare Committee, A. 8. 1928, IV, pp. 6, 10–11, (Geneva: Series of League of Nations Publications IV)

Report of the Traffic in Women and Children Committee, C. 184, M. 59. 1928. IV., pp. 43–5 (Geneva: Series of League of Nations Publications IV).

NEW ZEALAND

Report of the Ministerial Committee of Inquiry into Pornography (1989) (Wellington: Department of Justice). Committee chaired by Joanne Morris.

UNITED KINGDOM

Report from the Joint Select Committee on Lotteries and Indecent Advertisements (British Parliamentary Reports from Committees: Vol. IX, 1908).

Report of the Committee on Homosexual Offences and Prostitution (1957) Cmnd 247 (London: Her Majesty's Stationery Office). Committee chaired by Sir John Wolfenden.

Report of the Committee on Obscenity and Film Censorship (1979) Cmnd 7772 (London: Her Majesty's Stationery Office). Committee chaired by Bernard Williams.

146 Hansard Series of Parliamentary Debates (England, 1857).

UNITED STATES

Report of the Commission on Obscenity and Pornography (1970) (New York: Bantam Books). Committee chaired by William B. Lockhart.

Attorney General's Commission on Pornography and Obscenity Final Report, Volumes 1 and 2 (1986) (Washington D. C.: United States Department of Justice). Committee chaired by Henry E. Hudson.

Pornography and Sexual Violence: Evidence of the Links (1988). (The transcript of public hearings on Ordinances to Add Pornography as Discrimination Against Women: Minneapolis City Council, Government Operations Committee, December 12–13, 1983) (London: Everywoman Ltd).

Index

Acton, W., *Functions and Disorders of the Reproductive Organs*, 103–4, 121, 252n
aesthetics, 21–5, 139
  as ethical practice, 16–17, 105–10, 118–34, 183–4, 190–2, 234–6
  legal incorporation of, 14–15, 139, 141, 143–4, 149, 152, 158–9, 164, 167, 176–80, 210–14
  limits of, 82, 100, 101–2, 176–80, 234
  and psychoanalysis, 106–7, 114–15, 115–18, 122
  and psychology, 24–5, 35–6
allegorisation, 155–7
American Booksellers Association v. *Hudnut*, 208–9, 232–46, 262n
  see also Indianapolis Ordinance
American Booksellers Association, Inc. v. *Rendell*, 220
American Law Institute (Model Penal Code), 26
Arcara v. *Cloud Book, Inc.*, 221
Archbold, J.F., *Pleading and Evidence in Criminal Cases*, 73
Archer, P. 249n
Aretino, 34
Arnold, M., 105
art and pornography, 8–10, 18, 36–9, 42, 59, 80, 92–3, 94–5, 96–7, 109–10, 138, 141, 151, 164, 176–80, 185, 190–1, 195, 212, 213
Ashbee, H.S., 254n
Attorney General's Commission on Pornography and Obscenity Final Report (Hudson Report), 219, 225–8, 246, 258n, 259n, 260n, 264n
audiences, 41, 50–1, 84, 88–9, 119, 126–8, 128–9, 138, 141, 146–7, 190–1
  cultural levels of, 10, 16, 42, 80–1, 93–4, 100, 135–7, 157–8, 213–14, 220–1, 239–40
  gender of, 195, 197, 222, 225–7, 243
  problem of, 27–8, 93–4, 99–100, 177–80, 214–15

typologies of, 17, 92–4, 99–101, 167–71, 178, 194–5
  see also variable obscenity
auto-eroticism, xi, 39–42, 96, 204, 222, 243, 253n
  see also masturbation

Baisch, D., 126
Balzac, H., 75
Barrin, J., *Vénus dans le cloître (Venus in the Cloister; or, the Nun in her Smock)*, 34, 49, 50, 52, 87–8
Beal, A., *D.H. Lawrence*, 126, 253n
Bedborough, G., 250n
Besant, A., 250n
Besig v. *United States*, 258n
bibliophiles, 136, 254n
Blackwell, E., *Counsel to Parents*, 12, 15, 19, 72, 77; *The Human Element in Sex* 123, 125, 136, 252n
body and flesh, 32–5, 36, 247n
Book Named 'John Cleland's Memoirs of a Woman of Pleasure' v. *Attorney General of the Commonwealth of Massachusetts*, 210
book sex (*biblio-erotics*), xi, 35–48, 92, 104–15, 118, 137–8, 186, 195, 222, 246
book-trade, 50, 63, 64, 65, 77, 80, 86–7, 88, 92–4, 100–1, 135, 137, 154, 157–8, 187, 217–18
Bourdieu, P., *Distinction: a Social Critique of the Judgement of Taste*, 128
Boyd, E., 120–1, 251n, 252n
Bradlaugh, C., 250n
Bradley, F.H., 179
Branit, J., 263n
Brigman, W., 264n
Brown, B., 176
Brown v. *Pornography Commission of Lower Southampton Township*, 259n
Burroughs, W., 55, 192, 193, 194

Index

Calder, J., 157
Carlin Communications, Inc. v. Federal Communications Commission, 258n
Carpenter, E., 105–15, 192; *Angel's Wings*, 251n; *The Intermediate Sex*, 108; *Love's Coming of Age*, 107; *Towards Democracy*, 109
censorship
 historians of, 48, 57–8, 59, 85, 86, 90–1, 97–8, 99–102, 214, 257n
 inadequacy of the concept, 48–56, 58, 73, 76, 86, 160, 243
Chaplinsky v. *New Hampshire*, 239, 257n
Chevasse, P.H., 104, 252n
Chidley, W., *Confessions*, 1, 7, 46
Chorier, N., *Satyra sotadique*, 34, 49
civic societies, 49, 53, 77–8, 80, 82, 84–5, 249n
classics, treatment of, 61–2, 70, 75, 80–1, 137, 150, 255n
Cleland, J., *Fanny Hill*, 38–9, 46
coercion, 88–9, 90, 164–5, 172–5, 200, 202–3
Collins, W., 93
Colquhoun, P., *Treatise on the Police of the Metropolis*, 59
Commonwealth v. *Dane Entertainment Services, Inc. (no. 1)*, 216
Commonwealth v. *Stock*, 217, 221
competences
 cultural, 40, 89, 90, 185, 237
 ethical, 96, 109–15, 119, 124, 198, 224–8
 literary, 39–40, 50, 96, 109–15, 137
 uneven distribution of, 9–10, 18–19, 27–8, 40, 42, 56, 64, 72–3, 80–1, 88, 92–4, 97, 135, 137–8, 156–7, 160–1, 177–80, 185, 198, 204–5, 206–7, 239–40, 250–1n
confession, ix–x, 30–3, 36–7, 43–5, 65, 66, 67, 88, 95–6, 103–5, 110–15, 188–9, 204, 243
Confessional Unmasked, The, 37, 66–73
contingency, viii, 4, 7, 18–19, 102, 117–18, 124, 135, 224, 243, 246
Cousins, M., 206
Cowan, James, 253n
Cowan, John, *The Science of a New Life*, 104, 119–21, 122, 123, 125, 136, 252n

Criterion Miscellany, The, 97–102
cultural history, x, 3, 6–8, 42–8, 97–9, 132–4
Curll, E., 49, 143, 188
Customs Consolidation Act 1876, 74

Davy, K., 244
Day-Lewis, C., 153
decriminalisation, 158–9
Defoe, D., *Robinson Crusoe*, 38–9
De Grazia, E., 247n
De Grazia, E. and Newman, R.K., 257n, 259n
Delaney, P., 252n
Delavenay, E., *D.H. Lawrence and Edward Carpenter*, 105, 108
desire and norm, 6–7, 20–5, 140
dialectics, xi
 and aesthetics, 21–5, 182–4
 and cultural history, 7–8, 42–3, 47, 97–9, 105–6
 as an ethical practice, 16–17, 121–5, 129–34, 137, 182–4, 234–5
 and psychology, 20–1
 and reconciliation, 43, 49
 and repression, 20–5
 sexualisation of, 22–4, 97–9, 105–15, 117–18, 121–9, 190–2, 251–2n, 253–4n
Dickens, C., 93–4, 117, 135
discrimination, 233–4, 238, 245, 262n
 see also rights
disinterestedness, viii, 71
distribution, 7, 18–19, 34, 40, 42, 51–2, 56, 64, 72, 73, 88–9, 92–4, 99–100, 101, 126–9, 134, 135–8, 140, 150, 159, 185, 212, 216, 217–18, 220, 223–4, 227, 240
Donzelot, J., *The Policing of Families*, 18, 258n
Draper, R.P., 127, 253n
drives, 33–4
 in aesthetics, 21–2
 in psychology, 20–1
 see also dialectics
Duggan, L., 263n
Durrell, L., 127
Dworkin, A., 231–46, 262n; *Pornography: Men Possessing Women*, x, 47, 166

education
  aesthetic, 21–3, 128–34, 183–4, 192
  and government, 128, 133–4, 168–71, 204–5
  legal reliance on, 179–80, 211–13
  popular, 128–9, 192–3
  see also novels
Eisenstein, E., *The Printing Press as an Agent of Change*, 40
Ellis, H., 47, 97, 123, 125, 192, 250n, 253n; *Little Essays of Love and Virtue*, 122, 252n; *Man and Woman*, 108; *The Objects of Marriage*, 121–2; *Studies in Sexual Psychology*, 47
Eliot, T.S., 127
ethics
  as an ability, 38, 118–26, 176–80
  and aesthetics, 105–8, 183–4
  and education, 128–34
  Foucault on, 118–19, 126
  and self-regulation, 16–17, 176–80
  techniques, 40–2, 184
  see also competences; confession; Puritanism
evidence
  expert, 14–15, 139–41, 147–8, 150–6, 254–5n, 256n
  sociological, 147, 225–8
  see also trials

FCC v. Pacifica Foundation, 239
Feinberg, J., *The Moral Limits of the Criminal Law*, vol. 1: *Harm to Others*, 173–4, 175, 178, 180–1
feminism, x, 100, 125–6, 160
  as aesthetic critique, 234–6, 245–6
  ambivalence of, 231, 233–6, 244–6
  and law reform, 9–10, 197, 231–7, 263n
  and liberalism, 17–18, 197, 230, 233, 242–3
  and pornography, xi–xii, 5, 15–18, 42, 149, 184, 231–3, 261–2n, 262n
  see also objectification
Fleishman, S., 257n
Forster, E.M., 92, 94, 97, 127
Foxon, D., *Libertine Literature in England 1660–1745*, 34, 248n

Foucault, M., ix, 29–33, 36–7, 43–5, 261n; *The History of Sexuality, Vol. 1, An Introduction*, 29–33, 43–5, 85–6, 102–3, 111, 128, 188, 228; *The History of Sexuality, Vol. 2, The Use of Pleasure*, 118–19, 124
Fowler, O.S., 121
Freud, S., *On Sexuality*, 114–15
Frohwerk v. United States, 199
Fuchs, E., 244

Galsworthy, J., 127, 128
Gay, P., *The Bourgeois Experience: Victoria to Freud*, 3, 6, 25, 39, 58, 119
Ginsberg v. State of New York, 214
Ginzburg v. United States, 195–6, 219
Gitlow v. New York, 199
Goldsmid, J.A., *Companionate Marriage*, 125
government, xi, 7, 50–2, 58, 59, 64–5, 82, 87, 128, 187–90, 229
  and education, 128–34, 168–71, 193
  and liberalism, 171, 230–1
  and norms, 44, 50, 75, 86, 134, 170, 205–6, 220–1, 226, 228, 234, 240, 243, 258n
  and police, 59–60, 64–6, 90
  and population, 7, 12, 18, 44, 52–4, 170
Grosskurth, P., 253n
Grove Press, Inc. v. Christenberry, 211–12, 213

Haiman, F.S., 200
Hall, R., 254n
Haller, J.S. and Haller, R.M., 252n
harm condition, 162, 165, 172–6, 185, 198, 200, 202, 205
  and offensiveness, 59, 65, 71–2, 73, 140, 160, 163–4, 172–6, 193–4
Heath, S., *The Sexual Fix*, 58, 115–18, 251–2n
Herbert, A., 142
Hirst, P., 206
Hirst, P. and Woolley, P., *Social Relations and Human Attributes*, 125
Hite, S., 47
Hixson, R.F., 260n

Index 285

Hoggart, R., 154
Hunter, I., *Culture and Government*, 128–9
Hunter, J.P., 247n
Huxley, A., 127

indecency, 74, 78, 79, 80
Indecent Advertisements Act 1889, 74, 248n
Indianapolis Ordinance, 261n
see also *American Booksellers Association v. Hudnut*; Dworkin, A.; MacKinnon, C.
intention, 67, 69–70, 132, 149, 155–6, 212, 217–18, 260n

Jackson, M., 252n
Jacobellis v. Ohio, 210, 218, 260n
Jeffreys, S., 252n
Jenkins v. Georgia, 258n
Joyce, J., 94, 193
Joynson Hicks, Sir W. (Viscount Brentford), 99–101, 250–1n
juridification, 9, 19, 49–52, 73, 87, 187, 248n
jurisprudence, 3, 8–10, 25–8, 48–9, 75, 87, 137, 155, 162–4, 171, 198–205, 220, 230–1, 235–6, 258n, 262–3n

Kappeler, S., 166, 237
Kaufmann, U.M., 247n
Kinsey, A., 47
Kittsteiner, H.-D., 256n
knowledge
and interests, viii
and pleasure, 30, 44–8, 109, 113–15, 121–4, 195–7, 198, 204, 244
the will to, 30–1, 102–4
Knowlton, C., 250n
Kopold, S., 125
Koselleck, R., 231, 261n
Krafft-Ebing, R., 47, 196, 197
Kronhausen, E. and P., *Pornography and the Law*, x, 20–1, 178

law
and aesthetics, 14, 21–5, 48, 234–6
and education, 179–80, 185, 203–4
and the 'infra-legal', 51, 53–4, 58, 71–3, 93, 134, 144–5, 159, 168–9, 171, 188, 195, 207–8, 209, 210–13, 223, 243
and literature, 24, 54–5, 57, 61–2, 81, 92–102
and medicine, 188–90
and morality, 8–10, 18, 28, 42, 50–1, 64, 159, 172–86, 194, 230–1
and norm, 44, 91, 138–9, 141, 142, 148, 158–60
and policing, 51, 59, 60–1, 63, 72–4, 75, 135, 138–41, 144, 189–90, 208–9, 215–19, 221–2, 225–8, 236, 240, 243–5, 255n
as processual, 10, 209, 229–30, 237–42
and psychology, 20–1
as repressive, 20–5, 48–56, 57–8, 73, 76, 86, 87, 89, 91, 99–102, 161
and self regulation, 16–17, 100–1, 138, 139, 143, 159, 179–80, 205–8, 209, 211, 215–16, 224, 228, 242, 243–5
see also obscenity law
Lawrence, D.H., viii, 21, 22–3, 48, 55, 76, 94–5, 97–9, 117, 119, 124, 125–7, 133–4, 140, 151, 154–5, 159, 171, 178, 184, 192, 193, 194, 195, 251n, 252n; *Fantasia of the Unconscious*, 107; *Lady Chatterley's Lover*, 95, 110, 112–15, 123, 124, 131–3, 137, 152, 153, 154, 211–12; *Pansies*, 140; *The Rainbow*, 95, 101, 111, 139–40, 154; *Sons and Lovers*, 111, 129–31, 154; *Women in Love*, 111–12, 154; 'A propos of *Lady Chatterley's Lover*', 212; 'Pornography and obscenity', 23, 48, 212; artworks, 140–1, 142
and Carpenter, E., 105–15
Lawrence, F., 127
League of Nations, 250n
Leavis, F.R., 131–2, 253–4n
Leland, C., 108
Libel Act 1843, 73
liberalism
and aesthetics, 21–5, 176–80

liberalism — *continued*
  and feminism, 17–18, 162, 166, 197, 230, 233, 242–3
  governmental, 171, 198, 207–8, 215–16, 228, 256n
  and jurisprudence, 25–8
  and law reform, 13–19, 172–3, 185–6, 194, 202–4
  limits of, 15–19, 172–86, 194, 198, 204–5, 207, 214–15, 224
  philosophical, 9, 160–1, 162–4, 171–2, 194, 196, 198–205, 215, 222, 228, 230–1, 256n
  and privacy, 8–10, 165, 176–80, 222–4
  and psychology, 20–1
  and representation, 164–5, 180–5, 198, 215, 228
  and rights, 179–80, 198–205, 207–8
  see also harm condition
libraries, 84
Lindsey, B.B., 125
literacy, 88–9, 101, 118
literary criticism, x, 21–5, 115, 129–33, 146, 151–6, 169, 253n
  legal recognition of, 14–15, 147, 153, 190–5, 212
  see also aesthetics; Romanticism
literature
  and education, 128–34, 135, 253n
  historicisation of, 36–9, 76, 92–6, 101–2, 117–18, 118–21
  and law, 24, 54–5, 57, 61–2, 75, 92–102, 210–12
  and sexology, 47, 121–6, 253n
  sexualisation of, 31–5, 76, 91, 102–15, 117–18, 121–6, 135, 137, 149, 190–2
Lockhart, W.B. and McClure, R.C., 14, 16, 19, 26, 27, 174, 177–80, 194, 202
lotteries, 53, 78, 82, 85, 249n

MacKinnon, C., 231–46; *Feminism Unmodified*, 233, 235–7, 240, 242, 262n
Macon v. *State*, 259n
magistrates, 60–1, 63, 66–7, 74, 79, 81, 216, 248n
  see also summary procedures
Manchester, C., 62, 77, 249n
Marcus, S., *The Other Victorians*, x, 25, 46, 57, 58, 119, 247n, 254n
masturbation
  as metaphor, 24, 98
  as social problem, 45–6, 103–4, 120–1, 227
Mauss, M., 124
Memoirs v. *Massachusetts*, 258n
mens rea, *see* intention
Metropolitan Police Act 1839, 73, 77, 78
Mill, J.S., 162, 165, 181
Miller, H., 21, 55, 127–8, 192, 193, 194
Miller v. *California*, 201, 213, 214, 215, 227, 239
Millot, M. and L'Ange, J., *L'École des filles (The School of Venus)*, 3, 5, 6, 8, 33, 34–5, 37, 39, 40–1, 49
Mishkin v. *New York*, 195–7, 218
Montano, L., 244
Morais, N., 262n
moralism, 59, 62–3, 64, 65, 71, 73, 76, 86, 91, 97, 98, 163–4, 167–8, 193
morality and law, 8–10, 18, 28, 42, 50–1, 159, 172–3, 194, 198–9, 209–10, 215
  see also ethics; self
Morpurgo, J., 149, 152, 153, 256n
M.S. News Co. v. *Casado*, 215
Murry, J.M., 127
Muir, E., 127

Nabokov, V., 192
Nagel, E., 175–6
National Vigilance Association, 77, 80
New Criticism, 146
New York v. *Ferber*, 215, 239
newspapers, 84
Nin, A., 127
norms, 5
  and desire, 6–7, 16, 20–5, 140
  and law 44, 60, 72–3, 85–6, 90, 138–9, 141, 144–5, 148, 205–6, 209–10, 213, 215, 220–4
novels, 92–5, 211–12
  and Puritanism, 38–9, 247n

of sexual education, 23, 55, 109–15, 149, 193
pedagogical use of, 54–5, 128–34, 136, 154, 193–5

objectification, viii–ix, 10, 17, 166, 234, 236, 237, 240, 245, 262n
see also aesthetics
Objectionable Literature Act 1954 (Q), 167
obscene libel, 50, 52, 60, 74, 79, 87, 89–90
obscene publication, 60, 62, 66, 74, 78, 83–4, 87, 88–9, 91, 187
and copyright, 95, 248–9n
Obscene Publications Act 1857, 52–3, 57, 59, 60–2, 63–5, 74, 77, 90, 93, 148
Obscene Publications Act 1959, 57, 66, 89, 100, 135, 138–9, 142–8, 149, 150–1, 153, 154, 155, 157, 158, 159–60, 162, 163, 164, 171
obscenity, 3–4, 97–101
  definitions of, 26, 68–9, 70, 81, 140, 143, 248n
  liberal consensus on, 2–4, 8–9, 15–16, 200–4
  and police, 73–4, 208–9, 216–17, 225–6
  as social problem, 7, 49–54, 99, 170, 188–90, 211
  tests of, 14, 52–3, 57, 66, 73–4, 78–9, 141–5, 156, 210–11, 213–15, 216–17, 239–40
  see also variable obscenity
obscenity law
  aestheticisation of, 14, 100, 156, 209–13, 245
  England: eighteenth century, 49–52, 86–90; nineteenth century, 52–4, 57, 59–76, 92–4; twentieth century, 94–5, 97, 99–102, 135, 138–9, 142–60
  infrequency of prosecutions, 75–6, 77, 101, 187–8, 250n
  policing of, 64, 189–90, 199, 208–9, 215–19, 221, 224, 225–8, 230, 259n
  reform of, 8–10, 13–17, 54–6, 75, 81, 138, 142–3, 162–6, 172–86, 202–4
  United States, 198–9, 208–11, 213–15, 216, 231–2, 237–41
Oestreich, G., *Neostoicism and the Early Modern State*, 59
offensiveness, 163–4, 167, 173–5, 193–4, 213, 215

Pack v. *City of Cleveland*, 259n
Paris Adult Theatre 1 v. *Slaton*, 201, 217, 259n, 260–1n
Paul, J., 182
People v. *Lerch*, 260n
People v. *Wiseman*, 214
perversions
  aestheticisation of, 110, 113–15, 137, 191–2
  'implantation of', 44–5, 102–3, 114–15
  pornography of, 46, 92, 192
Pepys, S., 1, 5, 7, 8, 9, 34–5, 39, 50
Phillips, J., 248–9n
Pittsburgh Press Co. v. *Pittsburgh Commission on Human Relations*, 257n
police, 66, 74, 83, 99–102, 159
  definition of, 59–60
  and law, 63, 75, 79, 99–101, 208, 215–19, 225–6, 243–5
  medical, 64, 71–3, 78, 92, 138, 143, 168, 210
  pedagogical, 168–71, 210, 213, 243–4
pornography
  aesthetic account of, 21–5, 35–48, 55
  aestheticisation of, 109–15, 140, 190–2
  and art, 8–9, 18, 36–9, 42, 92–3, 94–5, 96–7, 109–10, 164, 176–80, 185, 190–2, 195, 244
  as conduct, 5–6, 40, 180–5, 220–1, 223–4, 225–8, 233, 238, 240
  effects of, 15, 26–7, 225–8
  and feminism, xi–xii, 5, 15–18, 166
  general explanations of, viii–ix, 2–3, 16, 101–2, 189, 234
  as genre, 21, 36–9, 109, 112–14
  harms of, viii–ix, 4, 12–17, 45, 65–6,

288 *Index*

pornography, harms of — *continued*
  99–100, 172–6, 204, 210–11,
  214–15, 225–7, 231–4, 244
history of, x, 3, 6–8, 31–5, 42–8, 96,
  162, 229, 246
and liberation, 3, 28, 30
medicalisation of, 1–2, 7, 12–16, 35,
  45–8, 55, 60, 64–5, 72–3, 90,
  102–5, 144
and men, xi, 18, 34, 39, 42, 195, 197,
  198, 222, 225–7, 230, 231–3, 236
and pedagogy, 45
'positivity' of, x–xi, 6, 28–35
and printing, 7, 9, 34, 40–1, 88–9,
  189
psychological account of, 20–1, 28–
  30
and religious practices, 5, 30–3, 36–9
as representation, 5–6, 40, 164–6, 172,
  180–5, 198, 226–8
Pornography and Sexual Violence, 244,
  261n, 263–4n
post-modernism, 86, 115–18, 244
Post Office (Protection) Act 1884, 74
postal regulation, 77, 82–3, 84, 99, 100,
  140, 216, 218–19, 249n, 254n
printing, xi, 7, 9, 34, 40–1, 50–1, 57, 65,
  86–7, 88–9, 90, 91, 92–4, 104, 189
privacy, 8–9, 165, 176–80, 185, 222–4,
  225, 260n, 260–1n
Proclamation Society, 77
psychology, x, 20–1
public good, 139, 141–2, 145, 147–8,
  150, 151, 160, 210–11, 213, 255n
Public Health Act 1875, 74
Public Service Board, Australia, 264n
Puritanism, 3, 34, 154
  misunderstandings of, 43, 49, 87, 89,
    91, 97–8, 187
  and the sexual self, 8–9, 35, 38–9

Queensland Literature Board of Review,
  166

Radclyffe Hall, R., *The Well of Loneliness*, 145–6, 147, 193
Radzinowicz, L., 249n
reading
  as erotic practice, 1–2, 8–9, 40–1, 92,
    97–8, 101, 115, 121–2, 127–8,
    137, 190–5, 222–4
  and reader response theory, 75, 76, 80
  see also book-sex; competences
realism, 5–6, 20–1, 28, 41
Rembar, C., 57
R. v. Curll, 50–1, 52, 87–90, 187
Reg. v. Read, 50, 87
Reg. v. Hicklin, 26, 27, 37, 52–3, 57, 60,
  66–73, 75, 135, 146, 148–9, 157,
  163, 165, 167, 170–1, 178, 189,
  197, 209, 210, 248n
Reg. v. Moxon, 70
Reg. v. Penguin Books Ltd., 135, 139,
  148–58, 159, 160–1, 255n
R. v. Sedley, 74, 87, 89
Reg. v. Thomson, 75, 146–7
*Report from the Joint Select Committee
  on Lotteries and Indecent Advertisements 1908*, 78–86, 134, 139,
  216, 249n, 254n
*Report of the Commission on Obscenity
  and Pornography* (Lockhart Report) 202–5, 216, 217, 219, 223,
  225, 243, 257n, 258n, 260n, 263n
*Report of the Committee on Homosexual
  Offences and Prostitution*
  (Wolfenden Report) 1957, 164
*Report of the Committee on Obscenity
  and Film Censorship* (Williams
  Report) 1979, 56, 57, 63, 68, 143,
  158, 162, 163–5, 172–3, 174–5,
  176–7, 178, 181–2, 249n
*Report of the Ministerial Committee of
  Inquiry into Pornography*, 263n
Report of the Special Committee on Pornography and Prostitution: Pornography and Prostitution in Canada,
  263n
representation, 116–18, 165, 230, 234–5
  and liberalism, 164–5, 172, 180–5,
    198, 215, 228
  pornography as, 5–6, 40, 164–6, 172,
    180–5, 198, 226–8
repression, 20–1, 28, 189–90, 194–5
  fable of, ix, 29–30
  and confession, 30–2, 121–4, 128
  in humanist historiography and politics, 3, 30, 42–8, 98, 203

see also 'repressive hypothesis'
'repressive hypothesis', 28–30, 43
Reynolds, R., 250n
Richards, D.A.J., 200–1, 214
rights
  civil, 58, 231–4, 236–41, 245, 264n
  conditionality of, 205, 206–7, 219–22, 224–5
  of expression, 82, 198–210, 215, 217–18, 219–22, 226–8, 233, 238–41, 259n
  and interests, 198, 205, 211, 220–4, 240, 259n
  of privacy, 176–80, 222–4, 225
  and the subject, 10, 198–9, 220, 222–3, 228
Roberts, R.F., 253n
Robertson, G., 160–1; *Obscenity*, 57–8, 62, 63, 68, 76, 90, 94, 143–4, 145, 146, 152, 158, 250n
Rolph, C.H., *Books in the Dock*, 58, 90, 141, 254–5n; *The Trial of Lady Chatterley: Regina v. Penguin Books*, 150, 151, 152, 154, 155, 156, 157–8, 160, 255–6n
Romanticism, 96, 105, 108–9, 146, 182–6, 190
  see also aesthetics; dialectics
Ross v. State, 216
Roth v. United States, 210–11, 213, 214, 215, 227, 247n
Rowbotham, S., 105, 252n
Rushdie, S., 160

Saliba v. State, 214
Saunders, D., 155, 247n
Schiller, F., *On the Aesthetic Education of Man*, 22, 183–4
Schorer, M., 253n
scienter, 217–18, 260n, 263n
Scott-James, A., 152–3
Seabury, F., 125
sedition, 90, 91
self
  formation, 8–9, 35, 39–40, 95–6, 102–5, 115, 183–4
  stylisation, 102, 105–8, 110, 118, 124–5, 126, 128, 133–4, 135, 137–8, 145, 149, 153, 193, 235

regulation, 16–17, 66, 128–9, 131–3, 206–8, 222–4
Sendler, W., 263n
sexology, 46–8, 102–8
  and feminism, 125–6, 252n
  and literature, 47, 121–6, 253n
  and pleasure/knowledge, 44–5, 47, 121–4, 195–7
sexual medicine, 12–15, 46, 102–5, 110–14, 119–21, 136, 142, 252n
sexuality
  aestheticisation of, 96–9, 101, 105–8, 137–8, 155–6, 190–2
  apparatus of, 43–5
  as historical construction, 6, 30–3, 43–5, 57, 91, 102, 124, 134
  and literature, 91, 96–9, 102, 108–9, 190–2
  and medicine, 102–5, 111, 119–21
  and pedagogy, 128–34, 192–4, 257–8n
Shaw v. DPP., 255n
Shienbaum, K.E., 262n
sin, 87–8, 91
Slights, C., 247n
Smith, J.C. and Hogan, B., 155
Smith v. California, 201, 217, 260n
social problems, 7, 49–54, 93–4, 170, 215–16, 225–7
Sparrow, J., 115
spiritual courts, 50, 87, 249n
St John-Stevas, N., 16, 24, 25, 48, 90, 140–1, 146
Stanley v. Georgia, 222–3
Star Satellite Inc. v. City of Biloxi, 259n
Starr, G., 247n
State v. Furuyama, 259–60n
State v. Summers, 214
Staten v. State, 214
Stephen, Sir James F., *Digest of the Criminal Law*, 70, 255n
Stern, L., 262n
Stone, G., 263n
Swinburne, A., 110
subject (the), 10, 27–8, 32, 41, 76, 86, 90–1, 230
  and feminism, 184, 186
  and liberalism, 172–6, 186, 198–203, 205, 215, 228

subject (the) — *continued*
  and philosophy, 181
  of pornography, 39–42
  see also competences; self
sublimation, 20–1
  see also dialectics
summary procedures, 53, 63, 74, 79, 82, 100–1, 139, 216–17, 248n
Swan v. *State*, 224

Theatres Act 1843, 73
Thomas, D., *A Long Time Burning*, 3, 5, 6, 48, 57–8, 62, 67, 90, 249n
Town Police Causes Act 1847, 73–4, 78–9, 248n
Transport Publishing Co. v. *The Literature Board of Review*, 166–71
trials
  and expert witnesses, 15; *see also* evidence, expert
  and juries, 74–5, 79, 82, 85, 139, 147–8, 149, 151–2, 153, 157, 160–1
  procedures, 145–8, 150, 216, 237–41
  as ritual, 74–5, 148–9
  see also individual cases
Tribe, D., 68, 248n
Trilling, D., 253n
Tsuzuki, C., 105
Twain, M., 21

United States Constitution, First Amendment, 14, 178, 199–203, 209–10, 211, 213–14, 215, 217, 226–7, 228, 238, 240–1, 249n
  Fourteenth Amendment, 233, 238
United States v. *One Book Entitled Ulysses by James Joyce*, 94, 258n
United States v. *Orito*, 223
United States v. *Patrillo*, 218
United States v. *Reidel*, 261n
United States v. *Smith*, 218
United States v. *37 Photographs*, 261n
United States v. *Roth*, 162, 171, 212, 258n

Upper Midwest Booksellers v. *City of Minneapolis*, 215, 260n

Vagrancy Acts 1824, 1838, 73, 78
Van de Velde, T., *Sex Hostility in Marriage*, 122–4, 126; *Ideal Marriage: its Physiology and Technique*, 124
Van Ghent, D., *The English Novel: Form and Function*, 129–31
variable obscenity, 10, 16, 27, 72–3, 75, 80–1, 135, 139, 146–7, 157, 194, 207, 210, 211, 213, 214–15, 221, 224, 225–7, 230, 237, 239–40, 244, 255n, 258n
  and communications technologies, 219, 243
  see also audiences; competences
Veyne, P., 95
Vice Society (Society for the Suppression of Vice and the Encouragement of Religion and Virtue), 77, 254n
Vizetelly, H., 75, 250n

Wagner, P., 34
Warren, S.D. and Brandeis, L.D., 260n
Weekend Australian, 264n
Weininger, O., *Sex and Character*, 108
West, A., *D.H. Lawrence*, 126
West, R., 155–6
Whitman, W., 192
Wilberforce, W., 77
Williams, J. and Williams, R., *Lawrence on Education*, 133–4
Williams, R., 153, 154; *The English Novel from Dickens to Lawrence*, 132–3
Wilson, C., 24
Witte, W., 183

Young v. *American Mini Theatres, Inc.*, 240

Zola, E., 75, 76, 250n